RESTLESS WATERS
of the
ICHHAMATI

Rimli Bhattacharya trained in Comparative Literature and works on literature, performance history and the arts. Her translations from Bangla to English include the autobiographies of Binodini Dasi *My Story & My Life as an Actress* (1998), Rabindranath Tagore's *Four Chapters (Char Addhyay)* and two other novels of Bibhutibhushan Bandyopadhyay, *Aranyak: Of the Forest* (2002, 2017) and *Making a Mango Whistle (Aam anthir Bhepu)* (2007).

Bibhutibhushan Bandyopadhyay was born in Ghoshpara-Muratipur village in Bengal on 12 September 1894. His ancestral home was in Barakpur (formerly in Jessore District) on the banks of the river Ichhamati. He moved to Calcutta for higher studies.

Bibhutibhushan spent his time writing and travelling intensively, particularly in the forests of Bihar, participating in literary meets and conferences, until his sudden death in Ghatshila on 1 November 1950. Besides numerous unpublished manuscripts, his oeuvre comprises seventeen novels, seven diaries-travelogues and over two hundred short stories. He was posthumously awarded the Rabindra Puruskar in 1951 for *Ichhamati*, his last published novel.

Source: *Diner Parey Din* [Anthology of Bibhutibhushan Bandyopadhyay's diaries], Calcutta, Mitra & Ghosh, Pvt. Ltd, rpt. BS Jyestha 1400.

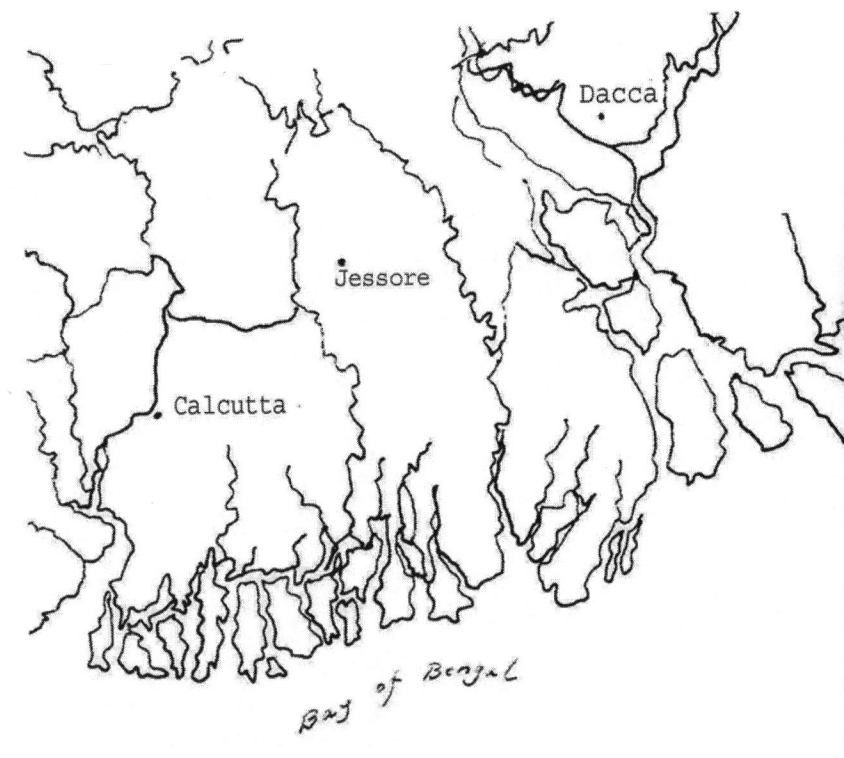

Jessore District in Bengal Presidency
Illustration courtesy: Rimli Bhattacharya
Map not drawn to scale

RESTLESS WATERS
of the
ICHHAMATI
Bibhutibhushan Bandyopadhyay

Translated from Bengali by
RIMLI BHATTACHARYA

Published by
Rupa Publications India Pvt. Ltd 2018
7/16, Ansari Road, Daryaganj
New Delhi 110002

Sales Centres:

Allahabad Bengaluru Chennai
Hyderabad Jaipur Kathmandu
Kolkata Mumbai

Translation and Introduction copyright © Rimli Bhattacharya 2018

This is a work of fiction. Names, characters, places and incidents are either the product of the author's imagination or are used fictitiously and any resemblance to any actual person, living or dead, events or locales is entirely coincidental.

All rights reserved.
No part of this publication may be reproduced, transmitted, or stored in a retrieval system, in any form or by any means, electronic, mechanical, photocopying, recording or otherwise, without the prior permission of the publisher.

ISBN: 978-81-291-XXXX-X

First impression 2018

10 9 8 7 6 5 4 3 2 1

The moral right of the author has been asserted.

Printed by XXXXXX

This book is sold subject to the condition that it shall not, by way of trade or otherwise, be lent, resold, hired out, or otherwise circulated, without the publisher's prior consent, in any form of binding or cover other than that in which it is published.

May the rivers flow...

Contents

Introduction / ix

Restless Waters of the Ichhamati / 1

Translator's Note / 359

Glossary / 365

Introduction

Ichhamati. Ichhamati. The restless waters of the river Ichhamati flow past villages carrying in whirls and eddies the stories of ordinary folk—subjects and subjectivities that do not find a place in the grand roll call of history. Both prologue and epilogue to Bibhutibhushan Bandyopadhyay's epic narrative *Ichhamati* cue us to a mode of reading. The gaze of a slow-moving attentive river-farer brings into view glimpses of vibrant plant life, traces of human habitation and changes of sky and water in the course of seasons. These are signs, evoking the flow of time in which generations unknown have lived and those unborn will live along the Ichhamati's banks as it wends its way through Jessore district towards the Bay of Bengal. Born of this tension between the ephemeral and the forever, the novel's own riverine course dispenses with chapter breaks—the writer's decision that my translation follows.

Bibhutibhushan had long wanted to write a novel with a 'vast canvas'—at least from the time he was writing *Pather Panchali* in the forests of Bhagalpur. Scattered allusions to impressions of people, places and incidents that would later be woven into *Ichhamati* are found from the late 1920s in many of his diaries or *dinalipis*,[1] as well as in his unpublished journal of 1949. The description of a certain 'Morrison Saheb's silk-cotton tree' in Barakpur, his native village, is quite similar to the banyan by the river under which Bhabanicharan, the protagonist, sits down to meditate and is interrupted by Grant Saheb.[2] Reflections of Bibhutibhushan's own fulfilment in marriage to a younger woman in his late life and his new-found joy in his infant son permeate the novel. A letter to his wife dated 1 December 1941 is about the Bonsimtala ghat and a picnic in which he misses her intensely.³ This emotional link between place and person is refracted in the novel's idealized female protagonist, Tilu, who thinks wistfully of Bonsimtala when the women decide to go bathing in a group to another ghat.

In a 1944 radio talk Bibhutibhushan emphasized how the warp and weft of his writings came from the minutiae of all that he had absorbed in his life.⁴ *Ichhamati*, the final novel to be published in the author's lifetime, is set in the village of Panchpota and the Mollahati indigo plantation in the second half of nineteenth-century Bengal. But the novel is interwoven with numerous strands of Bibhutibhushan's entire experiential life.

≈

Ichhamati does not aspire to be a historical novel. Historical references appear like flares, lighting up mundane, often intimate, moments in the lives of a cross section of people of nineteenth-century rural Bengal. The author internalizes, to some extent, the dialectics of history in the way affective ties are shaped and hierarchies are played out in a chessboard of race, caste and gender. The indigo plantation *sahebs*, the occasional *memsaheb*, the never-quite *mem*, and the multitude of people whose lives are bound visibly and invisibly with the plantation economy make for a localized yet expansive canvas evoking other lands in the invisible chains of imperial economy.

The indigo dye or *nila* was known since *c.* 500 BC in the Indian subcontinent and production and dyeing processes were brought to a fine art along the western coast extending to the north up to Punjab, Sindh and Multan, but indigo was a late entry to Bengal.⁵ Summing up the indigo trail in a global context, a historian observes: 'From the seventeenth to the twentieth centuries indigo was a fugitive among industries, wandering from Gujarat in Western India to the West Indies and then back to Bengal in Eastern India.'⁶ In fact, it was shortly *after* British planters in the West Indies turned to coffee and sugar as more lucrative crops, that indigo was introduced to Bengal on a big scale, to be manufactured by European planters by 'West

Indian methods.'[7] The British in turn had followed the French, the Dutch and the Spanish—nations embroiled in 'economic rivalries' in what is known as 'the Caribbean era of indigo'.[8] The 'regional' in Bibhutibhushan's narrative is thus already bound by the ebb and flow of capital, labour and goods across oceans.

Is *Ichhamati* then a 'plantation novel', revolving around life in one of the numerous *neelkuthis* or indigo factories that dotted Lower Bengal under Company rule? ('Lower Bengal' is the geographical term for the deltaic region, where the floodplains were particularly suitable for growing indigo.) There is enough in the novel about the coercion that went into indigo cultivation, the intricate nexus between the English manager and the brahman dewan, the peasant subjects, Musalman and Hindu, including episodes from the Indigo Revolt, sometimes called the 'Indigo disturbances', of 1859–1862.

Clearly though, the plantations in Bengal were distinctive from say, the ones in the West Indies; the latter were worked entirely by slave labour transported from thousands of miles away from Africa.[9] Besides, drawn slowly into the episodic flow of his narrative, we realize that Bibhutibhushan did not wish to write an ethnographic treatise of indigo production. Shades of indigo-neel seep into fragile alliances and the bonds of custom and law, into the unrealized possibilities of unexpected love in oppressive sociopolitical contexts of 'native' and 'saheb', upper caste and outcast, renunciate and householder. The novel is not made of sharp breaks, twists and turns, dramatic denouements. Rather, the 'highlights'—if they may be so called—lie in the glint of an ornament encircling Tilu's arm in the light of the oil lamp, Nistarini stumbling upon the pearl-seeded oyster as she emerges dripping and exhausted after a long swim in the river, a child's babble that sends his father into a meditative trance; Gaya-mem, teasing, flirtatious and heroically steadfast—an icon of dignity and endurance—even if she was 'given' as an adolescent to the Burra Saheb by her own mother. The reader holds on to such moments for their extraordinary resonances.

Yet, it is colonial ethnography that initiates us to this world in the persona of the English travelling artist, 'Grant Saheb', intrepid recorder of native life. The narrator of the novel abruptly and solemnly informs us of the 'existence' of his characters in colonial records: 'The two sketches, "A Bengalee woman" and "An Indian Yogi in the Woods" that appear on pages 54 and 57 of Colesworthy Grant's *Anglo Indian life in Rural Bengal,* published in 1864, are of Tilu and Bhabani Barujje respectively.' Should it matter that the portraits of Rajaram, Bhabani or Tilu are not to be found in the book that the *real* Colesworthy Grant (1813–1880) wrote?[10] A different notion of critical empathy impels Bibhutibhushan's claim to authenticity. For even Grant Saheb, the curious white man, can only paint the appearance of individuals who become generic types in his book.[11] After all, the only word the sympathetic saheb has mastered is the imperative *Jao!* Go! What would a Grant Saheb know of the erotic tryst that Bhabani plans with the most beloved of his three wives, Tilu? She arrives at the riverbank resplendent in her *dhakai* sari, ostensibly to become a subject of the saheb's painting. Painting over, she has to find the way back home through secret paths, for tongues would wag if she were to be seen outdoors walking with her husband. Such obscure cow paths and undertows the author tracks in *Ichhamati*, privileging moments of reflection and meditation, even silent communion between people, and between humans and nature.

Bibhutibhushan's vision of contemporary rural Bengal was hardly idyllic. In *Urmimukohor*, a journal written in his mid-life, he records his close relationship with Barakpur.[12] There are moving and tender vignettes of people, many of who find their way to the novel.[13] But even as he writes of the pleasures of bathing in the Ichhamati that flows past his native village, he expresses his fear about the danger of stagnation, of being stifled.[14] On another occasion he notes the destruction of 'the green wild banks of the Ichhamati' with the large-scale cultivation of crops like *potol* or pointed gourd.[15]

The rural Bengal of his novel is hidebound and restrictive. Often violent. In a shifting tapestry of names, occupation, livelihood and community, the politics of caste are played out through rules of inclusion and exclusion with strategies of calibration and negotiation. Satish Kolu, whose last name signals his lineage as oil-presser, begins as an itinerant fellow vendor with Nalu Pal. His flight of terror at the approaching white man in his buggy sets the tenor of the opening pages. Eventually though, pooling together their resources, experience and merchantile drive, it is they rather than the traditional *banik* community of Bengal, who make good. The two buy up the defunct Bengal Indigo Concern, and turn the indigo plantation into a profit-driven zamindari. Nalu also turns into a multi-tasking *aratdar*, an agent who earns a commission selling goods, regularly advances money to cultivators for seeds and lends money to zamindars. Others, such as Teenkori of the lowly *kaora* caste, tap into the colonial economy to diversify, producing oil as well as breeding pigs for the sahebs' table.

Seen through the eyes of Bhabani, the insider-outsider brahman protagonist of the novel, the region is shown as impoverished in other ways too. By way of religious entertainment, Bengal only has her medieval verse narratives of *Mangalchandi*, the songs of *Manasa'r bhashan*. To gain an insight into the Upanishads or other scriptures, the scholar-brahman has to travel westwards. True, that Durga Puja and other festivals offer the rare space of communal amusement and sharing—food for the hungry, and *jatra* and *kobi-gaan* sessions thrown open to the masses—sponsored by the zamindar or by the white man turned native, the 'Burra Saheb' of Mollahati. But even on festive occasions, destitute brahman women and their children have to fill their bellies stealthily under the cover of darkness. When the sponsor of the puja is the self-made entrepreneur Nalu Pal, the better-off brahmans ostracize their poor brethren who would wish to eat their full in the home of a *sudra*.

Brahmans come in for the sharpest critique. At least thrice in the novel the narrator comments directly on the idle group of landowning brahmans who while away their lives in the *chandimandap*, smoking and playing board games, gossiping and passing judgement on the hapless in their midst. Bhabani the *kulin* brahman and erstwhile celibate wanderer, observes to the like-minded Ramkanai: 'Aah, Kobiraj-moshai, the world is running on the wheels of lies and deception. Just look around you—in our very own village. Each one concerned only with wealth and property. Oppressing the poor, tricking people of their land, criticizing, gossiping, busy slapping lawsuits on each other at the slightest chance. Frogs in the well, deluding themselves every moment of their life.' For all the humility he professes and his dependence on brahmans to confer social rank, Nalu Pal speaks slightingly of them. Even the murderous dacoit Hala Pekey expresses his contempt for brahmans in general.

Of all brahmans, kulins bound by strict laws of hypergamy, were ranked the highest in Bengal. An enormous social and emotional energy was spent in fine-tuning hierarchy amongst the kulins and other brahmans; sharing of food and the brokering of feasts were also way of negotiating caste mobility. Nalu Pal finally seals his status by sponsoring the Durga Puja and by holding a feast for brahmans in *his* home. Ramhari, a slightly 'inferior' brahman in status, triumphs by virtue of leveraging sheer numbers from neighbouring villages to Nalu's feast. Gradations between a '*baruri* brahman' and a '*shrotriya* brahman' become crucial in setting up marriage alliances and other social relationships. (A *strotriya brahman* is one who is well versed in the Vedas and Upanishads. *Shrotriyo brahman* has a negative connotation: one who lacks one of the nine qualities and hence, not of the highest order; i.e. not kulin.)

Bhabanicharan Bandyopadhyay, in his urban satire *Kolikata Kamalaya* (1823), had offered an early exposé of the double life led by brahmans who had dealings with sahebs in the colonial city. This entailed a separation of spheres, keeping the *vishaykarma* or sphere of worldly matters apart from sacred or ancestral duties—*daivakarma* and *pitrikarma* respectively. In *Ichhamati*, Dewan Rajaram enacts this daily separation with scrupulous strictness: he has a bath after every encounter with a *mlechha* or untouchable, doesn't drink a drop of water while at work in the Neelkuthi, and piously performs his *sandhyanhik*, evening prayer, on his return home. Purificatory rituals undertaken in the realm of the domestic are meant to function as antidotes to his 'worldly affairs' that include perjury, forgery, murder and pimping. Speaking to his *guru-bhai*, Chaitanyabharati, Bhabani makes a rare caustic comment about Rajaram: 'This village is steeped in darkness. There's only the Neelkuthi and the sahebs, land, money, crops and assets—that's all they care about. My brother-in-law heads the list—he is the dewan of the Neelkuthi. The "Saheb" is his chosen deity.'

The rituals are a balm to the actual exercise of raw power in ensuring profits for the distant sojourners who have come to rule the land. In the process the Dewan consolidates his own power and wealth, even as he plays the considerate husband and the loving elder brother to the three sisters. Rajaram's favourite phrases are *praja jabda kora* and *praja jabda rakha*—putting down the peasant subjects, and, keeping them under one's thumb. They translate into a policy of terror-induced suppression, of maintaining the upper hand with calculated outbursts of cruelty. In the chain of command it seems quite 'natural' that Shipton Saheb should threaten his dewan with the same refrain, albeit in his archaic Bangla: '*Ami tomake jabda koriabo.*' I shall teach you a lesson!

Rajaram is a kulin brahman: his sisters are condemned to wait till they find a saviour in the guise of Bhabani, the handsome if elderly groom. Considered to be the highest among brahmans, kulins could only marry among themselves. A girl born in a kulin home had to wait until a groom was found, however old he might be. It was perfectly acceptable for kulin men to have innumerable marriages simply to 'save' the women's family from dishonour. The marriages entailed no responsibility since the women (and the children born of the marriage) usually continued to live in their natal homes. Marriage was livelihood, even profitable business. The starkest critique of kulinism had actually come in mid-nineteenth century when a pandit of Calcutta's Sanskrit College, Ramnarayan Tarkaratna, wrote *Kulinkulasarvasya Natak* (1854), a prize-winning play in a competition sponsored by reformists in Calcutta. Almost a hundred years later, the grim play finds a rather innocuous mention in *Ichhamati*.

Alongside this critique, the novelist seems simultaneously to seek redemption from the violence of indigo cultivation and the enmeshed oppression of caste and gender in the figure of the exceptional brahman. Ramkanai Kobiraj traverses the ravages of physical intimidation and social ostracism before he surfaces as an exemplar of dispassionate service in his capacity as the ideal *kaviraj*— as indigenous healer and passionate lover of god, capable of forgiving even those who would have murdered him. The woman who is 'cast out', Gaya-mem, and Ramkanai establish a special kinship that breaks through taboos of caste and gender. Similarly (though less dramatically), Bibhutibhushan has Bhabani initiating his eldest wife Tilu and their son (and subsequently, Nistarini) into a conscious awareness of Brahman, the Supreme Being. Not surprisingly, spiritual discourses in *Ichhamati* take place primarily between Bhabani and Ramkanai Kobiraj on the one hand and Bhabani and Chaitanyabharati on the other. The emphasis however is on seeking joy in ever-present signs of the divine. Bhabani himself, the perennial wanderer, is presented as the seeker who wants to find the cosmos in the grain of the everyday, as the spiritually inclined householder, ambivalent husband to two of the three sisters he has wed, and perhaps most emphatically as the doting father. Bhabani is poised to discover his own path. It is one of living in *sansar*, with all the responsibilities and acts of compassion that it entails, yet maintaining a certain detachment (*vairagya*). He distances himself from the material wealth his wives and son stand to inherit from Rajaram. In this he follows the basic tenet of the Upanishads: 'It is by a strictly personal effort that one can reach the truth.'[16] He attempts to weave together 'different strands' by 'sympathetic interpretation'.[17]

Khoka, the only child of the three marriages, combines the clouds of glory of the Romantic child and the clear-eyed seeker of truth exemplified in Nachiketa of *Katha Upanishad*. This is an abiding theme in Bibhutibhushan's oeuvre: numerous short stories anticipate entire sections of *Ichhamati*—of the little boy afraid of the forest, but eventually entering it with complete faith in his father.[18] In the novel, it becomes a leitmotif of the search for divinity in the mundane rounds of *sansar*.[19] Bhabani finds in his son the middle path of devotion, lit with the celebratory incandescence of the Upanishads and the unpredictable, difficult innocence of the child. The predominant emotion in *Ichhamati* is of *vatsalya rasa*. Bhabani muses: 'It is only now that I have become a father myself, after Khoka's birth, that I have begun to understand the love of the father in the Divine. How would I have known all these years how a father might feel!'

The texts most frequently cited in the novel include the Upanishads (*Isa, Prasna* and *Svetasvatara*) and a few other *Advaita-Vedanta* texts alongside the *Gita, Srimad Bhagavat* and *Chaitanya Charitamrita* constituting the range of Vaishnav scriptures, with their emphasis on faith in a personal god. An underlying motif connecting discourses and texts from various schools is that of renunciation, as a voluntary surrender of possessions for self-realization. The search is summarized in the passionate prayer of the fifteenth *sloka* of the *Isa Upanishad* (mistakenly referred to as the fourteenth) on the nature of truth, which Bhabani shares with Tilu: 'The face of truth is covered with a golden disc. Unveil it, O Pusan, so that I who love the truth may see it ... '

Bibhutibhushan's father was renowned as a *kathak-brahman*, a reciter of scriptures. He was an unworldly householder, a dreamer and a poet. Apu's father in *Pather Panchali* was cast in his likeness. Late in his life, the author of *Ichhamati*, in repeatedly affirming the joyous manifestation of the Supreme Being as one who delights in His own creation, was not only recalling his own father—part of an impoverished brahman literati—whose learning did not extend into colonial forms of knowledge, but also echoing the *Brahma Sutra* which refers to 'the creation of the world as an act of *lila*, play, the joy of the poet, eternally young...the Supreme [Being] is described as a *kavi*, a poet, an artist, a maker or creator, not a mere imitator.

Even as art reveals man's wealth of life, so does the world reveal the immensity of the Divine.'[20]

≈

With his intense awareness of the broken dreams and aspirations of most village women, it must have been difficult for Bibhutibhushan to represent with equilibrium both the oppression and the spaces of freedom available to Hindu women in nineteenth century Bengal. It is significant that while several of the male Muslim peasants are delineated in rough but powerful sketches, no Muslim woman even makes a fleeting appearance in *Ichhamati*.[21] The women's world in the novel is essentially of upper and lower caste Hindu communities—brahman and *bagdi*. Denouncing kulinism in recurrent episodic strands (the river a mute witness to sorrowful tales of women such as Tilu's aunt), Bibhutibhushan tries—at least in the realm of fiction—to propose a happier fate for the three sisters that Bhabani marries. Here too, doubts surface, in the somewhat orchestrated conversations between Bhabani and Chaitanyabharati, but more poignantly in snatches of conversation between Bhabani and Bilu, the second sister who dies untimely. Bibhutibhushan shies away from a representation of *sati*, ubiquitous in colonial accounts, though he alludes to it in passing, when the murdered dewan's wife desires to immolate herself in her husband's pyre but is dissuaded by her sisters-in-law.

Cutting across caste and class, the women in *Ichhamati* appear stronger (physically and mentally) than their men, more protective and caring. A few are singled out for their frankness and integrity, as with Tilu, Nistarini and Gaya-mem. Others like Setho Kumudini Jeley (from the fisherwoman's caste) feature anecdotally: Kumudini is sketched almost in mythic proportions for the fierce affection with which she looks after her flock of pilgrims. Iconic figures like the Rani of Jhansi (with whom Kumudini is compared) become part of popular lore through the tales of pilgrim-travellers.

Mediated through Hala's bloody tales of night raids with his gang is a recurrent image of the goddess like daughter-in-law who becomes Shakti incarnate in her violent defence of the menfolk, the home and her honour. Disguised as a Musalman fakir, Hala compulsively returns to the scene of the crime to see this woman, as if to reassure himself of her mortality. In recounting the hair-raising episode he manages to pique the curiosity of the *sannyasi*, Chaitanyabharati, who also wishes to glimpse this incarnation of Devi. Tilu is repeatedly 'imaged' as goddess Jagadhatri; other characters celebrate their conjugality: 'Like the divine consorts Shiva-Shivani—the two of you!' Tilu is the true *ardhangini*, woman as a complementary half, *sahadharmini*, helpmate, possessing appropriate virtues of benevolence and self-sacrifice coupled with self-preservation. Endowed with practical skills of housekeeping and child rearing, trained in the martial arts, she is beautiful and frank, and capable of enchanting a range of men—Grant Saheb, Hala Pekey, Chaitanyabharati, Ramkanai Kobiraj and Ramhari Chakrabarti, among others. In a sleight of hand essential to fiction, Bibhutibhushan's rescue of his young wife from drowning is transformed into Tilu braving the dark waters to rescue her husband from sure death. [22]

More persuasive than these flashes of the archetypal Bengali female as the mother goddess is the casual way in which Bibhutibhushan weaves into the narrative a range of expressive forms—songs devotional/erotic, poems, riddles and proverbs—marking their transactional spaces as peculiarly feminine. Exchanging riddles, 'cutting' impromptu verse, singing amongst a group of teasing and bantering women comprise modes of socializing, a frank acceptance of the erotic, with touches of the bawdy. The scenes at the river *ghat* where women routinely go to fetch water, bathe and generally let their hair down, conjure up an uninhibited occasion for merriment, homo-eroticism, of day dreams and dreams of desire in the sensuous abandonment of water and foliage. Women such as Nistarini who have come from elsewhere carry with them fragments of semi-classical forms such as the *tappa*. ('Nidhu-babu's tappa', became a byword for erotic lyrics composed by Ramnidhi Gupta of the early nineteenth century.) With her strong body, her unfettered movements, her powerful singing voice and superb gestures Nistarini appears seductive in a 'mannish' way to the more docile women at the ghat who are initially hostile to her unconventional ways. Of course, Bibhutibhushan tames this impulsive strong woman by showing her complete surrender to (and undoubted attraction for) Bhabani, just as the fierce Hala Pekey follows Tilu about like a loving 'pet' within the confines of her modest home! Memories of songs haunt even the ruthless Prasanna Amin as he recalls his unattractive but loving first wife: 'When she believed herself to be alone, she would sing devotional *rasakali* songs in that moaning nasal voice of hers.' And at the very beginning of the novel Nalu Pal is belting out a *shyamasangeet* (devotional song to goddess Kali), although Nalu is usually cast as a Vaishnav for the remainder of the novel.

While underlining changes in the celebration of traditional 'womanly' rituals and 'allowing' Bhabani entry into an all-female outdoor gathering, Bibhutibhushan finally affirms a kind of continuity, at least for the period he is depicting. *Ichhamati* does not offer any major rupture in gender roles, even though focalized through Bhabani, dynamic (*tejaswini*) women characters are consistently foregrounded and there are allusions to reform movements in distant Calcutta that promise female education and emancipation.

≈

Ruins of indigo plantations dot the landscape of Bengali fiction, and of Bibhutibhushan's oeuvre as a whole. An entire chapter is devoted to the child Apu's perception of one such abandoned neelkuthi even in the abridged children's version of *Pather Panchali*, called *Aaam Anthir Bhepu* (*Making a Mango Whistle*). In his short story entitled 'Neelganjer Fulman Saheb', Bibhutibhushan drew a fairly sympathetic portrait of a certain family of Farmour sahebs.[23] The last of the line, Farmour/ Fulman has gone native to the point of enjoying *krishnajatras* and *panchalis*, much like Shipton in *Ichhamati* who is keen on *kobi'r ladai* and encourages his new dewan to book a renowned jatra troupe during the Durga puja at the Mollahati Neelkuthi. In these moments of individuation, *Ichhamati* distances itself from the stark black and white characterization of sahebs in much of Bengali literature. Even rapacious Indian collaborators such as Dewan Rajaram and Prasanna Amin have a human face.

The history of forms of land-holdings, land and occupancy rights, tenancy and revenue rates in colonial Bengal that constitutes the economic base of the novel is too complex to be delineated briefly. Only a few critical aspects are touched upon here. The interested reader who wishes to delve deeper may turn to some of the texts in the references. As already mentioned, the *rayiats* or cultivators in colonial Bengal were legally 'free men', unlike the slaves who had been transported to power indigo plantations set up in colonies elsewhere in the world. However, the accepted process of forcibly giving out 'advances' (*dadon*) to rayiats and the nexus between a complex legal system, banks and the community of planters (usually English and Scotch) and merchants (represented through agency houses—'a group of some 15 Calcutta firms') in Calcutta *and* London effectively meant an 'exit closed' situation for the cultivator. The rayiat was therefore *bound* to cultivate indigo, often on the most fertile soil at his disposal, the price of the crop being subject to speculation on the London/global market.

The Permanent Settlement Act of 1793 had already reconfigured the revenue system with the creation of a new class of landholders in Bengal. From early nineteenth century onwards, European planters 'negotiated' forcefully between Bengali landlords and different classes of peasants with the sole intention of bringing as much land as possible under indigo cultivation. Since the planters oversaw the entire labour-intensive process of manufacture—transforming crops cut in the fields to the pressed indigo 'bricks' ready for export in the families, they hounded the rayiat—individually and collectively, to realize their quota, the price of which was governed by a speculative market. The risk of crop failure too was borne entirely by the rayiat.

Professional *lathiyals* (literally, wielders of sticks or *lathis*) comprised the armed guards that every planter (and zamindar) employed against recalcitrant peasants or a rival estate. Lathiyals surface with unexpected ties in *Ichhamati*: Aghore Muchi, freshly released from jail where he had been serving time for banditry, speaks familiarly to the three sisters, addressing them variously as 'Didimoni', 'Tilu-didimoni' and 'Bor-di'. He looked after them when they were children; clearly, he has been in Dewan Rajaram's employ. The conversations between dacoit, lathiyal, respectable householder reveals the porosity of occupations, of livelihoods induced by empty bellies. Following the Bengali zamindars, the European planters also retained bands of lathiyals and spearmen, 'hiring levies from the surrounding villages' when necessary.[24] In the 'contests between planters and zamindars...the rayiat was the chief victim. Whoever won, his crops were destroyed, his villages looted, and his cattle driven off.'[25]

There are other dimensions to land and labour in the novel. The upper strata of brahmans, their ignorance matched by arrogance, are shown as living primarily off the income from their land. This comprised inherited holdings that were in the nature of rent-free grants such as *debottar* (made in favour of the deity of a temple), *brahmottar* (personal grants made to brahmans), or, *dharmottar* (endowments to institutions or congregations.) Bhabani too derives his sustenance from the land he receives as dowry from his dewan brother-in-law! The novel hints at shifts in the nature of education, learning and employment with the more ambitious amongst the brahman literati moving to the metropolis primarily to work as clerks. Bhabani's son Tulu with his serio-comic rendering of English will mark a break from the relationship with traditional learning, land and labour.

Amongst the diverse strata of people in the novel, representing different histories of belonging to the region and the land, are the *bunos*, literally, the wild ones. The nomenclature is a reference to their histories—of being transported from their natal regions and recruited to clear the jungle—*buno* or wild terrain. According to a historian, 'the *buna* coolies, the tribals who were employed each season by the planters for the manufacturing process' were also emboldened during the time of the tumult to ask for more advance and pay.[26] Theirs is a flickering presence in the novel, signaling forgotten trajectories of internal migration, new modes of livelihood and labour with initiation into the colonial economy, but always on the margin. Khepi, the 'crazy one', who sets up her ashram just outside the village of Panchpota and attracts a range of followers, says she is from the lowest Hanri-Dom caste, but is regarded as a buno.

The hamlets in *Ichhamati* are shown segregated into localities or *paras*, with spatial hierarchies determined along access to resources such as drinking water: thus, bagdi-para, duley-para, kaora-para, brahman-para. The Neelkuthi, with its imposing proportions and adjoining property stands out in every way from other spaces. Nalu Pal's shop, Khepi's ashram and the village chandimandaps (when transformed to the weekly court), comprise intersectional locations where otherwise segregated groups meet either by need or choice. But subtle and explicit distinctions in seating, eating, smoking and modes of address in the treatment of one caste/class and another impact interpersonal relationships in these common spaces as well.

≈

Bibhutibhushan's choice of Jessore district for his novel follows history. It is generally agreed that the Indigo Revolt or *Neel Bidroho*, as it was known in the Bengal countryside, began around February–March 1859 'when thousands refused to grow indigo any more', and the 'earliest sparks' began in Jessore.[27] Ashley Eden's 'vernacular note' mandating that peasants had a choice of crops provoked fresh organized resistance. On the whole, peasant resistance to the cultivation of indigo was one of defiant non-violence, but there were 'expressions of militancy' which included fighting off mercenary armies of the planters, refusing to pay rents, and even organizing marches with peasant *lathiyals* on indigo factories with the intent of destroying them. One such factory was Mollahati, celebrated in the popular song *'Mollahati'r lamba lathi'* (The long sticks of Mollahati)! After the Indigo Act (Act X of 1860), which for a time, strengthened the hands of the planters, peasants resorted to withholding rents; 'thus the rent strike merged into the indigo strike.'[28]

The novel is peppered with historical references, with liberties taken in chronology. Some of these are directly related to the role of the liberal Bengali bhadralok and Britishers in the Indigo Revolt: Ramgopal Ghose's lectures, Harish Mookerjee's fiery editorials in the *Hindoo Patriot*; Rev. James Long's agitation and involvement in the *Neel Durpan* case (the anti-planter play written by Dinabandhu Mitra); the rebellion of the peasants in the districts of Nadia and Jessore; and so on. Other occurrences are often not only historically inaccurate but reduced almost to a farce in their treatment, as in the case of the uprising led by Titu Mir.[29] Personages such as Rammohun Roy, (Iswarchandra) Vidyasagar and (John Drinkwater) Bethune, are alluded to by Bhabani. Lord Mayo's ('Laad Meo' in the novel) assassination and one of the Afghan Wars lie on the periphery of the general consciousness of the people in the novel. It is beyond the scope of this introduction to provide an exhaustive gloss on each of these referents; I offer below a particular example of Bibhutibhushan's complex configuration of history, nature and subjectivity.

The steamboat and the steam train make their almost mandatory appearance, while the motorcar (machine-gari) and lamps with kerosene oil (replacing castor oil) are objects of wonder to the villagers through hearsay. They are not intended to function exclusively either as exact historical referents or as markers of colonial modernity. The Chhota Laat (Lieutenant Governor) and his entourage on a steamship puffing along the Ichhamati function less as agents transforming the entire collective of Mollahati, than signaling possibilities for some in the new generation who which will use the English language as a capital for social mobility in the city. As the Chhota Laat sails down the river the peasants wait patiently by the banks, and chant the *jigr* (the word is from the Arabic *zikr*), successive chants or cries in praise of Allah.

According to a contemporary report, when 'Lieutenant Governor J. P. Grant...[was] on his way up the Kumar and Kaliganga rivers through the heart of Kushtia...numerous crowds of raiyats appeared at various places, whose whole prayer was for an order of Government that they should not cultivate indigo'.[30] 'At one point... two hundred rayiats assembled on either side of the river, joined hands and called out for justice with a loud lamentable [sic] groan.'[31] Perhaps this is a case of mistranslation in the colonial records: the 'loud lamentable groan' in the report is the jigr raised by (Muslim) peasants in the novel!

The novel's strength lies precisely in the mingling of custom with the visible manifestation of colonial power: the good government versus the bad planter, the benevolent but distant 'Maharani' versus the proximate and fearful 'Neel Saheb'. Bibhutibhushan plants vignettes of 'objective history' amidst everyday local rituals: the narrative begins with a group of children engaged in a seasonal custom of identifying and picking the 'fourteen kinds of greens' along the bank on the very day that the Chhota-Laat is to sail by. And it is within this 'customary and natural' event, juxtaposed with a sweeping 'image from history', that the author picks up the emergent aspirations of an intermediate group of people. Neither peasants nor sahebs themselves, members of this class/caste throng the bank along with the aggrieved peasants: Tulu (Bhabani's son) receives his first glimpse of the sahebs and has his first taste of English on this occasion.

Coming soon after the 1857 Uprising, but in contrast to the former, the *Neel Bidroho* saw the beginning of organized protests in Bengal, with small landholders and moneylenders, better off rayiats, journalists based in or educated in Calcutta coming together in support of the rayiats. Missionaries as well as sympathetic white officials joined in the larger debates and legal action against the planters and merchants. But it never developed into a full-fledged anti-British movement.[32]

The consensus amongst historians is that at the time of the

Revolt, indigo farming was already turning non-profitable—the 1830s–40s were the decades of maximum profits.[33] In any case, synthetic aniline dyes invented in Germany would soon flood the market. Bibhutibhushan encapsulated the two events in *Ichhamati*, bringing forward in time the discovery of the chemical dye, to suggest a 'natural death' of the indigo industry. In the waning years of indigo farming only Shipton Saheb stays behind in Mollahati nursed by Gaya and a few other faithful retainers. Ironically, he spends his last days not by the river Ichhamati; he wanders back to his childhood fishing trips to Lake Elterwater in the Lake District, and hears again the church bells pealing in the English countryside as he lies dying. His final words to Gaya add to this distance.

≈

> From behind the waves of the ulukhagra flowers that surrounded Shipton Saheb's grave a woman's figure rose up with a start, hurriedly, and stood still in that hazy moonlight like a marble statue.

Ichhamati does not end either with a panoramic view or with a strong closure. Gaya-mem, a ghost of her former vital beautiful self, is discovered by her one time admirer, Prasanna Amin, laying flowers at the grave of the Burra Saheb on his death anniversary. In this triangulation working with presence and absence, past and present, she reminds us obliquely of a tale unfolded elsewhere—in the ending that Dickens finally chose for *Great Expectations* (1861-62) when Pip and Estella meet in the deserted garden, the ghost of Miss Havisham around them. But Gaya is a bagdi-mem who provokes a revisionist reading of *Ichhamati*.

Bagdi girls/women feature in many of Bibhutibhushan's stories.[34] In *Ichhamati* he enmeshes them in the very workings of power in layered hierarchies of caste, race, class and gender, and above all in the dynamic physical beauty, strength and vulnerability of the labouring body. The fraught ending of the novel only underlines how Gaya-mem, dispossessed of community, livelihood and social status, bereft of her protector Shipton Saheb, remains with us as a spectral presence, returning us willy-nilly to the residual trauma of indigo cultivation. Like the surveying chain which marks out the gift of land that will allow her to eke out a living, in excess of her speech and her engagement with various characters, is the way she is emplotted as a physical presence in her movements (even that of making dung cakes) and of certain kinds of actions she will never be able to perform. Her in-between spectral 'being' is perhaps best captured in the stinging 'judgement' that cousin Niri (Nirada bagdini) delivers, when Gaya, facing penury and starvation, asks her kinswoman to teach her how to thresh paddy:

> You won't be able to do it, not you,' said Niri, at the end of her account. 'Aunty raised you differently, spoilt your chances. You didn't become a memsaheb and you didn't become a labouring bagdi girl. How will you live? You've lost out both ways.

Notes

1. Successively published as *Smritir Rekha, Utkarna, Urmimukhor* and *Heye Aranya Katha Kau*. Mollahati and the names of other familiar landmarks in the novel appear in *Trinankur, Bibhuti Rachanabali*, vol. 4, p. 349.
2. See letter 21 written from Barakpur, postmarked 4 March 1947, in *Bibhuti Rachanabali*, vol. 4, Calcutta, Mitra & Ghosh Publishers, BS 1385, rpt. 1388, p. 836.
3. *Bibhuti Rachanabali*, vol. 8, G.K. Mitra & T. Bandopadhyay, eds. Calcutta, Mitra & Ghosh Publishers, rpt. BS Aswin 1403.
4. 'Amar Lekha', Radio Talk, June 1944, *Bibhutibhushan Galpasamagra*, p. 1.
5. See Lotika Varadarajan, 'Indigo: The Indian Tradition' and other essays in Kapila Vatsyayan, (ed.) *Culture of Indigo in Asia: Plant, Product, Power*, New Delhi, Niyogi Books, 2014.
6. Blair B. Kling, *The Blue Mutiny*, p. 15. From Bengal, indigo cultivation moved to Bihar where the major 'disturbances' occurred in 1874.
7. Kling, pp. 17–18.

8. Prakash Kumar, *Indigo Plantations and Science in Colonial India*, p. 27.
9. The global route of the 'Atlantic triangular trade' was brought to my notice through the aquatints and copper engravings exhibited at Chateau des ducs de Bretagne/ Musée d'histoire de Nantes. Nantes was a major slave port. See for example, an illustration from 1770 showing an indigo plantation at http://www.spiegel.de/fotostrecke/photo-gallery-of-nantes-slave-trade-memorial-fotostrecke-81493-4.html. Accessed on 15 October 2015.
10. Anuradha Roy, 'Ichhamati'r prabaha ebong ichhamayi itikatha', p. 81.
11. Grant, a self-taught artist, became well known for his lithographs of British warfare in Burma and Afghanistan.
12. Written between May 1935—September 1936; published in August 1944.
13. Editorial gloss of *Urmimukhor* in *Bibhuti Rachanabali*, vol. 6, p. 804.
14. *Urmimukhor*, p. 374, p. 385.
15. *Urmimukhor*, pp. 386-387.
16. Radhakrishnan, Introduction, *The Principal Upanisads*.
17. Ibid., Preface, p. 8.
18. The conversation between father and son is almost similar in the short story 'Khela'/Play (*Kushal Pahari*, *BR*, vol. 6, p. 811), though here, the narrative ends in death by drowning. The story was published posthumously in December 1950. According to Rusati Sen, the story was first published in *Jugantar Saradiya*, BS 1356.
19. 'The *Brhadaranyaka Upanishad* teaches that, while those who put their trust in the intellect cannot attain to a knowledge of Brahman, yet there is an apprehension of His being by those who are childlike.' Radhakrishnan, *The Principal Upanisads*, Introduction, p. 100.
20. Ibid., p. 86.
21. Hindu and Muslim peasants united in the Indigo Revolt.
22. Death by drowning is a leitmotif in his works; his beloved sister Jahnavi drowned in the Ichhamati in 1939, the year he met his future wife, Roma Chattopadhyay.
23. 'Neelganjer Fulman Saheb', *Bibhuti Rachanabali*, vol. 6, pp. 206–214.
24. Kling, p. 54.
25. Ibid., p. 55.

26. Ibid., p. 166.
27. Subhas Bhattacharya, 'The Indigo Revolt of Bengal', p. 14.
28. Ibid., p. 15.
29. Titu Mir (1782–1831), born Syed Nisar Ali, well educated, influenced by the Wahabi movement successfully organized Muslim peasants against Bengali Hindu zamindars and the British. He was eventually defeated by a large British force in 1831.
30. Kling, p. 168, fn. 64. Buckland, Lieutenant Governors, I, 192.
31. Ibid.
32. Subhas Bhattacharya, p. 19 and p. 22.
33. 'In the peak year of 1842 indigo accounted for 46 per cent of the value of goods exported from Calcutta.' Kling, p. 21.
34. Turning adolescent Durga's death (in *Pather Panchali*) into an interrogative marker, Rusati Sen scrolls down Bibhutibhushan's work where bagdi women live fiercely independent lives but are often condemned to miserable deaths. Rusati Sen, 'Ekti anibarjo mrityu', pp. 112–113.

References

Bandyopadhyay, Bibhutibhushan. *Ichhamati* (Aswin 1382), Calcutta, Mitra & Ghosh Publishers Pvt. Ltd. Rpt. BS 1419.

Bandyopadhyay, Bibhutibhushan, *Bibhuti Rachanabali*, vol. 4 (BS 1385), Calcutta, Mitra & Ghosh Publishers, rpt. BS 1388.

Bandyopadhyay, Bibhutibhushan. *Bibhuti Rachanabali*, vol. 6, Calcutta, Mitralaya, 1944.

Bandyopadhyay, Bibhutibhushan. *Diner parey din* [Anthology of diaries], Calcutta, Mitra & Ghosh Publishers rpt. BS Jyestha 1400.

Bandyopadhyay, Bibhutibhushan. *Bibhutibhushan Galpasamagra*, Taradas Bandyopadhyay et al (eds.) vol. 1, Calcutta, Mitra & Ghosh Publishers, rpt. BS 1401.

Bandyopadhyay, Bibhutibhushan. *Bibhuti Rachanabali*, G.K. Mitra & T. Bandopadhyay (eds.) vol. 8, Calcutta, Mitra & Ghosh Publishers rpt. BS Aswin 1403.

Bhattacharya, Rimli. Introduction to *Aranyak, Of the Forest*, Calcutta, Seagull Publishers, 2002.

Bhattacharya, Subhas. 'The Indigo Revolt of Bengal', *Social Scientist*, Vol. 5, 12 (July 1977), pp. 13–23.

Bhattacharya, Suman. 'Jat and pater panchali', in Rusati Sen (ed.), *Bibhutibhushan Bandyopadhyay'er Sandhane*, pp. 30–47.

Bhattacharyya, Ananda. *Indigo Rebellion, Selections (1859–1862)*, Calcutta, Dey's Publishing, 2012.

Chatterjee, Partha. *The Land Question*, vol. 1, Calcutta, KP Bagchi & Co., 1984.

Chakravarty, Bikash. 'Bibhutibhushan Bandyopadhyay, 'Kalpanar bhugol o bhugoler kalpana'. *Visva-Bharati Patrika*, Magh-Chaitra 1412/January–March 2006.

Marriot, John and Bhaskar Mukhopadhyay (eds.). *Britain in India, 1765–1905*, vol. 3, Education and Colonial Knowledge, London, Pickering and Chatto, 2006.

Kling, Blair B. *The Blue Mutiny, The Indigo Disturbances in Bengal, 1859–1862* (1966), Calcutta, Firma KLM Private Ltd, rpt. 1977.

Kumar, Prakash. *Indigo Plantations and Science in Colonial India*. Delhi, Cambridge University Press, 2013.

Radhakrishnan, Sarvepalli (ed. & trans). *The Principal Upanishads* (1953), London, George Allen & Unwin Ltd, rpt. 1968.

https://ia802507.us.archive.org/10/items/PrincipalUpanishads/129481965-The-Principal-Upanishads-by-S-Radhakrishnan_text.pdf. Web.

Roy, Anuradha. 'Ichhamati'r prabaha ebong Ichhamayi itikatha' in Rusati Sen (ed.), *Bibhutibhushan Bandyopadhyay'er Sandhane*, pp. 65–88.

Sen, Rusati (ed.). *Bibhutibhushan Bandyopadhyay'er Sandhane*, Calcutta, Akshar Prakashani, 2014.

Sen, Rusati. 'Ekti anibarjo mrityu' (An inevitable death), *Bibhutibhushan Dwander Binyash* (1993) Calcutta, Papyrus, rpt. 1998.

The Ichhamati is a small river, at least that bit of it flowing through the district of Jessore. Moving southwards, the Ichhamati is transformed into a vast salty river replete with crocodiles, sharks and tortoises, melding into the jungle of *sundari* and *garan* trees in some faraway Sunderban until it merges with the Bay of Bengal—of this, no one from rural Jessore keeps track.

Only those who have had a chance of witnessing that stretch of the Ichhamati running through the districts of Nadia and Jessore know of its exquisite beauty. But only they who have actually lived for long in this region, along the banks of the river, will have truly experienced it. Green with creepers and foliage, resounding with bird song, both banks of the river are wondrous creations of God.

Take a boat from Morighata or Bajitpur right up to Chanduria ghat, and you shall see the bright red flowers of the poltey and madar trees on either bank, the aquatic foliage of the *bonnyeburo*, the radiance of the yellow flowers of the wild *titpalla* creeper and the floating leaves of topa-pana; sometimes, along a high bank, you will spy shrubs of *uluti-bachda* and *bainchi* in the shadow of ancient banyan and pipal trees, the nesting holes of river-mynahs, and everywhere the pleasing spread of creepers and all manner of greens. Few people live along the banks where the river broadens out: there are only the newly risen sandbanks, char-lands now covered with tussocks of fine green durba-grass, only the sandy ghats, shrubs thick with wild flowers and forests filled with cries of a multitude of birds. You might spot a dozen or so dinghies moored to a village ghat. On occasion you may sight a vulture sitting atop one of the crisscrossed branches of a tall silk-cotton tree in a stillness suggesting a higher state of spiritual realization—like a wash painting done by a Chinese artist. On some ghats women are bathing, while others, climbing up the steps with pitchers of water in the crook of their arms, stop to chatter with their companions who are still in the water. Perched on a high bank, the longish shed of a primary school on a grassy patch comes into view with its thatched roof and fencing of bamboo strips or cane; the only bits of furniture—a couple of benches and a rickety half-broken chair tied to a stake.

When the moonlight falls on the green grassy fields that have sprung up on the sandbanks where white clusters of *akanda* flowers blossom in the summer, and the mild breeze from the river sways the golden laburnum along the banks, travellers journeying along the river will sight the remnants of old ruined homes now covered with a profusion of wild akanda; perhaps too, a couple of termite mounds rising from the abandoned foundations. As you pass by these ruins of homes you will dream of bygone days, of a mother and her son, of a brother and a sister, whose lives were once entwined with these living signs of habitation.

From one century to another many are the unwritten histories of joy and sorrow that lie on their breasts, like the tracery of lines on water in the rains. Over them the sun spreads its rays, the late autumn sky rains down dew and the full moon pours its liquid light. Their voices, their stories, are the real history of our nation. Not the conquests of kings and emperors, but the unsung histories of the mute people of our land.

The year 1863. Bengali Era 1270. The floodwaters have barely receded. The paths still lie thick with mud, the fields submerged in water. On an afternoon, a drongo comes to perch on the thickly flowering branch of a babul tree. Nalu Pal is on his way to the weekly market of Mollahati, a load of betel nuts and leaves on his head. All along the road to Mollahati stand sturdy banyan trees planted by the sahebs, dating from when the indigo plantations came up in the region. Beneath the deep shade of one such banyan an exhausted Nalu Pal put down his load and twirling his thin strip of towel, sat down to rest.

Nalu was dark and scrawny, about twenty-one years old. He wore his hair long, hanging in slick locks. Around his shoulders he had wound a strip of brightly coloured towel, considered fashionable in rural parts. He hadn't married as yet: he'd been raised by his maternal uncle and, until recently, didn't have a cowrie to his name. It was only a year since Nalu had begun vending his goods of *paan-supari*, always on the move from one weekly market to another. An aunt of his had somehow put together for him the seed capital of seventeen rupees. Within the year he had increased the sum to fifty-seven rupees—that, after all his expenses were paid. Net profit.

Nalu was in high spirits. He had found it difficult lately to stomach the food he got at his uncle's, doled out without any affection or respect. It really didn't suit a twenty-one-year old to be such a burden. The way his aunt had lashed out at him—all because he had wanted a bit of oil to groom his hair with! 'And where is one to get so much oil from, may I ask?' she'd said with a toss of her head. 'Look at the airs he puts on, this boy! Growing his hair so long! You need to *earn* your own keep I say, if you want to be *so* fancy.'

Nalu Pal would probably have dozed off beneath the shady banyan; it was still a while before the market would open and he could snatch some rest in the meantime. But just then someone rode up and reined in exactly where he was sitting. Nalu Pal hastily got up and addressed the rider with great deference, 'Ray-*moshai*, how are you? My respec'ful greetings to you this morning.'

'Blessings on you, my man. Nalu, aren't you? Off to the market?'

'Yes, sir.'

'Sit up straight. Shipton Saheb's coming this way.'

'Should I leave the path then and get on to the field, babu? I've heard he beats up people something terrible.'

'No, no! Why should he beat you up! That's nonsense. Keep sitting here.'

'Will he be riding?'

'I think not; he'll come in a tom-tom most likely. Well, I shan't stay any longer.'

People were scared to death of Shipton, big boss of the Mollahati indigo plantation. Tall and stocky, with a face as round as a tiger, he always went about with a whip in his hand. 'Shyamchand' was the name the locals had given the whip. Since there was no saying when Shyamchand would land on anyone's back, people were terrorized when they heard the Saheb was out.

In the meantime, Satish Kolu, another itinerant vendor, appeared on the scene with a huge earthen pot of mustard oil perched on his head-cloth. Spotting Nalu who was still sitting by the wayside, he asked, 'Aren't you goin'?'

'Sit down...have some tobacco.'

'Don't have any.'

'I've got some; but wait, let Shipton Saheb go by.'

'An' who's tole you that the saheb's a comin'?'

'Ray-moshai said so. Sit.'

Suddenly, Satish Kolu looked ahead fearfully, and then, cutting past the bushes of shanra and sheora, he scrambled right down to the paddy fields that lay below the road. 'Come away!' he called out to his friend as he disappeared into the standing crop, 'The saheb's out!'

Abandoning his load of betel nut and leaves, Nalu Pal followed suit. The jingling of bells from the tom-tom could be heard approaching and soon, driven at a furious pace and raising a cloud of dust along the dirt road, the saheb's carriage came into view. As fate would have it, the tom-tom pulled up by the very banyan tree where Nalu Pal had sought some rest.

'Hey! Whose loat be this?' the saheb let out a cry in his semi-archaic Bangla, as his eyes fell on the huge bundle by the wayside, apparently ownerless. He spoke in a curious mix of colloquial and literary Bangla with his own rules of declensions.

Half-hidden in the stalks of rice in the field below, Nalu Pal and Satish Kolu were petrified. Nafar Muchi—of the tanner community and now employed as the Saheb's orderly—barked out from behind the carriage, 'Hey there! Which fellow's left behind his load by the tree?'

'Answer!' cried the saheb. 'The loat belongs to which intividual?'

Looking most woebegone, Nalu Pal slowly climbed up the incline. Joining his palms in a respectful greeting, he said, 'It's mine, saheb,'

The saheb kept looking at him without saying a word.

'Yours?' demanded Nafar Muchi.

'Yes, *huzoor*.'

'What were you doing in the rice field?'

'Huzoor, your Honour...'

'I knows. All hite when they see me. I a snake or a tiger—me, huh?' asked Shipton.

The question was directed at Nalu so he fearfully mumbled, 'No, saheb.'

'Right. And the bundle, be what?'

'Paan leaves, saheb.'

'Takes it to the Mollahati market?'

'Yes.'

'What be your name?'

'Sri Lalmohan Pal, huzoor.'

'Put back upon your head! In future, do not hite if you see me. I'm not a tiger; I don't eat up people. Now go—you understand.'

'Huzoor...'

The saheb's tom-tom sped away. Nalu's heart was still going pit-a-pat. Whew! That was quite a close call. 'O Uncle! Uncle Satish!' he whistled and called out. Satish Kolu had gone far away from the road by this time, managing to keep under the cover of the paddy. Moving up cautiously behind the paddy stalks, he answered, 'Comin'!' and finally got up on the road.

'Oof! You really ran away some ways! Did you break out through the rice field when you heard him call me out?'

'What's one to do! We're po'r folks. If he was to lay on a stroke of Shyamchan' on our back, what could we do? And what was the saheb a-tellin' you?'

'Spoke well enough.'

'An' what was Ray-moshai a-tellin' you?'

'Saheb's on his way, sit up straight. That's what *he* said.'

'An' wouldn't he be saying that! The saheb's middlemen—that's what they are. Straight out business, that's what Ray-moshai's doin'— being a *dewan* to the indigo house. Built himself that huge two-storeyed house a few years ago...'

≈

Ray-moshai's full name was Rajaram Ray. He was the dewan of Mollahati's indigo plantation that the locals referred to as the 'Neelkuthi'. They hated him for his sycophancy to the sahebs as much as they feared him for the kind of suffering he brought upon the peasants on behalf of the sahebs. No one dared to utter a word though.

Rajaram Ray lived in the neighbouring village of Panchpota. The afternoon sun had already gone down the dense green of his garden when he dismounted. Bhoja the syce, a cousin of Nafar Muchi, ran to get his horse. Glancing towards the semi-enclosed *chandimandap* Rajaram found quite a crowd gathered there, waiting for him—a common enough sight at his place the whole year through. People came from far and near to the dewan's open court, each one to present his complaint or appeal. Someone's crops might have been destroyed, someone's land seized and the owner forced to grow indigo; in some other case, the plantation *amin* or surveyor may have disregarded the land marked out and kept aside for indigo cultivation and had taken over a much richer plot instead, marking it anew. All sorts of grievances could be heard at the dewan's. Some must have been attended to; would people have thronged his durbar otherwise, day after day? No bribing was necessary. Rajaram Ray was not the sort to accept bribes. If, however, at the end of a piece of legal business, someone wished to give him a big carp or a giant taro, or send over two earthen pots of special liquid molasses as a gift—no record exists of any of these expressions of gratitude ever being returned.

Rajaram's wife Jagadamba was once known for her beauty. In her unbleached red-bordered cotton sari, an assortment of ornaments on her arms that included a *bauti*-bracelet, an old-fashioned armlet, the iron bangle and white conch bangles of marriage; a big round of vermilion on her forehead, and her well-endowed figure, she looked every inch a prosperous matron.

Coming forward to welcome her husband, she said, 'Don't go outdoors right away, first complete your prayers.'

'Keep this,' said Rajaram, handing her a small pouch. 'Why, is there anything by way of refreshments?' he added with a smile.

'Of course there is. I've roasted some chana-grams and puffed rice.'

'That's good. But let me wash my hands and feet. And where are they—Tilu, Bilu and Nilu?'

'Busy cutting vegetables'

'I'll be back. Ask Tilu to get me some water.'

Tilu had already laid out a *kusha*-grass mat for her elder brother.

It was very late by the time Rajaram sat down in a corner of the open verandah to perform his ritual recitation. He did so for over an hour, reciting a number of Sanskrit verses in praise of various gods and goddesses. He was in the habit of paying obeisance to numerous deities, male and female, after he was done with the regular evening ritual. Amongst the goddesses, the ones he felt he must daily appease were Lakshmi, Saraswati, Rakshakali, Siddheswari and Ma Manasa. It wouldn't do to offend any one of them. After all, it was they who ensured that his affairs went well. Lest any of the goddesses should miss his prayers, he enunciated every syllable clearly and loudly, drawing out each line of praise.

'Dada, will you have some tender coconut water now?' asked Tilu.

'No. Isn't there any palm-candy water?'

'No, Dada, we've no palm candy at home.'

'Let the coconut water be; get me something else.'

Tilu brought him puffed rice and roasted chana-grams generously doused in oil in a huge metal bowl which could hold at least half a *katha* of puffed rice. Bilu came in with a bell-metal plate heaped with ripe jackfruit and finally, Nilu brought him a tumbler of water and some date-palm jaggery in a stone bowl.

'Come, sit down Nilu,' said Rajaram affectionately to his youngest sister. 'You'll have some of the jackfruit, won't you?'

'No, Dada, *you* have all of it. I've had lots.'

'Bilu, will you have some?'

'It's for you, Dada.'

Jagadamba joined him after finishing her prayers. 'You've worked so hard all day. Why don't you eat? How will you survive otherwise? Those red-faced sahebs wear you down to your bones at the Kuthi.'

'Isn't there any green chilly?' asked Rajaram. 'Send for a couple.'

'Shall I fan you?' Jagadamba asked her husband. 'O Tilu, ask your sister-in-law to bring a green chilly—and O Netya-aunty, the dal's on the fire; check on it—seems to be getting scorched. Chhoto-bou, will you take a look?' said Jadagamba, reeling off commands to the various women of her household.

'Don't rush off once you've finished eating; there's something I have to tell you...' she said, once she was seated beside her husband, fanning him.

'Well, what is it?'

'I'll tell you. Let the sisters leave.'

'They've left. What's going on?'

'There's an eligible man who has come to our village. We must try and make a match for the sisters.'

'Who would this be?'

'He'd become a sannyasi. Quite handsome; he's related to Chandra Chatujje—a nephew of sorts. I've heard he's leaving tomorrow; do visit them once.'

'How did you come to know?'

'Didi came and told me. She's been here twice to see me.'

'Let's see.'

'Won't do to simply say: "Let's see"! Tilu is thirty now, Bilu, twenty-seven. Tell me where shall we be finding a groom for them later? Won't do you any harm to get away from the daily grind of the Neelkuthi for *one* day.'

'Well then, let me be off. Give me my cotton shawl. I'll set off as soon as I've had a smoke.'

Rajaram didn't go past the crowded chandimandap; there was no way he could get away if he did so. Mehrauli Mondol's property was to be divided and settled; it was Rajaram who had set aside the day. They must all be sitting there—Ramjan, Shukur, Prahlad Mondol, Banamali Mondol and all the other elders of the Musalman locality. No, he would never be able to get away.

Chandra Chatujje, who he was to visit, also enjoyed a high status in the village. His was a prosperous household that ran on the income from seventy-two bighas of land. Their land, designated as *'brahmottar* property', was in the nature of an endowment to a brahman and so exempt from revenue. Not a single man of the brahman locality of Panchpota either held a job or worked for wages. Each owned a plot of land. It was their usual routine to stay up late in somebody or the other's chandimandap until ten or eleven at night, whiling away the time playing dice games like *pasha,* or *daba,* a form of chess.

Chandra Chatujje stood up to welcome Rajaram. 'Come, come babaji! Rains from a cloudless sky! Such an unexpected treat! What brings you here today? Do take a seat. Here, let's play a round.'

'Ah, it's Dewanji himself,' cried out Nilmoni Samaddar. 'Come dear brother and give me a hand: save my knight.'

'Come and sit by my side, brother—right here. Shall I get you some tobacco?' asked Foni Chakkarty.

Rajaram smiled at everyone in general and remarked, 'Do sit down all. Uncle Chandar, I see you have a real *adda* going on here.'

'Well, *you* never so much as step by our place,' Chandra Chatujje responded. 'Here we are lying by the wayside, you never spare us a glance.'

Rajaram had barely stepped on the colourful patterned carpet when every one of those present vied to make space for him.

Nilmoni Samaddar being a householder of very humble means in comparison to the others had no choice but to try and please everyone in whatever he said. 'How will Dewanji ever come down to visit us!' he exclaimed. 'Look at the crowd in *his* chandimandap—a regular *cutchery*! You can't find your way through that mass of people—accused, plaintiff and the whole lot. How would *he* ever find the time to come here for a game of chess?'

'As though we don't know!' retorted Foni Chakkarty. 'You're not telling us anything new.'

'You're such a good player; won't you join us for a round?' asked Nilmoni again.

Rajaram came forward to accept the hookah that Foni Chakkarty offered him. But he did not wish to smoke in front of the older Chandar Chatujje out of deference to him. He retired to a room inside the chandimandap and after having several puffs came back and handed over the hookah to Nilmoni before taking his place in the gathering.

It was not until ten at night that the game wound up. One by one people drifted homewards. Only then did Rajaram tell Chandra Chatujje quite frankly the reason for his arrival. Chandra Chattujje beamed in delight.

'And is that all, babaji?' he exclaimed, holding Rajaram's hand. 'There's nothing to it. But you know, baba, Bhabani had become a sannyasi—I must share that with you.'

'Let me go home and inform the women. And I have to tell Tilu. It's for them to decide.'

'Certainly!' said Chandra Chatujje. Lowering his voice, he went on, 'Another thing: it's my desire that Bhabani should settle down here, amongst us. You get him married to all three of your sisters— and you'd have done your job, be out of harm's way. Give away five bighas of the brahmottar land as part of the dowry. I can settle it all right away.'

'But Uncle, I cannot confirm *anything* till I've spoken at home,' said Rajaram with a worried look on his face. 'I'll let you know tomorrow.'

'You go ahead with the marriage without any qualms. It's not because he is *my* nephew. They are from a family of *baruri* brahmans from Katad Bandhigati; a break in their *kulin* lineage only in one generation. I'll have the matchmaker recite the entire family genealogy for you. Real-to-goodness kulins they are—every one knows them!'

'How old would the groom be?'

'Close to fifty I would say. But then, your sisters aren't young either. If Bhabani hadn't turned sannyasi, he would have fathered seven sons by now. Have a look at him first—you'll find him by the river every evening absorbed in his meditation for an hour or so, and then wandering around at will. Impressive build—the biceps on his arms are quite something.'

'Would Bhabani agree to marry all three sisters at the same time?'

'That, babaji, is in my hands. You can be easy on that score.'

The way back home through the bamboo copse was somewhat dark. Fireflies flickered in the thick foliage of the babul and *kunch* trees. From the nearby forest wafted the delicate fragrance of *chhatim* flowers.

≈

It was very late at night by the time Tilottama got to know of the news. The waning moon had risen from above the bamboo grove by the river. She called out to the sister who was next in age, 'O Bilu, has *Bou-didi* told you anything?'

'Course she has! Why wouldn't she! About marriage, isn't it?'

'Go hang yourself, you wretch! Aren't you ashamed to speak like that!'

'What's to be ashamed about? Was it *such* a wonderful thing to remain old and unmarried?'

'We're going to be painted with the same brush—you've heard that, I presume? The same deal for all three.'

'Yes I know.'

'Willing?'

'If you ask me how I feel, I'd say that whatever might happen, let it happen.'

'I feel the same way. Must ask Nilu for her consent tomorrow morning.'

'What's *she* to say! A slip of a girl: she'll do whatever we do.'

Tilu stayed up on the terrace till the early hours, pensive and thoughtful. She was thirty years old. The idea of ever gazing at a husband's face had been like a dream never to be fulfilled. She couldn't believe it—even now; was she really going to be married? Actually set off to live in her husband's home? Did it matter that she was getting married to the same person along with her sisters? It was so in every other family like theirs which claimed a kulin lineage. Uncle Chandar's father had seventeen marriages—common enough in kulin households.

Had her brother decided on the wedding day, she wondered. How did it matter that the groom was fifty years old; she was hardly a young girl herself. In her excitement Tilu did not sleep that night. All she could hear was the fierce buzz of the mosquitoes in the bushes and in the forest.

≈

At the same time that Tilu was staying up the night on their terrace, Nalu Pal had come back from the Mollahati market. He had cooked his own meal, settled his accounts and then gone off to sleep.

Nalu had hatched a scheme. It had struck him that he *did* have a good head for business. He had sold seven rupees and nine annas worth of paan-supari. The net profit he made was one rupee and three annas. He had spent two annas on two and a half seers of rice, and two paise for one *poa* of *khoira* fish freshly caught from the *gaang*, where the river turns briny. He had really wanted to buy half a seer of fish, but didn't have enough oil to fry so much fish. The price of mustard oil had gone up…used to be three annas a seer, and was fourteen paise now. Could he afford it?

He *would* have to increase his capital. But that could never happen so long as he dealt only in betel nuts and paan leaves. He'd have to do business with cloth pieces—that's what his friend Mukunda Dey had advised. And, he could start off the cloth business only when he had thirty rupees saved. Nalu Pal did not feel like sleeping. At least he had found a way out of being a burden on his uncle! He wasn't a kid anymore to put up with his aunt's unending barbs.

Nalu felt a great surge of energy. On this moonlit night throbbing with the cry of crickets, when all the world was asleep, he felt he could see his life's path stretching out far ahead of him.

≈

As soon as it was morning Rajaram set off on horseback for the Neelkuthi. The path was cool and shady, green with wild creepers and plants. A host of birds perched all over the *juggidumur*-fig tree chirruped and sang out noisily. It was mid-June and thick clumps of golden laburnum bordered the edges of the field.

The Neelkuthi buildings were laid out along the Ichhamati. The white bungalow with huge pillars was Mr Shipton's. Rajaram dismounted a fair distance away from the Kuthi, and tying his horse to the stake, walked up towards the building. He peered this way and that most cautiously before he took off his shoes and entered the big hall. Indoors, he found another saheb besides Mr Shipton and his wife.

Shipton called out to him in Bangla, 'Dewan, come here,' and then switched to English to introduce him to the visitor, 'Look here Grant, this is our Dewan Ray…'

The other saheb was a newly arrived Englishman who wished to travel all over India. He was tall and of medium built, in his early thirties. He was wearing a high collar, like a padré. His name was Colesworthy Grant, and he was known as a writer and an artist. Right now, he was engaged in writing a book on rural Bengal.

'Yes, he will be a fine subject for my sketch of a Bengalee gentleman, with his turban—' said Mr Grant, looking up to smile at Rajaram.

'That is a *shamla*, not a turban,' Shipton Saheb corrected him.

'I would never manage it. Oh!'

'You would, with his turban and a good bit of roguery that he has.'

'In human nature I believe so far as I can see him—no more.'

'All right, all right—please yourself.'

'I'm not going to see you fall out with each other, wicked men that you are!' said Mrs Shipton.

'So I beg your pardon, ma'am,' said Mr Grant with a laugh.

Bhoja Muchi's elder brother, Sriram Muchi the bearer, entered the room with coffee for the sahebs. All those who worked as house servants for the sahebs came from the lowest social strata of *muchis* and *bagdis*; almost none were Muslims. There were exceptions like Madar Mondol, the syce at the cutchery, who was a Muslim.

Rajaram stood there waiting, all hot and streaming with sweat.

'You go, Dewan,' said Shipton Saheb to him. 'He wishes to make a painting from you. He will painting you be.'

'Yes, huzoor.'

'Take a look at the *dadon khata*, will you?'

The dewan was soon engrossed in the registers that recorded the dadon, advances forcibly given out to peasants to cultivate indigo.

In a short while though Sriram Muchi appeared at the office with a summon for Rajaram.

'Ray-moshai, they've sent for you. That new saheb is going to be looking at you and pinting—just see what he gone and stringed up there under the Ingleesh tree in this terrible afternoon sun. Go see for yourself what a show. An' Ray-moshai, do speak to the big boss and ask him to give me a rupiya, will you? The price of grains has gone up—it's only eight measures of rice to a rupee! Can't make do.'

'Let's see. It won't do to say anything to the Burra Saheb. It will have to be David Saheb—he's the man.'

Rajaram went and stood under the tree by the river, anxiety written all over his face. It was an Indian cork tree. Shipton Saheb's predecessor had brought it over from the Narangarh plantation in Patna district where he had been the manager. The sapling had been transplanted to Bengal some twenty-five years ago. It had grown into a huge tree, the spreading branches bending downwards, almost touching the river. People hereabouts had never seen such a tree, so they referred to it as 'the English tree'.

Rajaram struck up a pose standing beneath the English tree. Some fun this was, he thought. What on earth was going on! What was *that* the saheb had strung up? Rajaram would have laughed out loud but for the presence of Shipton Saheb's memsaheb. What was the wench up to now? What a fix he was in!

Colesworthy Grant took up a coloured pencil and surveyed his canvas this way and that.

'Will he be so good as to stand erect and stand still, say for ten minutes, madam?' he requested the memsaheb to translate.

'Stand straight, Dewan,' she said to him in Bangla.

'Alright, huzoor.'

Rajaram promptly straightened his back and puffed out his chest; he had a plaintive look on his face.

'No, no,' Grant Saheb immediately cried out, 'Your dewan wears a theatrical mask, madam. Will he just stand at ease?'

'Not *so* tall. Correct your chest!' the memsaheb instructed

Rajaram, gesturing with her hands.

Rajaram found her Bangla quite incomprehensible and made greater efforts to stick out his chest until he was bent over backwards like a bow.

'No, no, my good man,' laughed Grant Saheb. 'This is how...' Walking up to Rajaram, he gently directed his body to a more natural position.

'I hope to goodness he will stick to this! God's death,' he said. The next moment he turned to the memsaheb and apologized, 'I ask your pardon, madam, for my words a moment ago.'

'Oh, you wicked man!' was her response.

Rajaram now settled down in his pose. That picture-painting saheb was after his life. The memsaheb too, standing right in front of him! Besides, the saheb had touched him! He had thought he wouldn't bathe again today, but now he had no choice. Sahebs and their lot were all polluted, *mlechha*, eating goodness knows what. He wouldn't be able to enter his home if he didn't have another bath.

It was an hour before he was let off. Oh! But that was excellent—what the saheb had done! An absolute likeness of him standing there! Though his face was yet to be done. Said he'd have to come again. Would he touch him again...? He wouldn't be able to bathe late in the day.

Late that afternoon, Colesworthy Grant got on to the buggy for a ride on the road along the Panchpota Baur, where the bend in the river had created a natural pool called the *baur*. Junior Saheb, David, and Shipton Saheb's memsaheb accompanied him. It was a straight and well-built road and the buggy moved smoothly enough. The crystal clear waters of the baur lay on one side; on the other, you could see open fields, plots of indigo plants, as well as crops of the quick growing autumn paddy called *aush*. Grant Saheb was not only a painter, but a poet and a writer as well. Rural Bengal had opened up new vistas before his eyes...dazzling laburnum trees dotting an unbroken sweep of fields, the clamour of unknown birds from the flowering bushes, shrubs and trees...That rustic David and bull-headed Shipton simply did not have the eyes to appreciate the countryside, he thought. After all, they were farmers who had come from the villages of Bligh and Faringford from the Western Midlands district of England. Had they not become managers of indigo plantations in India, they would've been ploughing the land in their farms under the landlord of Pantok Manor. Here, they were like veritable kings ruling over the poor black people—the *kaala aadmi*. Dear Lord! He had come not only to see the sights, but also to write about life in the mofussil. About the everyday life of the people who lived here, the wonderful river and the unknown trees and the thick vegetation of the jungle—these were to become the pictures in his book. He had already worked out his ideas for the book. It was to be called *Anglo-Indian Life in Rural Bengal*. He had gathered a lot of material on the subject.

Nalu Pal was on his way back from the market at Mollahati carrying another load of goods on his head. He had made twice the amount of profit this week than he had the last. He was lustily singing a devotional hymn to Kali:

> 'In your sinuous dancing pose you stand
> In the joyous temple of my heart—'

He found himself almost face-to-face with Grant Saheb.

'Let me have a good look at the man. Stop him, will you?' Grant Saheb called out to David. 'Oh, that's good. What does he do?'

David Saheb had turned into a full-fledged Bengali living in these parts for many years. The Bangla he spoke was the rustic speech of the region. He turned with a laugh to the memsaheb and said, 'He can have his old yew cut down, can't he, madam?'

To Nalu, he said in Bangla, 'Well master, bide here for a while.'

Nalu Pal had fallen straight into the tiger's lair. Fortunately, it was the younger saheb and not Shipton, who was known for beating up people. And who was the mem? Probably the Burra Saheb's wife...

Nalu Pal stopped in his tracks: 'Salaam to you, sir. What would you be saying?'

'Stand there, over there.'

'Will he stand there for a bit? I'll go around him.'

'Stop here! This saheb will look at you and make a picture of you.'

'What does he do?' Grant Saheb wanted to know. 'Quite a fellow! Good-looking chap. Come, let's go.'

'He comes to our weekly market to sell his goods. Will you want him anymore?'

'No, I want to thank him David, or shall I—?

Even as Grant Saheb put his hand in his pocket, David fished out an eight-anna coin from his pocket and tossed it at Nalu: 'Take it! Saheb has given you *baksheesh*.'

An astonished Nalu Pal picked up the eight-anna coin from the dust. 'Saheb, may I take your leave now?'

'Go.'

≈

It was a lovely afternoon at Panchpota Baur.

The slightly warm breeze carried the scent of fragrant flowers. Beyond the green spreading fields of autumn-paddy you could see the radiant sky in which rosy clouds had piled up like mountains. Flocks of river-mynahs and magpie-robins were chattering away in the late afternoon. For long, Colesworthy Grant's gaze rested on the horizon. His whole being was suffused with a deep sense of peace. A feeling that carried you elsewhere, filled with the conscious touch of the infiniteness of the sky, an appeal as tender and poignant as the strains of the flute.

This is India, Bharatvarsha…Colesworthy Grant mused. He had been wandering all over the country, spending his time in Bombay, at the polo fields of the Poona Cantonment and in the Anglo-Indian clubs. Such strange creatures his countrymen were, too. Who knows why they turned so strange once they set foot in India? The India that he had glimpsed through Monier Williams's translation of *Shakuntalam* and in the poetry of Edwin Arnold—for which he had come so far; now at last in all his sojourn he had a sense of a different world, exquisitely beautiful, resonant with poetry—on the banks of a river in this obscure little village in the fading afternoon light. He felt it had been worth all his travelling.

≈

Rajaram's three sisters were aged thirty, twenty-seven and twenty-five respectively. Tilu was the eldest. But she was also the best looking—a beauty, one might even say. All three sisters were fair and Rajaram himself was a handsome man; but Tilu's complexion had a tinge of red like that on a ripe *sabari*-banana; she looked particularly beautiful if she had been out in the sun or cooking by the open fire in the kitchen. On her slender strong frame hung heavy tresses of hair; she had big expressive eyes and a wonderful smile. You really couldn't take your eyes off Tilu once you saw her. For all her beauty she was a gentle soul, rather like a bashful young village girl. She did not have the amorous glances of fiery youth; had she been married earlier, she would have been quite the matron by now, mother of several children. But they were unmarried and all three still had a certain childlike innocence and freshness in their gesture and speech, in the way they expressed their affections, their demands and desires.

'Get ready to pound the rice, *Thakurjhi*,' instructed Jagadamba calling her sister-in-law Tilu to her side.

'What about the sesame for the sweets?'

'I've told old Dinu to bring it over; she'll come by this evening. And tell Nilu to get the ritual tray ready to welcome and bless the groom. I'll be caught up with the cooking.'

'Don't you leave the kitchen! A huge festive affair this...things are bound to get stolen.'

The three sisters got extremely busy making preparations for their own wedding. Neighbours were constantly scurrying to and fro, helping them. The middle daughter-in-law from the Ganguly household teasingly said, '*Thakurjhi*, no matter how busy you are, you must decorate the bridal chamber yourselves. I'm telling you now—that's not something *we* are going to do!' Turning to Jagadamba she said, 'Didi, isn't Tilu looking quite ravishing! And this, even before she has got married. Wonder how many heads she's going to turn—our Tilu-thakurjhi—once she's married!'

'The things my sister-in-law says!' exclaimed Saraswati, the widowed sister of Ganguly-moshai. 'Why should Tilu find someone else—let her turn her *husband's* head—if she's going to be turning heads at all.'

The women burst into laughter.

≈

The following day, at the auspicious twilight hour, the three sisters were married to Bhabani Barujje. It had to be said that the groom was handsome. He was about fifty years old, but his hair was still black; he was well-proportioned, fair and very good-looking; had a fine pair of moustaches too. His body was firm and strong, like that of a disciplined wrestler's.

Once the womenfolk had left after their fill of teasing, singing and reciting verses in the bridal chamber, Bhabani Barujje sat himself down and turned to the eldest—'Tilu, introduce me to your sisters.'

Tilottama had on a variety of jewellery. Her fair and shapely arms were adorned with golden *poinché*, she wore scalloped *kharu*-bangles of gold on her wrists, anklets of *gurjaripancham* bells, a gold string of *murki*-shaped beads on her neck and a red bridal veil. With a shake of her poinché, she replied using the respectful honorific *aapni*, 'Don't you know them?'

'You could tell me...'

'She is called Swarabala—and she, Neelanayana.'

'And *your* name?'

'I don't have a name.'

'Tell me truly. What is your name?'

'Ti-lo-tto-ma.'

'Has the Creator crafted you bit by bit, like the sesame seed?' said he, punning on the Bangla word *til*, for sesame.

The trio—Tilu, Bilu and Nilu—laughed merrily at his words.

'Not so, moshai! Don't you know the scriptures!'

Bilu began, 'From all the beauties of this earth, the Maker...'

'...took the most beautiful part of each,' chimed in Nilu.

'... and, little by little...' went on Tilu.

'Yes, I've got it. He moulded Tilottama.'

'And didn't you know that?' exclaimed Tilu with a laugh.

'We're going to box your ears,' declared Nilu and Bilu in unison.

'For shame! What's that you're saying!' Tilu reprimanded her sisters.

'Didn't Sati didi actually box his ears a little while ago? Didn't she?'

'Well, *she* is permitted to, according to kinship terms. But it's not the same with you. Do you have the authority to box your husband's ears? Think before you speak.'

'Tell us then, what are we to you?' asked Nilu.

'Not again,' said Tilu, glaring at her sister.

Bhabani smiled and said, 'You are—each one of you—my partner in dharma, *sahadharmini*—my helpmate.'

'How old are you?' Bilu wanted to know.

'And you?' asked Bhabani in turn.

'You're old.'

'Not again!' warned Tilu with a glare.

≈

Bhabani Barujje was to live on the piece of land gifted by Rajaram. A simple dwelling had been put up, but for the time being he lived at his in-laws. It was altogether a new life for him. He had left home to become a sannyasi and had wandered all over the land from one pilgrimage spot to another, and finally—in his old age—had fallen into the trap of domesticity!

And yet, it wasn't so bad. Tilu was a loving wife, a wonderful housewife; Bhabani was filled with joy whenever he thought of her. It was as though she girded him protectively with numerous arms—like the nurturing spirit of the earth, goddess Jagadhatri herself. No chance for the slightest bit of discomfort or the slightest disregard.

Bhabani Barujje had set aside some time for his daily meditation. It was a practice from his sannyasi life that he continued even now.

'Come home early,' Tilu would say, 'or you'll catch a cold.'

He had been late returning one evening. Apparently Tilu had gone crazy with worry. Bilu and Nilu were frisky youngsters in his eyes. Bhabani didn't pay them the same attention. But there was simply no way he could get around Tilu.

As he was about to set off one evening, Nilu said with mock-solemnity, 'Hold on, O gallant, O stealer of hearts! No going out now.'

'Why must you be so cheeky! Nilu, speak to me with some consideration for my age.'

'And why must a gallant, a stealer of hearts, get into such a temper!' Nilu rolled her eyes and made a strange gesture.

'You know what's wrong with the two of you—a rich brother, and you've been pampered to the hilt! You've not learnt anything about your duties and responsibilities. Is it right of you to hurt me in this way? Bilu's the same as you—precocious and cunning. Look at your eldest sister!'

'Precocious. Cunning. Are *those* nice things to say?'

'I wouldn't have said so. You made me.'

'Good that we did! And we shall go on saying so.'

'Say on. Is there anything that restrains the two of you!'

In the meantime Tilu had come back from the ghat with a load of clothes she had scrubbed with fuller's earth. She overheard the last part of her husband's speech as she came up to the guava tree. 'What is it?' she asked.

Bhabani Barujje felt as though someone had finally thrown him a lifeline. Simply to see Tilu was a delight. With her by his side, there was a way out of everything.

'It's your sister; she's been saying all sorts of obscene things to me.'

'What sort of things?' said Tilu, as though she did not quite understand what the row was about.

'All right, Didi,' broke in Nilu, 'it's for *you* to decide. Didn't they use words like "gallant", and "dandy" the other day at the *jatra* when they were performing at Panchanantala? I said the *same* thing to him. So why should I blamed? Can't I say it to my husband!'

'Listen to them!' said Bhabani in despair.

'Will you ever grow up, Nilu!' exclaimed Tilu.

'They're both the same. Bilu is no less.'

'Don't be angry,' said Tilu calming her husband. 'I shall scold them both. But where are you going now?'

'For a walk across the fields.'

'Don't stay out too long. Come home by evening for a drink of water and have a bite of something. Bou-didi is planning to make a special treat for you—*mungtakti*.'

'You're wrong. You *can't* make mungtakti now. it's only at winter end when the new crop of mung-dal will come up, that you can make them.'

'You're soon going to find out whether they're made or not. You *must* come home early—upon my life.'

'And mine too,' added Nilu.

'Get away with you!' said Tilu.

≈

Bhabani almost heaved a sigh of relief as he came out of the house. Autumn was in the air—the season of *Sharat*. The harvesting was over and the fields of *aush*-paddy lay fallow. Yellow titpalla flowers had blossomed all over the shrubs in the jungle. Bhabani always enjoyed this sense of space. He found it stifling sometimes with three wives when he was indoors. Then too, it was not *his* home. However respectful they were towards him, there was no sense of freedom. What was all this about getting back by a certain hour? What on earth for!

Bhabani sat down beneath a banyan tree, rather discontentedly. It was a huge banyan whose branches had come down going deep into the soil, transforming themselves into pillar-like slender trunks. Beneath the shady banyan was the peace of solitude. Flocks of local birds perched atop. There were also migratory birds that sought a resting place on the spreading tree—flocks of *shyamcoot*, ducks and *silli*. Besides, *khoro*-ducks, egrets, kites and a couple of vultures had set up their permanent habitat on the tree. Smaller birds like mynahs, babblers, magpie-robins and waterbirds like jacanas neither liked to rest on the banyan nor did they nest there.

Bhabani had found his way to this tree on earlier occasions and had observed the birds. Small clusters of *sandhyamoni* flowers bloomed at the foot of the tree. Bhabani looked around before he sat down. He needed a lonely spot. The peasants tended to be curious; if they chanced upon him, they would come to gaze at him and would bombard him with unending questions about why he was sitting there and so forth. This was the time of the day when he liked to be alone and meditate.

On this late afternoon he sat down to meditate by a flowering sandhyamoni creeper. Some time went by. He was suddenly aroused by an unknown voice speaking in a foreign tongue. The speaker was none other than Colesworthy Grant. He had been standing some distance away admiring the beauty of the banyan; he was drawn to admire it from close quarters and entered the arches and pillars made by the roots-trunk. As he wove in and out he came across Bhabani immersed in meditation.

'An Indian Yogi!' the saheb exclaimed in an awestruck but respectful manner,

There was no one else with the saheb. His buggy stood some distance away on the road. Syce Bhoja Muchi was sat in front, holding the reins.

'Oh, I'm so very sorry to disturb you. Please go on with your meditations,' said Colesworthy Grant who had come up closer and was speaking in a reassuring tone.

Not understanding a word, Bhabani Barujje simply looked at the saheb in surprise. It wasn't as though he had not seen this particular saheb a couple of times, but never at such close quarters.

'I offer you my salutations—I wish I could speak your tongue,' the saheb went on.

Bhoja Muchi sensed that something was up by the banyan tree. He tethered the horses and joined them. He didn't know Bhabani either, but tried to mediate.

'Accept my salutations, *baba-thakur*,' he greeted Bhabani, using the respectful honorific of *thakur* to address a brahman. 'You see, this saheb's a-pinting pictures, so he set off that early in the mornin' from the Kuthi, makin' me take him all over the place, over hill and dale, into woods and jungles and what not. He likes you, your 'pearance—that's what he's a-sayin'.'

Bhabani joined his palms in greeting and smiled gently at the saheb.

Grant tried to return his namaskar but didn't quite succeed in imitating him. 'Let me not disturb you. I sincerely regret I have trespassed into your nice sanctuary. May I have the permission to draw your sketch?—You man, will you make him understand?' Grant Saheb turned to Bhoja Muchi and sought to explain to him with much gesticulation the business of sitting for a portrait.

'Says he wants to pint your picture. You see, I know that's the way of this saheb—just you set still for a bit,' Bhoja Muchi explained to Bhabani.

This was a blow. Here he had come to meditate in a quiet spot and now look at what he had got into. How long would he be sitting for? Oh well! Might as well find out where it would all lead. Might as well sit it out. Bhabani kept sitting.

'Don't you stand agape, just go on and bring my sketching things from the cart,' said Grant Saheb to Bhoja Muchi. Then with a gesture he said to him in Bangla, 'Go!'

It was the one Bangla word that Grant had learnt well enough in all the months of his sojourn.

≈

It was quite late by the time Bhabani got home. He found Tilu wiping something away from the threshold of their room with a rag.

'What's that?' he asked her.

'Some castor oil got spilt. The lamp broke and the water spilt on the floor,' replied Tilu, her head still down, busy at the job.

These double-storeyed earthen lamps were common in rural places. The water in the bottom half was supposed to cut down the use of oil. Bhabani found some broken bits of the earthen lamp beneath his bed.

'It's all clumsiness with you...must've broken the lamp?'

'Not I.'

'Who then? Was it Nilu?'

'No, my dear sir; now be quiet. I'm not going to speak to you.'

'Why, what have I done?'

'Indeed! Did you listen to *any* of my words? Didn't I ask you to come home early and rest and have something to eat?'

'Listen to me—there was no chance of coming early. Fell into such a danger!'

'Danger! What was it? Wasn't a snake that got after you, I hope? Cobras all over that field...' Tilu turned around to face her husband with enquiring eyes.

'No my dear, it wasn't a snake; it was a mad saheb! The syce said that he was visiting his friend at the Neelkuthi. Come from his land to visit ours. There I was, sitting quietly under the banyan tree, and suddenly, he appears and stands gaping at me. Said all sorts of things hit-mit-dhit—strange stuff like that. Wants to paint your picture, the syce said to me.'

'Oh, it's that picture-pinting saheb, is it? Yes, I've heard my brother speak of him. And did he pint one of you?

'Didn't he now! Had to sit still, all frozen and stiff, for almost half an hour.'

'Goodness!'

'Now tell me who is to blame?'

He happened to look attentively at Tilu the next moment. Wasn't she looking beautiful! Perhaps not a perfect beauty, but she was exquisite...a smiling countenance, her arms so finely shaped and those delicate grooves around her neck...her complexion too... In the warm light of the waning afternoon she looked like a goddess.

'If the saheb had made a picture of you, he'd have know what *real* beauty is.'

'Go on—as if you...'

After a while she said with a smile, 'Wait, I'll get you some food. Shall I get ready the place for your prayers?

'Yes, do.'

'O Nilu! Come here...and bring the little mat with you.'

Nilu joined them and laid out the mat. She also brought the boat-shaped vessel carrying holy water. Tilu used one end of her sari to carefully wipe clean the space where he would sit down to pray.

Even as he sat down to his prayers Bhabani could only think of one thing: the saheb had asked him to come to the banyan tree the following day. It was the saheb's order; he had to go. They were like kings in this land. But, what if he took Tilu along with him? She was a beauty. How wonderful it would be if the saheb could make a picture of her! But it was taking her there that presented a real challenge. If anyone got to know of it there would be a hue and cry in the village. He would be ostracized. Both he, as well as his brother-in-law, Rajaram Ray.

Tilu was back with a plate full of delicious treats—*sandesh* made of coconut, roasted parched rice, and sweets made of mung-dal—the promised mungtakti!

'There!' she smiled at him, 'Not the season to make mungtaktis, you said! Now tell me, what will you give me?'

'*I* am going to give your ears a nice twist,' said Nilu to her husband.

'Nonsense! Shame on you! Do you know whom you are speaking to? Saying such things!'

Bilu, who had been hiding, suddenly appeared and burst into merry peals of laughter.

'Here comes the other one who's at the bottom of it all,' said Bhabani in a tone of annoyance. 'What's there to laugh about! You blurt out whatever comes to your head; the two of you stop at nothing. Shame!'

'No need to go on saying "Shame! Shame!" I'm telling you.'

'We're not such trash,' added Nilu, 'that you need to go on crying "Shame!" at us all the time.'

'Please don't mind them or take offence,' said Tilu to Bhabani. 'They are spoilt, childish too. Dada never disciplined them at all. He's only pampered them, praised them to the skies.'

'Now, my dear companion, *you* needn't act as a go-between!'

'Didi's playing our rival, taking away our man, don't you see?'

'For shame! Spouting that obscene stuff again?'

'Yes, of course, it's only obscene speech and obscene that,' retorted Bilu angrily. 'So what are they supposed to say? They've barely spoken a couple of words and right away they're told it's obscene speech. Well, we *shall* go on speaking obscene speech—what can you do about it! So there!'

'Get away, the two of you,' Tilu scolded them, 'Go and fetch some paan.'

Turning to Bhabani she asked, 'Shall I get you some more of the mungtakti? Did you like it? Bou-didi dunked some in syrup for you. I shall give you those when you have your meal later.'

'Can I say something, Tilu?'

'Yes, what is it?'

'See if there's anyone around.'

'There's no one. But tell me...'

'Do you think you could come with me to the banyan tomorrow?'

'Why?'

'I will have the saheb make a sketch of you. Wear your fine *dhakai* sari. Can you come?'

'Goodness!'

'Why, what's wrong!'

'Is that possible? How will I come outdoors with you in broad daylight? Already, there are many speaking ill of me because I'm seen with you during the day. One's not supposed to meet one's husband except for late at night—you know that's how it is with us in the villages. I've no choice but to walk over to my Bou-didi's: she can't manage everything on her own.'

'Listen, we'll have to plot a bit. I'll have to be there by late afternoon—the same as today. You start off for the ghat with your pitcher and your towel. And I'll come by and pick you up from the ghat. No one will ever get to know! Tilu, my dearest, I have such a wish...'

'You have such nonsensical wishes! This sort of thing will never be tolerated in our society. You've been a sannyasi, wandering all over the land—never kept track of what's acceptable and what's not in our social world. There's no way that I can do whatever I like.'

Finally though, Tilu had to give way to her husband's desire. She simply couldn't bear to hurt him in any way. Resplendent in the finely woven dhakai sari of many motifs, the water-pot balanced on her head, she walked towards the ghat. No one sighted her but Bada-vaishnav's wife, addressed as 'Boshtom-bou' by the villagers.

'O *Didimoni*! What's all this dressin' up for?' called out Boshtom-bou. 'Where are you off to—all shinin' and glowin' in your beauty?'

'That's enough! Going to bathe in the river and to wash my sari...'

Tilu's heart was beating wildly. She had been forced to come up with an excuse, as though she was an accused. Thank goodness Boshtom-bou didn't dawdle to carry on a conversation but simply went her way. Thank goodness that there was no one at the ghat in the late afternoon.

Spotting Tilu from a distance Grant Saheb doffed his cap and exclaimed in a respectful tone, 'Oh! She is a queenly beauty! Oh! I am grateful to you, sir...'

Then, with great attention, he began making a rough sketch of Tilu's bashful face, her gentle bearing.

The two sketches, 'A Bengalee woman' and 'An Indian Yogi in the Woods' that appear on pages 54 and 57 of Colesworthy Grant's *Anglo Indian Life in Rural Bengal*, published in 1864, are of Tilu and Bhabani Barujje respectively.

No one in the village found out. Bhoja Muchi, the saheb's syce, had been told by Bhabani to keep mum about the sketching. The only trouble was that it was a moonlit night, so they had to be careful coming back. Tilu brought her husband home, guiding him through this field and past that one. He was a stranger to these parts and did not know his way about the village in the sure-footed way she did.

'Ooh! What a scrape you've got me into!' said Tilu. 'There's dew everywhere; don't you catch a cold! The saheb was quite handsome looking. Never seen a saheb from this close. As for you—you're a brigand.'

'Shame on you for saying such obscene things to your husband!'

≈

The Chhota Saheb had sent for Rajaram Ray. Rajaram knew well why he had been summoned. It would be to forcibly mark out some raiyat's land for indigo cultivation. Rajaram was a mighty terrible dewan; he didn't have to be taught about how to keep the raiyats down, fix them well and good. It was over eighteen years since he had been associated with this English company. It was his talent at dealing with the peasants with an iron hand that had made him a favourite of the Burra Saheb.

Panchu Sheikh lived in Teghora Sheikhhati. The Sheikhhati peasants had expressed their opposition to the Neelkuthi's demands. 'Dewanji,' they said, 'why don't you grow indigo in your *khas*-land? We're not going to let you force us this time to grow indigo in the raiyat's land.'

Rajaram had nevertheless forcibly marked out plots for indigo on Panchu Sheikh's land, and on land belonging to Panchu Sheikh's father-in-law, Bipin Gaji, as well as that of Nobu Gaji, the latter's brother. Both were amongst the well-to-do people of the village. Bipin Gaji owned about eight stacks of grain, two dozen or so bullocks fit for ploughing and six pairs of ploughshares. Nobu Gaji had recently made quite a pile giving out loans at a high rate of interest. Between the two, at least a hundred bighas of prime aush-paddy was harvested. The villagers treated them with respect, while on their part the brothers unreservedly threw themselves into the fray if ever they were called upon for help.

It was Nobu Gaji who had come directly to the Chhota Saheb with a complaint. Was that why Chhota Saheb had sent for the dewan, Rajaram wondered. At any rate, Rajaram was not scared. Let Nobu Gaji do what he could.

A long-time resident, the Chhota Saheb could speak the local Bangla as well as any native speaker.

'O Rajaram, what was that Nobu Gaji a-tellin' me?' he enquired of the dewan.

'What is it, huzoor?'

'Believe you've gone and put a mark for indigo cultivation on his tobacco plot.'

'No other way to keep that village under our thumb, if I don't.'

'Says you've even included their pir's *dargah* in your markin'.'

'That's a lie, huzoor. Have him come here.'

Nobu Gaji was a full-blooded young man, impetuous and upfront. But now, standing before the Chhota Saheb and Dewanji, he was a veritable image of meekness. Was there any raiyat who could speak in a normal voice or stand up straight within the precincts of the Neelkuthi?

'So, Nobu Gaji, done any of your molasses an' the fragrant palm candy this year?' David Saheb began.

'No, saheb, we've not yet tapped the trees this season,' replied Nobu in a tone of low supplication.

'Won't you give me some of your palm-candy when it's done?'

'If we don't give them to you, who else shall we be a-givin' them to?'

'You will, won't you?'

'Of course, saheb!'

'Rajaram, believe you've marked out the land on which their holy man's mausoleum stands?'

'No, huzoor! It's just that the plot of land is called *"dargah-*

tala"—the place of the dargah—that's all. That's what it says in the old revenue books. Ask him if there's either a masjid or any pir's mausoleum on that plot. Is *there* a dargah, now?'

'Use to be. Not now, dewan-babu.'

'So there! What a lie you've cooked up for the saheb!'

'Babu, look upon us kindly! We *do* perform our *hajat* on that plot of land. In the winter solstice in the month of *Aghraan* we do a lot of cookin' and fastin' in membrance of our holy man. Whether it's true or not, you can come and see for yourself. Why would I lie to you—you are the kings of the land. Beg of you—let go my land!'

Chhota Saheb looked at Rajaram and said in the tones of an appeal, 'Oh a'right—let his land go. Says they perform that…'

'Hajat,' offered Nobu Gaji.

'And what is that?'

'As I said Saheb, it's cookin' a lot of rice an' meat in the name of *Khuda* in the month of Aghraan, feedin' the wanderin' fakirs and the mendicants and then all of us comin' together and havin' a meal of whatever's left.'

'That's a good thing!' said Chhota Saheb with pleasure. 'You must show it to me sometime.'

'Course I shall, saheb,' said Nobu Gaji bending forward and almost touching the ground to express his gratitude. But Nobu wasn't a fool; he knew exactly what the Dewanji was capable of. He went out and stood waiting behind a tree.

'Huzoor,' said Rajaram to the Chhota Saheb, 'you've messed up everything.'

'Why?'

'That was prime land—number one. On an average you would get about three and half maunds of indigo per bigha. Letting go of such land! And if you are going to be spoiling the raiyats in *this* fashion, will anyone ever bother listening to me? Or ever pay heed to me!'

Chhota Saheb walked away whistling.

Rajaram fumed with indignation. He proceeded to *Sudder Amin*

Prasanna Chakravarty's office to hold a parley with him.

Prasanna Chakkarty as he was called, was over forty, dark-complexioned, of medium build. He sported a huge pair of moustaches and his eyes were like two balls of fire. Everyone said that he was the wickedest amongst those employed by the Neelkuthi. He was a master at turning day into night. As surveyors, amins enjoyed a lot of power. The simple villagers knew little of the complexities of measurements and of land surveying. The amin's work was to fiddle with Ram's land and make it appear to be part of Shyam's, falsify measurements and to acquire and mark out—by any means—the best land for indigo farming. The raiyats were afraid of him and so they bribed him. Rajaram had a share in the bribes.

'If it goes on like this, O Dewanji, no one's going to listen to *us*,' Prasanna Chakkarty opined, pulling away on his flat-bottomed hookah.

Rajaram was only too well aware of this. 'Well, what's to be done now? Why don't you suggest something?'

'Go tell it all to the Burra Saheb.'

'Who's to enter that tiger's den?'

'Who else but you!'

Burra Saheb Shipton was a grave and awe-inspiring kind of man. The Chhota Saheb was somewhat generous; he was a bit of a drunkard—that's why. At least, that's what everyone said. Few dared to approach the Burra Saheb. But Rajaram had no choice. His honour was at stake.

Shipton was seated in his room looking through some papers and puffing away at his long pipe: a foot long it must have been, as he held it in his hand. His chair made of the wood of a jackfruit tree stood next to an enormous table, almost the size of a bed, heavy and solid. The saheb had personally supervised their making. The craftsman was Musabbar Mistri from Satberey. Then the saheb had polished and stained the table himself. Fat leather-bound books were piled up on one side of the table. On the walls hung numerous portraits of sahebs and mems. In one part of the room was the fireplace where thick logs were always blazing away, right up to mid-February.

The Burra Saheb looked up at the wall and said, 'Good morning.'

Rajaram, who had already done his salaam, now performed a more exaggerated greeting, thinking that the Burra Saheb had not seen his earlier one. His mouth felt dry. This was not the easy-going Chhota Saheb before him. Sombre and reserved, this one was famous for his terrifying ways. Capable of anything he was. They were not a lot to be trusted—these sahebs. That mad saheb who went around making pictures was a good sort though. Had secretly made sketches of Tilu and brother-in-law Bhabani. Rajaram had even managed twenty-five rupees as baksheesh from that fellow, casually mentioning it to the mad saheb on the eve of his departure. Bhabani was as bad as the mad saheb, doing whatever pleased his fancy.

'I am well, by your grace, huzoor,' said Rajaram in response to Shipton's greeting.

'And what is it you neet? Any particular work? I am very busy now. Little time I have.'

'Nothing much, huzoor...I had marked out some land of a subject in Teghora; Chhota Saheb has nullified it—excused the man.'

Shipton frowned and said, 'Whatever orders he hath given, that will be done. In this, what is not worth following, it seems to you?'

Such nonsense the Burra Saheb spoke with aplomb when he didn't really know Bangla, or at least, not well. It was a real misfortune that had befallen him to have to endure such outlandish creatures, simply to survive. No point correcting the saheb: it would only anger him. You just had to accept whatever these spoilt brats said.

'No, huzoor, there's nothing wrong. But if we carry on with this sort of a thing it would be tough ruling the raiyats.'

'What cannot we do?'

'Can't keep them under our thumb. No cultivating of indigo.'

'If there's to be no cultivating of indigo, why have we appointed you?'

'That is absolutely right, huzoor. If I am to be insulted before the raiyats, tell me huzoor, how am I to get any work done—'

'Insult? Oh, you are in disgrace, you old scoundrel, I understand. What be done by you then?'

'I leave it to you, huzoor. I had marked out some land belonging to a bad character called Nobu Gaji. I was ordered by Chhota Saheb to let go off that land. Now there's no question of marking out *any* piece of land in that entire village. How will there be any farming of indigo?'

'How much land have you marked out this year—must show me tomorrow. Have you prepared the Impression Register?'

'Yes, huzoor.'

'Now go. Shall be fined if you can't show the register. You will bring it here tomorrow.'

That was that.

Rajaram went back to Prasanna Chakkarty with a sullen face. No, nothing had worked out, he told the amin. 'They're concerned about the prestige of their own people above everything else. Pig-eating rascals they are, after all. They care nothing for your honour or mine.'

Prasanna Chakkarty was a fish of deep waters, secretive and cunning. He had known all along that it would turn out so.

Pulling on his hookah, he recited: '*Apamanang puraskrityam manang kritva ch prishtake*...Learnt it as a schoolboy, Dewanji—this sloka by arch-strategist Chanakya. Once you've come to work for them, no point thinking of honour or insult. You had better be on your way to work.'

'And instead—the threat of fining *me*!'

'What's that! Fined you, did he?'

'Not for that; I've to show him by tomorrow all the accounts for all the land marked out for this year. If I can't, said he will fine me.'

'Well, that's how they dispense justice.'

'Instead, to be treated with such pettiness!'

As soon as the disgruntled Rajaram came out of the Kuthi, his eyes fell on Nobu Gaji who was standing with some of his people by the main gate. Nobu, grinning from ear to ear, was recounting something to the clerk, *Karkoon* Ramhari Tarafdar. But he was yet to know Rajaram; the saheb himself didn't!

'Here, Nobu Gaji, you come this way and listen to me,' Rajaram called out, his voice grave.

Nobu Gaji's smile vanished in an instant. He hadn't been laughing about what had happened in the morning. He didn't have the guts to. It was a tale about a cow of his that had been stolen by a dishonest peasant who worked on his land and who had the temerity to sell it off in Nobu Gaji's own weekly market at Nahata. Nobu Gaji's laugh was one of complacent pride as he narrated how he had outwitted the rogue. His heart skipped a beat as he quickly came up and stood most deferentially before Rajaram.

'What is it, babu?'

'Indigo will be sown right on the land that I had marked out. Got it?'

'But, babu, didn't the Chhota Saheb himself say…?' Nobu Gaji protested in amazement.

'Chhota Saheb may well have said so. There's a boss above the boss—every father has a father. This is the Burra Saheb's order. I've just come out of the Burra Saheb's office. You can't go over someone's head, got it, Nobu Gaji! I'll have you imprisoned in the lime shed at the Neelkuthi and stuff your mouth with paddy, or my name's not Rajaram Ray Chaudhuri, let me tell you! I know you in and out. Won't rest till I see that you are finished off good and proper.'

Nobu Gaji shrank in terror. There was not a soul in the vicinity of the indigo plantation who was not afraid of Dewan Rajaram. There was much that he was capable of doing, if he so wished.

'Forgive me, Dewanji,' he said with folded hands, 'have mercy on me. You are like my father and my mother—if *you* choose to, you can kill me and beat me down. And if *you* wish to, you can keep me alive. I'm a poor ignorint man, your own child. Do not be angry upon me…shall die if that happins.'

'Do you think that's all there is to it? I shall mark out land for indigo in your very courtyard. And may your good father the Saheb rescue you! Let's see what you are capable of...'

Nobu Gaji came forward and fell at Rajaram's feet, embracing them with both his hands.

'No, don't you come to me,' the dewan said roughly, 'go to that saheb father of yours.'

Nobu Gaji continued to clutch on to Rajaram's feet.

'What is it?' Rajaram said finally.

'I wouldn't live if you don't save me. Ignorint that I am—went and did somethin' today. Have mercy on me, babu...you are my father and mother.'

'All right now, straighten up. I can let your land off, but—'

'Babu, you don't have to tell me. I know how to honour you...'

'Go now. I'll let your land be. Amin-babu will be there tomorrow to settle it. But make sure that you pay the labour costs for removing the stakes for the marked out areas. Go now.'

Nobu Gaji once more prostrated himself and fell at Rajaram's feet as a mark of obeisance. He walked homewards along the side of the baur across Kantapora.

Dewan Rajaram Ray and Head Amin, Prasanna Chakkarty, were all smiles again. This was how their rule had been enforced. The Burra Saheb or the Chhota Saheb might relent a bit, but they never did. They went ahead and marked out prime plots of the peasant's land, and that of wealthy householders too—it became obligatory to cultivate indigo in these plots. There were ways of dealing with those who did not oblige.

The Burra Saheb was also the *faujdari* judge in these parts, handling all the criminal cases. Thrice a week the Neelkuthi served as a court. This was where judgements were pronounced on cases ranging from the theft of cattle, to fights, riots and other assorted complaints. On court days, a whole lot of people came from villages far and near to put up their respective cases at the big bungalow. Recently, a gallows had been strung up at the Tematha intersection, on a field adjoining Sanakpur. Rajaram had been going around announcing that the Burra Saheb had received permission from the government to order hangings as well.

It had to be said though that the Burra Saheb was a fair judge. He never gave a decision until he heard out both sides with great attention. And, he thought long and hard before he pronounced his verdict. To the guilty he was the very devil. Heavy punishments were regularly meted out for light offences. If there was slightest neglect of the indigo company's work, even the dewan couldn't get away with it. Yet people still preferred the Burra Saheb to the Chhota Saheb.

The Burra Saheb would say to his dewan, 'You will be proberly tealt with if I stuffed you in the lime shed.'

'As you wish, huzoor,' Rajaram would respond. 'If you had a mind to do it, you could do anything.'

'You have a very oily tongue I know, but that won't cut ice this time—I know how to fix you.'

'Of course, huzoor, you do. You are my benefactor—my mother and my father!'

'Mother and father! Ma and Pa! You will be tealt alright insite the lime shed.'

'As huzoor wishes.'

'Go! Ten rupees fined.'

'I shall obey you, huzoor.'

That was how Rajaram's work went.

≈

The District Magistrate was to visit the Neelkuthi. Dewan Rajaram had been on his toes since early morning. It was his duty to ensure that the best sheep and fish, the choicest mangoes and *ghee* were procured for the occasion. These events of grand dining and wining—*khana-pina*, when sahebs and such like came as guests to the Neelkuthi, took place at least twice or thrice a month.

He had sent for Teenkori of Muropora to get a healthy pig off him. Teenkori, a *kaora* by caste, had grown rich doing business in pigs. He now had a double-thatched brick house, stacks of grain, a pond stocked with fish, and labourers aplenty. Even the upper-caste brahmans and kayasthas treated him with respect. Teenkori had wanted to give Rajaram ten seers of cold-pressed mustard oil that he produced at home, but Rajaram had returned the gift. He wouldn't allow anything to come into his home that had been gifted by a low-caste kaora.

Teenkori was telling him, 'There's one that's five months old, and 'nother of two years. You may have whichever you choose—let me know. But pardon me for saying so, Dewan-babu, you people jest don't know how tasteful it is. You'll never be able to forget the taste of it, if you've had it once. That five-month piglet, jest fry it in ghee—'

'That's enough, you rascal!' cut in Rajaram with a laugh. 'Mind your tongue! Is that how you speak to bamuns! You've got money alright, but caste will show.'

'Oh no, babu! Plain forgot that you don't eat all that—do forgive me.'

'No, your words don't make me angry. But keep this in mind—you've got to organize the pig.'

'What's to keep in mind, babu? I'll have both sent over—the five-month piglet and the two-year-old. Will my people deliver them to your home?'

'Certainly not! Why to my home? Send them over to the Neelkuthi. Pigs in a brahman home, indeed! What am I to do with this rascal!'

As Teenkori made as if to leave, Rajaram said, 'Do you think you're going to leave without any *persad* from my home, or *should* you be doing so? Just because you've made some money, you think you can grasp at the moon, that everything's changed, do you?'

'Don't even say such a thing,' said Teenkori making an apologetic click with his tongue. 'We've all grown up picking up the leftovers from the berahman's plate, Dewanji. Even if you were to spit out something from your mouth, we'll raise it to our forehead and honour it. But you've hurt me real bad today, sadden'd my heart today.'

'Why, what's happened?'

'Got that good quality oil, 'pecially for you, and you've not accepted it.'

'Well, I didn't take it, meaning that in our lineage we're not allowed to accept gifts from *shuddurs*—you shouldn't be sad on that account, Teenkori. Alright, since it's given you grief, let me pay you something for it and then you may leave the oil here.'

'Payment! And how much will you pay?'

'A rupee.'

'That's as good as paying for five seers of oil, master. Did I come here to sell oil to the babu? Well may I be a low-born critter, but won't you show me some comppussion?'

'No, Teenkori; don't take it to heart. You have to take that one rupee. Can't accept the oil if I take any less. Hey, anyone there? Sitanath, take this jar of oil from Teenkori.'

The Chhota Saheb came in hurriedly. He was about to say something to Rajaram, but stopped himself on finding Teenkori there.

Rajaram stood up and announced, 'A piglet of five months has been procured, huzoor.'

'Oh, the sucking pig is the best! Five months is too old. Can't you get me one that's still suckling?'

'No, saheb, there's none o' those. Where will I get such a little one from?'

'The *hakim* is going to be visiting from the district. If it was a little one, it would've been just right for the meal.'

'We will keep one ready the next time,' assured Teenkori. 'Saheb, my salaam! And *pernam* to you, Dewanji!'

One look at the Chhota Saheb and Rajaram knew that he must have come with news of grave import.

'What has happened, saheb?' he asked as soon as Teenkori had gone.

'A big mess! The Muslim peasants of Rasoolpur and Rahatoonpur are up in arms—they say that they won't grow any indigo.'

'Who said that?'

'Our karkoon had gone to mark the land. They wouldn't let him touch the soil; chased him off with sticks and staves.'

'What insolence!'

'Tell them to get the horses ready. Let's ride to the spot, the two of us, right away. Don't tell the Burra Saheb anything at this point.'

'If it turns out to be true, you needn't tell me, saheb, about what I ought to be doing. But be kind enough to save me from any faujdari enquiry or any criminal case, if it comes up.'

'No, no, you are too rash—you'll end up doing something or the other. That's why I don't believe in you.'

A little later, the two of them set off on their horses for the offending village.

No one knew when the dewan returned, but next day, the news spread that the village of Rahatoonpur had burnt down overnight. Everything in that village of well-off peasants—some of whom had a score or more of paddy stacks in their courtyard, and homes of eight to ten thatched rooms—had all been burnt to cinders. Nothing remained. No one knew how the fire might have started. However, the evening before, Dewanji and the Chhota Saheb had both been seen at the headman's home. The raiyats had been summoned and asked to explain why they wouldn't grow indigo. They couldn't be made to agree. The dewan and the saheb had left the village after eleven that night. In the last hour, a fire had sprung up and soon the entire village was burnt to cinders. Everyone suspected that there was a strong link between one event and the other.

The next morning the District Magistrate Mr Duncinson arrived with his party at the big bungalow of the Neelkuthi. Only the Burra Saheb and the Chhota Saheb were at the main gate to receive him when he got off the phaeton sent by the Kuthi. Dewan Rajaram had been stationed by the table in the drawing room to hand over the box of cheroots. Duncinson was here not merely to accept the hospitality of the Neelkuthi; the Burra Saheb had invited the magistrate with a specific purpose.

The Burra Saheb called over his dewan: 'You must tell him what you have seen. He is being the District Magistrate; and, this man is our dewan, Mr Duncinson, and a very shrewd old man he is too—go on, go on, what did you see in Rahatoonpur?'

Rajaram bent low, almost to the floor, in making his salaam. 'They had turned furious,' he began. 'About to beat me up with sticks, they were. Wouldn't allow any indigo to be grown. I kept pleading with them, practically begged them, and touched their feet.'

Duncinson turned to the Burra Saheb and asked, 'What did he do—he says?'

'Entreated them.'

'I understand. Ask him how many people were there.'

'How many people were there?'

'About two hundred, saheb. They'd all come armed with sticks and staves—'

'Come with lathis and other weapons.'

'Oh, they did, did they? The scoundrels!'

'And then, what tid you to?'

'I came away, saheb. I came away saddened, brooding about so much good indigo land going waste. No planting, no harvesting. A big blow to the Neelkuthi.'

In a little while, the field in front of the main Kuthi swelled with a huge crowd. People had come to complain directly to the magistrate that the Dewanji had come and burnt down their village Rahatoonpur to ashes. The entire village had been razed to the ground.

The magistrate sent for Dewan Rajaram, 'What have you did? Setting on fire?'

Rajaram expressed great astonishment. 'Fire!' he said, raising his eyebrows. 'What do you mean, saheb? Fire?' As though he had no inkling of what the word meant.

The magistrate grew suspicious. He grilled Rajaram for quite a while. But the veteran Rajaram had emerged unscathed through many such grillings; he was not going to be flustered now.

The magistrate called on many of the villagers of Rahtoonpur and questioned them at some length. But standing right there, within the boundaries of the Neelkuthi, they were too terrified to speak out. After all, the Magister Saheb was here today and gone tomorrow; but the Chhota and the Burra Sahebs and the Dewanji were the eternal bogeymen, particularly the Dewanji. To stand before *them* and to speak against them; no, it was impossible!

Then the magistrate himself went on an inspection of Rahatoonpur, accompanied by the Chhota and the Burra Sahebs. Two big elephants were got ready for the expedition. A mass of villagers gathered at the field adjoining the village of Rahatoonpur.

It wasn't a big-sized village, Rahatoonpur: a stubbled field lay on one side and to its east, the village. It did not have a single brick house; the thatched huts of peasants and the relatively better-off upper-castes stood cheek by jowl. Now, everything was burnt to ashes. Some blackened half-burnt poles of bamboo still stood witness to where a hut had once stood. The earthen walls had turned a fierce red—they looked like the firing kiln of a potter's home. Two mature bulls used for ploughing lay charred in their cowshed belonging to Kabir Sheikh. In every courtyard there were half-burnt stacks of paddy. The women were trying to salvage what they could of the grains, winnowing and keeping aside something to fill their bellies with.

Many came up to the Magistrate Saheb and broke down in tears. Many of them said that the Dewanji had a hand in the fire, but there was not much by way of proof. It couldn't be proved that one person had actually seen him or any of his men start off the fire. The magistrate did go through with the investigation as he best could. Finally, he called over the Burra Saheb. 'I'm really sorry for the poor beggars,' he said, 'we must do something for them.'

'I wonder who has committed this black deed,' said the Burra Saheb. 'I suspect my oily-tongued dewan.'

'You think it is a case of arson?'

'I can't tell. Years ago I saw a case like this, and *that* was a case of arson—my dewan was responsible—the Devil!'

The Magistrate Saheb released a fund of a hundred rupees as

relief; the Burra Saheb promised two hundred more. The village resounded with praise for the sahebs. You have to admit, said everyone, such judgement was rare. After all, they were the red-faced ones!

≈

That night there was much dancing in the big ballroom in the Neelkuthi. The red-faced sahebs had drunk quite a bit. They danced holding on to the memsahebs' waists, and sang English songs. Syce Bhoja Muchi, now dressed in the uniform of an orderly, was serving them liquor. There was not a servant in the Neelkuthi who was not a Bengali. *Khansamas* and other house servants for the plantation were recruited from *dom*, bagdi and muchi castes from the neighbouring villages. As a result, the sahebs and even the memsahebs spoke a smattering of some kind of Bangla. They did not know any Hindi.

Seated in the outer courtyard of his little dwelling, Amin Prasanna Chakkarty was pulling on his hookah. Sitting before him was Barada Bagdini. Barada was older than Prasanna Chakkarty—her hair was jute-like, thick and white. Prasanna often called her over to get some of his own work done.

'And how is Gaya?' he asked her.

'She's well enough, by your blessings.'

'A nice young woman...not seen one like her in these parts. Barada, there's something—'

'What is it?'

'A bottle of good English stuff—ask Gaya to get me one. A lot of good things have been ordered for tonight's khana for the saheb-lok—you know how it is. Haven't had a swig of any quality stuff for long.'

'Well, can't promise, can I? Gaya's not here right now. She doesn't stay here when the sahebs have their feasts.'

'My darling Didi, won't take no for an answer. You must do some scouting around, Didi. Now get up, do, and just see if you can get a hold of even one bottle, through Gaya.'

Barada Bagdini went off to fulfil the amin's request.

Barada Bagdini was treated with enormous deference as the mother of the famous Gaya-mem. Gaya, who was Barada's daughter, was intimate with the Burra Saheb. That was why she was known in these regions as 'Gaya-mem'—an almost memsahib. Every single raiyat under the Mollahati plantation knew and obeyed Gaya-mem.

Gaya was not a bad sort. If you approached her with a request she would entreat her saheb on your behalf. People came to her with their troubles, big and small, and she had managed to help them. She had a woman's heart after all. She may have stepped into a life of sin, but she had kept alive within herself a sense of right and wrong. Gaya was young, not yet twenty-five, fair-complexioned, with lovely big eyes and lustrous black hair that cascaded down her back when she left it untied. Her features were not particularly fine, but she had a freshness and bloom on her face, and a fine figure. All in all, she could have put to shame many a beauty from a respectable household. You felt strongly drawn to her as she walked down the village path.

No one of course had actually seen Gaya-mem with the Saheb. Yet, everyone knew of the matter. She was the Burra Saheb's ayah who lived in the yellow bungalow, the special one belonging to the Burra Saheb. She wore nothing but freshly washed black-bordered saris, a gold poinché on her arm, arm-clasps and big *makri*-earrings. Like a path through a deep mountaneous forest, a gold necklace strung with thin murki-beads swung in her cleavage.

'Gaya-didi certainly knows a trick or two,' observed the dom and bagdi women.

Those who considered themselves respectable, said scornfully, 'A curse on such ill-gotten poinché and arm-clasps!'

There must have been many who were envious of her. There was evidence enough: several others had tried to compete with her but had failed. Certainly, there was reason for envy.

For this same Gaya-mem to put in an appearance in Amin Prasanna Chakkarty's little hut was an unexpected event.

'Oh, here you are Gaya!' said Prasanna Chakkarty's getting up to his feet with a start. 'Come in my child, do come in...wherever shall I give you a seat?'

'That's all right, *Khuro-moshai*,' she replied, addressing him respectfully as one would an elderly uncle, 'I will sit down on the wooden seat. You had sent word; what was it about?'

'Can you manage to get us a bottle, my child?'

'Now look at what you are up to! Mother came and told me that you must get *thakur-moshai* a high quality bottle. See, I've got you one: what kind is it do you reckon?'

From within the folds of her sari Gaya took out a squat white bottle and stood it before Prasanna Chakkarty. His beady eyes lighting up in greed and joy, the amin quickly stretched out his hand for the bottle and said, 'Aha, mother of mine—let's see now, there's something written in English; can you read it?'

'No, Khuro, this *injiri-finjiri* we can't read.'

Prasanna Chakkarty looked at Gaya with admiration in his eyes. Perhaps there was a bit of adoration in his gaze as well. Gaya-mem's nubile youth made her an object of desire to many. But she was far too precious and rare a fruit; hardly someone that you could aspire to, or reach out for.

'So, Gaya,' asked Prasanna Chakkarty, 'what exactly happens when the sahebs and the memsahebs are a-dancing, eh? Seen something of it?'

'No, Uncle, they don't let me stay there.'

'I believe Shipton Saheb's mem dances with the Chhota Saheb?'

'A cursed lot they are! Grabbing hold of each other's waists and dancing away. Let them all go to...I quite die of shame, Uncle.'

'Horrors!'

'That's so, Uncle. I'm not lying, one bit. Why don't you go and have a peek yourself? Nafar Muchi, the Burra Saheb's bearer, is standing right outside the verandah.'

'Where's Bhoja Muchi? He listens to me somewhat.'

'He's there too.'

'And the Burra Saheb?'

'Him too, of course! Where else would he be?'

'And what sort of a person is the Burra Saheb? I mean the real him.'

Gaya shyly lowered her gaze to the floor as she replied, 'Oh, he's all right. He's not such a bullish sort as it might appear from the outside. Oh, it's all quite decent, but their bodies are so...'

'Smelly?'

'Well, there is that goat-like smell of course, but it's not that... all that prickly heat. At night the rash flares up, he'll ask me for my hair pin to stick it in those...'

As soon as she'd said these words Gaya felt that she shouldn't have said them to the elderly Amin, especially someone that she addressed as 'Khuro-moshai'. She was momentarily consumed with shame and got up hurriedly to overcome her embarrassment. 'I'll be on my way now, Khuro-moshai; it's getting on to be quite late. Would you like some biskoots? If you do, I can get you some. And there's something else they eat—that's called "chizz". Very smelly! I had put a little piece in my mouth for a taste and almost threw up. But they say it makes you strong.'

When Gaya had left, Prasanna Amin opened up the foreign bottle and with the greatest of pleasure had a sip of the English liquor. It was true that from time to time a fair bit of money came to his hands, by the grace of Dewanji. But it wasn't only a question of money to have access to this stuff—you had to know *where* to get it. There was no point telling Dewanji: a dry sort that man, not a drop of feeling. Only good at sparking off fights, riots and clashes. Look how he got all of Rahatoonpur reduced to ashes overnight. As though Prasanna Amin didn't know what had really happened. Didn't all the hatching and plotting go on right under his nose, in this very room! Let the magistrate or whoever, come inspecting. Once within the boundaries of the Neeelkuthi, mum's the word. Besides, wouldn't the ruling class—that breed of kings, speak up for their own kind? Why should they take sides with the blackies?

Go on, eat drink and be merry, clutch on to the women's waists and dance away!

≈

Bhabani Barujje was living quite contentedly. It was now almost two years since the family had settled in the two thatched rooms that he had built on the edge of the bamboo grove, some distance away from Dewan Rajaram Ray's house. Tilu had given birth to a son. Bhabani Barujje didn't have to earn a living; he had received about four bighas of rice-growing land as part of the dowry for his marriage. It yielded enough grain to tide them through the year.

That saheb who had sketched them had sent him a letter and a book, all the way from England. Rajaram had brought over the letter and book from the Neelkuthi.

'So Bhabani, how did Tilu's likeness get in here, eh? Did the saheb sketch her then?' Rajaram had casually remarked. How wonderfully he had done it—with such dedication, Rajaram went on. And what a beautiful pose! But how did the saheb actually get to sketch her, huh? Well, it didn't matter really, but be sure not to show it to any one else in the village. You never know who might take offence. An English book! No one could say what the contents might actually be. All one could make out about the book was that it was about our land—this very village, and lots of pictures of our Jessore region. He was a good man, that saheb.

'Have you seen how nicely my picture has come out?' said a smiling Tilu.

'Mine too.'

'Show it to Bilu and Nilu, it will make them happy. Wait, let me call them.'

Nilu kicked up a fuss as soon as she saw the book. Why should Didi be the first for everything, as though *her* likeness wouldn't come out well! Would that Krishna-like-teaser forget for a moment his devotion to Didi's happiness?

Nilu's exuberant outburst notwithstanding, the two younger

sisters had mellowed in these last two years. Their speech had lost some of the earlier girlish boisterousness. Bilu had changed even more than Nilu; she was expecting her first child in another month or two.

Most amazing though was Tilu. Coming as she did from a wealthy family where she had been pampered throughout her childhood and youth, how wonderfully she managed everything now. Her presence lit up those two little thatched huts of Bhabani Barujje. She had carved out little niches here and there and crafted shelves for their home. She fetched dung and carefully plastered and smoothened the floor with fresh mix of dung and earth every day. You would see her choosing the best clay she could find from the pond to keep their earthen stove in good repair, and evenings you would find her spinning the ritual cotton thread that brahmans wore across their shoulder. Not for a moment would you find her sitting. She whirred and hummed like a top through the day.

Bilu was of great help too. The eldest cooked, but the younger ones got everything ready in the kitchen. Bilu and Nilu were quite devoted to their sister—Didi's was the last word on anything. For all these years it was Didi who had made up their world. Now, gradually, they were beginning to know another person, their husband. They enjoyed their fill of long chats with him too.

Sister-in-law Jagadamba would say in a tone of gentle rebuke, 'O, Nilu, you never seem to step this way at all.'

'There's so much work to be done at home,' Nilu would reply shyly. 'Didi can't manage all by herself if we don't...'

'Yes, of course! As though *we* never had a home; only you do! Isn't that so?'

'Say what you like...'

'That's why I was a-telling Tilu, just this morning—'

'Goodness! Didi wouldn't go to *heaven* even if she was invited, if she had to leave behind her little boy and her husband!'

'Don't I know!'

'We've got to manage Khokon because Didi can't do it all alone.'

'Our Tilu is such a darling. Do send her over later in the evening. It was Tilu who always got the hookah ready for him when he came back home from work. And to this day he always says, "Now that Tilu is not here anymore, there's no light at home."'

'I shall tell Didi so.'

'She shouldn't bring Khoka along once its dark.'

'Didi won't be able to come until your son-in-law gets home. As for him—that paragon of virtues—he comes home only late at night.'

'Where from?'

'That I can't say.'

'You must ask about where he's been gallivinting. That's always a problem with menfolk.'

'Bou-didi, your son-in-law is not that sort. He's a different sort altogether...like a sannyasi. You know, don't you, that he had actually become a sannyasi? He is simply not interested in worldly affairs. And whatever Didi says or does is fine with him.'

'A good man! I wish I could meet with him oftener. You must ask both of them to come over this evening. Our son-in-law can break his fast after he completes his prayers at our place.'

That evening, as soon as Bhabani came home from the river, Nilu cried out, 'Do listen! Our Bou-didi from the other house has ordered that Didi and you must go over as a couple, to visit them this evening.'

'What about Bilu and yourself?'

'Does anyone care for us! It's enough if the dandy and his lady love goes on a visit.'

'Back to your old ways of speaking?'

'I do beg your pardon. I'm so sorry, my dear sir!'

Tilu who happened to come in just then, laughed at the exchange, 'A lot of chattering going on I see! Here, the seat for your prayers is ready and waiting.'

'Nilu says that your Bou-didi has invited us both,' explained Bhabani.

'Let's go; Khokon can stay with them,' said Tilu.

Soon after it became dark, the sky was awash with moonlight. The last of the cold weather was still with them. Tiny clusters of mango blossoms had begun peeping out. It was not yet that time of the year when the fragrance of mango blossoms spread out far and wide. Every now and then, a cuckoo called out from the slender-branched *bakul* tree.

'Shall we sit awhile, Tilu?' asked Bhabani. 'Come, let's go to the river and sit together for a bit.'

Tilu seemed to have no opinion of her own nowadays. 'Let's go,' she agreed, 'But no one will see us, I hope?'

'And what if they do!'

'Whatever you wish…'

'Let's go from the back of that old ruined house of the Rays; people don't go that way…they say it's haunted.'

Soon they were at the riverbank, standing over a carpet of dry leaves in the bamboo thicket.

'Wait!' said Tilu, 'Let me spread out my sari-end for you to sit.'

'Don't unwind your sari; you'll feel cold.'

'I don't feel the cold; do sit.'

'It's very nice here, isn't it?'

'Yes, it is,' agreed Tilu with a laugh. 'One is hardly able to get away from the daily grind nowadays. It's one pile of work after another. Have to keep a lookout for everything too. Bilu and Nilu hardly know a thing, still so childish; I have to tell them what to do.'

Bhabani Barujje savoured the peculiar rural strain of Jessore Bangla that Tilu spoke—he found it sweet to his ears. He was from Nadia himself; the Bangla they spoke was very measured, whether in pronunciation or in the mode of speech. The Jessore Bangla he heard for the first time only when he moved to this region.

'Here, let me tell you how you speak in your land,' he said laughingly to his wife: '*Shibee'r mati, pubee'r ghar, mugeer dalee ghi dili khiree'r tar hoi,*' as he went on to elongate the ee-sound in every word, particularly in the possessive.

'What, what did you say?'

'*Mugeer dalee* means...in the mung dal.'

'Hmmph! You don't have to tell me what it *means*! Where did you pick up that phrase from?'

'There, see! Now you're speaking like a real native...you needn't tell me where you picked it up. Then why do you hide it most of the time and speak differently?'

'I feel ashamed to speak before you in my own tongue.'

Bhabani drew Tilu even closer. The moonlight fell in a slant all over the body of beautiful Tilu. She was over thirty but from the day she had 'found' her husband it was as though she was transformed to a youthful girl. Years of longing as a young girl for that most precious treasure of a kulin maid—a husband, and such a gem of a husband, who was now hers, after an aeon...she could hardly believe it herself, even though they had been married for over two years.

'You know what I think?' said Tilu. 'It's because *you* hadn't come, that we were not able to get married all these years. Marriage for a kulin woman...'

'There's something I don't quite understand. You carry the surname of Ray. Rays are not kulins! Rays are *strotriya* brahmans.'

'You must ask Dada about those sort of things. How would I know—I'm a woman. It's true though, that we *are* kulins. I had two aunts—my father's sisters. After my younger aunt died, a good kulin groom from the back of beyond came to marry my elder aunt; they took her away to some obscure place in East Bengal.'

'You can hardly speak of "Bangals" and back of beyond! You are a *Bangali* from Jessore yourself—is it any better than where you are, the way you turn every sound into those long eees...*mungeer dalee ghi deeli khireer tar hoi...*'

'Oh, go on with you! You only know how to tease. And how do you people speak—all the verbs ending with *gelumm-khelumm, halumm-hulumm*, like tigers roaring! Hee hee...'

'You've made your point! Now go on with what you were saying.'

'Aunty must have been over forty by the time she got married. She was so happy about it. The children by her husband's first wife were all grown up, about twenty or thirty years old, if not more. The first wife was dead; but these children made her life hell. Aunty endured it all silently: she felt that she had finally a household, a husband. But the widowed daughter who had come back to her father's home couldn't stand her; she would even hit her with kindling and abuse her—"And you! Who might you be! Married to my father: hardly his real wife! He's married you only because he's lost his mind." Things like that...Still Aunty would bear it silently. Then, her husband who was in his early seventies, died one day—'

'And then?'

'Then the stepsons and daughters ganged up and began torturing my aunt. Aunty would beg them for a bit of a place to stay. She'd weep and tell them, give me a mite of space in my husband's home. But they didn't. Threw her out on the streets. She was a woman of those times: how did it matter that she was old in years, she felt and behaved like a shy frightened bride. Some people felt pity for her and took her into their home. How she wept. It was those people who brought her back to her maternal home. But for her, it was all her husband. She didn't have to observe the widow's fast for too long on her return: the good lord took her away—that devoted chaste woman.'

'When would all this have happened?'

'Long long ago: I was still very little. I don't recall her; I've heard about her life from my mother and my Bou-didi as I was growing up. Bou-didi was herself a little thing then, a child bride who'd just married into our family.'

Tilu fell silent. Bhabani Barujje was silent for a long time. He felt that it was for nothing that he had once become a sannyasi. He was willing to be born in this world again and again if he could serve in any way these victims of oppression. All thoughts of personal liberation and salvation seemed trivial in comparison.

The Ichhamati flowing before them bore the sorrowful memory of an unfortunate kulin maiden from long ago. The salty tears of the unfulfilled yearning of a woman for her husband, of so many years ago, had merged into the riverwater. It was as though on this moonlit evening, fragrant with the scent of water hyacinths it was she who came down from heaven to tell him, 'My son, that yearning of mine which stayed unfulfilled, you must fulfil for the young woman by your side. Be a good husband to the women of Bengal; all that I could never realize in my own life, may they all be fulfilled...my blessings on you.'

Bhabani Barujje enfolded Tilu in his arms and held her in a deep embrace.

≈

By the time they reached the dewan's house, the evening was gone and night had fallen.

'Oh there you are! Where were the two of you, Tilu?' said Jagadamba. 'Nilu had dropped by a little while ago. Said that you had left home ever so long ago. Here, I've been sitting and waiting for our son-in-law to come and perform his prayers and then have a bite to eat! Oh, the two of you are simply...'

'Don't tell anyone, Bou-di,' interrupted Tilu, 'he'd taken me to the riverside. You better give him some of the food you've kept for him right away. I'm missing my little fellow; haven't seen him for hours. What did Nilu say? Hope Khokon wasn't crying and fretting?'

'No, Nilu said Khokon was fast asleep. Why don't you eat too?'

'Let him finish his prayers. Hasn't Dada come home yet?'

'They've taken his horse out to meet him.'

As she spoke, Jagadamba spread out all the food before the son-in-law of the house. Bhabani looked upon her with the respect that was usually accorded to mothers-in-law, although she was the wife of his brother-in-law. Jagadamba always had her face half hidden by her sari when she came out before him. On this evening a spread was laid out for him of high quality palm candy, sprouts, little balls of coconut sweets, other sweet delicacies like *chandrapuli*, *khirer chanch*, crunchy *feni batasha*, date-palm syrup, along with a bowl of thickened milk.

'Did you give something to Bilu and Nilu?' Tilu wanted to know.

'Nilu came and had her meal here, and she took some for Bilu.'

'I *must* go home now, Bou-didi: Khokon might be fretting.'

'Come again with your husband. I would love to make a couple of *andosa* for our son-in-law. And I shall make him a special dessert with the date-palm syrup. Could've made some today, but that brother of Bhoja Muchi's—he gave me only one pot of the syrup.'

'Listen Bou-didi, d'you know your son-in-law says that I speak Bangaal, he mimicks my speech...He's even composed a line that goes: *mugeer dalee ghi dilee khiree'r taar hoi*...Hee, hee.'

'Aha, a fine fellow he is, our son-in-law. Quite an urbane dandy! I shall tell him off one of these days. It was not so long ago that he was sporting a beard. Why, when I first set my eyes on him, he had a beard this long—like the sage Narad!'

'Bou-di, you deal with your son-in-law, I must be off. Khokon must have woken up by now. I'll come by again, the day after tomorrow.'

As they walked homewards, Bhabani went on ahead and Tilu followed him, her sari well draped over her head like a good wife. They had to go through the village. It wouldn't do at all if they walked together or if they were seen actually having a conversation along the way.

Their path went past Chandra Chatujje's chandimandap, famous for hosting long sessions of board and dice games that went late into the night. Tilu was now related to Chandra Chatujje by marriage, as he was Bhabani's uncle. Tilu's heart began beating wildly: What if such a senior kinsman happened to see her now? Here she was, walking out so late at night with her husband.

When they had come up very close to the chandimandap, someone from the crowd called out, 'Who goes?'

'It's me,' said Bhabani, clearing his throat.

'Oh! Bhabani, is it?'

'Yes.''

'Oh!'

The man fell silent. Tilu briskly went on ahead and then asked in a whisper, 'Who called out just now?'

'Mahadeb Mukhujje.'

'What a nuisance! Did he see me?'

'What if he did! You stay by my side—what's there to be so afraid of?'

'You don't know about the goings on in our village. They might start a scandal about it by tomorrow. They'll say, such and such's wife was walking along quite brazenly with her husband in public.'

'Who cares! All this is going to change Tilu; I can see it coming. Our life might go on this way, yours and mine. But if little Khokon lives on, he will be able to walk along this village path side-by-side with his wife, and no one will mind.'

≈

Nalu Pal had set up a shop. The bend in the river where the current was obstructed was known as the baur of the Ichhamati; it had once been its old course. Now stifled with vegetation it did not flow this way any more. Nalu Pal's shop stood along the baur. While carrying his wares on his head to the Mollahati market he'd often thought that a grocery store on this location would do very well.

A customer came to Nalu Pal's shop. He was a *buno*, one of many whose ancestors had been brought from the Santhal Parganas to work as labourers in the indigo plantations. Over time they spoke Bangla quite well, the women wore their saris in the Bengali fashion and they worshipped the local goddesses, Kali and Manasa.

'Will you give me two paise's oil and some salt? It's clouding up, going to rain...' said a young girl.

Another girl untied four paise from her sari's end; she had come to get change for her cowries. Each paisa fetched five *gondas* of cowrie—twenty cowries. She needed to buy spinach and brinjals at the weekly market of Sabaipur.

Nalu Pal was terribly busy. It was market day. The market at Sabaipur was half a mile away; people would stop at his shop on their way back from the market to pick up goods. He had separate boxes for paises and cowries. The sales were brisk; he barely had time to toss the cowrie or the paisa into the right box and get on with his business.

He knew how to make a profit without stirring from his shop. He'd spot a woman on her way to the market with a bundle of *lau*-greens.

'How much is that for?' he would call out.

'Eight cowries.'

'Nonsense! Got one for six just yesterday. Greens for eight cowries indeed! Never heard-a such a thing! Here, give it to us at six.'

'But that's as good as selling it at a loss. It's freshly picked, jes' now.'

'Now give it, dear. 'Course it's fresh: whoever heard of stale greens selling!'

A man was walking past with two tender green gourds in a basket on his head. Nalu's alert glance immediately shifted to the gourds, 'Here, brother Dabiruddi, listen, won't you—this way!'

'What is it? I'm telling you, you won't be buying these gourds—can't give 'em to you cheap.'

'What's the rate?'

'Two paise each.'

All those hanging about the shop looked up at the asking price. They stared at each other in amazement.

'Must be jokin'?' said one.

Dabiruddi put down his load and taking up the hookah from one of the group, said with a laugh, 'An' why *should* I be jokin'! Are the likes of us worthy of makin' jokes!'

Nalu laughed as he replied, 'You're saying it the other way round—are *we* worthy of your jokes? That's what it should've been. Now tell me, how much?'

'Give me one paisa, ten cowries, then.'

'No. Take one paisa, five cowries. Don't pester me any more, my man—be happy with this. And give me the pair.'

Ancient Hari, the barber, was putting together the burnt tobacco grounds from the hookah into a leaf.

'What's that you're doing?' Bhudhar Ghosh asked him curiously.

'Goin' to polish my teeth with it later. Thought I'd buy a gourd, but didn't dare buy one, the price bein' so steep. Right here at the Mollahati bazar, when Johnson Saheb was a rulin', bought myself a gourd like this for six cowries. You could get *two* such for ten. I'd just got married. And at the wedding feast of Parshanath Ghosh's eldest son, with a cart-load of vegetables—an' one rupee it cost—the *whole* cart. Musta bin some twenty such gourds in that lot. Pointed gourds, pumpkin, spinach, cucumber, brinjal, banana flowers, banana-spathe, countless numbers of ridged gourds—all the vegetables you can think of!'

Akrur fisherman sighed deeply, 'Nyaah! Humans are goin' to stop eatin' girdually the way things are becomin' scarce. This very Sabaipur—milk you could get twenty-two, even twenty-four seers, to a rupee. No one's willing to give more than eighteen seers now.'

'Hardly eighteen seers, Uncle, they'll be giving you!' said Nalu Pal. 'You won't get more than *sixteen* to a rupee in our village. Went to Aghore Ghosh for some cottage cheese, thought I'd make some sandesh; now *that's* come up to two annas an earthen *khuli*. An' you get five poa cottage cheese at most in one little khuli.'

'Nyaah! Poor folks like us are a goin' to die starvin',' sighed Akrur fisherman again.

'Aye, that's what it's all come to,' someone seconded.

Feeling that he had been criticized enough by the company, Dabiruddi wanted to quickly sell off his gourds at one paisa each before he headed off to the market. Nalu Pal gave him a paisa and said, 'Here, you do something for me. Get me a paisa worth of shrimps. Not much fun to cook the gourd without any shrimp. Get me some really fresh stuff caught in the bamboo fish-trap.'

Hari barber had his own tale, 'Went to the thatcher's—thought I'd get the hut thatched. Used to be four annas daily wages for the job, always; but Sona thatcher sed that day he couldn't do it anymore for four; would have to be *five*. So, five annas for the thatcher, and one helper—two annas...figger out how much would it cost to do five roofs, I ask you my sons? Not less than six rupees, surely?'

Poor Akrur was so disheartened by the current state of affairs and at the high prices, that he stopped smoking altogether. Dumping his hookah on the ground, he almost rushed out of the gathering.

But after going a short distance he had to come back. Akrur fisherman's home was in the neighbouring village of Pustighata. His elder son had set up a catchment for fishing at the Sabaipur Baur. Suddenly, this son was sighted walking beneath the fig tree some distance away. They could see a huge fish almost spilling over from the basket atop his head.

Akrur stood frozen. Was it *his* son who had caught such a huge fish! It was hard to believe. As it was, he didn't have any money to go to the market.

As his son came closer, Akrur's face lit up. O my! What a grand fish it was!

'Where you going, Baba?' called out his son from afar.

'Was going home. Whose be the fish?'

'Caught in the *bundh*. Jes' got trapped.'

'Weight?'

'Eight seers and one *chhatak*. You take the fish to the markit.'

'An' you?'

'I kep' the boat by the side of the baur. 'Twill fly away if a storm whips up. You take the fish now.'

Nalu Pal's shop saw a lot of customers every evening. That was the time he liked to chat with people. Now everyone drew around Akrur wanting to look at the fish. Aah, quite a fish it was! However did it get caught so late in the day?

'Give us the fish, Akrur-da,' said Nalu Pal.

'Tek it then. Saves me, it does. Won't have to go to the markit so late now.'

'The price?'

'Give me four rupees.'

'Reflet on it a bit, Akrur-da; clearly, you haven't sold a big-sized fish for a long time now—you wouldn't know the price. Uncle Hari, what would you say it should be?' said Nalu.

Hari barber examined the fish this way and that before he pronounced, 'When we were lads, a fish like this would go for one and a half. Well, you could give it for three, now.'

'Forgive me. That's simply not possible. That's to get badly cheated.'

'Oh, a'right! You shall get three and a half rupees. Not one word more, Here, you take two rupees right away, and take the rest tomorrow.'

No one was particularly happy after buying their share of the fish because they hadn't been able to cheat Akrur fisherman right and proper. At they most, they had whittled down the extra half a rupee he would have got as a fair price at the market.

'Which ones of you want a share?' asked Nalu Pal. 'Ready money only! Throw down your cash and pick up your stuff—and you're all my pals.'

About half a dozen agreed to pay ready cash for their share of the fish. They sat down in the shade of the bamboo grove behind the shop and got ready to slice up the huge fish. Then they wrapped up their individual pieces in huge taro leaves that they had picked from the jungle.

As for Nalu Pal, he took away only half of one of the shares.

'Why have you only taken a half? Don't you want a full share?' asked Akrur.

'Not really. The shop isn't doing too well, you see. If I were to eat that much fish, it would finish me off for sure.'

'But there's only you, your mother and your younger sister—not many mouths to feed!'

'I'm not going to do anything till I put the business on a sound footing.'

'Bring home a bride before this winter, by Aghraan... and we'll all come to celibrit!'

'Let's get the business going first. The rest will follow.'

Nalu Pal could not go on bantering for a sudden rush of people entered his shop. Most of these were small-time customers who paid in cowries, not paise. Nor did anyone ask change for a rupee. In fact, no one took out a rupee. Yet waves of customers kept surging into his shop till eight in evening. Finally, when everything had quieted down it was late night.

It was an hour past midnight when Nalu Pal sat down at his till to make up his accounts. He counted each and every cowrie and heaped them up on one side and did the same with the paise. Two rupees, seven annas and five cowries—it came to.

Nalu Pal was astonished. Almost two and a half rupees worth of sales in one evening alone! It was unbelievable. He certainly had a gem of a shop. If only it went on so every single day, by the grace of Ma Siddheswari! Two and half rupees in *one* evening...Nalu Pal had never imagined that the takings would be so good. He had started off his business selling basic cooking spices, carrying his load on his head from one weekly market to another, come rain or shine, through mud and water. His body had endured it all. The big shopkeepers and wholesalers at Gopalnagar had never thought him worthy of any conversation. He was a poor creature who went all over the country toting his wares on his head.

Well, the times were-a-changing now. He had a shop, nicely thatched, with strong mud walls. He sold his goods now sitting like a proper merchant on a solid wooden seat, with bolsters by the side. Not for him any more the rushing here and there at all hours of the day. No rain or sun to rough out. His very own shop, and himself the proud owner. And a fair crowd gathering on the bamboo seats outside the shop, exchanging gossip every evening. Everyone respected him and looked up to him because he was now a full-fledged shopkeeper.

So he had made two and half rupees. Wonderful as it was, he had to sell more. He could call himself the rightful heir to the late

Govardhan Pal if only he could raise the daily sales to at least five rupees.

May Ma Siddheswari grant me such a day!

For some time now he had been looking out for some good rice-growing land. When he reached home that night he made up his mind to visit Kanai Mondol of Satberey first thing in the morning. He had been told that there was good land to be had next to the waterbody in Satberey.

As for marriage...Hari barber hadn't been far off the mark in bringing it up. What was a home without a wife? Besides, he *had* spotted such a one whom he would like to bring home as a bride— Ambik Pramanik's middle daughter, Tulsi, of Binodepur.

How Tulsi had stolen a glance at him as she was watering the fragrant jasmine creeper in their home! Nalu had noted: not once, but twice she had looked his way. Tulsi was eleven if not more, dark and large-eyed. Hard to describe the beauty of her limbs: you had to see her to appreciate her. No wonder his visits to his aunt at Binodepur had gone up. Even his aunt did not know why. But no, that wasn't quite all...

He knew very well that Tulsi's father would be in seventh heaven if he happened to mention that he wished to marry her. But, if he *were* to marry, he needed a father-in-law who would be like a guardian to him. He didn't have any one to support him, enthuse and encourage him in his ventures; he needed someone that he could turn to in times of difficulty. He had been thrown into the whirlpool of life, surviving and fending for himself. Ambik Pramanik was a small-time wholesaler in the village, dealing in mustard, pulses like mung and *kalhai*. He had a couple of paddy stacks in his home, but wasn't a prosperous man who could suddenly produce fifty or a hundred rupees on demand—the kind of support Nalu needed at this stage of his business. He needed capital. Goods were now available at cheap rates. He needed to quote his prices right away. This was the moment to really expand his business. He seemed to have understood the business of buying and selling well enough;

but where was he to get the capital from…

Nalu's mother sat waiting for him by the kitchen door with his food.

'Nalu my son, have you come home?' she cried out when she saw him. 'Been setting here so long, gone all sleepy.'

'Serve me the rice. Am hungry.'

'Go and wash your hands and feet. Moyna's kept the water ready by the wash-up place.'

'Where's Moyna?'

'Asleep.'

'So early?'

'My, what are you saying? Won't the young uns want to sleep when it's so late?'

'She'll have to go to another's home…at most, a year from now. They'll make her slave before they give her a bite. Won't let her sit around. *They're* not going to listen if she falls asleep.'

Nalu sat down to his meal. A vegetable dish made of bitter gourd, and some kalhai-dal—that was it. The glow of contentment that spread over his face as he put in the first mouthful of the red *aush*-rice mixed with the kalhai-dal, was touching.

'Dada, shall I get the hookah ready?' asked Moyna emerging from inside the house.

'Yes, do.'

'Ma says you were upset because I'd fallen asleep.'

'Course I was. A big girl like you, as though you've no housework…snoring away like a buffalo, so early…'

'I shall sleep—so there!'

'A chit of a girl and look at her talk! Big mouth!'

'I'm telling you Dada, don't you abuse me. Do I eat off you!'

'Course you do, you wretched girl! Who feeds you then?'

'Ma does.'

'Huh! Ma earns all that money and gets you the food, doesn't she! You're a monkey, that's what you are! Wait till I get you an old man for your husband, and once married too—'

'*Eesh*! Won't I chop off that old husband's nose with a cleaver! Dada, do tell me, when are going to get me a sister-in-law?'

'Let me get rid of you first. Unless I chase away a fearsome sister-in-law like you—'

'Huh, listen to him! You shall see how much work this fearsome creature will do for her sister-in-law. Now, where's the palanquin I'd asked you for?'

'Didn't get one. They don't keep them ready you see. But I've told Suro potter to keep one. He'll paint it up for the chariot festival.'

'I'm going to get my doll married during the rains. You *must* buy me a palanquin, Dada, otherwise—'

'Run along now and fetch me my hookah. What a load of rubbish!'

Moyna brought him the tobacco. After a few puffs Nalu Pal unrolled a mat on the verandah outside the kitchen and lay down to sleep.

It was summer. The breeze carried the sweet fragrance of custard apple flowers. A faint moonlight spread across the sky. In the back garden of the Nandi family a fox began to howl. At that late hour the entire neighbourhood had fallen silent.

Moyna came out again to her older brother: 'Shall I massage your feet, Dada?'

'No, no, you be off. Such caring!'

'Let me...'

'It's late. Get off to sleep. Wake me up early tomorrow morning. I'll be going to Satberey to check on some land.'

'I'll do that. Don't have to massage your feet then?'

'No, get going.'

≈

Every night on his way back home, Nalu Pal would make an offering of half a paisa at the sannyasini's little settlement, known as her *akhda*. Nalu had immense faith in the blessings of the gods; only their grace could bring him success in his business. The sannyasini's akhda was along the edge of the road running past the Baur, beneath an ancient banyan tree. Hidden by dense thickets of thorny *sai-babla*, you couldn't see it from the road.

The sannyasini's native village was Dhopakhola. It was said that she had a dream in which it was revealed that beneath an ancient banyan of such and such a village was a sacred spot dedicated to Kali in her manifestation as the goddess of the cremation ground—Shamsan-Kali—going back some three hundred and fifty years, now lost in oblivion. Some seven years ago, the sannyasini had made her way to this spot, cleared the jungle and set up her own little akhda. Gradually, she had attracted quite a crowd of devotees and disciples. People came from far off villages to offer pujas, to make vows so that their wishes might be fulfilled and so on.

Come evening, and a crowd of hemp addicts found their way to the little thatched hut by the side of bainchi bushes, over whose roof hung the branches of the ancient banyan festooned with innumerable hanging nests of tailorbirds, not to mention the scores of tiny bats that hung upside down. People came and smoked their ganja in the darkness of the night.

Srihari fisherman—or Chihari, as he was called—would cry out as Nalu went by, 'An' who be that? Nalu, is it?'

'Yes.'

'Come for what?'

'Come to give my offering to the Mother; I come every day.'

'Off'rings?'

'Ah, yes.'

'How much?'

'Ten cowries, half a paisa...'

'Set down. Won't you have a puff?'

'No, that's not for me. You carry on. Who's there along with you?'

'Not any, right now...but Hari Boshtom—he comes, and Monu Jugi, Dwarik Karmakar, Hafeez, Mansur Nikiri—they all come...'

Nalu was about to reply when he saw something that struck him dumb. He had sighted the Dewanji's son-in-law, Barujje-mosahi, walking past the pipal tree. Was *he* too one of those hemp smokers?

Nalu stood quietly by the washing-up place, outside the little hut.

Bhabani Barujje came up right to the seat beneath the ancient banyan. There was no image or idol, only a vermilion-smeared trident stuck into a mound beneath the banyan that people referred to as the 'seat' or *asan*. After Bhabani Barujje had quietly sat there a while, the sannyasini came and sat near him. She was dark, about thirty-five years old. Her features would have put a demoness to shame. Two locks of densely matted hair came down from both sides of her face to meet on her lap.

'So, Khepi, how goes it?' asked Bhabani, for she was known as Khepi, or the mad one.

'Thakur, how is it with you?'

'Have you been doing any austerities?'

'By your grace...We're lowly *hanris* and doms by caste—what sort of spiritual austerities can we do? Haven't yet gained God's grace.'

'I shall come the next moonless night and show you the discipline.'

'That won't do, Thakur—giving me the slip again. You must teach me.'

'Nonsense, Khepi! What do I know...I don't perform any austerities; I simply come to look in on all of you, that's all.'

'You can't keep putting me off, Thakur. You come here every evening. All sorts of people, without any thought of wisdom or light come crowdin' here day and night. Fetch us medicins, fetch us this or that court verdict, win me that case, let me beget a son... that's how it goes.'

'You needn't have allowed them from the start. Why did you let them turn it into a place for boons, wanting cures?

'You forget. This is hardly the white saheb's bungalow—why do you think so many turn up? Not for religion. It's to improve their lot. Turn around their luck. Win lawsuits.'

'That is so.'

'I'd entreat you to stay behind some day. Come while there's daylight. What's left to see so late at night! Every one's gone. I'm in such a fix! Prayin' and meditatin'...it's all going to seed. I'm pretendin' to be a healer and all that. Cure this one and that one—it's all come to that.'

Nalu Pal overheard this exchange, understanding only some of it. He had seen Bhabani Barujje often enough. That son-in-law of the dewan was a handsome man, no doubt. And, he inspired respect.

'I saw something wonderful today, Ma,' he said to his mother on returning home. 'You know, the sannyasini's guru is our own dewanji's brother-in-law. The husband of the eldest sister; well, he's the husband of all three sisters. Couldn't follow everything that he said, but the sannyasini who is herself such a mighty person, she's awestruck too.'

≈

'You are so late tonight,' said Tilu to her husband by way of a greeting. 'The rice must have gone dry. Nilu, come this way; will you lay out the mat? Where's Bilu?'

Nilu came in rubbing away sleep from drowsy eyes.

'Bilu's fallen asleep,' she said, as she swept clean the kitchen verandah. 'Where has our gallant been all this while? Have you found something new, interesting?'

'Is that the sort of thing you—?' Bhabani Barujje replied, with displeasure on his face.

'Hee, hee, hee!'

'As if it's all taken care of with a laugh.'

'What do I have to do, may I know?'

'Look around you—see how everyone is working. Isn't there something more you aspire to having been born a human? Is it only eating and speaking nonsense?'

'My dear, there's no need to give me advice. *You* are all in all to all of us—in this life and the one to come. If there's anything else to be done, you are welcome to go ahead and do it. We are going to have our rice and fig curry, and we will keep squabbling with you. That's *our* idea of heaven. Do take Khoka in your arms once you are done eating,' concluded Nilu.

Bhabani held Khokon and caressed him and played with him for a long time. His eight-month-old lovely child...The little fellow stared in wonder at his father, like a simple-minded creature. Suddenly, a radiant toothless smile lit up his face for no apparent reason and he gurgled in joy.

'Right, that's right,' Bhabani would say.

'Hey... yaa....a... a... g... gg...aa'

'Right, my son.'

Khoka stares in amazement at his own little hands that he turns around this way and that as though they are remarkable. Bhabani can see before him a stretch of the boundless sky. Fireflies twinkle in the bamboo grove. There is the heady scent of ripe bakul, *ghentukole* and the flowering wild *malati* filling the darkness. Constellations have flowered in the sky. A sky so vast, with a multitude of stars...The eastern horizon is aglow with the light of the moon, in its third phase. The darkness, the child and the starry sky are all part of a vast painting made by the same hand. Like his infant son, Bhabani too is lost in amazement, wonderstruck.

'When are you going to have the first-rice ceremony for Khokon?' Tilu asked, breaking into his thoughts.

'When he is older, he can have his sacred thread ceremony,' came the reply.

'How could that ever be! No, no, you must look up an auspicious day for his rice ceremony. I'm not going to take no for an answer.'

'It's done one way in your Bangladesh, and we do it differently in our Nadia-Santipur. Now, pet him a bit, won't you?'

Tilu brought her beautiful face close to Khokon's and shaking the golden makri-rings in her ears began fondling him in her own inimitable manner. 'O my little Khokon, my little ruby-red, whose darling Khokon are you? Whose golden precious jewel?'

Immediately, Khoka lunged at his mother's dark flowing tresses and tried to stuff some strands into his mouth. Then he smiled a radiant toothless smile at his mother.

Bhabani Barujje could not but look up at the boundless sky studded with constellations once more before his eyes returned to the mother and child before him...There must be a loving mother who lay hidden within cosmic Nature. How else could there exist such boundless love if it were not part of the cosmos? Bhabani had walked along many paths, searched out sadhus and sannyasis in hills and mountains, practised yoga for years; but before this most intimate of bonds between mother and child—all his yoga, his efforts at seeking a cosmic union, had been simply washed away.

Everything rests on experience. It was as though he could sense the entire mystery of the cosmos through perception, experience. Was it not the same sensibility that moved poets and seers, the mystic seekers of divine love in every age? It is because of that all-pervasive love, that the world contained mothers and children, flowers, affection, sacrifice and devotion, the lover and the beloved— that all of them existed.

Bhabani remembered listening once to a famous *khayal* singer in Kanpur. He was called Kanhaiya Lal Santara and was the fellow disciple of the famous Hanumandasji. He would first treat his listeners to such a meticulous and mature rendering of a composition, then proceed to create the most exquisite embellishments...the notes flowed out from his throat like the liquid gold of the veena; even now, some thirty years later, Bhabani could still hear with his eyes shut, the gems of a rendering of the courtly raga, *Darbari Kanada*. A great artist's music steals imperceptibly into the innermost recesses of the listener.

Bhabani thought in wonder of how, manifest within the child, one might discover the same Immortal Artist's truth in pure melodious utterance. Some were able to discern it, and others not.

A nightbird, probably come to drink the honey from the *jiuli* tree, cried out from the nearby bamboo thicket. The fishermen were at the Baur, fishing with the help of lights. You could hear their thuds while they were at work. Only after he had come here had Bhabani Barujje learnt that you needed to hit the boat when fishing with lights at night. Well, it *was* a nice place to live in.

The cool waters of the Ichhamati had washed away the grime of his own thoughts. Those who wish to experience the mystery of the world, let them walk around with their eyes open, observing at all times. It was as though the river gave him the mantra of a vision that would be gained not by renouncing the world, but by becoming a part of life itself...*kalasvana amritadharavahini ichhamati*...nectar immortal borne in the music of the Ichhamati's flow.

What God was it whose music did not bring in its wake any hope and joy?

'But tell me, honestly, when will you have the ceremony?' came Tilu's voice.

'You are so naïve. We are poor. We shall have to invite ever so many people if you want to go by the prestige of your own family and your brother's status. It will have to be a grand affair. I don't care for that kind of burden.'

'I shall take care of everything. You don't have to worry about a thing.'

'Do what you like. How much will it cost?'

'I will bring the rice and the dal from my brother's. And I shall get a cartload of vegetables for two rupees. Five blocks of palm candy—that'll cost about a rupee and a quarter. Half a maund of milk: that's another rupee. And, fifteen rupees at the most, for a maund and half of fish. That's it!'

'How many guests?'

'That's enough food for about two hundred people. I've worked it all out. Dada is obsessed about feeding people. There's always some gigantic feast or other in our home, all the year round. For this one, the costs won't go beyond thirty rupees, I assure you.'

'You are done simply having said it. Is it easy to get thirty rupees? It doesn't matter to you—you're a rich man's sister. You said it as though it was nothing.'

Tilu bent her neck at a certain angle to show her anger. 'I'm not going to listen,' she declared, 'you *must* have the first-rice ceremony for Khoka.'

'Won't you have the ceremony?' said Nilu making a sudden appearance. 'Then why did you have the urge to marry?'

'Why are *you* here?' said Bhabani in a tone of rebuke. 'We're having a conversation—'

'Isn't he *my* son too?' asked Nilu.

'Yes, but what does that mean?'

'It means that you have to hold the rice ceremony in the coming days!'

≈

The rice ceremony for the child recently born to Bhabani Barujje unfolded with Tilu, assisted by all the young women of the neighbourhood, making five full baskets of coconut-ball sweets.

Khoka was lovely: anyone who saw him fell in love with the child. Tilu had asked her Dada to have a gold chain made for the boy. Rajaram put the necklace around his nephew's neck.

Tilu was not rich any more since her marriage. But Bhabani Barujje did not leave out a single person in the village: everyone was invited. The day before, all the young girls had come and had helped to peel and cut vegetables into mountainous heaps. They stayed up all night cutting up the huge fishes and frying the pieces.

Kushi-thakuron, an old brahman woman of the village, was considered an expert cook. Just before daybreak she got the cooking going. The widowed daughter-in-law of the Mukhujjes' and Nau-thakuron came to assist her.

The rice was cooked outdoors, where a shallow trench had been dug for the firewood over which the vessels would be placed. Chiru Ray and Hari barber gutted, cleaned and then cut up the remaining fish and took it all to the trench to fry up the huge pile of pieces. Those who were busy cooking the rice cried out that they had no time now; the others had better cut a fresh trench for themselves and fry the fish. The two groups fell to quarreling until old Bireswar Chakkarty finally stepped in and resolved the matter amicably.

A distant relation of Rajaram had recently come from Calcutta. He was employed as a *nakalnabish* or copyist for the Amuti Company. With his sacred thread draped around him like a garland and a bright red towel flung on his shoulder, he went around supervising everything and everyone. He was bragging about the latest from the city.

'There's a new kind of oil,' he said with a dramatic gesture of his hands, initiating them to the mysteries of kerosene. 'It's called earthy-oil, *metey tel*—comes from deep inside the earth. The sahebs use it in their homes for light. It smells, though.'

'Can you use it for lamps?' asked Rupchand Mukhujje.

'No, works only with the lamps that the sahebs use: you know, the ones with the *gelash* outside. And who is to bring it *here*? It's very costly.'

'Don't keep talking to us about Kolkata this and Kolkata that all the time. Whatever's to be found in Kolkata, will first come to our Neelkuthi. There's no sahebs like *them* in your Kolkata, I can tell you.'

'As if! What have you seen of Kolkata, may I know? Never ever been there, have you? Come, I'll take you there by boat.'

'Is it true that there are machine-*garis* moving in the land of the sahebs? Naderchand Mondol from the Neelkuthi heard so—directly from the Chhota Saheb. Said pictures have been printed in the papers and sent here. Imagine a carriage run by a machine!'

And so the chattering went on.

On the auspicious day, Bhabani Barujje took Khoka in his arms and set off on a round of the village. Rajaram himself followed them, scattering flowers and puffed rice along the path. Dinu Muchi played the dhol as he accompanied the procession while his son followed playing the flute. Bhabani Barujje carried his infant son through the various localities grouped according to caste—of the Rays, the Ghoshes and the eastern settlement. People began blowing their conches in celebration. The women poured out of their homes to have a glimpse of little Khoka.

When the guests were being fed, the invited brahmans began competing with one another about who could polish off the most kalhai-dal or pieces of fried fish. For dessert there were the coconut sweets. Many remarked that they had not partaken of such delicious coconut-*nadus* in recent years. A single guest easily tossed off thirty or more of those sweets and an equal amount of *ananda*-nadus made of sesame seeds that had also been fried for the ceremony.

The feeding of the brahmans was almost done when notorious Hala the pikeman, otherwise known as 'Hala Pekey', appeared and prostrated himself before Bhabani Barujje. Bhabani being a newcomer to the village did not know who he was. But everybody else began treating Hala with great deference.

'Come Baba Haladhar, do come and sit down, my son—,' Dewan Rajaram invited him.

'Baba Haladhar, how are you keeping these days?' enquired Foni Chakkarty.

Haladhar—the terrifying leader of dacoits that he was—could easily cover forty *kos* in a single night on his stilts; killer of countless human beings, skilled at looting, and now freshly released from jail. The same Haladhar Pekey clasped his hands together and said with great humility, 'By the grace of your b'essed feet, all of you baba-thakuron—'

'When did you come?'

'Got out this Saturday...after noon past, baba-thakur. I'll get a bit of persad from the home of a brahman, I thought—'

'Of course; do sit down, son.'

The Neelkuthi had sentenced Hala Pekey to three years of imprisonment on charges of dacoity. Hala was back as a free man, the villagers noted fearfully. He was worth looking at: a huge young man, tall and broad-shouldered, sturdy and strong and dark as night. He could whirl his shield with one hand; and there was none to beat his mastery over the ringed bamboo stick. Completely fearless he was. He had once overturned Moody Saheb's carriage by the side of the Ghodamari Field. It was said however, that he held great respect for brahmans as the twice-born and, so far, had never mounted a raid on a brahman's home. The brahmans of the region did not set much store by this.

Everyone gathered around Hala Pekey as he sat down to his meal.

'Baba Haladhar,' one by one they coaxed and urged him, 'do eat your fill.'

Haladhar on his part did not need much persuasion. Two huge pots of kalhai-dal, two *kathas* of rice, one pot of creamy sweet rice-*payesh*, eighteen gondas of coconut-nadus and one big stone bowl of sweet and sour chutney he polished off, washing it all down with two metal potfuls of water.

Then he said, 'I'll have a look at Khoka.'

Tilu was terror-stricken on hearing this. 'Oh, no! He's a murderer; I'm not going to bring out my little boy before him.'

Eventually, when Bhabani Barujje himself picked up Khoka and placed him on Hala's lap, Hala took out a gold necklace from a knotted end of his garment and put it around Khoka's neck. 'I don't have anythin' else, my little brother; there was this—and I'm a givin' it to you. It's like servin' the Lord Narayan himself. '

Bhabani cast a suspicious glance at the gold chain: 'No, don't give him this necklace. Why should you gift him such a valuable thing? Why not buy him some sweets?'

'It's not what you believe it to be, baba-thakur,' said Hala with a laugh. 'It's not stuff I've looted. Used to belong to the one in my home...she's gone to heaven some twenty odd years ago. It lay inside an earthen pot buried in my house. Took it out and polished it up with tamarind, jes' yesterday. I've sinned a lot. Baba-thakur, it's not as though I respec' brahmans—a bad lot they are, all! But little Khoka here is God inca'nate. If I give him my necklace, it's my way to the life to come. Bless me.'

All present greeted Hala's words most enthusiastically. Bhabani was in a quandary. When he brought over Khoka to Tilu, she too insisted, 'Oh, but you *must* return it to him. It doesn't seem right to have it on Khokon.'

'He won't take it back. You think I haven't told him so! Besides, he will feel hurt. He begged me to accept it.'

'Let him beg. Go and give it back to him.'

'That's not possible. What if he be a sinner? Someone who has begged for forgiveness in all humility and who understands his own mistakes—can one be angry with *him*? You can get the gold melted and give away the money for some good work.'

Tilu did not protest any more. But her expression suggested that she could not agree wholeheartedly with her husband.

From that day onwards Hala Pekey began turning up everyday at Bhabani Barujje's place. He never said anything but would call for Khokon and after gazing at him for a while would take leave.

'Come, have a seat,' said Bhabani to him one day.

A slight afternoon shower had made the air moist; the fragrance of bakul flowers enveloped them. Hala Pekey sat down and prepared the hookah for Bhabani Barujje. It was as though he became a different person when he visited them. He would relate many of his own crimes, not with any pride though; rather, one might detect a faint note of remorse.

'What can I say, baba-thakur, as to the things I've done. That one time I used bamboo poles to climb up to the second story of the Gosain house. I climb up and find husband and wife fast asleep on the terrace. He was a young feller—came at me with a spear. I aimed my ringed stick at them and threw it hard. The young woman went down first. The husband, he kind of whirled around, spewin' great bursts of blood from his mouth he was. Both polished off.'

'What are you saying!'

'That's right, baba-thakur. What's the harm of saying what I've gone and done? That was me at a young age, never understood it all. It hurts me bad, now that I've realized it.'

'Those stilts that you spoke of—how far can you travel on them?'

'Not much these days; but that time, when I went to loot the Ghosh's home at Haludpukuri, I set off on stilts around midnight.

And was back at my village before dawn. Eleven kos it was.'

'You can't do more than that?'

'Went up to fifteen kos once: Nandipur to Kamarperey. Murshid, the headman's granary it was.'

'You better leave all that behind you. Think upon God.'

'That's why I keep on coming to you baba-thakur; something's a-happ'n to me after seein' you. Does somethin' to my heart. My heart keeps sayin' that a way will be found. Somethin' will come out of it—that's what.'

'There *is* a way. But I must tell you that unless you completely break off all ties with wrong deeds, nothing can be done.'

'That's your kindness,' said Hala Pekey, suddenly springing up and touching Bhabani's feet. 'Haladhar isn't afeard of Yama himself— by your blessins. I can get on on my stilts and cut off the head of Yama himself—like the time I cut off Tushtu Kolay's head at Ghodadanga—want to hear that story?' And Hala let out a loud ringing laugh.

At that instant Bhabani glimpsed not the meek and mild Haladhar frightened about the life to come, but the fearless unconquerable and fierce Hala Pekey who played with the heads of men just as easily boys would play with a *pituli* fruit. This awesome giant, huge and strapping, wasn't ready to listen to the warning about transience and illusion in the *Moha Mudgara* slokas attributed to Sankaracharya; the murderous dacoit in him was still alive.

≈

In the last year and a half Bhabani Barujje had come to fall in love with the village, the region. Never in his life had he come across such a cool and shady place. Bainchi, bamboo, neem, laburnum, *roda*, kunch creepers and all kinds of wild bushes filled the countryside. At all times of the day you heard birdsong—mynahs, magpie-robins, babblers and *bou-katha-kou*. With every season came new flowers, not a month went without some new blossoms—*dhundhul, radhalata, keya*, mango blossoms, *bilwa-pushpa*, suo, bonchatka, nata-kata flowers, all growing wild amidst thorny bushes.

Here, the riverbanks were overgrown with dense foliage, for no one actually lived in this part of the Ichhamati. From the time he had got married, Bhabani Barujje had dreamt of fashioning a little hut by the river where he could meditate. But during the sowing season, the Neelkuthi amin invariably marked out this stretch for indigo. It was hard to get even a bit of land that was not already marked out.

Rather than get entangled in squabbles and battles related to land matters, Bhabani preferred to sit by the broad river beneath the shadow of a juggidumur fig tree on silent solitary afternoons. He was getting by, wasn't he? Life was all too brief; why should he get caught up in that mess. He was fine, the way it was going.

A fellow disciple of his guru, whom he called his 'guru-brother', lived in an ashram at the foothills near Mirzapur in western India. A renowned pandit of Vedanta, he went by the sannyasi name of Chaitanyabharati Paramhansadev, formerly called Gopeshwar Ray. They had studied together at the same village school; subsequently, Gopeshwar had worked at the renowned Ray zamindar's estate of Patuli, Balagarh. Bhabani did not know what had suddenly impelled him to renounce the world and become a sannyasi, but his friend occasionally wrote to him once he settled down in the Mirzapur ashram.

The same Gopeshwar, now sannyasi Chaitanyabharati Paramhansa, suddenly came to visit Bhabani one day with a salt-and-pepper beard, in the ochre garment of the renunciate, his slender bedroll tucked under one arm and a pair of iron tongs in his hand. Tilu attended to him with great care. He didn't wish to live in a house, but preferred to spread out his blanket in the bamboo grove near their home.

'Paramhansadeva, you'll be bitten by a snake,' Bhabani tried to dissuade him. 'Don't blame me then.'

'I'll be fine, my brother,' replied Chaitanyabharati.

'What will you eat?'

'Everything.'

'Meat and fish as well?'

'I don't mind. But can't digest them any more, so have stopped eating them.'

'May my wife cook for you?'

'I shall cook the food myself.'

'As you wish.'

When Tilu heard this, she came out before the sannyasi and entreated him with folded hands, 'Dada—'

'What is it?' asked the Paramhamsa.

'Will you not eat any food cooked by me?'

'Didi, I've never done so. But if you wish to cook you may. Don't cook any fish or meat though.'

'Not even fish in a light gravy?'

'No.'

'*Koi* fish?'

'I see you are incorrigible. Do as you wish.'

So every day after a ritual bath and change of clothes, Tilu began cooking for the sannyasi. Bilu and Nilu would lay out the seats for the meal, and the three sisters served him and Bhabani Barujje.

≈

Towards evening, the guru-brothers were seated beneath the juggidumur tree by the Ichhamati.

'I say,' began the Paramhansa, 'it's tough enough to deal with one—and now, three of them…'

'You *know* that kulin daughters never find husbands. Our hearts cry out for them. If I can't do any meditation or perform any austerities in this life, it can all wait till the next one. At least let me do something to wipe away some suffering of mortals while I am alive. You cannot imagine the pain of kulin brahman women in these parts.'

'The three women are really nice. And your Khoka I liked very much.'

'I'm fifty-two. If I live long enough, I'll make a pandit out of him.'

'There's something greater than knowledge. Teach him devotion.'

'Sounds odd coming from you: you are a sannyasi following the path of the Vedanta. Doesn't that sound false?'

'You must know that it is not easy to be a vedantic. You first have to go through the texts of Nyaya and Mimansa. It is hard indeed to gain any understanding of Brahman.'

'Why don't you teach me for a couple of days?'

'It is not something to be achieved in a few days. Just learning Nyaya will take up a considerable amount of time. You can begin with the *Nyayashastras*, and I shall come and instruct you in Vedanta. But then you need to immerse yourself in it. Only reading will not do. You've got yourself all entangled in domesticity; how will you meditate, worship? Not in this life!'

'Not to worry! That is why I have chosen the path of devotion—bhakti.'

'And is that so easy? It's harder than the path of knowledge. Knowledge may be achieved by teaching oneself, whereas bhakti is different. It should be born spontaneously, from within. The most difficult thing is to be a true follower of bhakti. None of this is easy, my dear fellow.'

'Am I to sit quietly twiddling my thumbs!'

'Sri Krishna says in the *Gita*: to those who are constantly devoted and worship Me with love, I will grant the consciousness of understanding by which they come to Me.'

'Well, you have given me a response.'

'You've messed up things a bit with your marriage. You will get too involved. And then too, three—one is bad enough.'

'Let me test it out in this life. I shall know the limits of His grace. In the *Bhagavat*, Sukdev says, "Only through enjoying the life of a householder will you overcome your desire to live with a wife and sons." That's what I'm doing.'

'In that case why did you spend so much time going on pilgrimages as a wandering ascetic? If all that time there was the desire to play the role of a householder?'

'I believed that all desires had been destroyed, then realized that they remained. Better then to exhaust them. Let me put it in Sukdev's words: "Go to the forest retreat only when you have renounced all desires. But not while you still have them." Besides, who has told you that one may not reach out to bhagwan whilst still a householder?'

'No one has said that one may not call out to the divine. One cannot—that's what they said. Neither devotion nor knowledge is possible in such circumstances.'

'Let us see. I don't think that bhagwan is as harsh as all of you are. At least I do not believe that if one lives the life of the world, one may not find faith in devotion. Why then did he create this universe? Was it only to deceive his naïve children? Those so vulnerable and helpless—would he as a father deceive them, only to enmesh them in the maya of worldliness? Will you respond to this?

'*Eshavrittirnam tamogunasya*: the power of *tamas*, darkness or confusion, is that it covers or conceals. Material objects, *vastu* manifest themselves as something else, i.e. they do not reveal their true nature, that is why *tamaguna* is known as *vritti*—waves of thoughts which conceal.'

'Why do you conceive of bhagwan so? If you study the Vedanta, you will understand differently. He does not do anything. The problem is with *your* vision. One of the powers of maya is *vikshepa* or projection, superimposition; that which is real and unchanging is superimposed in the mind by an ever-changing manifest world of names and shapes. This projection has enamoured you and is preventing you from obtaining a clear vision of bhagwan.'

'Well, let me see how it will turn out if I take refuge in bhagwan. I've told you, I'm willing to see how far I can go with his compassion. However great the power of *mayashakti* and all that, the power of the One is greater than all. How can one think of mayashakti without bhagwan? Everything in the world he has created is his. Mayashakti is not *without* the divine; where else would maya come from? It would be false to believe that.'

'Not false. You've not at all understood what I've said. It's been said in the *Svetasvattar smriti*, "No creation is ignorant. The one who is the lord of the world in all its compositeness, it is he who as the individual, as the doer, is *jiva*, the individual soul. Advaita Vedanta says, the consciousness in all its compositeness is called *karya*. That is to say, *Iswar* is the doer, *karta*, and *jiva*, the action. But in their fundamental nature, *swaroop*, both are the same. Only the names of reference are different. You are your own lord, who else would the lord be?'

'First you said one thing picking up a sloka from the *Gita*; and now you are bringing in a doctrinal view from Advaita-Vedanta!' objected Bhabani.

'What harm have I done by citing a sloka from the *Gita*?'

'The *Gita* is a text of bhakti; Advaita-Vedanta one of knowledge. Do not mix the two.'

'Don't say that! It hurts me to hear this from your lips. In Vedanta, Brahman is the only verifiable subject; other schools of philosophy have not even acknowledged Iswar. It is only the Vedanta that has privileged Brahman. And this Vedanta you say does not believe in bhagwan!'

'I haven't said that it is atheism; I said it is not part of bhakti-shastra.'

'You don't know anything. I will teach, you *Chitsukhi* and *Khandana-khanda khadya* this time, and you shall realize the immense respect with which they have searched for Brahman. But then, they are very difficult texts to access. You won't understand unless you are familiar with Logic. You'll find in the Vedanta how they have explained the gaps in other distorted interpretations or any corrupt arguments. And you're telling me—'

'I've not really said anything. There's a world of difference between the two of us. You are a man of great wisdom—a *mahajnani*, and I, a mere householder. How can I presume to say anything over and above your words? I shall tell you my thoughts some other time.'

'Do tell me, for you are both an attentive listener and a good speaker. It is satisfying in making you listen and speak.'

'I'm happy to have had even this conversation with you. This village is steeped in darkness. There's only the Neelkuthi and the sahebs, land, money, crops and assests—that's all they care about. My brother-in-law heads the list—he is the dewan of the Neelkuthi. The "Saheb" is his chosen deity. Terribly oppressive! But my eldest wife is the lotus in the mud.'

'Good, is she?'

'Extremely so. Perhaps too good.'

'And the other two?'

'Good, but they're still to outgrow their girlish ways—spoilt little sisters of the Dewanji. Honest, though.'

≈

In the following days Bhabani Barujje and the Paramhansa were often found by the river discoursing. It was decided that the latter would initiate Tilu, Bilu and Nilu as his disciples.

That night, Tilu asked her husband, 'Do you have a guru?'

'Why do you ask?'

'Aren't you going to be initiated?'

'Aren't you the wise one! How could the sannyasi be my "guru-brother" if I did not already have a guru.'

'Of course! I won't be initiated by him either.'

'Why?'

Tilu did not reply; she smiled mischievously. She kept looking at the bauti around her wrist as she turned it around by the light of the lamp. Then she began grinding *agar* and other slow-burning incense into a small earthen incense holder. This was something that Bhabani cherished. Tilu lavished her attention on this one little fancy of a husband who otherwise had no demands, no wants or greed. Every night before they went to bed she delighted in preparing the incense, asking him every now and then, 'Can you smell the fragrance? Isn't it nice? Do you like it?'

Bhabani saw that Tilu was about to leave the room. 'Where are you going? And where is Khoka?'

'As if you don't know! It's Nilu who will come tonight. It's Wednesday, don't you remember? Khoka is with her; she will bring him to you.'

'No, *you* stay here tonight. I've to talk to you about something.'

'How could one do such a thing! Nilu has been waiting eagerly with Khoka; she is wearing her fine dhakai sari.'

'It would have been really nice if you had stayed, Tilu. Well, alright...'

A little later, Nilu came in carrying a sleeping Khokon in her arms. The necklace gifted by Hala Pekey was on his neck. Bhabani Barujje felt he had never seen so lovely a child. Not only beautiful to look at, but everything he did or said was beautiful. Then he would stop to ponder sometimes: did not other parents also regard their children the same way? Even when their child was ugly? Surely that was not false affection?

Nilu laid down Khoka most tenderly. Bhabani gazed his fill at the sleeping child whose eyelids dropped so heavily. He gently picked up Khokon and put him in a sitting position. Khokon kept his eyes shut like a miniature Buddhadeva, tranquil in repose. Bhabani had to support his neck otherwise his head would have fallen back.

'What are you doing!' exclaimed an agitated Nilu. 'It will break his neck! Really, don't you have any sense!'

Bhabani marvelled that the little fellow was sitting there, looking like a little clay model of Krishna fashioned by the skilful potters of Krishnanagar.

'Just look at him,' he said to Nilu, 'Quick, go and call Tilu. Call your Didi—'

'My, my!' said Nilu sarcastically. '"Look at how he is sleeping with his eyes shut." Why are you hurting him? For shame! Lay him down this instant.'

'What is it?' said Tilu coming in.

'See how lovely Khokon is looking!'

'Aah...yes.'

'Not a tear, not a sound from him.'

'But how *would* he speak! He's fast asleep!' said Tilu. 'Would the poor fellow know that he's being made to sit up or anything of what's been done to him?'

'Now you *must* put him down,' said Nilu. 'O my dearest darling... must be hurting. Lay him down. Didi, of course, won't say a word to his face!'

As he lay Khoka down, Bhabani felt, this was right. How can one leave out the parents, if one wished to enjoy the child's beauty? The child, his father, his mother were strung in the same golden thread. The very laws of creation had ordained that they would love each other, understand one another. It wouldn't do to leave one self out. This too, the Vedanta has spoken of, *dashamastvamasi*: you yourself make up the tenth. Why should one exclude oneself?

≈

Hala Pekey came over the next morning with his follower, the ferocious dacoit Aghore Muchi. The sisters were delighted to see Aghore Muchi who had taken care of them and played with them when the three of them were children.

'Come, Aghore-dada!' Tilu welcomed him. 'And when were you set free?'

'Jes yes'erday, my little sisters,' he replied. 'Hev come to see you all. And I say to myself let me stop by at the sannyasi-thakur and pay *him* my respecs. It will be like takin' a dip in the Ganga. Where's he?'

'Will he ever live in anyone's home! There he is—in the bamboo grove next to his fire. But Aghore-dada, do sit down for a while. How about having some ripe jackfruit? The two of you both be seated.'

'Want to see Khokon, Didimoni. But first let me prostrate myself at the feet of the sannyasi.'

Chaitanyabharati was sitting silently in the bamboo grove. His sacrificial-fire had not yet been lit. Hala Pekey and Aghore Muchi both prostrated themselves before him.

'You are...?' asked the sannyasi.

'It's us, baba.'

'That's my disciple—my *shagird*, Aghore; jes' set free yesterday. Lives in this village.'

'Why was he jailed?'

'Wouldn't hide anything afore you. The two of us we led a dacoity. Got sentenced, both of us.'

'Both of you look extremely strong. What's the harm if you put your strength to some good work?'

'No harm, baba. Jes' that we get all work'd up like. Can't keep away from it.'

'Let that keep happening: that very mind which gets worked up and makes you restless, you must keep it busy always with some good work. And your mind will change for the good, on its own.'

Hala Pekey was sitting down and listening quite attentively. Aghore Muchi didn't look like he was relishing this talk. His thoughts were with the ripe jackfruit that Tilu-didimoni had offered him.

In the meantime Nilu came out and called out, 'O sannyasi-dada!'

'Yes, my didi?' asked Chaitanyabharati.

'I'll be bringing along some ripe bananas and cut pieces of papaya now. Have you byethed?'

'Not bathed yet. You bring them along, not a problem. But why do you say "byethed" in these parts?'

'What then?'

'Nothing then; Jessore Bangals—the lot of you! Now be off. Bring me the food...'

'If you say such things, shan't bring you any food—I'm tellin' you now, dada.'

Hala Pekey stood up, 'Well, let me get on to my stilts.'

'What will you do with the stilts?' asked the sannyasi with a laugh.

'I'll be gatherin' some bananas, radishes and stuff for you. Now that Nilu-didi's annoyed.'

'A ripe jackfruit for me,' said Aghore Muchi. 'O didimoni, hunger's really tearin' me apart!'

'Go back to the house and call out to our eldest; Bor-di's sure to give you food.'

'No, didi, you come alonger me. Bor-di's bound to give me a terrible scoldin'. Why were you put into jail? What've you been upto? I'll have to give her a thousand and one 'cuzes. And everyone knows I'm a thief and a dacoit. Don't get enuff to eat; must rob and loot. Would I ha' done it, if I got enuff to eat! What I find in the village now—the prices are somethin' unbelievable. One katha of rice is two annas ten paise. Better to have stayed behind bars for a while, I say. How am I going to eat that rice—so dear—and what am I going to feed the little uns with? What do you say, baba-thakur?'

'Do whatever you consider is best, my son. But don't kill men. That's not right,' said the sannyasi.

Hala Pekey had been sitting quietly all this while. At the sound of the words 'kill men' he suddenly sprang to life. Hala was a murderer at heart. Many a head had he cut off. Any talk of murder excited him.

He came closer to Chaitanayabharati and entreated him with his palms joined in supplication, 'Baba-thakur, I beg of you, don't take it badly. Let me tell you something. Went that time to Panchitey to mount a raid on the village headman's home. When we were a-climbin' up to get upstairs, the junior headman stopped me. I stood where I was. He had a fishing spear in his hand. One blow of my ringed stick an' I sent that spear flyin'. Would a young fellow be able to wield a stick afore me! Then he picked up a brick and came at me. I sed to him, "Don't try and fight 'gainst me, step aside." But his destiny must have said his time has come: would he stop to listen, not he! Hurled abuse at me. Then an' there, I split his head in two with a blow of my stick. He tumbled down the stairs, rolling like a pum'kin.'

'How horrible!' cried out Nilu.

'And then...?' asked Chaitanyabharati.

'Then...listen to this most wonderous event. The headman's daughter-in-law, and a grand lookin' woman she was, a beauty, not more than twenty she would be—her hair untied all flyin' around her, she's standin' right there—where the *chanpa shiri* is, with a long spear in her hand—'

Chaitanyabharati, who had long left the worldly life, interrupted with, 'What is a "chanpa shiri"?'

'Oh, haven't you seen one?' said Nilu. 'I'll show you; we have one in Dada's home. It's like a second door. If you're climbing up the stairs, and when you stand on the landing, the people above can throw the chanpa shiri over your head, like a trapdoor. The latch to the door is at an angle above your head. Then the dacoits can't push it up and come up to the second floor, you see.'

'Why not?'

'Didimoni couldn't explain it to you porperly,' cut in Hala Pekey. 'You simply can't climb upstairs once they throw down those stairs. It becomes too difficult. The regular ones, you can hack away at the latch. But here, the latch is jes' above you, at a tilt—so you can't get at it...you understand?'

'Anyway, what happened after that?'

'Then, baba-thakur, I see afore me the goddess Kali herself—the very image of her...long black hair all loose and flowin', wonderful form, big beautiful eyes and face; and she's graspin' the spear like a veritable ten-armed goddess Durga, her face glowing with sweat and oil, eyes blazing fire. I'm a tellin' you the truth, baba-thakur. Many a woman I've seen; never seen one like *that* one. And how she was playin' with the spear! An absolute master she was. Swings it sharp with such a twist that you know that if it so much as touches you, it's bound to pull your guts out. I tell myself, that's some sight now. All praise to you! By my life, you've given me a dose, you have. I swear, she had the right spirit in her, that woman.'

'Then? Then what?' Chaitanyabharati was so excited that he sat up straight by his fire.

'I thought once, I'll fight it out, come what may. Then 'gain I thought, no, better back off. Doesn't bode well for me today. I was jes steppin' back, when Biro Hanri says—'

The next moment Hala stuck out his tongue and chided himself,

'Oh no, I've let out the name of one of the boys! Anyways, am sure you won't be rushin' off to the Neelkuthi sahebs to tell on us.'

'What on earth will the Neelkuthi sahebs do?' asked Chaitanyabharati.

'Oh, don't you know, baba-thakur, it's the Neelkuthi sahebs who do all the jedgin' around here. Aghore and me got put behind bars because of what that Burra Saheb said. Listen now to what happened. Biro Hanri marched on ahead. "Shame on you!" he told me. "You lost out to a woman at the end; are you a man!" And he climbed up the stairs with a mighty tread. I turned around to watch. If Biro Hanhri was a goin' to lay hands on a woman, I'd see to it that it was going to be a fight between him and me. Just then, Biro lets out a scream, "Help me!" He comes tumblin' down, right down to the foot of the stairs. And then he stumbles to his feet and pulls at somethin' in his abdomen. Like a rope it was and he's pullin' at it with both his hands. And I'm wonderin' what on earth is that. I go up close and find that his stomach is slashed and his bloody guts are going up all the way up the stairs right to the point of the spear. The more that daughter-in-law yanked at the spear, the more of his guts simply came out and gets pulled out by her. In the blink of an eye I got him out of there. Carried him in my arms right outside o' the house and sat down. Couldn't get a drop of water to give him in his dyin' moments. I knew he was 'bout to go.'

'And his guts still pierced by the spear?'

'I'd torn away the guts with one thrust of my stick. Else how could I have brought him out of the house! But that son of a Hanri had nine lives. Just wouldn't die. He moans and cries out for water. Can't even make out what else he's sayin'. Meanwhile people were about to ring us, such a hullabaloo I could hear around me. What to do—I carried him somehow to a pond behind the house; he's still moanin' away and tryin' to say somethin' with his hands. The earth is awash with his blood, baba-thakur. Not a minute left before that crowd was goin' to get us. Quickly I took Bemo Muchi's bill-hook from him and sliced off Biro's head, threw the body into the pond, carried the head back with me, so they wouldn't be able to identify the corpse. That head of Biro Hanri's—his eyes keep looking at me like they are scoldin' me. I still seem to see those eyes of his tellin' me all kinds of things.'

'What happened to that woman?'

'That I don't know. But, two months later I made for the headman's house once more, but in the guise of a fakir to take a look at that young housewife. "Give me a fistful of alms!" I cried. It was afternoon. That night in the dark, I couldn't see her so clearly. Now I could see her right close, a grand figure, complexion all shinin' gold—the very image of Jagadhatri. You had to respec' her. I was filled with reverence...

"I'm hungry, Ma," I says to her.

"What will you have?" she asks.

"Whattever you give me," says I.

She went indoors and brought me half a *khunchi* of puffed rice and pressed rice and poured it all into my sling bag. Here I was—dressed as a *mochalman*; had I prostrated myself full length afore her, she might a bin suspicious, so I lifted up my hands and said "Salaam, my mother," and I came away. But what I really felt like was to humble myself at her feet, take the dust of her feet. So I came away.'

Nilu had been listening to Hala's account, standing stiff like a wooden puppet all this while. 'And if he is dead and gone, dada,' she burst out, 'why did you stick out your tongue when you said he's part of your gang? To this day no one knows how he died.'

'What would you know, didimoni! Those Neelkuthi fellows would have gone and roughed up those two little boys of his. Would have asked them, "Where's your Pa gone?" This happened some six-seven years ago. Most people believe that Biro Hanri's settled down with a second wife somewhere by the Ganga. It's *our* fellows that have spread the rumour. So his sons can at least plough the soil in peace. The elder one's going to be a real strong chap, like his father was. '

'And you've never seen that young wife again?'

'No, had a two-year stint behind bars soon after. But that was for something else. This dacoity has never been traced.'

'After listening to your tale, I feel like paying a visit to that young wife,' remarked Chaitanyabharati. 'What caste did you say they belonged to?'

'*Sadgope.*'

'I shall visit them. Women with such power—they embody Shakti, they are the very manifestation of goddess Jagadhatri. You were right to say so.'

'Baba-thakur, you've probably never lived in these parts before. There are some more of that kind here. But other than that young wife, never met any such in a *bhadra* upper-caste household. But among the bagdi, *duley*, muchi, *namashuddurs* you'll find many a woman who are masters at wielding spears, billhooks and tapering blades, I can tell you.'

'I know,' chimed in Nilu. 'That time when there was a riot in the Neelkuthi, my brother saw with his own eyes how two young duley wives were inside a little thatched hut raining down arrows with such fierceness that the armed *burkandwaj* of the Neelkuthi had to back off.'

'That's wonderful! It makes me so happy to hear that, didi. If I can once meet any of these powerful women, it would be the very bliss of experiencing Brahman. Hail Ma Jagadamba!'

At that very moment Bhabani Barujje was returning home, water-pot in hand. 'What's this I heard brother—you hailing Ma Jagadamba? Have you quite demolished the pile of Vedantic knowledge, then?'

'As soon as you come down to the everyday, to the divine play of *lila*, its inevitable that you will think in terms of relationships—mother, father and so on. How does that demolish or tarnish in any way the Vedantic, I'd like to know. Didn't I tell you the other day that Vedanta is not such an easy philosophy? You need more time to grasp Advaita-Vedanta. Jiva Goswami's Vedanta is rather easy in comparison.'

'Well, let it go. What were you talking of?'

'Lila, divine play—the sheer energy and strength of the women in these parts of Bengal! It is all the mysterious play of the divine Mother.'

'And here's something else,' chirped Nilu, '*Our* Bor-di is very skilled at shield and stick play. She had a bout once with Akbar Ali Lathiyal with shield and stick. Akbar Ali is a renowned lathiyal of the Neelkuthi. Bor-di was such a good defender: he couldn't touch her with his stick, even once! Bor-di's a tough one, and really strong too. She can carry two huge metal pots filled with water, one on her head, and the other in the crook of her arm. She still does.'

Bhabani went back to the house with Aghore Muchi and Hala Pekey in tow. 'O Tilu, do listen, O Tilu…'

Tilu was busy feeding Khoka. She came out a little later with Khoka in her arms. 'What's this! A gang of dacoits in my home!'

'Bor-di,' said Hala Pekey, 'my stomach's a ragin' with hunger. Give us somethin' to eat, otherwise there'll be lootin' for sure.'

'I know how to wield a stick,' Tilu retorted laughingly.

'That I know.'

'Shall I take out my stick and shield then?'

'What's your stick made of?'

'Moina-wood.'

'Bor-di, I'm asking you truly, have you still kept it up?' Aghore Muchi wanted to know.

'So, shall we have a go at it one of these days? You remember those times when we played at the akhda where the Jagannath chariot is stored? I would've been eighteen at most.'

'Ooh, that's *such* a while ago. Yes, we did play a lot with sticks and shields at the akhda. I remember it well.'

'Now, sit down, I'll be right back.'

A little later Tilu came back swinging two heavy ripe jackfruits, holding each by the stalk. She put down the pair before the two men. 'Eat them up, brothers. Let's see how strong you are.'

'What's the tree? What kind of jackfruit, Didi?'

'Malshi.'

'Crispy or pulpy?'

'Bit of both, I'd say. Can the fruit be juicy, once the *Ashad* rains begin? Now eat it up—the two of you.'

Aghore Muchi polished off his jackfruit in a little over ten minutes.

'Ustad,' he said, addressing his teacher Hala Pekey, 'how come you're still at it?'

'Ate a load of mutton last night...'bout two seers,' said Hala Pekey. 'Not so hungry now.'

'Now *that* won't do, dada,' said Tilu. 'You can't throw away anything; you'll have to finish it all. Shall I fetch one for you? Won't be from that malshi tree though; there are four left over of the *khayerkhagri* kind, and those would be a bit overripe.'

'Well, give me the smallest one then.'

'Eat it up, Aghore my friend,' advised Hala Pekey, 'they're out of season now. You won't get one such for less than an anna at the markit. Me, I won't be able to start a second one; am older than you, remember? Here, didimoni, will you give us some jaggery water now?'

'So dada, you've lost to your follower! And why should I give you only jaggery-water? Two ripe coconuts I've kept for the pair of you—break them up and have them with the jaggery-water. But I warn you, can't give you too much of the palm candy. This time there's a lot we are using up at home. There's only a pair of palm-candy cakes left from the ten we had bought. *He* simply loves eating gur, you see.'

The day ended on a happy note. Hala Pekey and Aghore Muchi performed yet another elaborate prostration before Chaitanyabharati before they finally set off.

≈

Bhabani Barujje loved to go swimming in the river with his wife every evening. Today was no exception. There were pearls to be found in the

Ichhamati, and only last winter, the pearl-diving fisherfolk had cut out a narrow path through dense bushes of *nal-khagra*, beneath the shade of the babul, juggidumur, pituli and *notkaan* trees. Following the path, Tilu and her husband had cleared a little ghat for themselves. There, in the crystal clear waters of the river, yellow flowers of the babla tipped over and plopped into the water, slender creepers of gulancha draped across the branches of the notkaan, tiny-eyed fish darted and frolicked around Tilu-sundari's breasts, flicking away and disappearing the very instant you stretched out your fingers to grasp them; in the evening how many were the birds that clamoured around the lush foliage and bushes. From the bank, no one can see the couple.

'Let's swim across,' said Bhabani Barujje to his wife, as he entered the water.

'Do let's,' chimed in Tilu, 'and we can pick some pointed gourds from the fields across.'

'Shame! Spoken like a rustic: don't you understand that's like stealing?'

'As you say! It's just that *we* used to pick lots of them.'

'Shall we swim then?'

'Come, let's. Shall we swim towards Go-ghata? You know—by the field with that huge aswath tree?'

Tilu was a marvellous swimmer. With her straight and slender body she would swim underwater silently. Bhabani Barujje usually swam by her side.

Suddenly, right where the waters were black and deep, Bhabani Barujje cried out, 'Tilu, O Tilu!'

Tilu had gone on ahead; she swam back to him. 'What is it?'

Bhabani who was waving his arms about helplessly, cried out, 'Get away, Tilu! A crocodile's got me. Get away...!' He was swallowing great gulps of water.

'But what is it, tell me?' asked Tilu, quite dumbfounded. 'How can that be!'

Bhabani who was still flailing his arms, choking in the water, could only gasp out, 'Look after Khok-a-aa, Khokaaa-aaa...'

Tilu trembled. Would the dark blue waters of the river of this rainy evening really turn red with the blood of her beloved? All the joys and desires of life to be quenched forever...so soon?

Without a moment's hesitation, she dived into the water. Either she would rescue her husband from the jaws of the crocodile or she would let herself be devoured by the beast. Beneath the waters she found that her husband's garment had got entangled in the thorny branches of the splaying roots of a huge silk-cotton tree, now lying on its side on the riverbed. A swift tug and she managed to tear away some of the cloth. Then she surfaced and swam to her husband's side to give him courage, 'There's nothing to fear. Your cloth is stuck in the *simul* thorns; stay afloat and I shall free you soon.' Taking a deep breath she plunged in again, tearing off more of the cloth this time. The failing evening light made it difficult for her to see clearly once she was underwater. It wasn't clear how his garment had got caught in the first place. She had to dive down three or four times before she could completely set him free; her husband was by now completely limp, almost unconscious. She half held and half floated him towards the shore where the water was shallow.

'Oohh!' Bhabani Barujje could only gasp and breathe in great gulps of air.

Tilu's sari was undone, her long and thick tresses untied; somehow, she managed to put herself in some order. She too was exhausted and panting, though her keen eyes were still on her husband. True, he was quite old but still so handsome.

What a narrow escape that was!

'You were getting us into a fine mess this evening!' she said to her husband with a smile.

Bhabani Barujje could only smile back.

'That's enough swimming for one day. Let's get home.'

'Thank goodness you dived, Tilu! Whoever knew that the roots of the silk-cotton tree were lying in wait under the water! I had given up: thought it was a crocodile that got me.'

The two walked home along the lonely dark path.

If something had happened to him…she shuddered at the thought. Would she have lived if her husband had died?

≈

Dewan Rajaram had been summoned to the Burra Saheb's office in the Neelkuthi. At this moment he was still standing before the Burra Saheb with his palms joined deferentially.

'Your work is not happening in the ride way,' observed the Burra Saheb, puffing away on his carved wooden pipe.

'Why, huzoor?'

'How did the figures for indigo cultivation come down so low this year?'

'If you give me leave, huzoor, I shall tell you the truth. It's after the affair at Rahatoonpur—'

James B. Shipton suddenly brought down his fist on the table with a thump. 'I don't wish you to spin that rigmarole here again. I want work. Work! We *have* to sow indigo across two hundred bighas of land this year. Understart! Don't want to listen to any of your nonsense.'

'Huzoor!'

'Mr Duncinson has been transferred. A new magistrate is come. He's with us. We've got to begin the marking of the land against the advances, briskly. I need the figures. Show me the dadon registers every day, you must.'

'Huzoor!'

Sriram Muchi entered with coffee for his saheb.

Rajaram pointed at Sriram and said, 'Huzoor, ask him. It's in *their* village of Chorpara where the muchi community will not let us grow any indigo—you can ask him.'

'What is that happening now?' the saheb asked Sriram in his peculiar Bangla.

Sriram was a favoured khansama of the sahebs. Forget about those lower in the hierarchy, the Burra Saheb himself did not inspire any excessive respect or fear in Sririam.

'Yes, it's all true,' he said frankly.

'What's true?'

'Golu and Hansa have ganged up with the others, huzoor. Won't let the indigo lines be marked.'

J.B. Shipton turned to his dewan quite enraged, 'You are no milksop—go and mark out the land in Muchipara today, right away. I shall ride out later to see it for myself. Have they forgotton the Shyamchand! Ramu Muchi has set himself up as a leader—straighten him out first.'

Sriram Muchi now stepped up with his palms joined in supplication, 'Saheb,' he said, 'I've got three bighas where I'm growing masur-dal—the winter crop. Dewanji may kindly not mark out that bit. As for Ramu Sardar, neither do I visit him, nor does he have anything to do with me.'

'All right, granted! Dewan, his lant is not be in the reckoning.'

'As huzoor orders,' said Rajaram.

'You can go now. That devil of an amin should go with you. Prasanna Amin will accompany you. Not Harish Amin.'

'As huzoor orders.'

Prasanna Chakkarty was busy cooking rice for his lunch. He quickly stood up when Dewan Rajaram entered his home. Thank goodness! It was only a while ago that Nobu Gaji and his companions had been here in this very room. They had come to plead that their land be spared somewhat from growing indigo this year. They hadn't come empty-handed with their request. Had they stayed on a little longer, he would've been caught. That old fox Rajaram was not to be easily hoodwinked.

'So, cooking rice, eh?', said Rajaram.

'Do come in. Yes, sir.'

'Let's go right away, Chakkarty; we've got to finish off those muchis today. The Burra Saheb's mad as hell.'

'May I say something? You won't be angry...?'

'No. What is it?'

'The marking's all done.'

'How's that!'

Wiping his hands on his thin towel after he had washed them, Prasanna Chakkarty opened a small tin box from which he took out the book of accounts and a map.

'Here's seven *pakhi* of land, two pakhi here and this one and a half a pakhi. Altogether—thirty bighas and seven kathas of land,' he explained to the dewan.

'That's good,' said Rajaram, looking at him approvingly. 'When did you do it?'

'Sunday. Past midnight.'

'Who was with you?'

'Karim Lathiyal and me; Sayaram Boshtom was the pinman.'

'Why didn't you report this? I should've known all this…Wouldn't have had to get such an earful from Burra Saheb. Anyway, come on now.'

'Please don't mind, Dewanji. Let me tell you why I didn't say anything earlier. Wasn't sure how it would work out. That's right. After that affair at Rahatoonpur…'

'Don't be afraid. That's no cause for fear *now*: the magistrate has changed. The Burra Saheb himself told me so.'

The dewan wished to take credit from what Amin Prasanna Chakkarty had already accomplished. The report was written accordingly and Prasanna Chakkarty's name was all but erased.

≈

However, that very morning there was an outburst of violence in Chorpara.

That distantly related nephew of the Dewanji's, the one who had impressed everyone with wondrous tales of steamships and trains, and who worked as a copyist in the Amuti Company—had turned up at the Neelkuthi to meet the dewan. Suddenly, the *paik* came to report that the raiyats had uprooted the stakes that marked out the plots.

Rajaram immediately raced off on horseback towards Chorpara.

There, he seated himself beneath a banyan, and one by one, he summoned all the muchis. He ensured that yet more land was added to the area that had already been marked out for each peasant. He got each one's thumb impression assenting to the new measurements and didn't listen to a word that any one of them had to say.

Ramu Sardar was summoned.

'Haven't you set up a fish bundh at the Panchpota Baur this year?' Rajaram asked.

'Yes, sir, Ray-moshai, I do set up one every year.'

'H'mm,' said Rajaram.

Ramu Sardar trembled inwardly. He knew Dewanji well enough.

As Rajaram was mounting his horse, Ramu came up to him and said, 'How am I to blame: have I done anything wrong? Please don't take offence simply because people have said something or the other.'

Rajaram was already on his horse and away in a flash.

Late that evening, Ramu Sardar was sitting by the Panchpota Baur having his smoke, chatting with some peasants and half a dozen *nikiris* (as the Muslim fisherman were called), when—from nowhere it seemed—about ten people rushed in and began smashing up his bundh.

Ramu Sardar sprang up and cried out, 'Who? What the...! Which ill-omened fella dares lay hands on my bundh?'

'Your father!' mocked Karim Lathiyal, striding up towards him.

'Don't you dare!'

Ramu Sardar was headman of the bagdis. He was not a coward.

As soon as he picked up his stick and charged at Karim, the lathiyal's stick flashed above his head. Ramu Sardar managed to stave off the blow and Karim yelled, 'On guard!'

Yet another powerful blow.

Ramu Sardar gave a return blow. '*Shabash*! Good show! On guard!'

Ramu Sardar was waiting for an advantage. The triumphant Karim Lathiyal had left his head unguarded. In a flash, Ramu Sardar swung his stick and called out, 'Better watch out—you beef-eating minion!' Like lightning, Ramu's stick twirled over and past the other's diagonally positioned stick. There was a terrific sound, like a wood-apple fruit exploding. Then, like a broken branch of a papaya tree Karim fell at the stakes of the netting by the bundh. But Ramu couldn't keep his balance. He too stumbled and fell forward. Immediately, Karim Lathiyal's companions fell on him with all their might, beating him until they had finished him.

The grass around the bundh was bloodied. Even the next day, passers-by could see the thick splotches of blood on the grass. Not a sign of the bundh remained. The band of lathiyals uprooted and broke off every bit of bamboo of the bundh, carrying off every single piece.

In a field adjoining the bundh, beneath a date palm tree, lived Ramkanai Chakrabarty *Kobiraj*, the local doctor of herbs, practitioner of ayurveda. Ramkanai was a wretchedly poor brahman. All summer long he lived on a bit of cooked rice and fried laburnum flowers. He picked these flowers for as long as the laburnum bloomed on the field by the Baur. He knew well his profession of healing, but in the remote rural area that he lived in, no one paid him in cash. Some patients gave him a quantity of grain, that too, after long intervals. If a patient happened to recover at the end of rains in the month of Sravan, he had to wait for another two months, till the beginning of *Aswin*, when the first crop of aush-paddy would ripen. He would himself have to go door-to-door collecting his share of the grain due from the peasant families he had treated.

On that day, Ramkanai was sitting inside his hut by the date palm reciting Dashu Ray's *panchali* verses, when the sudden commotion at the baur made him shut his book and step outdoors. He walked on ahead and saw that some of the lathiyals employed by the Neelkuthi were untying the bamboo from the bundh. A little later he heard someone cry out murder. Ramkanai was walking back home when he saw fish-sellers Haru Nikiri and Mansur Nikiri race past him.

'O Haru! O Mansur! What's up?' called out Ramkanai. 'What's happened?'

Soon Hajrat Nikiri came rushing and followed the others into the darkness. As he went by, he said, 'Who is that—oh, Kobirajmoshai? Don't go that way. The Neelkuthi lathiayls have killed off Ramu Bagdi and they're looting the bundh right now.'

Ramkanai walked back home fearfully and shut his door.

Out of this incident something else emerged, that was quite extraordinary. It was bigger than the murder and the raid and loot of the bundh.

≈

The next day there was a huge outcry that the Neelkuthi people had smashed to bits the Panchpota bundh and murdered Ramu Sardar. People rushed in droves to the site where it all happened. Some remarked that it was because the Neelkuthi Saheb had all along wanted to gain control over the water revenues. Many others went to Dewan Rajaram's house.

'Murder?' said Rajaram in astonishment. 'What do you mean! Certainly it wasn't anyone from the Kuthi; must be the work of outsiders. Ramu Bagdi was an epitome of wickedness. *He* didn't lack for enemies! You people are the limit...whatever happens, you have to blame the Neelkuthi for it, don't you? It's too much!'

The Burra Saheb summoned Rajaram: 'What's this I hear aboud a murter? A murter done by *whom*? Who hath done the murter?'

'Not one of ours, huzoor,' was the reply. 'He had a whole lot of enemies—that Ramu Bagdi. How would we know who has gone and killed him?'

'Dit our lathiyals go or not?'

'No, huzoor.'

'We shall have to prove this to the police.'

To the Chhota Saheb the Burra Saheb said, 'I think that man has overshot his mark this time. I don't appreciate this murder business, you see. Too much of a trouble, when I am the enquiring magistrate.'

'Sir, I ordered only that the fish bundh be swept away.'

'I know, get ready for the trouble this time.'

Prior to the police enquiry, Ramkanai Kobiraj was summoned to Rajaram's home. Rajaram told him what he was to say at the enquiry: he had seen people from the Buno-locality kill Ramu.

'Ray-moshai, how am I to utter such an absolute lie?' said Ramkanai Chakrabarty.

'You have to. Don't whine! You will do as you are told.' Rajaram was using the polite honorific to address Ramkanai, but the threat was plain.

'Sir, Ray-moshai, you've put me in great trouble.'

'We shall reward you, give you paan-money from the Kuthi.'

'Ram! Ram! Don't even say such a thing. I'll not do this work for money.' Ramkanai was horrified at this euphemistic offer of a bribe.

Ramkanai was summoned during the enquiry. The *daroga* was someone much obliged to the Neelkuthi in former times; now, he tried his best to overturn Ramkanai's statement as a witness.

But Ramkanai was unwavering in his statement: he had seen the Neelkuthi lathiyals come running away from the bundh. He had also seen Ramu Sardar's dead body. But as to who had actually done the killing, he hadn't seen anything of that.

'Didn't you know that Ramu was on fighting terms with the folks at Buno-para?' the daroga insinuated

'No, Daroga-moshai.'

'Did you see *anyone* from Buno-para at the spot?'

'No.'

'Think hard,' said the daroga, 'whether that was indeed the case.'

'No, Daroga-moshai.'

The daroga called Rajaram aside before he left, 'Dewanji, that old kobiraj is a real stubborn creature. We'll have to try and win him over somehow. Give him lots of coconut water to soften him up!'

A paik was sent to bring Ramkanai over to the Neelkuthi. Prasanna Chakkarty Amin now began to work on him: 'Kobiraj-moshai, the Burra Saheb Bahadur has said he will make you happy. Only tell us what you would like. He's very pleased with you.'

'What can I ask for? I'm a poor *bamun*, Amin-moshai, whatever he may choose to give...'

'All the same, do tell us what you would like. For example, money, or grains...'

'Some paddy would be very good.'

'So I shall tell Dewanji right away.'

Ramkanai Chakrabarty was then taken to the Chhota Saheb's own office.

Ramkanai was a poor man and he had never entered the premises of the sahebs' Neelkuthi. He entered the room trembling. Chhota Saheb was sitting there, pipe in mouth.

'Come here,' he said in a stern voice.

'Yes, sir, Saheb-moshai, I salute you,' said Ramkanai.

'What do you do?'

'Sir, I'm a kobiraj.'

'Good, will you practise your healing at the Neelkuthi?'

'Sir, who shall I treat, Saheb-moshai?'

'Us.'

'If that is your desire...I shall certainly do whatever you wish.'

'You will?'

'Why not, sir?'

'Then you will be given ten rupees a month.'

Ramkanai Chakrabarty couldn't believe his ears. Ten rupees a month was close to the earnings of important men like the Dewan-moshai! Why were they suddenly so pleased with him today?

He exclaimed, 'Ten rupees, Saheb-moshai!'

'Yes, that's the amount.'

The cunning Chhota Saheb then called Rajaram: 'Draw up a contract with this man and get him to sign it. You will pay him ten rupees from the Neelkuthi's cash box every month for his doctoring. Give him an advance of ten rupees.'

'Right, huzoor.'

The next morning Ramkanai was once more summoned to the Neelkuthi. The evening before he had come back feeling most contented with the promise of ten rupees. He wondered why was he being called again this morning. Ramkanai was told to report to the dewan's chief record keeper, his *seresta*.

'So you have now become one of us...' began the dewan.

'It is their kindness,' responded Ramkanai with great humility.

'No, no, *that's* not the point. You are a good kobiraj. And on our part, *we* need you. Have you received the ten rupees?'

'Yes, sir.'

'One more thing: now that all this has happened, and you are beholden to the Neelkuthi, you must sing their praise.'

'Sir, the compassionate Burra Saheb, Chhota Saheb and Dewanji—their praises shall I always sing. I'm a poor brahman, and the kindness that you have shown me—.'

'Enough of that! You will have to stand witness in our favour in that murder call. You can do us this kindness.'

Ramkanai was dumbstruck. 'That? That's all over, isn't it? You have already said what you had to before the police; why bring it up again?'

'No. No. You will have to speak up in the court. We shall put you forward as our witness. You will say that you saw Bhontey Buno, Nengta Buno, Chikistho Buno and Patiram Buno from Buno-para rushing away with lathis in their hands.'

'But Dewan-moshai, I didn't see any of that.'

'Well, if you haven't, you haven't. Don't speak like a fool! You have now been made the official kobiraj of the Neekluthi at a fixed monthly salary. You get extra baksheesh if you can cure the sahebs and mems. Besides, there is the fixed payment of ten rupees per month. You will get a room as well, from tomorrow. That's what the Burra Saheb has said. You are now one of us, our own. Just say this one thing in our favour—only this one thing, and it's all settled. You needn't say any more. Just that one line: you will say that you've seen such and such buno run away with sticks.'

'But, but...' Ramkanai mumbled in a despairing way.

'No buts! You have to say it. What do you want? Burra Saheb has showered his benevolence over you. He will give you whatever you want. And you will come up in life.'

Ramkanai was silent.

'Well, you better be off now,' the dewan went on. 'I would have offered you the Neelkuthi horse to ride back home, but then you don't know how to ride. So, will you go home in the bullock cart?'

Ramkanai joined his palms in supplication and said most humbly, 'Dewan-moshai, I'm very poor. Don't put me in a spot. I've heard that one has to swear in court before giving witness. Sir, I won't be able to live if I do so. Please forgive me. My father would not drink a drop of water until he had performed his *trisandhya* ritual. No one ever heard him say a lie. I am not worthy of our lineage, so I have to take money for my healing skills. Sickness should be treated and the ill restored to health without money changing hands. I know it all, but am too poor; so I do accept some money. Dewan-moshai, I shan't be able to stand in court and speak untruth.'

'This one's a scoundrel!' said Dewan Rajaram, infuriated beyond measure. 'Stuff the creature into the lime shed for the night and let's see if we can knock some sense into his head with a bit of pressure. If that won't cure him—there's Shyamchand, don't you know!'

Paik Nafar Muchi who was standing by, said, 'Come thakur-moshai.'

'Where will you be a-taking me?'

'Dewanji told me to take you the lime shed, didn't you hear? You are brahman, god-like—I'm not going to touch you; otherwise I'll commit a grievous sin. You come on ahead of me.'

'Which way?'

'Better follow me.'

When they had walked for a while, Rajaram sent for Ramkanai again.

'So you are off to the lime shed? It's the sort of place that will make you cry your heart out...I'm warning you about it because after all, you are a bhadralok.'

'Why are you sending me there, Dewan-moshai? Please don't send me there.'

'Here you are, a decent bhadralok, a *salaried* employee of the Neelkuthi, and yet unwilling to do us a little good deed.'

'It's not that, can't say a lie on an oath. That means sure damnation. I'd be fallen.'

'Then go and elevate yourself in the lime shed. Take him and lock him up, Nafar.'

≈

It was almost ten at night.

Dewan Rajaram went alone to the lime shed and unlocked the door. Ramkanai Kobiraj had fallen into an exhausted sleep. The lime shed of the Neelkuthi wasn't exactly the most comfortable of places for a good sleep. The 'lime shed' had in fact not much to do with the storage of lime, as it had with unruly peasant subjects. Whosoever dared to stand up against the interests of the Burra Saheb or the Neelkuthi inevitably had to sojourn in the 'lime shed'. He would be kept locked up in this room which was sunless and airless, except for what came in through a couple of holes near the ceiling, until such time when the Burra Saheb, or the Chhota Saheb, or the Dewanji, might choose to give the order for his release. A big madar tree used to stand just outside the shed. Once, a certain indomitable raiyat from Rashmonipur who had been locked up inside, managed to climb out through one of the holes and swing himself out with the help of a low overhanging branch of the madar tree. He had made good his escape. The then Burra Saheb, John Saheb, had forthwith ordered the tree to be chopped down. Another story went that one of those imprisoned had fainted on sighting a ghost in the shed.

Rajaram was rather afraid of ghosts. He would normally have never come so late at night all by himself to the lime shed. Tremors of fear had been assailing him as he walked to the shed; but once he saw Ramkanai, he felt a little reassured. No matter that the fellow was asleep; at least he was a flesh and blood human being.

'O Kobiraj-moshai, O Kobiraj...' he called.

'Who is it?' cried out Ramkanai startled out of his torpor. 'Oh, is that you, Dewan-moshai...do come in...' Ramkanai began looking around as to where he might seat his unexpected visitor, as though it was to his home Rajaram Dewan had stepped into.

'That will do,' said Rajaram. 'I haven't come here to sit and chat with you. Come along with me, now.'

'Where to, Dewan-moshai?'

'I said, come along.'

'I'm coming. But don't stuff me into such a room again, Dewan-moshai; it's thick with mosquitoes. They've practically bitten me to death.'

'It's all your doing! Otherwise, here you are—the Neelkuthi's own appointed kobiraj—why should you even have to step in here! Well, whatever's happened has happened. Now you come along with me.'

'Wherever you might be taking me to...d'you think I would be able to sleep a bit?'

'You've changed your mind...?'

'No, Dewan-moshai, I'm a-begging you with folded hands, don't make this request of me. I'm a healer, a kobiraj, if I see someone is ill, I will go out and pick and choose the right ingredient from the field and forest. I'll make them into pills and mixtures; you'll never find me wanting in any of *that* work. But don't involve me *please* in all this having to do with cases and courts. I beg of you—'

Ramkanai was a simple man. He had no clue as to how the Neelkuthi sahebs worked. Nor did he have a clue about these servitors of the saheb: that they could go up several notches higher than their masters. A mere hint or an oblique order from a saheb was enough for them to murder in cold blood, remove any 'obstacle' in accomplishing the order. The corpse would disappear in the waters of the Gazipur Lake. Could Ramkanai Kobiraj have learnt any of this from the manuscripts of the masters of traditional medicine, Charak or Sushruta, that he had studied for so long?

The Chhota Saheb was seated in the long verandah, doing the accounts. Beside him lay the 'bundles' of indigo. The Calcutta-based Amuti Company had sent tenders for the indigo. In another three days, their representative, House Manager Roberts Saheb, would be here to check out and examine the bundles. That was why the Chhota Saheb was busy supervising the making of samples. Prasanna Amin, who excelled at detecting the quality of the indigo, was also present along with Kanai Ganguly who was employed as their *jamanobish*, an accountant. Syce Bhoja Muchi hovered in the background, waiting on them.

'Oh! Here's the dewan,' said Chhota Saheb, 'come in, come in! Tell me Dewan, did you say that lot number 363 from Akaipur will mix well with those from Deuley, Sarabpuri and Ghoga?'

The fact was that they were mixing the good stuff with the bad. Not all the plots yielded the same quality of indigo. Those who were experts could grade the different varieties and rank them accordingly. They could immediately warn, don't mix this lot with that, otherwise, the broker from the Amuti Company will catch you out.

'They'll mix very well indeed,' replied the Dewan. 'Kalibor agent won't be coming this year; and, Robert Saheb doesn't know the first thing about indigo. The indigo from Ghoga, our Mollhati, and Panchpota can all be nicely mixed and no one the wiser. Here, huzoor, I've brought you that kobiraj of ours.'

'How did you enjoy your stay at the lime shed?' asked the Chhota Saheb, turning his gaze on Ramkanai.

'Saheb-moshai, my salutations,' Ramkanai said with folded hands,

Dewan Rajaram clicked his tongue and raised his hands in exasperation.

'Huzoor, you're asking him about the place! How would the kobiraj know! He was put in there and he promptly went off to sleep.'

'Really! You were a-*sleeping* in the lime shed? So it must have been a most comfortable sort of place. How about staying on for a few more days?'

'Sir, I don't understand at all what saheb-moshai's telling me.'

'Course you do. You are a sly one—no use pretending. John David is not going to let go off you. Tell me, are you going to testify in the case or not? If you do, I shall raise your salary right away by another ten rupees. There, do you agree? Don't have to say anything but this: you saw Chikistho Buno and a couple of others from Buno-para running away with their sticks. Willing?'

'Sir, saheb-moshai...'

'Calling me "saheb-moshai" is of *no* use. You've got to do it. Testify, and I'll see that you prosper. You shall be the Neelkuthi Kobiraj with a fixed salary. Dewan, raise his salary to twenty rupees from the month of June.'

'As huzoor orders,' Dewan Rajaram Ray promptly repeated like a pet parrot.

'Well, take him away. The kobiraj is willing; take him away! Prasanna Amin, won't you be able to give him a bed in your home for the night?'

'Certainly, huzoor,' said Prasanna Amin, jumping to his feet. 'My bed is already made, he could even sleep there.'

Ramkanai turned pale. His tongue was parched with thirst. But he couldn't drink a drop of water touched by sahebs and the low caste muchis. He had just seen that bearer Sriram Muchi had brought in liquor in a glass bowl for the saheb. It was actually not liquor but coffee. Too much of caste pollution going on here, he thought; if he was to pursue his kobiraj profession in these premises, he would simply have to manage with coconut water.

'Then we better be going: it's late at night,' Prasanna Amin said.

Dewan Rajaram was a man of business, not one for half measures. He wanted to firm up things. 'So it's been decided that Kobiraj-moshai is to testify, right?'

Prasanna Amin looked enquiringly at Ramkanai.

'Saheb-moshai, how can I do that?' I've already said so to Dewan-moshai,' said Ramkani.

'You are not going to be a witness?' cried the Chhota Saheb in a fury.

'No, saheb-moshai, I won't be able to tell a lie. I beg of you, I beseech you with folded hands, my father was a brahman pandit—'

'Oh! I see that you're not yet straightened out. You won't begin to think right without some help. Bhoja—call out to Nafar, will you? Let this fellow have ten solid ones of Shyamchand.'

Nafar Muchi was a tall young man, black as ebony. He had killed many a man. Outside the boundaries of the Neelkuthi in the outlying villages, he was regarded with terror. Nafar had probably been sleeping when he was summoned. He came in behind Bhoja, rubbing his eyes.

Chhota Saheb turned to Ramkanai and said, 'So, shall we bring Shyamchand down on you?'

'Sir, saheb-moshai, I'll die for sure if he does so. Don't tell him to kill me. I've been very weak since the month of Ashad, suffering from gout and phlegm...'

'It won't matter *a bit* to me if you die. Take him away, Nafar.'

'As you say, huzoor.'

Nafar took hold of Ramkanai's hand and practically dragged him away. Before he left, he addressed Dewanji, 'So I'm to take him to the stables?' He rested his steady gaze on the dewan for a few seconds.

'Take him there,' said the dewan.

Ramkanai went along with Nafar like a sacrificial goat about to be slaughtered. In any case he was a bit of a simpleton; although he had heard the order he still wasn't able to comprehend that Nafar Muchi's powerful arm would flay his back to strips with a couple of lashes of Shyamchand.

Nafar made Ramkanai stand in the stable; looking at him in the faint moonlight, he asked, 'How many will you 'ave?'

'Don't kill me, my son. I suffer from gout and rheum, catarrah...I shall die for sure.'

'Go and die then. I'll set you floatin' in the baur waters. No need to worry about that. I've floated away many a corpse with these hands. Now turn around and get ready.'

Two lashes of Shyamchand—and Ramkanai went down on the floor writhing in pain. Nafar stopped to get some old dusty jute sacking that he threw over the prone body of the kobiraj. The dust flew into his mouth and nose, choking him, and his tongue was filled with grit. Meanwhile Nafar was wielding Shyamchand with all his might, shouting out, 'RAM, TWO, THREE, FOUR...!'

After completing 'Ten', he said to Ramkanai, 'You're a berahman, after all. Whatever Saheb might say, ten lashes of Shyamchand would've killed you for sure...Don't move an inch from here, tonight. The game will be up if the Chhota Saheb comes to see you.'

All night long Ramkanai lay corpse-like on the floor of the stable.

≈

It was market day and Bhabani Barujje was planning to buy some rice. Nilu had just told him that they had run out of rice. He was standing beneath the bakul tree by his home that morning. Tilu came out with their year-old boy in her arms.

'Don't give him to me now,' said Bhabani, 'Take him away; I have to visit my uncle.'

Khoka however, put out both his arms, ready to jump into his father's embrace. When Tilu tried to take him away, he began crying, waving his tiny right hand, as though calling out to his father.

'All right, give him to me. Wait, here comes old Dinu, I'll have a look at the rice she's selling,' said Bhabani and took his son in his arms.

Khoka began tugging at his father's ear in delight, pointing to the road, 'Eeee...there...there.'

'No, it's *not* time for your walk now. I'll take you out later in the day.'

Khoka didn't understand, of course. He kept pointing to the path with his fingers making strange sounds.

'No, not now.'

'Well, if you are going to Uncle's, why don't you take him along?' said Tilu.

In the meantime, Khoka had got hold of his father's sacred thread in his little fist, and was urging him on to the road.

'No.'

At this reprimand Khoka began crying.

'He really loves going out with you, take him, go on,' urged Tilu.

'Why? He has three mothers; can't he manage without me?'

'No, he can't. Even when he's with us in the kitchen, every now and then he looks outside and cries out, pointing outdoors. He's trying to say that he wants to be with you.'

Right then old Dinu appeared, her bamboo container of rice balanced on her shoulder.

'Let's have a look at your rice,' cried out the sisters.

Dinu Buri was almost eighty years old. She looked exactly like Annada—the archetypal old woman described by the poet Bharatchandra, right down to the iron bangle she wore. She came up to them with a beaming smile and put down her load.

'It's double *nagra*, didimoni!' she said, describing the rice. 'Our son-in-law there?'

'Yes, my dear,' said Tilu. 'What's the going rate?'

'Six pice.'

'It's an anna in the market.'

'No, didimoni, I've lived off your bounty all these years, and would I be cheating you? Well, if not six pice, give me five. Here, just chew on some of these grains and tell me if they're not sweet.'

'Come indoors. We'll have to keep some of the money pending though.'

'Of course, why should that matter? Give it later in the day.'

'Not today; won't be before Tuesday.'

'Well, do that.'

Seizing the opportunity Khoka grabbed a fistful of rice from the container and stuffed it into his mouth. Some grains fell on the ground.

Bhabani quickly took away the rest of the rice from him and said, 'Open your mouth Khoka, wide…'

Khoka promptly opened his mouth as wide as could be. This was a trick that Tilu had taught him, for he would at any moment dig up something with his two fingers and it would find its way to his mouth. His mother would say, 'Now open your mouth, Khokon, that's a good boy!' and Khokon would oblige while his mother would gently probe and remove whatever he had put inside. 'That's enough,' his mother would say. 'No need to open it so wide.'

Bhabani Barujje was gently taking out all grains from Khokon's mouth when he saw Foni Chakkarty approaching him; following him was Bhabani's uncle, Chandra Chatujje.

'Tilu, you better go in with old Dinu, and take Khoka along with you as well.'

The two older men came nearer, but even as Tilu tried to take away the boy, he clung fiercely to his father, embracing him around his neck. He screamed out his protest.

'What am I to do?' said Tilu. 'Once he's in your arms, he doesn't want to go to anybody.'

Bhabani laughed. Momentarily, he saw his child as though he was already a young boy, wise and learned. His son had set up a traditional Sanskrit school—a *tole*, where he was teaching poetry, philosophy and the devotional scriptures to a group of students. He was an honest man, spiritually pure. Why shouldn't it be so? He was his child after all. Certainly it would be so. His son would be known far and wide in the land.

At that same moment he saw Tilu, as she preceded old Dinu and disappeared inside the little door of their home, as though he was seeing her afresh. Women were like goddesses, presiding over all that life meant: every moment of their life they bring from the eternal a touch of divinity into that which appears material and circumscribed. The strong affection with which they nurture the helpless newborn babe; how many the sleepless nights that string together the lives of generations, inscribing the unread obscure pages of history with selfless devotion born of intense sorrow and love!

'Tilu, listen,' said Bhabani. 'Will you take Khoka?'

'I've told you he will not come to me.'

'But wait a minute, let me see...'

'Ooh! What's to see!' retorted Tilu and with a mischievous smile she entered the little door of their home with her easy swinging gait.

Bhabani marvelled at her grace and her dignity. She radiated the noble immortality of motherhood.

'Sit down, my man,' said Foni Chakkarty.

Everyone settled down comfortably.

Bhabani Barujje prepared the hookah and handed it over to his guest.

'Baba, there's something you will have to do for us,' began Foni Chakkarty

'What would that be, Uncle?'

'You will have to pay a visit to my house. I'm thinking of making a trip to Gaya and Kashi. Your uncle will also join us. You know everything about the roads and the best way of getting there, what to do, and so forth.'

'Will you walk?'

'What else! Would anyone be hiring palanquins for us! Of course, we'll walk.'

'And will you leave from here?'

'No, that won't do. Iswar Boshtom, the pilgrim leader, will be coming along with us. He knows a little; but *you* are a veritable ship of learning. We want to hear *you*. Do come over this evening for a little snack of roasted rice and grams. Many will come to hear you speak.'

'Wonders will never cease, my dear,' remarked Bhabani to his wife, after the company had left.

'What is it?' she asked fondly, slipping into her rustic speech.

'Apparently, Foni Chakkarty and my uncle Chandar Chatujje are getting ready to leave for Gaya and Kashi. At this rate, your Dada might say *he* wants to go on a pilgrimage too!'

Nilu and Bilu who were close on the heels of their elder sister immediately protested, 'Why, isn't our Dada a human being? What a thing to say!'

'Of course, he is a human being. Anyway, why should I start the day by criticizing my elders; better be quiet.'

'My, my! Listen to his manner of speaking!' said Bilu. 'Here comes the greatest poet of them all, Horu Thakur! What do you say, Didi?'

Tilu was silent. She rarely disagreed with her husband, and even if she did, she didn't like to express it to others. People praised her wifely qualities. Such devotion was unparalleled, they would say.

Others, more mischievous, were less enthusiastic. 'Isn't that but natural?' they would counter, and recite

'I'm a kulin's daughter looking for my man

Wandering all over the land,

Over hill and dale, dying in vain...

So finally, the kulin's daughter has got herself a mate at a ripe old age. On top of everything, she's given birth to a boy. No wonder she's devoted! She has got what she was not fated to.'

'Damn lucky they are—the sisters, to get a man when they've turned so old.'

Another, wanting more salacious comments, would provocatively say, 'Well, anyhow, he's a *husband* after all...'

'That he is, but then...'

'What then...?'

'Far too old.'

'Go on! What's age got to do with a kulin male?'

Nevertheless, they could not but agree that Bhabani Barujje was truly a good husband and an honest man. No one could really find anything mean or nasty to say about him. It was no small thing to remain untouched in the gossip sessions every evening at the chandimandap where the gods themselves, Brahma and Vishnu, were not spared.

≈

Well before evening fell, Bhabani Barujje was at Foni Chakkarty's chandimandap. It was the month of Kartik before winter set in: the afternoon light had waned and the hedges of *bherenda*, the moss, the clumps of akanda were cast in shadows. The cool evening breeze carried the fragrance of the *bonmorche*-creeper's flowers. Flowers were blooming too, by the side of Foni Chakkarty's fence, in his field of serrated gourds. Atop the haystacks and grains piled up in the courtyard flocks of mynahs chattered away.

Foni Chakkarty's was an old-fashioned chandimandap. On a particularly skillfully carved wooden pole someone had inscribed: 'Shri Shivasatya Chakrabarty, under the patronage of the year 1172. Madhav Gharami and Akrur Gharami have constructed this chandimandap; know this to be the place of the gods.'

So the chandimandap was almost a century old. People came from faraway places to marvel at the structure. The particular style and mode of thatching, the fine intermeshing of specially cut sticks called *rola* and *shola,* the split-cane work, the bamboo fretwork, and the image of the two pigeons fighting done of straw—all of it marked a level of craftsmanship that was soon going to disappear from the land. It drew the admiration of the discerning.

'It's come to down to laziness and cheating these days,' Dinu Bhattchaj would opine. 'They're making all these fancy bungalows at the Neelkuthi for the sahebs and such like, and everyone thinks, I'll make one for myself too. Thatched roofs are going out of style. And then, where would you get ahold of a master thatcher now?'

'The other day,' said Rupchand Mukhujje on a different note, 'a nephew of Rajaram told me that there's a new kind of carriage in the country. A machine that runs the carriage, and pictures printed on paper—he's seen them both.'

'Machine-run too, babaji?' enquired Dinu.

'That's what I've heard. All sorts of new fangled stuff we shall be seeing with the passage of time. And Uncle, have you heard this—there's something called *metey*-oil, from the earth it comes, and you can light lamps with it? He's seen it all in Calcutta.'

'Forget it! A city of damnation, end of the world, Kali Yuga—that Kolkata! Our mustard oil is *just* as good, or rapeseed oil for that matter, equally so. What do we need this metey-oil for—goodness knows whether it is from the earth, or made of wood! Yes, Bhabani

Babaji, now tell us something about the road and the directions. You've travelled around a-plenty, been to all kinds of places. What do hills and mountains look like, babaji?'

'What's all the fuss about mountains and hills?' Rupchand Mukhujje cut in, taking over the hookah from Dinu. 'What would they be like, do you think? Mounds of earth, what else! Haven't you seen those hillocks by the Debnagar Fort? Something like that; perhaps, a little bigger!'

'Where did you see mountains, grandfather?' Bhabani asked him.

'Not actually seen them, but *heard* of them.'

'That's right.'

Bhabani did not wish to offend the gathering of old men by smoking in front of them, so he retired to a corner with the hookah.

'Where would you like to go?' he asked them after he was back.

'We don't know anything really,' confessed Foni Chakkarty. 'Iswar Boshtom is a professional guide; *he* said he would take us along. Let him join us; someone's gone to fetch him.'

Just then, Binod, Foni Chakkarty's elder daughter began serving each of those gathered with a bowl of roasted rice and fried gram with salt and oil to taste; finally, she brought water for everyone. It was the usual kind of snacks offered every evening to those who turned up at the chandimandap. Besides, there was an unending and generous flow of tobacco—about one and half seers was consumed everyday. Foni Chakkarty was famous for his hospitality during these evening sessions.

Iswar Boshtom now joined them.

'Which is the route you are planning to take to Gaya and Kashi?' Bhabani asked him.

Iswar first did a low pranam to pay his respects and said, 'Well, you're askin' me all a'sudden: it will be by way of Bardhaman. From there, the road that goes straight to Gaya.'

'Right. And which is that road?'

'Well, in English, they call it the Gang Tang Road. We call it Ahilyabai Road.'

'How long have you been acting as a guide?'

'About twenty years. Never go alone; a whole group of companion-guides—*sethos* as we're called—start off from Bardhaman, Chakdah and Ulo. There's a person called Dhirchand Bairagi who lives in Hoogly. And there's Kumudini Jeley, from the fisherfolk, who lives in Hajra-para in Hoogly district.

'Kumudini Jeley...a woman?' asked Rupchand.

'Yes, sir, she's a woman alright, but she'll put to shame many a man. And such beauty, the very image of the goddess Jagadhatri.'

'If you go via Bardhaman, you will get on to the big road that was built by Sher Shah. It has nothing to do with Ahilyabai; it was built by the Nawab Sher Shah.'

'Which Nawab? From where?'

'Murshidabad. Sirajuddaulah's father.'

'Is it true, babaji,' asked Dinu Bhattchaj, 'that the Saheb Company still pays taxes to the Nawab of Murshidabad?

'That might well be the case; I don't keep track of it. Today, I'll tell you something about two sannyasis that will please you.'

'Yes, babaji, do tell us,' said Rupchand Mukhujje. 'I've not much use with those nawabs and all! We're just frogs a-lying in the well. Don't have the money to travel to foreign lands; and frankly, babaji— the very *thought* scares me. I don't know any other place. The moment I step out of the village, it feels foreign and strange. Went to the fair at the time when we go bathing in the Ganga, right up to Chakda; on the other side, I've gone as far as Nadey-Shantipur on a boat along the Ichhamati. Went to sell coconuts at the fair; made a fair profit that time.'

The men made a ring around Bhabani; Dinu Bhattchaj came up right in front.

'All of you know,' began Bhabani, 'that some days ago, one of my guru-brothers came on a visit here. His ashram is in Mirzapur.'

'And where might that be, babaji?' asked Dinu Bhattchaj.

'To the west, far away...you wouldn't understand. Wonderful hills and jungles—and there, a sadhu lives. He is from Bengal. His name is Hrishikesh Paramhansa. Lives in a little shack night and day. The forests are full of flowers, shirish and kanchan blossoms, there are peacocks by the waterfalls in the hills, wood-apples galore ripening on the trees...'

'Amazing!' said Rupchand Mukhujje, deeply moved by Bhabani's words. 'We've never seen such a place.'

'Never seen a hill in our lives,' added Dinu Bhattchaj, 'and to imagine springs and waterfalls along with that!'

'We are lying in a muck-heap, in a hole full of dung. Any chance for *us* to see anything like that! Getting on to be sixty-five. You ever been in those places, babaji?' asked Chandra Chattujje.

'I was there with Paramhansa Maharaj for six months. He is my guru. Though he doesn't initiate disciples with mantras or anything.'

'Maharaj? A king? Where from?'

'Not a king, "Maharaj" is a form of address for holy men.'

'Oh, I see! But what did you eat in the jungle?'

'Gooseberries, wild mangoes, wood-apples...and a profusion of custard apples that would just drop off the trees all over the ground—ten or twenty baskets you might fill. Foxes would feast on those ripe fruits. Sweet and fragrant...you would never have set your eyes on fruits like those.'

'So, babaji,' said Rupchand Mukhujje, 'You just tell Iswar Boshtom how to get there, and I'll go and have my fill of those custard apples.'

'Oh, who cares for those custard apples!' said Chandra Chattujje. 'A glimpse of those sadhus and holy men would be worth a lifetime. You are ancient enough now, brother, not to run after custard apples. But tell us more, babaji—'

'So I spent six months there. And I went to Bithoor, to the Valmiki ashram—'

'You mean Valmiki the sage? The one who wrote the Mahabharata?' asked Rupchand Mukhujje.

'"You know everything, don't you!' said Dinu Bhattchaj. 'Why on earth would Valmiki have written the Mahabharata! He wrote the Ramayana.'

'That's right,' said Bhabani. 'I spent some time there too in the ashram with another sadhu.'

'How do we get there, babaji?' said Rupchand.

'It's not the sort of thing that householders can do on their own. Particularly, if you go with Iswar Boshtom; how far can he take you? Better that you go to Bardhaman, take the highway to Gaya, and then to Kashi. From Kashi you could go to Prayag. Muni Bharadwaj he lives in Prayaga, The one utterly devoted to the feet of Rama.

'In ancient times, there was indeed an ashram of the sage Bharadwaj in Prayaga. Sadhus and holy men and women come there during the Kumbh mela, held once every four years. I was there during the last one. But it's very difficult getting there. You would have to walk all that distance. On the road that Nawab Sher Shah built there are inns called *sarais*—where travellers halt, cook their food and rest before they carry on with their journey.'

'Cook rice and dal?' asked Rupchand Mukhujje.

'Oh, you will get *every* thing at a sarai. There are shops too. But it's best to go in a large group. There are dangers along the way.'

'What sort of dangers?'

'All kinds—thieves and dacoits, gangs of thugs...Once you leave Bardhaman, the entire route is through dense jungle and hills, tigers, bears and other wild animals.'

'Oh baba!'

'He's right,' said Iswar Boshtom. 'That one time a pilgrim left for Khabrapota, wanting to visit Gaya. On the way in the west, one evening he said to us, I'm going for a little wash. Wouldn't listen to what I was a-saying to him. There were forty of us camped beneath a tree. He left with his water-pot and made for a thicket of palash. End of story. Never came back. Tiger got him.'

'You don't say!' said the group in a chorus.

'Yes. Such a terrible night it was...folks weeping and wailing. Searched high and low all morning and found his bloody clothes laying here and there. We found marks where the body had been dragged 'long.'

'Horrors!' cried out Rupchand Mukhujje.

At this point, Nalu was seen to approach the chandimandap. He was given a woven mat of date-palm leaves for a seat. He had opened a big shop now, his business was doing well, and he had also married recently. Many of those gathered at the chandimandap were obliged to get their monthly provisions on credit from Nalu Pal's shop. There was no option but to treat him with deference.

'Come Nalu, have a seat. What brings you here?' Dinu welcomed him.

Nalu bent low to greet the gathering and addressed them with folded hands: 'I have a wish and you must indulge me. I hear you are all setting off on pil'mige. It's my great desire to feed the brahman pilgims. You must give me permission, and I'll send the stuff to Chakkarty-moshai. Give me the order—what are the kind of things I should send and how much of it, and so on.'

Chandra Chatujje and Foni Chakkarty held the status of the village patriarchs. No one dared overturn their ruling—excepting, of course, Dewan Rajaram Ray. However, although everyone *feared* Rajaram as the Neelkuthi's Dewan, on questions of social status he really didn't have a say. On his part, he didn't give a fig for social approval. He often did exactly as he pleased. The patriarchs, fearing him, kept their silence.

'Will you be giving us a meal of curds and pressed rice and fruits—a *falaar*?'

'Yes, sir, whatever you order,' said Nalu with folded hands.

'Fine quality pressed rice—half a maund; curds; and to go with it, fine-grained *khanr* jaggery; feni batasha, bananas, sugarcane, *mothh* sweets and...'

'Murki,' added Foni Chakkarty.

'How much murki?'

'Ten seers.'

'How much of the mothh sweets?' Nalu wanted to know.

'About two and a half a seers. Keshto sweetmaker makes very good sweets: the mothh you can ask him to make, and tell him we've asked him. If he makes us the kind of mothh where the sweets are hardened nicely, they'll go well with our fruit feast.'

'You should decide how much you will gift each brahman.'

'What would all of you suggest?' asked Nalu.

'Foni, why don't *you* say something? I've said as much as I could.'

'Give us a quarter each, that's all.'

'But master, that's too much, isn't it?' protested Nalu. 'It will kill me if I have to give twenty *shikis* to twenty brahmans!'

'It won't kill you. On the contrary, our blessings will make you prosper. You've also a son born to you recently, don't you?'

'Sir, he's not my son. He's yours,' replied Nalu with his usual humble expression.

Chandra Chatujje turned his face away to hide his smirk at Nalu's response.

Eventually, Nalu Pal made them agree to a gift of two annas each. When he went out, possibly to have a smoke, Chandra Chatujje piped up, 'Hmm, so what did our Nalu say just now?'

'What?' said Foni Chakkarty.

'I used to think that whatever your character might have been in the past, you've settled down in your old age. Since when have you been making up to Nalu's wife, eh?'

A general round of laughter greeted this quip. Foni Chakkarty puffed furiously at the hookah and said, 'Yes, that's just like you Chandar-da, always suspecting...'

'Baba, you settle the date for Nalu Pal's feast,' Chandra Chatujje finally requested Bhabani.

'I remembered something while we were discussing Nalu Pal's feast...There's a place called Bhursooth near Jhansi. Every Kartik, a huge fair comes up in honour of the goddess Ambika. I was living there, used to eat whatever was offered by way of alms. There was a prince who lived nearby, deeply respectful of sadhus and sanyasis. Wanted to know how I managed to get food. I said, I beg. From that day on, he would send me rice and roti, cooked vegetables, curds, sweets and dessert for me, enough to feed two people. When we had become close friends, he told me the story of his life. He came from a small kingdom called Udiana, near Jaipur, and was the eldest son. His father had numerous other children. After the old king's death, according to the Mitakshara rules of succession, the eldest was to inherit the throne. That's why the younger queen served poisoned food to her step-son, the prince—'

'Your story, babaji, is as long as the Ramayana,' interrupted Dinu Bhattchaj.

'That it is. Uncle, there's nothing good about wealth, fame and prestige. That is why I had renounced everything. But listen to my tale: such terrible intrigues were being hatched in the kingdom that he found it impossible to stay on. Along with his wife he came away to a small house in the village of Bhursooth. Didn't tell anyone about his real identity. He confided to me that he didn't ever wish to become a king. He had become disgusted with kingship having been witness to the mysteries of royalty.

'But why wasn't he a king already?' asked Foni Chakkarty.

'The old king was still alive, almost eighty years old; this son was about my age. Makes me sad to remember all this after so many years. Many a wonderful moonlit night we spent sitting on the raised stone courtyard of the Ambika temple, a huge pond before us and a little temple to Ramji in the middle of the pond. The young stepmother had poisoned his food. A loyal servant had discovered the plot and had warned him in time. He pretended to eat the food, said he was feeling ill and dizzy, and retired to his chamber. The stepmother had laughed when she heard of his illness—this too, he learned from the trusted servant. That very night he fled the place knowing the terrible intrigues against him. The younger queen's clique was determined to murder him; the old king a mere puppet in her hands.'

'What a stepmother, capable of doing anything!' said Dinu Bhattchaj. 'A case of—"If you don't run off, it's off with your head", huh! Scares you, just listening…'

'And then?' asked Rupchand Mukhujje.

'Well, then, I spent about two months in Bhursooth. Every afternoon and evening he had food sent for me to the inn next to the Ambika temple. Many words of wisdom I've heard from him. Grieved that he had been born into a royal family, felt he would have been at peace had he been poor. He would discuss the philosophy of the Vedanta with me. His wife I saw when she would come to offer worship to goddess Ambika. She was young Rajput woman, tall and youthful, with a huge nose ring. I saw her once having a smoke on a special hookah, called a *farshi*.'

'A woman?' exclaimed Rupchand Mukhujje.

'Yes, they do, in those parts of the country. She was very beautiful, like the image of goddess Durga ready to strike the evil demon. I wondered at the stepmother-in-law who had brought her to such a situation. After a couple of months I left for Bithoor, near Kanpur. I saw that the Rani of Jhansi had come to worship at the Ambika Devi temple. I heard later that the Rani of Jhansi had died fighting the British. She was also very beautiful, in the manner of the women of those regions.'

'You don't say! Such strange things you've been telling us babaji! A woman waging war against the Company! Never heard of such things in my life! Where did all this happen?'

'How would you hear of such things, uncle? You've never stepped out of your village. If you do travel now...'

Nalu Pal appeared once more, looking anxious. He had to get home: it was market day and he had his work cut out. He could take leave once they decided on the day for the feast.

'The next full moon night,' suggested Bhabani Barujje. 'What do you say, Uncle? Would it be a problem for anyone?'

'I've got rheumatism,' said Rupchand Mukhujje. 'I shan't eat food that's offered to Lakshmi on a full moon night—but no harm in that; fruits, milk, mothh sweets—*those* I can eat. So let the day be fixed.'

Iswar Boshtom had been quietly listening to Bhabani's tales. Now he spoke up, 'What was that queen you were speaking of? And who did she fight? I was constantly reminded of Kumudini

Jeley—listening about her.'

'Oh, for god's sake!' said Dinu Bhatchaj, 'Comparing *her* with *her*! Rani Lakshmibai and your Kumudini Jeley! Who is she anyway?

Iswar Boshtom got up in extreme agitation. 'You're saying such things, khuro-thakur,' he said, gesticulating with both hands, 'because you don't *know* the pilgim leader, Setho Kumudini! If you'd seen her, you would have to say, "Yes, what a woman!" Such a fine figure of a woman, and in her looks too, like a ten-armed goddess. Likewise in courage and intelligence! Once, two pilgims fell ill with cholera on the way to Gaya. My! How she looked after them and nursed them back to health, like a mother would. And then again, the way she fought with a priest at Gaya—he was trying to squeeze out more money from the pilgims, you see. You should've seen her then—"Don't you know" she said to him, "my name is Kumudini. I bring about two hundred pilgrims to Gaya every year. You make more trouble and I'm going to take *all* of them to some other chap." The fellow was scared stiff. Not a squeak out of him. You get my point, don't you—if you can't respect the sethos, you simply don't get *any* pilgim as your client. Never seen a woman like her. Catch anyone trying to come close to her, try and get a bit intimate! Whew!! No one would dare. She knows better than anyone how to protect her dignity.'

'Why don't you bring her over sometime?' said Bhabani Barujje, 'And we shall have a glimpse.'

'Yes, yes,' chorused the rest, 'why don't you? You know her well. Let's have a look.'

Iswar Boshtom did not reply.

'Well, can't you?' persisted Dinu Bhattchaj.

'Sir, she's very high up—she's head of all the pilgim leaders. She won't come here at my request. Besides, she lives very far away: her home is in Hooghly district; don't know which village exactly. We meet up every Kartik at Chakkarty's inn and then set off on our travels. If you set off on the pilgrimge, you're bound to meet her. Anyway, I better be off now.'

'Have any one of you met the sannyasini who lives in the jungle here?' Bhabani Barujje suddenly asked the company. 'She's called Khepi; has any one of you seen her? You will like meeting her, do visit her.'

'A brahman can't keep his prestige if he goes to suchlike places. I've heard that female is a buno. I'd say babaji, *you* shouldn't be going there either.'

'Forgive me, Uncle; I shan't be able to keep your honour. Everyone is the same when you think on God—what's a buno and what's a brahman!'

'Buno and brahman—the *same*? Equal!' cried Foni Chakkarty in astonishment.

Everyone stared at Bhabani.

Chandra Chatujje let out an exaggerated sigh, 'That is exactly why I've gone on being a fakir rather than a king, all this while.'

His words were greeted with laughter.

'Look at him! One joke after another!' said Foni Chakkarty. 'To come back to the work at hand: who's going on this pilgrimage? When are you going? And, when is Nalu Pal going to feed us?'

'You, and brother Chandar here—are you definitely going?' Roopchand Mukhujje queried.

'Quite sure.'

'Who else will be going, Iswar?'

'Amongst the fisherfolk, Bhagirath Jeley's eldest daughter-in-law; then, Crazy Jeley's Ma; Narahari's wife from our neighbourhood, from the brahman locality—the two of you; and seven from Hamidpur—all my clients. We are to meet up with Kumudini Jeley's group on the day of Kartik Puja. There's a sarai in Raniganj: we rest there for a couple of days, and then set off. Two or three other groups will be joining us at the inn. All worked out and arranged for.'

'Let me talk to my eldest,' said Rupchand Mukhujje, 'let's see what he has to say. My body isn't what it used to be. The old energy's gone. But listening to Bhabani I felt like running off to the ashram he spoke of, and that sannyasi-thakur...Those flowers a-blooming, gooseberries to pluck off gooseberry trees and peacocks wandering 'bout—jest wish I could see them with my own eyes. Never really seen anything in my life, babaji!'

'You shall come, Mukhujje-moshai,' Iswar Bosthtom reassured him. 'I know all the folks, everywhere; I'll make sure the priests at the temples charge you a bit less.'

'Let's go then,' said Chandra Chatujje. 'There will be five of us; we'll manage somehow.'

≈

On the day of the brahmans' feast held at Chandra Chatujje's home, besides the actual pilgrims, there were others who were being treated by the devout Nalu Pal. Bhabani Barujje, Dewan Rajaram and Nilmoni Samaddar had come. The last of the three was not even a regular brahman. Tilu had come along with her little Khoka to help in the preparations. Bhabani swiftly cut out the banana leaves, washed them and laid them out as platters in neat rows for the guests in the inner covered verandah. Tilu first washed seven to eight kathas of fine-grained pressed rice (of the kind called *benamuri*) that she stored in a huge vessel. She then sat down to sift the sweet murki. Another vessel was filled with enormous piles of mothh-sweets and feni batasha; half a dozen big pots of curds sat waiting for the guests.

'Nalu Pal has done us proud—quite a spread,' said Rupchand Mukhujje with a broad smile. 'A good boy!'

Unlike wives who had come from other villages, Tilu, being a native of the village, could appear before the brahmans. She served them attentively and quickly.

Chandra Chatujje didn't wish to sit down to his meal with the others. After all, the feast was being held in *his* home; he would eat after all the guests had been fed. Bhabani Barujje joined Tilu and the two worked beautifully together, serving everyone with equal care. Otherwise, as frequently happens in the provinces, the best half of the foodstuff might have mysteriously found its way into the secret store of the house owner.

'The mothh sweet is really well done!' remarked Foni Chakkarty. 'Keshto's is a seasoned hand at confectionary. Bhabani, you may serve a couple of more mothhs on this platter.'

'In that case, you may add one to mine at the same time,' added Rupchand Mukhujje.

'Why so shy, uncle?' said Tilu with a smile. 'You only have to tell me how many I should give you—two or three?'

'Make it two, my child. So tasty—the khanr-molasses don't compare with it.'

'One more?'

'No, my dear! Not any more! W-e-ll, all right, you may give me *one*, since you're so keen,' said Rupchand Mukhujje diffidently, as Tilu's strong fair arm girdled with the bauti dropped off two more pieces of golden mothh on his platter. Poverty-stricken Rupchand had never partaken of such a marvellous feast in which such delicious mothh sweetened the fruits and curd.

≈

Rupchand Mukhujje was to remember these mothh-sweets on his way to Gaya along the Gang Tang Road (as they called the Grand Trunk Road). They ran into great danger one dark night near a forested and hilly place called Barkatta. The little group of pilgrims was resting, huddled beneath a tree, when dacoits fell on them and stripped them of all they had. Fortunately, the larger part of the group that had gone on ahead and had already taken refuge in a government rest house, had the money in their safekeeping.

Why was it that on that dark night, looking at the terrifying lonely beauty of the forest and the hills, it was the image of Tilu's fair slender arm encircled with the patterned bauti that flashed before the hapless Rupchand Mukhujje eyes? Even in the midst of danger he felt as though he had experienced life differently, in all its wonders... as though, leaving behind the past fifty years of his life, far away from his tiny village, he recognized life itself anew.

It was twenty years since his wife died. It was all like a dream, but from this distance, everything was dreamlike. In that tiny village by the Ichhamati the family goat may have wandered into Nibaran milkman's garden of brinjals...they were all running around with sticks; perhaps his eldest son Jatin had come back home today and was sleeping in the eastern room with his wife and his two daughters. The poor boy...he works for only five rupees a month at the Saktkhirey estate. Comes home once every three months, can't see his children grow up...how much he longs for them! So it is fated for the poor.

What a good lad his son was.

When it was decided that he would go to Gaya and Kashi with the others, the eldest Jatin had come to ask him, 'Baba, do you have enough money?'

'I'd kept aside some...'

'How much?'

'About thirty rupees it would be. I'd secreted it away inside the coconut husk for bad times. That will be enough, my son.'

'Baba, listen to me. That won't do; I'll—'

'It will, it will. You don't have to give me more—'

His eldest had then insisted on giving him another fifteen rupees which he tied up in a knot at the end of his father's scarf. His eyes filled with tears at the memory. What a beautiful starry sky above him and the vast grassy field that seemed to be freedom itself, the trees like a line of ghostly shapes...lying there, his eyes turned moist remembering that expression on his Khoka's face...

His heart grieved for that poor boy of his, he had never been able to afford even a special dhoti for him...He worked as an ordinary jamanobish far away from home, earning little. Rupchand was like a spirit floating around in the darkness across the earth—Where are you my Khoka, where are you my two granddaughters...

≈

It was a hot summer afternoon in the month of *Jyestha*, and once more, Nalu Pal was offering a feast for the brahmans at Chandra Chatujje's chandimandap. All those greatly fortunate ones who had come back successfully after the pilgrimage had been invited by Nalu Pal for another feast of curds and pressed rice and fruits.

Nalu Pal, standing at a distance with his palms joined, a scarf slung around his neck, was supervising everything. Huge quantities of mangoes and jackfruits lay piled up for the feast.

They were all present—Foni Chakkarty, Chandra Chatujje, Iswar Boshtom, Nilmoni Samaddar…Rupchand Mukhujje alone was missing. He had passed away on the path to Benaras; a letter had been sent to his home, but Jatin had never got the letter.

Chandra Chatujje was regaling Nilmoni Samaddar with tales of the journey, how they had been waylaid by dacoits at a certain stretch of the Gang Tang Road; how the temple priest at Gaya had with incredible resources found out from his notebook the name of his grandfather, Bishnuram Chatujje, and had recited the family genealogy to him.

'Feel very sad when I think upon Uncle Rupchand. He was blessed indeed, so he died on the way to Kashi. What happened to him?' asked Nilmoni Samaddar.

'We couldn't really figure out, brother. He got delirious and kept asking for his son, "Where's Khoka? Where's my Khoka? Khoka, I want some tobacco…" that's all he said. Poor Jatin sobbed out loud, when we told him 'bout it the other day.'

'Jatin is full of filial piety,' observed Nilmoni.

'Well, brother, it has to be a mutual love for any sort of devotion. Uncle Rupchand was mad about his son too. That's what I've seen all my life.'

Nalu Pal had made wonderful arrangements: the pressed rice was most delicate, and the seasonal mangoes and jackfruits were aplenty.

Mixing the juice from mangoes and jackfruit into the thickened milk, Foni Chakkarty remarked, 'Chandar-da, think of that day—and now this! Never thought I would actually return. That Satkori from Kumudini Jeley's group had warned us: just you cross Bardhaman, and the dacoits will get you. An' wasn't that exactly what happened!'

'All I can think of is that valley where we were—mountain

springs flowing along, those big shady trees, you know, where Uncle Rupchand lay down forever. The old man loved such places; he kept telling me, "It's like the sage Valmiki's ashram..."'

Nalu Pal said with folded hands, 'I am indeed most fortunate that you allowed this poor man to serve you with a few grains of food. Give us your blessings that the boy who has been born should live long, that the lineage continues.'

≈

When Bhabani came back home Bilu's greeting was, 'Where is your beloved wife? Still not come? Khoka just fell asleep...he's been crying his heart out.'

'She has not yet eaten. The feast for the brahmans has just got over.'

Nilu had been lying down inside their room; it was quite late in the afternoon. Awakened by her husband's voice, she came rushing out.

'Come, come, our man-about-town—haven't seen you in ages! What was the fruit feast like, eh? What did you eat?'

'The older you get, the more you spout these obscene phrases. Why, your Didi never—' Bhabani said gravely.

'But of course, Didi can get away with anything!' retorted Bilu. 'Could *she* ever do *any* thing bad? Didi is quite the celestial beauty, a veritable *apsari*! All I want to know is, where's the food for *us*? It's going to be pressed rice and murki in store for us. We are the outcasts—lowly doms and doklas: we'll sit in the wash-up place, eat our meagre repast and head off home praising you and exclaiming how good it was! Isn't that true or what?'

Nilu who had been relishing this banter from the wings, now declared, 'Let him be. Our dandy is looking crestfallen; don't say any more, Didi! I'm almost beginning to feel sorry for him. You know he won't accept anything you say. He says...Oh, what's that Sanskrit word now? Not something that the likes of us can even utter, Didi!'

Bhabani Barujje's home consisted of only one room which had four tiers of thatching, and another smaller room with two tiers of thatching in the northern end. Bhabani lived in the smaller room and whenever he had some time, studied the scriptures. Tilu stayed with him in this room, while Bilu and Nilu shared the bigger room. Khoka was normally in the little room with his mother. Now, Nilu suddenly took hold of Bhabani Barujje by the hand and dragged him to their room. Khoka was fast asleep, lying flat on his back, his big expressive eyes shut like the reclining Vishnu.

When Bhabani went to pick up the boy, Nilu cried out sharply, 'Don't pick him up, I'm telling you! He'll start howling and who is going to look after him then?'

Bhabani nonetheless picked up the sleeping boy and put him upright in a sitting position. Khoka sat there with his eyes still shut, not stirring one bit. How beautiful he looked! His pure innocent face! As though all the mysteries of the cosmos lay waiting in some endless expectation behind this child. From the superior worlds to the most humble realms that were eagerly awaiting his footfall, one sensed in his creative play, whether in hope and despair, that message fluctuating between hope and despair written in the luminous language of every star in the firament.

'His neck will snap, don't you know! It's still too tender!' cried out Nilu in alarm.

Bilu ran to pick him up and lay him down again. Just as he had sat silently, so he went on sleeping soundlessly.

Bilu and Nilu sat down on either side of their husband.

'Ooh! Such sweaty heat today; not a leaf stirring! Do you know, both our jackfruits have ripened!'

The still air in the room was in fact filled with the fragrance of the ripe jackfruit. Bhabani felt very affectionate towards Bilu at the happiness in her voice. 'Oh! Have they both ripened? What kind are they—hard and crispy or sticky?'

'*Beltoli* and *kadma* jackfruits they are—one is crispy *khaja* and the other sticky *rasa*. Will you have some at night?'

'Am I the demon Bakasura to devour everything in sight? I've barely come back from a feast.'

'If *you* don't eat, then *we* don't get to, you see. Such a lovely fruit—it will go to waste...become overripe. Have one segment at least,' said Bilu.

'Give me some at night.'

'No, you'll have to eat it right away. Nilu's told me that she wants to eat the jackfruit right away. She's still so young, can't wait to eat.'

'So young! Above thirty if not more, and even now—'

'Enough! You don't have to go reciting your scriptures at us. It's all bad with us; and all good with Didi.'

'All right then,' said Bhabani smiling. 'If one little segment of jackfruit opens up the doors to your eating some, let it be so.'

Late in the evening Tilu entered their little room. Bilu brought back Khoka to his mother.

'How was the food?' Bhabani asked her.

'Good. And how are you?'

'Very well. Your sisters are angry that we went to the feast. True, we didn't bring anything for them; they have a right to be upset.'

'You don't have worry about it, dear; I made sure to bring back something. Didn't I ask Aunty now to give me some of that fine pressed rice and all the rest? You know, it would have been nice if you were to sleep in their room tonight.'

'Shall I leave?'

'Yes, do. They will feel hurt. As it is, we went and had a meal, leaving them to look after Khoka. And if you were to stay on in this room, how do you think they would feel? You had better go.'

'Your studies will be interrupted. I had thought we would have completed the Upanishad. I would ask you to explain the fourteenth sloka—"The face of truth is covered with a golden disc. Unveil it, O Pushan, meaning Suryadeva, so that I who love the truth may see it'." In the Vedas, the sun is spoken of as the light, the radiance of the poet. The poet's divine radiance is likened to or expressed in the Sun God.'

'Let me read this fourteenth sloka tonight. You'd said you would initiate me into *Narad Bhatkisutra*...But sit, do sit down for a while. Haven't seen you for so long!'

'All right. I'll stay.'

'If I were to die today, would you take care of Khoka?'

'H'mm.'

'Oh! Not a word of sorrow; only a "H'mm"—how could that be!'

'You and I will nurture and leave behind a lineage in the soil of this very village: I can see how in this very bamboo grove of ours, five generations will live on; they will farm and have paddy stacks here, ploughs and threshing rooms, a cowshed filled with cattle...'

Tilu put her head on her husband's lap and lay down.

'I cannot bear to be away from you. Such a wrenching goes on in my heart,' she said gazing at him. 'Do you miss me the same way? *Avajananti mang murha manushi tanumasritang*...You must be thinking that I am a mere woman? You are ignorant, that is why you would believe so. Do you know who I am?'

Bhabani kissed her beautiful large eyes glinting with love and mischief and gathering together her mass of hair in his hands said, 'You are Devi, the goddess herself, I have recognized you! Whether you cook a dish of the banana flower or cook something with *kochu*-greens—there's no way that I can even have a bit of your spicy dishes! The colour is as exquisite as the fragrance—*akarosadrishya pragya*—'

Tilu lifted up her head from her husband's lap and said in mock anger, '*Vishwashghatakang stwang*! So, the kochu-greens I cook are poor? No one has ever said—'

'That's incorrect Sanskrit. Your ears have to be boxed! Is that how you are studying grammar? What should you have said? What is the correct declension?'

'Can't think of it now...feeling sleepy. Think of all the hard work I had to do the entire day. Single-handedly, I had to sift and clean the pressed rice for such a large number of people, then washing it all. Peeling all those mangoes and jackfruits.'

'Go to sleep. I shall go to the other room.'

Bilu and Nilu were astonished to see their husband.

'Ah, the man-about-town has lost his way, it seems!' quipped Nilu. 'Wonder what was the first auspicious thing I saw this morning...'

'Won't let you sleep tonight,' declared Bilu. 'We shall chat away, all night long. What do you say, Nilu?'

'But of course! As they say, *"Like a bee hovering over those coal-dark eyes..."* You will have the jackfruits, I hope? Both the crispy ones have ripened. Shall I send some for Didi? What are you going to do today?'

'You teach Didi *every* night. Why don't you teach *us* too?' said Nilu.

'How am I to teach you? Are you the sort who will even sit down to study? Do you know, these days a saheb called Bethune has started an ishkool for girls in Calcutta. And there are many girls who are studying in his ishkool.'

'Really?'

'Of course, it's true. I've a newspaper, *Sarvasubhakari*; a famous pandit Madanmohan Tarkalankar has written about all these developments. It is important for women to be educated. Simply eating jackfruits, not interested in seeing anything or learning anything is a waste of the richness of human existence.'

'I'm warning you, don't you tease us about eating jackfruits. Is it bad?'

'And if I do eat some, will you learn how to read and write? See how your Didi is learning Sanskrit; and she can already read in Bangla. She has memorized the poetry of Bharatchandra Ray. And the two of you—'

Nilu raised her hands in a gesture of mock anger, 'Don't you dare make a dig about eating jackfruits! You'll have to eat *at least* ten segments. You've never had this kind, it's called *kadma*; why don't you try some?'

'Do you know what *swadhyay* means? It means learning on one's own. You must read something of the shastras every day. Don't you desire to know something about bhagwan? What is the point of wasting one's life? Jackfru—'

'Again!'

'All right! But don't you wish to know about bhagwan?'

'We know.'

'What do you know? Nothing!'

'So Didi knows more than us?'

'She is learning to read the Upanishads along with me. You will not understand at this stage what the Upanishads are. If you begin your studies, you will learn about it by and by.'

'Where did *you* learn all this?'

'There isn't much happening in Bengal. I find that people here are mostly into *mangalchandi* songs, Manasa's *bhashaan*-songs, Shiva's wedding—that sort of thing. At most, it would be something to do with Ramayana and Mahabharata. About the Upanishads—I was initiated by Hrishikesh Paramhansaji in his ashram in the west. Another disciple of his—the one you have seen when he visited us, really opened up my eyes; and that is why he is my guru. True, he did not initiate me as a disciple with mantras, but he opened up my vision. I did not know then that there was someone in Calcutta called Rammohun Roy—a great scholar and a great man, who was also speaking on the Upanishads. He's written books on it, I believe. So it's said in the newspaper called the *Sarvasubhakari*.'

'That's to become a *khishtaan*! Whatever our forefathers have done—'

'Nilu, how much do you really know of what our forefathers have done? Do you know that the dharma of the Upanishads is the composition of sages? It's getting to be quite late; we'll let it rest for now.'

'No, why don't you go on? It's quite interesting.'

'You are intelligent, even more than your Didi. But you are idling away your time in childish ways.'

'Now don't get into all that!' said Bilu. 'Have some jackfruit. We shall start our studies from tomorrow. But you must speak to us *along with* Didi. Not separately.'

Meanwhile Nilu had already broken a part of the jackfruit and now she served it in a stone bowl to her husband.

'Have I to eat so much?' asked Bhabani.

Nilu picked up only two segments and said, 'You must have the rest. It's a kadma jackfruit. Sweet as honey. Do we like it if our man-about-town does not have a bite? And you're not going to have such a delicious treat! Go on, eat away.'

'And after you've had it, you must have a jackfruit seed with some salt. Then you'll never be ill. Oh! Isn't that Khokon crying out from Didi's room? She must have fallen into a deep sleep after all the hard work she did the entire day. Nilu, go and find out, hurry...'

Nilu ran out of the room.

Outdoors, the moonlight was white as the petals of the ghentu flower.

≈

For the past one year Ramkanai Kobiraj had been homeless and without any refuge. He had been imprisoned for three days in the lime shed of the Neelkuthi, Dewan Rajaram constantly trying to make him see the light, offering him baits, but finally unable to persuade him to give false witness. Courtesy Shyamchand, he lay unconscious in the lime shed. But how could he even drink a drop of water in the premises of the Neelkuthi, where the sahebs lived? They let go of him eventually, fearing he would die on them.

He came back to his little thatched hut. The hut still stood, but he found his meagre store of earthen cooking utensils smashed up, his collection of roots and herbs tossed away; all the trouble he had taken over a long period of time to collect them—grounds of dried laburnum flowers, purarnaba, the leaves of the halhali-greens, khetpapra, the nalimul creeper—all gone. His savings of ten annas in a knotted-up rag—that too, was gone. It was as though a rogue elephant had been on a rampage inside his home, turning everything upside down. Not a grain of cereal or dal remained. He couldn't even drink any water when he came home: neither his pitcher nor the little drinking pot was to be found.

Ramu Sardar's murder case dragged on for almost six months. Finally, the District Magistrate intervened and resolved it in some manner.

Even those few patients who would consult Ramkanai in former times now stopped coming. They were afraid of antagonizing the dewan. Ramkanai practically starved the next three or four months. Around the end of Paush, in mid-winter, he fell ill. Suffering from fever and chest pain, barely alive, he lay on a makeshift bamboo cot in his broken-down home. There was no one to tend him, no one to even look in on him. No one dared to step in for fear of the Neelkuthi.

One day, Ramkanai was extremely startled to find at the door of his poor dwelling a woman in a freshly washed sari, wearing a stitched blouse such as memsahebs wore.

'Come in my child, take a seat. Where be you coming from? Don't seem to recognize you...'

The woman made him a respectful pranam from a distance, prostrating herself on the floor.

'You won't be recognizing me; my name is Gaya.'

Ramkanai had heard the name.

'Gaya-mem?' he asked with a start.

'Yes, baba-thakur, true enough—that's what they call me.'

'Why have you come, my child? How fortunate I am!'

'Among the sahebs, it's the Chhota Saheb who has been very angry with you. The Dewanji, too. But the Burra Saheb—he doesn't know anything of the torture and the terrible things done to you. How are you?'

'Fever. The chest hurts...very weak.'

'I'd brought you some milk.'

'Can't boil it and have it, you see. Can't get up at all. You better take back the milk, my child.'

'No, baba-thakur, brought it 'specially for you—won't take it back. If you won't drink it, I'll pour it at the feet of the wood-apple tree now. Can I ever hope for such good fortune that a brahman like you will accept my milk from my hands!'

'Ma, I do not take any gift from a sudra,' Ramkanai frankly admitted.

Gaya was an intelligent woman; with a smile she replied, 'But from your *daughter*, baba-thakur, why wouldn't you accept an offering? And, if you feel all anxious and doubtful 'bout it, you give the price for the milk your daughter's brought for you, once you're well. That wouldn't be a problem, would it?'

'No, that wouldn't.'

'Well, then let it be so. Now you accept this offering of milk.'

'I'm wondering who will boil it. Don't have the strength to get up...'

'Baba-thakur, shall I?' asked Gaya with great diffidence.

'Yes, do that. I have nothing to say about that. It's only about accepting gifts, you know. And you mustn't be hurt by it; my father or grandfather—none of them—ever accepted any. If I do now in my old age, I will be fallen from the path of dharma. But I shall eat whatever you have got for me. I've become useless as you see. Who will give me anything?'

'Won't I be giving you, baba-thakur? Don't you worry! While this daughter of yours is alive, you needn't worry about a thing.'

≈

That evening the Burra Saheb Shipton sent for the Chhota Saheb.

'Good afternoon, Mr Shipton,' said the Chhota Saheb.

'Good afternoon, David! Now, what about our poor Kaviraj? I hear there's something amiss with him?'

'Good heavens! I know very little about him.'

'It is very good of you to know little about the poor old man! My ayah Gaya was telling me, he's down with fever and of course she did her best. She was very nice to him. But how is it you are alone? Where is our precious Dewan?'

'He's there. Speeding up the accounts, the *mark-khatians*. Shall I send for him?'

'No. And after that rather unsatisfactory experience you had of his ways and things, see that he does not get a free hand in chastizing and chastening people. You understand?'

'Yes, Mr Shipton.'

'Well, what have you been upto all day?'

'I was checking up audit accounts and—'

'That's so. Now, listen to my words. Our guns were intact but they ceased fire while you were standing idly by with your wily dewan waiting for orders. No David, I really think the way you did it was ever so odd and tactless. Mend up your ways to Kaviraj; I mean it. You know, there aren't any secrets. You see?'

'Yes, Mr Shipton.'

'Now you can retire. I am dreadfully tired. Things are coming to a head. If you don't mind, I will rather dine in my room with Missus.'

'Please yourself, Mr Shipton. Good night.'

The Chhota Saheb had left the room and gone out to the verandah, when Shipton called him back, 'Look here, David, there's a funny affair in this week's paper. Ram Gopal Ghose, that native orator who speaks like Burke, has spoken in the Calcutta Town Hall last week in support of Indians entering the Civil Service! What the devil the government is up to I do not know, David. Why they allow these things to go on, it's beyond me. Things are not looking quite as they ought to. Here's another—you know Harish Mookherjee, the downy old bird of *The Hindoo Patriot*?'

'Yes, I think so.'

'He led a deputation the other day to our old Guv'nor against us planters. You see?'

'Deputation! I would have scattered their deputation with the toe of my boot!'

'But the old man talked to them like a benevolent blooming father. That is why I say David, things are coming to a head. Tell your precious dewan to carb his poop. Shall I order a tot of rum?'

'No, thank you, Mr Shipton. Really I've got to go now.'

≈

Dewan Rajaram came home from the Kuthi very late that night.

'Gurey!' he called out, dismounting from his horse.

Syce Gurudas Muchi came running to take over the reins.

'Bring me some Ganga water,' Rajaram called out to his wife, entering the house. He found her in the puja room busy with her worship. He recalled that it was a Saturday, so she must be worshipping the deity Saturn. When he had washed up, Jagadamba asked him, 'Who will read the scriptures?'

'Wait, I'll be back. I'll change my clothes first.'

Dewan Rajaram was a conscientious brahman. He sat down in his pale-golden silk garment, on a kusha-grass mat, and with great devotion read out the verses in praise of Saturn, Lord Shani. The puja was meant to secure him and his family against Saturn's evil eye, increase his wealth and prestige. He then went through his daily evening prayers. This last was particularly necessary because he was obliged to keep the company of the sahebs: he had to purify himself with Ganga water before he could even step indoors.

Jagadamba placed a bowl full of murki and the offering of *shirnni* made traditionally for Shani puja.

Rajaram finished the meal, and chewing on a paan said, 'Do you know what happened at the Kuthi today?'

'Shall I get you some wood-apple sherbet?' his wife asked.

'Why don't you first listen to what I'm saying! Let the sherbet be.'

'Yes, what is it...?'

'Burra Saheb has given the Chhota Saheb a big talking to.'

'Why?'

'We had dealt a tad firmly with Ramkanai Kobiraj. You don't have to teach me how to deal with his wickedness. The rascal's really lowered the prestige of the Neelkuthi over that murder of Ramu Sardar. Just as well that Duncinson Saheb, the district magister, is very respectful of our Burra Saheb, so we could patch it over this time. I had given that sisterfucker such a thrashing, made sure he woudn't get a grain of rice in these parts. But I believe the Burra Saheb's given orders not to do such stuff any more. He said the Sarkar Bahadur's been informed about the goings on at the Neelkuthi. Some fellow called Harish Mukhujje from Calcutta—he's been writing up a load of rubbish in the newspapers. Stirred up a lot of commotion. It's going to affect the planters. The Chhota Saheb called me over and told me, "Gaya-mem's the one who has brought it to the Burra Saheb's notice. That wench is a devil at heart."'

'Why, isn't Gaya-mem very respectful of you?'

'Forget it! One who is characterless herself—does she have anything! *Her* respect is of no consequence! Just that I can't do anything about it; otherwise, Dewan Rajaram Ray doesn't need to be taught how to fix people.'

'Has the Chhota Saheb reprimanded you?'

'Will he dare reprimand me? No indigo will grow if I'm not around—it'll only be the wind blowin' through an empty Neelkuthi. Without me and Amin Prasanna Chakkarty, not a single katha of land can they mark out for indigo! Who straightened out Nobu Gaji? Who fixed the peasants of Rahtoonpur? Let me tell you, neither the Burra Saheb nor the Chhota Saheb, not *any* saheb, can do any of this work. If this Rajaram Ray were ever to be laid down, then right away—'

'Oh! Oh! How can you say such inauspicious things on a Saturday evening!' Jagadamba exclaimed, very distressed. 'Dugga! Dugga! Ram! Ram! Don't ever say such things.'

'Did Tilu or the others come by?'

'Nilu came by with Khoka. Khoka pinched my cheeks and caressed me. What a precious creature he is, may he live long! He gives them such joy and hope. How sweetly he nibbled on the cottage cheese I gave him to eat.'

'Don't give him any of that, it will give him a stomach ache.'

Before he had finished Tilu appeared with Khoka.

Khoka was growing up to be as intelligent as his father. He spotted Rajaram and waving his hands, cried out, 'Bor-da!'

'How can I be your elder brother, my precious; I'm your uncle.'

'Bor-da,' persisted Khoka.

'It's because I call you Bor-da,' Tilu explained. 'He's decided that this person can only be called Bor-da.'

'So, I am to be your mother's Bor-da, and yours as well!' said Rajaram planting a kiss on the boy's cheek. 'And what is Bhabani doing?'

'He and Uncle Chandar are having a chat. I broke open a jackfruit for them, and I've come to get a ripe coconut. They want to have some muri with grated coconut.'

'Take as many as you want from your Bou-didi. Why only one?'

Jagadamba who was at the window said to her husband, 'There's someone calling you, dear.'

'Who?'

'How would I know; Gopal Mainder told me so.'

Rajaram was very astonished when he found that it was the Burra Saheb's orderly, Sriram Muchi, who had come to fetch him. What could be so urgent that Saheb had sent his orderly so late at night?

'What's up Remo?' he asked Sriram, using the familiar form of his name.

'Master, there are two sahebs sittin' up at the big bungalow. Drinkin'. Somethin' urgent has turned up. "Tell him to ride back right away," they sed to me.'

'Do you know what it's about?'

'That I won't be able to tell you, master. Must be somethin' big, though. Otherwise why would they send for you so late? I've brought along my spear. You come with me. Our enemies are all over the place...better not go out alone at night.'

Rajaram laughed. Sriram Muchi was trying to tell *him* what he ought to do! One shout from him as he rode by made entire villages tremble. There was not one who did not know him in a radius of ten or twenty *mauja*.

Within half an hour Rajaram was at the plantation, making his salaam to the sahebs. They were seated in front of small table with glasses and a bottle. The Burra Saheb was puffing on a silver hubble-bubble; the sweet strong fragrance of the tobacco filled the room. Chhota Saheb did not smoke, but he liked his paan and *zarda*, though he took care to hide it from his superior and the latter's wife. The Burra Saheb said something to the younger one in English, who then turned to Rajaram and said in Bangla, 'Dewan, we've fallen into a dangerous situation.'

Rajaram had realized that quite some time ago.

But he nevertheless asked, 'What is it, saheb?'

'News just come in from Calcutta—there's great anger about indigo cultivation. The Government is with them. A lot of important people have caused a stir in the newspapers. Now what are we to do? Shulko, Shubhoratnapur, Ulushi, Satberey and Nahata—can you tell us how many bighas have been marked out in these villages?'

Rajaram calculated mentally and said, 'Roughly, seven hundred to seven hundred and fifty bighas.'

'How much lant is markt?' asked the Burra Saheb.

'As I said, saheb,' answered Rajaram respectfully, 'about seven hundred bighas.'

Just then Bibi Shipton was seen alighting from her tom-tom in front of the bungalow. Bhoja Muchi ran up from behind the carriage and, taking the reins from her hand, helped her dismount. Rajaram wondered where she had gone out on such a pitch dark night, but he didn't have the courage to ask.

The memsaheb turned to them with a smile and said something in English.

Good lord! What was *that* Bhoja Muchi was picking up from the footrest of the buggy—a dead rabbit! At a gesture from her, Bhoja respectfully laid down the creature near the sahebs. Memsaheb had a gun in her hands. She'd have gone to shoot rabbits in the field by the river!

As soon as she came in both the sahebs rose to their feet. Such nonsense! Rajaram thought. They laughed and chattered for a bit amongst themselves. Then she asked Rajaram in her archaic Bangla, 'What do you think of the shikar?'

'Excellent, sir!' said Rajaram, dripping humility.

'Is it good?'

'Very good! Where did you shoot it, memsaheb?'

'By the baur. Over there. There's straw.'

'Straw?'

Bhoja Muchi glossed her words: 'Kharer Field in Sabuipur—belongs to the Bisheshes.'

'Oh, you'd gone quite a ways so late at night.'

'I have a gun,' she replied, 'What is there to fear? Ghosd won't eat me up!'

'No, no! Where would ghosts come from!'

'Bhoja was telling me that there are ghosds in the field. There are lights. They come and go, come and go. What name are they called, Bhoja? The light-ghosd?'

Before Bhoja could reply, Rajaram said, 'Oh, I know. *Eley bhooth*, we call them. I've often enough encountered them on my way home. But they don't harm humans.'

'Ghosd indeet!' the Burra Saheb broke in with a laugh, 'Not ghosd, but that be gas. The gas flames up and you see a ghosd. (He said something to his wife in English that Rajaram did not catch.) How is the rabbid?'

'Very good, huzoor.'

'You eat?'

'No, saheb, I don't. Some amongst us do; I don't.'

At this moment Prasanna Chakravarty Amin and Girish Sarkar, the *mohuree*, entered with a huge pile of account books. Rajaram was sharp. He knew immediately that he would have to spend the night in the Neelkuthi office. But why had they brought the markkhatian books now, at this late hour?

The Chhota and the Burra Sahebs discussed something at length in English pointing to the books.

The entire night passed with the Chhota Saheb, Prasanna Amin, Girish Mohuree and Gadadhar Chakrabarty Mohuree along with Dewanji changing all the figures of the amount of marked land that had been put down in the ledgers.

David Saheb ordered them to make up new figures replacing those about the land actually surveyed.

'There's an important matter, saheb...' began Rajaram.

'What's that?'

'We shall need matching thumb impressions of the subjects. We had taken them while we were doing the mark-khatian; why would they want to give us a fresh set for these new figures? Rascals that they are! Ever since the Nobu-Gaji case, they've completely turned against us, especially Rahatoonpur; and since the murder of Ramu Sardar, the lot at the bundh are angry with us. Now tell me what I should do.'

'We'll simply have to forge the thumb impressions. '

'That's a messy business, saheb. Better think twice about it.'

'It will not do if you get scared and back off, dewan. Don't you remember Duncinson's words—one khana and couple of pegs of whisky?'

'It's not one khana, saheb, but many. Just think about it. I'm sure you remember what took place at the Gallows' Field? It's we who had ordered the hanging of fisherman Giridhar. There's a huge difference though between *then* and *now*. Sriram Bearer has to arm himself with a spear if he is out at night, saheb. Heard it from him this very evening.'

Work went on in the Neelkuthi office until dawn. They were all wiped out by then. David Saheb had kept up with the rest of them in every way.

The Burra Saheb turned up before sunrise. They spoke with each other in English and the Burra Saheb asked, 'Have the mark-khatian been changed?'

'Yes, huzoor.'

'All in order?'

'Still three more days of work needed, saheb. But what shall we do about the thumb impressions? Where can we get so many of them, do you think?'

'Hast to be tun.'

'I'm not able to figure out how. Shall I end my days in jail then? How will we forge the thumb impressions?'

'If everything coot be forged, why shoot *that* not be? Work your brains. If money is spent, all will be tun. From this month on, Prasanna Amin and you will get a raise of two rupees in your salary.'

'Saheb, it's because of you that we've flourished,' said Rajaram bowing his head low and standing with folded hands, 'You can keep us secure, you can bring us down—it's all because of you.'

The Burra Saheb left the room muttering something in English.

≈

It was afternoon.

Prasanna Amin had carried forward quite a lot of the work. Girish Mohuree asked his counterpart in a low tone, 'O Gadadhar, any arrangements for food?'

'Why don't you ask Rajaram-thakur?' responded Gadadhar, taking off the string attached to his spectacles and glancing around nervously.

'Can't. I feel shy.'

'What's to be shy about? Aren't you terribly hungry?'

'Terribly.'

'Then say so! I can't.'

Just then Narahari Peshkar called out from the verandah, 'Dewanji! Amin-babu! Have you all bathed? The food is ready. You may bathe and come.'

'I have much more to do,' replied Dewan Rajaram. 'Go ahead and eat, all of you.'

They all sat down to eat together, excepting for the dewan. He never touched food at the Neelkuthi; didn't eat a morsel till he had bathed and done his ritual prayers. He could do neither here.

Narahari Peshkar was a good brahman cook; he was assisted by another brahman, Gopal Pandey. It was a hearty meal. No! You had to admit that the sahebs knew how to make you work *and* how to reward you with good food. Fish curry made from an enormous carp; each of them got about half a dozen pieces of fried fish as well, sweet-sour chutney, a dish made with the fish head and finally, yogurt.

Gadadhar Mohuree, who was quite a glutton, couldn't help saying, 'O Peshkar-moshai, when you've done so much, why not some sweets as well?'

Rasagolla and other such fancy sweets were not in vogue in rural Bengal. Sweets would mean the same round of sugar-mothh, batasha and monda.

'Didn't occur to me,' said Narahari Peshkar. 'Otherwise, the Chhota Saheb was quite willing.'

Tucking in mouthfuls, Gadadhar remarked, 'The sahebs really know how to treat you right. What do you say, Prasanna-dada?'

Prasanna Chakrabarty Amin had been absent-minded for the last couple of days. He was constantly brooding over something. He was simply not in a frame of mind to respond to Gadadhar. How he would have enjoyed this pressure of work, the pleasure of feasting on such a big fish at any other time! But now, he was eating simply because he had to, working because he had to—like a wound up mechanical toy. There was only that one thought, one dream, one focus.

But what *was* that one thought, one dream, one focus?

Prasanna Amin had fallen in love with Gaya-mem.

It would be impossible to describe the intensity of his enamourment. And with whom could he speak about it? Gaya-mem was a rare and elusive prize. An ordinary person such as Prasanna Chakkarty—could he dare reach for her? It should be of great consolation to him that she had at least looked upon him with favour. It meant that she had come to know of his love, and that she was not unhappy about it; rather, she encouraged it from time to time.

Here he was eating with the others, but in his mind's eye whose graceful form, whose large coquettish eyes and whose pretty face came floating up every moment? He could barely swallow his mouthful, so constricted was his throat with tears that threatened to break out any moment. Even the Chhota Saheb's liquor-inflamed arrogant strides he was willing to disregard—all for whose sake?

It was after years that Prasanna Amin felt some joy in his life. No woman had ever looked upon him with favour. His first wife had a nasal moaning kind of voice although she was named after Saraswati, goddess of speech. However that might be, she was devoted to her husband. Prasanna was barely twenty at the time; his father ruled over him with an iron hand. It was his father who had arranged the marriage; he was too timid to say a word.

Saraswati would serve him with leftover rice and mix it up nicely with a squeeze of lemon, spicing it up with tamarind, chilly and oil. Even if he bought her a plain sari from the Charak fair, her face would light up with innocent delight. 'Come to my parent's home,' she would say, 'and I shall cook you a dish with bitter gourd and jackfruit seed. Huge jackfruits growin' in our garden, you know!' And she would spread her arms wide to show him the size.

When she believed herself to be was alone, she would sing devotional *rasakali* songs in that moaning nasal voice of hers. He had never found it funny; rather, it made him very sad. True, she wasn't in the least good-looking—she was dark-skinned and had buckteeth. But with time, one comes to regard with affection even a stray cat or dog.

But Saraswati kicked the bucket the very first time she was going to give birth to a child.

He was married off again, this time to Sanatan Choudhury's youngest daughter Annapurna, from Rajnagar. Annapurna was good-looking and—possibly, because she was fair—very proud. She was still alive, but now lived in her natal home. They never had children. She'd never really respected her husband and accepted his home as hers. Perhaps it was because her parents were prosperous people. She spoke of the fine grains of rice from which they made pressed rice and the special yogurt they would have at their home. Seven stacks of paddy they had in her father's courtyard!

Annapurna had really left behind a scar. All because of money! Stacks of paddy make you *so* arrogant! How many did the late Sanatan Choudhury have anyway! Well, if he Prasanna was indeed a man, a true son of Ratan Chakkarty, *he* would show this very Annapurna one day what stacks of paddy meant!

He remembered how once—it was *Chaitra* month, hot and humid—behind the bamboo copse around their home ghentu flowers had blossomed—Annapurna had asked him, 'Will you have these bangles melted and get a bauti-bracelet made for me instead?'

Prasanna Chakkarty was not well off those days. His father had died and he himself earned very little, working at the cutchery of zamindar Hariprasanna Mukhujje of Ganrapota.

'Why, they're quite pretty, and they look quite nice on your arms!' he had said.

'Rubbish! They're part of my wedding jewellery, some cheap gilt stuff. You get a bauti-bracelet made for me.'

'I will, in another two years.'

'I'll die in two years.'

'For shame! You shouldn't say such things.'

'Say that you don't have the gumption to spend even a cowrie! And my father had to get me married to such a man! Is marrying a widower a *marriage*! If that man had looked after me at least, I could've borne it. A curse on my destiny...' And that grown up seventeen-year-old starts crying and howling, sprawling on the floor. Doesn't that hurt?

The next year in the month of Aswin she left for her natal home, and never came back. That was eight years ago.

Even after this episode he had gone to Rajnagar a couple of time to fetch his wife. Annapurna's mother had told off her son-in-law in the most humiliating manner: 'If you've got the guts, go marry again. My daughter's not going to go and slave away in your home, boiling rice and husking grain. If you ever have the means, come an' fetch my daughter in a palanquin!'

Prasanna Chakkarty had never gone back.

≈

Prasanna Amin was sitting by the lake. Gaya-mem and her mother Barada Bagdini usually came to the lake around that time. All he wanted was to see Gaya, just once.

His heart danced with joy when he saw Gaya-mem from far. He waited with beating heart.

Gaya was alone. No mother with her.

'Oh Khuro-moshai, sitting here all alone?' she said coming up to him.

'Yes, it's because you will be passing by.'

'How does that matter to you?'

'Nothing. I mean...where's your mother?'

'Ma is husking rice. She'd boiled and sunned other people's paddy; the way it's raining now! An' won't she have to give them their rice? Would they be willing to wait! You sit here, I'm off.'

'O Gaya...'

'What is it?'

'Won't you stop a while?'

'How will that help *me*? Won't I get drenched if it starts rainin'?'

Prasanna Chakkarty was gazing at Gaya with admiration.

'What are you starin' at?'

'Nothing,' said he, slightly abashed. 'What's there to see? If you are before me, is there anything *else* that I can see?'

'Why, what happens if I'm there?'

"I'm thinking...such a nice day...'

'I don't have the time to listen to such nonsense now! I'm off.' She sounded annoyed.

'Just a moment, Gaya...will the world come to an end if you stop here a minute?'

'No, can't be standing here like a clown. Look at how threatening the sky is.'

Dense black clouds of *Sravan* had piled up over the green paddy crops and the indigo saplings planted on fields on the other side. Flocks of white egrets were flying into the distant horizon; a sudden gust of cold wind blew from the open green spaces, there was a distant whistling sound and the other side of the lake seemed to disappear in a haze as the streams of rain fell. The clear waters of the lake embraced by the rain-fed banks rippled like the centre of a chariot wheel.

'Gaya, you'll get wet; it's going to pour,' said Prasanna Chakkarty, all in a flutter. 'Come, come to my home.'

'No. I'm on my way to the Kuthi.'

'O Gaya, *do* listen to me. You'll get wet.'

'I'll get wet, so what?'

'Gaya, am I not saying this for your own good? There's no one in my home. Come.'

'No, I shall not. Don't I call you Khuro-moshai?'

'How does it matter if you do call me by that name? What have I said that's wrong? You'll get wet in the rain, and so I'm telling you that my home is nearby, come and take shelter. Is that *bad*?'

'No. I don't have time to listen to rubbish. You better run, just look up, above the lake...'

'I hope you are not angry with me...Gaya, O Gaya, listen, I swear Gaya, do hear me out.'

'No, no,' cried out Gaya, as she quickly walked away. 'Mad creature! Never knew such a one!'

'Don't tell anyone please,' shouted out Prasanna Chakkarty in a tone of entreaty, 'O Gaya, by my oath...!'

'Get home, Khuro-moshai, don't get wet, go home—'

Gaya-mem's words came blowing in the wind and the rain from far off.

Does the snail living by the lake expect any more by way of blessing from the moon? Wasn't this already a lot?

≈

Ramkanai Kobiraj could not but be astonished that the people from the Neelkuthi were not troubling him any more.

This morning, Gaya-mem had stopped by with some milk. Every now and then she brought him some little offering of food. At first, Ramkanai had refused to accept anything because he knew he could not pay for any of it. But over time she had established a comfortable daughterly relationship that made it easier and natural for him to accept her gifts. Others too had once more begun to call him to attend to them. They'd give him a gourd or some such vegetable by way of payment; rarely did he get any money, and then too, it was only in small change.

Nalu Pal's wife Tulsi was pregnant and suffering from a pain in her abdomen. Harish doctor had been treating her for a while, but the problem persisted. Get a good kobiraj for your wife, Nalu was advised. Ramkanai did not fall into the category of a 'good kobiraj'—he was far too poor. People respected money, not integrity or excellence. Had Ramkanai Kobiraj visited his patients riding in a palanquin, he could easily have demanded half a rupee per visit, as did Harish doctor. But Nalu Pal, whatever might be the reason, did call Ramkanai Kobiraj to treat his wife.

Ramanai examined the patient and said, 'I'll give her the medicine, but I will also have to prepare the *anupan*—what's to be taken *before* the medicine: the juice of kalmi-greens boiled in sea salt; the mixture has to be left standing in an earthen pot for seven days.'

Nalu Pal was no more the Nalu Pal of yore. His business was thriving and his fortunes had changed. The year before he had got a biggish elaborately thatched house built for his family. In these parts, building a house with an eight-tiered roof was a sign of wealth; of course, the ultimate mark of social status was if you could hold the week-long Durga Puja celebrations in your home. That too, Nalu Pal had done last year. He had fed an enormous number of people. He was now recognized as a 'big man', someone who mattered.

He had new almirahs in his home that were decorated with cowrie shells; from the ceiling hung multicoloured skeins of rope with beautifully embroidered stands to hold pots, woven floor-mats with fancy bindings on the side, bell-metal containers for paan, brightly scoured and polished lamp stands of brass—all those objects that distinguished a prosperous man's household.

When he saw that Ramkanai's appreciative eyes were taking in the furnishings inside the sick woman's room, Nalu Pal said, 'I've decided that this time I'm going to get some of those painted clay fruits that the potters at Ghurni are famous for. That cowrie-shell worked clothes-stand you see over there—bought it for two and a half rupees from a brahman's daughter at Binodepur. She made it herself.'

'Good. It's an excellent piece.'

'Kobiraj-moshai, will she get cured?'

'If she doesn't, that treatise of *Madhav Nidhan* is one big lie. But you know, it is important to have the anupan and the *sahapan* in the correct manner—before and after the medicine. She must have the juice of kalmi-greens—that is the anupan. You understand?'

'Yes, sir.'

The refreshments that were served included cucumber slices and high quality batasha, little coconut sweets, as well as freshly grated coconut. It had to be food of a special kind, for Ramkanai would not touch any greens that had been cooked in a sudra household. He also got by way of fees half a rupee, one kantha of rice and *boris* made of *matar*-dal.

Bhabani Barujje, who happened to meet him on the way, said, 'Kobiraj-moshai, my salutations to you.'

'I hope you are well, son-in-law?'

'I am well, by your blessings. You must come to our home for a bit. The little boy's been down with a fever and a bad cough the last few days. Do come and take a look at him.'

'Certainly, I shall. Let us go.'

Khoka was asleep, wrapped up in a light embroidered quilt that his aunt had stitched for him. 'It's a bit of fever,' said Ramkanai after examining his patient. 'His pulse beat shows some irregularity. I will give him some medicine—you have to mix it with the juice of *sheuli* leaves and honey and feed it to him.'

Tilu and his other mothers were all standing around looking worried and agitated. They were all daughters of the village, so they were allowed to come out and speak with men outside of the household.

'How did you find Khoka, Kobiraj-moshai?' asked Tilu tearfully.

'It's nothing much, what we call the early fever. It's all over the place during the monsoon. Don't be afraid.'

'He'll be cured, won't he?'

'What are we here for, if not to cure?'

'I beg of you Kobiraj-moshai', said Nilu, 'do tend to Khoka very carefully.'

'My child, I assure you that he will recover in about three days if he has this medicine. You must not be afraid.

'That strange whistling sound in his throat?'

'It's cough and phlegm; his pulse is affected. It happens. Don't you worry! Just grind up this little ball of medicine and feed it to him right away, in front of me. Do you have a stone pestle for medicines?

'I'll get one from Uncle Sidhu.'

'It's quite late, Kobiraj-moshai; you must have a meal and then go home,' said Tilu.

'It's rice and greens—all that a poor man can provide,' Bhabani Barujje added with folded hands.

Ramkanai was overwhelmed by their graciousness, their humility and the unaffected way in which they presented their meagre resources. No one had ever shown him such affection, or given him such respect. And then too these were people who were part of the Dewanji's family.

Tilu laid out two large low stools for the men to sit down. Had anyone ever sat down beside Ramkani Kobiraj, offering him this or that delicacy with such love? At least, he couldn't recall such loving hospitality. Fried pointed gourd, mung dal, fish cooked with a spicy gravy, a sour-tart preparation of hog-plums, and homemade yogurt, along with ripe jackfruit and lovely *martaman*-bananas. Oh! An auspicious day indeed! Ramkanai was in a daze of wonder.

After the meal was over, Ramkanai suddenly came up with a serious question for Bhabani Barujje: 'Son-in-law, you are learned, wise and like a sadhu. Everyone praises you. We've barely been educated; haven't studied much. Just some basic Sanskrit, and then studied traditional medicine—Ayurveda, from the late Patitpavan Kobiraj of Teghora Senhati (here he paused to express with a gesture his respect for his late teacher). What do we really know of anything! Tell me, what is the *Adi Samvad*—the Primeval Cause. Let me hear it from your lips.'

'I'm sorry, what did you say? What samvad?'

'Adi Samvad?'

'I didn't quite follow what you said.'

'Brahma, Vishnu and Maheswar—the three of them together created the universe, didn't they? Now will you explain to me the inner significance? I lie awake at home at night very often thinking about these things. How did it all happen?'

Bhabani Barujje fell into a quandry. Brahma and Vishnu had certainly not consulted *him* in creating the universe; how was he to know of the inner meaning or significance? What could he say! He knew the philosophy of Patanjali, Sankhya, he recalled the Vedantas—but before a simple village kobiraj—No! It wouldn't do. It would all sound meaningless. He found it quite laughable. Adi Samvad indeed!

Suddenly, Ramkanai said, 'You know, there's something that I've been thinking of for quite long, all by myself…Whatever you may call him—Brahma, Vishnu or Maheshwar—they're all one and the same. The One in the Three, and the Three—the One. What do you say?'

Bhabani Barujje could have not been more astonished at these words than if Ramkanai Kobiraj had suddenly been transformed into the four-armed Vishnu himself, with his two upper arms raised in the mudra of boon giving, and pronounced, *vatsya varang brinu— ihagatosmi!* My son, ask me for a boon, I have come! From the mouth of this ordinary village kobiraj to hear the liberating gospel of *Advaita Brahmavad* in his simple homely language! And that too, in the dank musty hut of a village ridden with unlettered, greedy, superstitious and envious people and their sentiments.

Bhabani Barujje fell completely silent for a while. He knew something of humankind; he had travelled much and seen much. Then he raised his face and addressed Ramkanai: 'You have spoken rightly, Kobiraj-moshai. What can *I* explain to you? You are a person of knowledge, of wisdom.'

'Huh, now you are saying the right thing, son-in-law! You've searched out a wise person indeed!'

Tilu too was very surprised. She had been studying with her husband, had learned a lot from him, and was familiar with the basic philosophy of Vedanta. But she had not imagined that Ramkanai Kobiraj would speak of such things with such simplicity.

'I have heard a lot about you,' she said to him. 'My brother has much oppressed you, so did the people of the Neelkuthi—all because you didn't want to bear false witness, taking bribes from the sahebs. You've suffered a lot, but no one could make you lie regarding the murder of Ramu Sardar. I know it all. I used to think I would surely see you some day; I never thought that you would come to our home, and that I would offer you food. After I've heard you speak, I feel that because *you* have taken refuge in truth, truth emerges from within you.'

Bhabani Barujje had not known that Tilu could speak so well. 'That's good,' he said to her with an approving look.

'What is?' asked Tilu smiling.

'You spoke well. Kobiraj-moshai, how old are you?'

'Born on the 17th of Magh 1234, Bengali Era. You may calculate then…'

'You are older than I. May I address you as my brother, Dada?' requested Bhabani.

'Me too,' added Tilu. 'You must come here every now and then, Dada, and have a meal. Won't you?'

Ramkanai Kobiraj blessed his stars: it had turned out to be such a wonderful day—to be honoured by such people.

'Of course I will. A hundred times I will. If I don't eat at my nephew's, where else would I! I take your leave today: there is another patient, in Sabaipur. Whatever I've given your little boy; his fever will be gone by late afternoon. I'll come by again tomorrow morning.'

≈

Nilu put in the final dash of spices into the mixed vegetable gravy she had been cooking and took the pot off the fire. Khokon had been left in her care while his mother had gone to ask after their brother. Their Bor-da was in danger; the sahebs had said he had to accompany them somewhere. Tilu had gone to find out more.

'Chho-ma-chho ma—' Khokon called out to his youngest mother.

'Yes?'

'Givv—'

'What shall I give you? No, no more jaggery for you.'

Khokon was a quiet child. Playing all by himself he upturned a bowl of oil and then came toddling towards the open clay stove.

'No! You'll get burnt like a scorched brinjal! Ooh! I don't know! Got to cook and look after the boy, and she's such a queen that she couldn't take her son with her. O Mej-di, Mej-di—' said Nilu calling out in vain to Bilu, the middle sister. 'Of course, there's no one around when you need them. Here, you sit down. No, here! I'm going to show you—picking up the bowl of oil again!'

'Bole!' said Khokon.

'Put down the bowl!'

'Ma!'

'Ma's going to come now. There she is.'

Khokon looked outside and said, 'No Ma.' Then, waving both his hands, he said, 'No Ma...no...Go...go...'

'Alright, she's not there. My darling, now sit quietly for a bit.'

'Baba!'

'Must be on his way home. Gone to bathe in the river.'

'Ma.'

'Goodness, can't keep on jabbering with you. Sit, here. That's hot. *Hot*! You'll scald your feet! Oh, you're going to stumble and fall right into the hot *shuktani*. Mej-di—!'

The slight note of admonition in Nilu's voice set Khokon wailing for his mother. Nilu came running to pick him up and tried to calm him down, 'My precious! No, don't cry my darling, my *ram-moni*, my *sona-moni*, my *shyam-moni*...hush now. My darling is crying, why is he crying? Mej-di...! Oh, damn the whole lot, leaving behind the boy and going off wandering.'

Khokon continued sobbing for his mother.

'Don't cry my little fellow, I haven't scolded *you*...now what shall I give you? Oh look! Is that a bird?'

Tilu entered with quick steps, 'Why is he crying?'

'If my voice goes up a notch, your spoilt little fellow goes all sulky. There's no way I can say a hard word. Did you find out where Dada has gone?'

'Dada has gone with the sahebs. There's a fellow called Titu Mir, fighting 'gainst Maharani Victoria—that's where the sahebs have gone with people from various plantations to join forces against him; taken along Dada too.'

'Titu Mir?'

'That's what I heard. Bou-didi's in such a state, weeping away. Battles are terrible; you never know who will come out alive from one.'

Nilu promptly plonked down on the floor and began to cry loudly, her legs spread out. The more Tilu tried to calm her down, the more she upped her wails. Khoka watched her, first in amazement, and then joined her with loud wails of his own.

'What's happened? What's happened to Nilu?' Bilu ran in to find out.

'She's crying because she's heard that Dada has gone to fight Titu Mir. Do calm her down. Dada loves her dearly, and she's still the child, always coaxing and cajoling him.'

'Hush now,' said Bilu, sitting down beside her sister. 'It will bring misfortune. What's to be afraid of when the entire Neelkuthi has gone with him? There, don't cry. If you don't stop, Khokon won't either.'

'And isn't he our Dada too? Are *we* crying? Don't go on like that, it's inauspicious. Dada might come back tonight. Come now…' Before Tilu had finished, Bhabani entered.

His first words were, 'Dada's come back from the battle with Titu Mir. Just saw him. What's this? Why is she crying?'

'She's crying for Dada. Thank goodness! When did he come?'

'There, he's just dismounting.'

Nilu had forgotten her tears; she stood up to listen and then said, 'Come Mej-di, let's go and meet Dada.'

'No, don't,' said Bhabani Barujje.

'Not go? But I really want to see him.'

'Let me go and get all the news. If you go, your precious Didi will also want to as well…and who is to look after Khoka?'

'It's better that he goes and finds out everything,' Tilu endorsed her husband.

If Bhabani forbade them to do something they listened to him.

But Nilu couldn't help adding, 'D'ye know something—you have a-none-too-innocent heart—it's all twists and turns. Only *I* know how I'm a-feeling about my Dada. Go on then; go and meet him!'

≈

Half an hour later, Bhabani was among the crowd of people gathered at Dewan Rajaram's chandimandap.

'Well, brother, hope you've not been wounded?' began Foni Chakkarty.

'No, Dada, nothing of the sort!' responded Rajaram. 'By the grace of your blessings, there was hardly a battle. I believe they'd killed a lot of people earlier—mostly innocent villagers.'

'And who be this Titu Mir?'

'Leader of the Musalmans—that's what I understand from their talk. I was there one day at the Kuthi when the Burra Saheb got a letter about how a fakir called Titu Mir has declared war on the Maharani.

He's furious with the Neelkuthi folks. Looting and killing...'

'And who sent that letter to the Burra Saheb?'

'The new magister who has come instead of Duncinson Saheb; he wrote to them saying, Come with all your people; and all the sahebs from different plantations gathered in one spot. We found them camped in rows in a mango orchard by the Jamuna. Lots of people, horses, guns and furniture; the Sarkar's army had also come out...pitched their tents on the other side—a huge affair it was, Dada! I quite enjoyed it. Prasanna Chakkarty Amin also joined us. He's an old hand; said, "I'll go and find out how and where that Titu Mir is." We weren't scared at all. There *was* no battle. He'd made a bamboo fort on the bank of the Jamuna.'

'Many sahebs gathered there?'

'All the plantation sahebs with their men, guns, bullets, ammunition—from Boalmari, Raghunathganj, Panchitey, Palpara, Dwighare-Bishnupur...The village folk were rushing around and getting hold of hens and ducks and goats to feed the sahebs. One woman had been beaten up so badly by Titu Mir's men that she was bleeding away from her nose and mouth. Titu Mir's fort was about one kos and three quarters away from where we were, near a mango orchard.'

'And the battle?'

'Titu Mir had told his men that the sahebs' bullets and cannons wouldn't do them any harm. That's because the Sarkar's sepoys fire blanks at first, you see. Titu Mir told them that *he* had devoured all the arms and ammunitions. But then the sepoys charged their guns with cartridges and fired. Twenty-two dead at one go. The rest just fled. Titu Mir was bound up and sent off to Calcutta. End of the battle! So we all came back home.'

'And here we were worried to death,' said Nilmoni Samaddar puffing away on his hookah. 'God knows we thought our Rajaram Dada's gone off to a mighty battle. After all, you are like the head of this village. Do we feel good if you are not around in the village? Shyam Bagdi's elder daughter Kusum ran away from her home, with her brother-in-law. Her father brought her back from Mamudpur. There was to be a judgement the day before. Couldn't be done 'cause you weren't there. It'll happen today, am told.'

≈

Shyam Bagdi and his daughter came that evening to the Dewanji's.

'What say, Shyam?' Rajaram enquired.

'Brought alon' my daughter 'fore you. Jedge as you will.'

Rajaram was an experienced man. Before pronouncing anything on the matter, he asked Shyam, using *tui,* the most familiar form of address, 'Where's your daughter?'

'Standin' in a corner—o'er there. Here, Kushi, come up…'

Kusum came up and stood before him. She wasn't more than twenty, ripe in her youth, her firm well-proportioned body like a gleaming dark sculpted figure. She had lustrous black hair, and her dark eyes were particularly beautiful. Rajaram had only seen such a figure in Gaya-mem. The expression on Kusum's face was one of innocence and gentleness.

Quite a piece of goods, thought Rajaram. Pearls in a pigsty…a glimpse of her, and the Burra Saheb would grab her right away.

'Your name?'

'Kusum.'

'Why did you leave your home, child?'

Kusum was silent.

'Why, don't you like your father's home?'

Kusum fearfully raised her eyes to Rajaram and said, 'My stepma doesn't give me food enough to fill my belly. She scolds me, beats me. My brother-in-law, he sez to me, he'll buy me a house, give me good things to eat—'

'And did he?'

'Did he have the time! Baba went and got a hold of me and brought me back.'

'All right, you shall have good things to eat—you stay on in my home. Will you?'

'No.'

'Why, my child?'

'I'll fret.'

'For whom will you fret? You'd left your father and gone away. Not for your step-ma surely. For whom will you fret, my child?'

Kusum did not reply.

Shyam Bagdi was quiet all this while out of deference to Dewan Rajaram Ray. Now he came up and said, 'Let me tell you how it is, master. My little boy—from this marriage—he's mad about her. An' that's the one she'll fret for—she's a sayin'.'

'If that be the case, how come you left him and ran away? What do you say to that? You people can't even think! Say one thing, do another, no head or tail in it. You will stay in our home, eat all kinds of good things. You don't have to work too hard—you can do the cowsheds in the morning.'

'Stay on then at the Master's,' Shyam Bagdi counselled his daughter. 'It will be good for you in every way.'

Rajaram summoned Jagadamba and said, 'Listen, this girl will be staying in our house from now on. She enjoys eating. Is there any murki at home?'

Jagadamba looked at them in surprise. 'Isn't that Kushi from the bagdi-para? She's come to our place ever so often with her grandma. Do you remember, my child?'

'Can't remember,' said Kusum shaking her head. 'Was little then.'

'Will you stay in our home?'

'Yes.'

'Good, you stay here. I'll give you some pressed rice and some sweet puffed rice to snack on. Come with me to the kitchen.'

'You will stay with us like a daughter,' went on Rajaram, 'and muck out the cowsheds and all. You ask your mother for whatever you want whenever you feel hungry. If you want a coconut, there's plenty of them; just grate one and have it. Lots of murki too! Do women have to run away from their homes just because they can't get enough to eat! The people of my village live off the food from my home, and a girl from *my* village is going to run away for lack of food! Tell your second wife, Shyam, it wasn't right what she'd done. I tell you, since she doesn't have her mother, who is going to look after her, huh?'

'Don't talk to me about that ill-thinkin' wimin,' began Shyam irritably. 'Fairly roasted my bones she has. Come back all wiped out from workin' in the fields, and never does she offer me a nice bite to eat. It's leftover rice-in-water, leftover rice-in-water, ever-y single day. If I say give me some freshly cooked rice, it'll take her till sundown to cook me a mouthful of rice and vegetables. Doesn't die neither. Could've married another then.'

Kusum was trying to hide her smile. She seemed mighty amused at her father's words.

≈

'Come, son-in-law, do come in,' said Ramkanai Kobiraj as he spread out a woven date-palm mat for Bhabani to sit on.

'What were you doing?'

'I was about to boil the root of *ishe*. I'm making all the preparations. It's pouring; where have you come from in such rain?'

It was getting to be evening in mid-Sravan. It had been raining incessantly for the last three days. Completely drenched in the downpour the titpalla bushes had taken on strange shapes. You couldn't speak for the sound of the rain. Water was running in channels all over, like tiny rivulets. In the bagdi-para, Noley Bagdi, Adhar Sardar and his three strapping sons along with Bhenpu Mali and others were wading knee-deep in the rushing waters of the bundh, armed with woven bamboo fishtraps. The fine spray from the rain had made a mist everywhere. In the tree behind Ramkanai's hut only a few clusters of laburnum still remained dangling limply. All over the field were vast pools of rainwater that could be mistaken for lakes. Not a soul could be seen outdoors. A young creeper of *telakochu* had pushed its way into Ramkanai's hut, new leaves budding on its tender green tip.

'Let me prepare some tobacco; you are quite wet! Do wipe yourself dry with this,' said the kobiraj.

'Been stuck indoors for three days. There's no one with whom I can have an honest conversation—all too worldly-wise. I've come to meet you,' said Bhabani by way of explanation.

'That is my good fortune, son-in-law. Will you have a bit of pressed rice? I've got some jaggery to go with it too.'

'I will, if you're going to have some.'

'Don't worry; the two of us will share it. A visitor's come home and what do I have to offer? Nothing really. Offered you whatever little I have. A bit of cow's ghee I have in this little bottle—shall I put some into the mix?'

'Let's have a look at it; do you buy it or did you make this yourself?'

Ramkanai took up a little bottle from a wooden seat and handed it to Bhabani, saying, 'I make the ghee myself. Gaya-mem brings me some milk everyday. Calls me "Baba". She's a good girl. She's brought me this bottle from the sahebs' Neelkuthi. I skim the cream that forms on the milk and make the ghee. Need it for our medicines, you know. There are many who buy ghee made from buffalo milk from the market and pass it off as pure ghee. Where it's a question of life itself, those who play tricks and deceive—how will they ever justify themselves when the call comes!'

'Aah, Kobiraj-moshai, the world is running on the wheels of lies and deception. Just look around you in our very own village. Each one concerned only with wealth and property. Oppressing the poor, tricking people of their land, criticizing, gossiping, busy slapping lawsuits on each other at the slightest chance… Frogs in the well, deluding themselves every moment of their life.'

Meanwhile Ramkanai had mixed some ghee with the pressed rice. From an earthen pot that was hanging on the hook he took out some jaggery. He offered Bhabani this simple fare in a stone bowl.

'Shall I give you a green chilly?'

'Yes, give me one.'

'Now, will you tell me something about Adi Samvad? What is

bhagwan like? Can one see him? Let me tell you, I often lie here alone in the dark of the night thinking, then who be this bhagwan? But who will give me a reply? Why don't you tell me something?'

Bhabani Barujje felt himself to be very vulnerable. Ramkanai Kobiraj was an honest person whom he respected. How could he answer such a profound question? Was he worthy enough to quench the thirsty soul of this venerable old man? Specially, since the questions concerned the Supreme Mover of the universe. He was always diffident about speaking of the divine in a casual or trivializing manner. He remembered the message of the Upanishad—'The unwise person though steeped in various kinds of ignorance, believes, "I am fine, I am fulfilled."'

Was he not himself one of those ignorant souls? Was not the old brahman before him a far worthier person? Was not the kobiraj one of those who...

> depending on alms, those most tranquil and wise men,
> who live in the forest, who with an attitude of respect are
> involved in *tapasya*;
> All those individuals without greed and attachments
> will journey towards the portals of the sun,
> where the immortal indestructible *Akshara Purusha* is to be found.

Had Bhabani Barujje come to sell needles at the ironsmith's?

'What will you hear from me?' he asked Ramkanai in a humble tone, and recited the Sanskrit verse: 'The One is vast, the Creator of this varied universe. Itself indestructible is Brahma—it is speech, the mind..'

Ramkanai Kobiraj was not unacquainted with Sanskrit. As he listened to Bhabani, he shut his eyes to submerge himself in the experience, only expressing his appreciation verbally every now and then. 'Aah! What wonderful worlds you have unfolded before me, my son-in-law! No one here speaks of such things. It has filled me with contentment. Please go on, say some more.'

Bhabani Barujje continued in his soft low voice, reciting and explicating with the utmost sincerity: 'The One is smaller than the smallest, greater than the greatest. The One lives in the heart of all living creatures. *Aasino durang brajati*...while standing the One travels far; sleeping, is present everywhere... the One, who is luminous, subtler than the atom. Within whom lie all three worlds and the living creatures of all those worlds.'

Ramkanai who had been munching on the pressed rice pushed aside his bowl. In his right hand he still held a half-eaten green chilly, he had a silly stupefied expression and tears streamed down his face. Bhabani Barujje was surprised at the kobiraj's tear-filled eyes.

In the clear sky beyond the river channel, the seven-day moon had come up above the babla tree. Hidden in the thickets of nalrushes a hutum-owl was crying out.

≈

It was very late at night when Bhabani set off for home.

Countless constellations shone in the clear Sharat sky in the season following the rains. The distant throbbing sound of a woodpecker lulling one to sleep, a couple of stray foxes howling—every single sensation seemed mysterious to him. He felt as though he was steeped in a kind of immortality, both mysterious and sweet. And immense and beautiful...so *intimate* a God. The One who was beyond sound, form, rasa, smell, unending and primeval—the night sky throbbed with its exquisite presence. Those who lived in these parts never spoke of that divinity; in their deafness, everything passed them by. For them, there was neither the rising of the constellations, nor the blossoming of the moonlight, focused as they were only on taking over the property of others, and planting their stake in their neighbour's possession.

O you peaceful, the supremely manifest and the unmanifest supreme One, just as the entire sky is girdled in darkness so it is within you. Be kind; be kind to all of us. Be kind to Khoka, there is no harm if he stays poor, only let him know You. Be kind to his three mothers.

Tilu was waiting for her husband. So late it was...he normally never stayed outdoors so late. Bilu and Nilu had been checking every now and then, coming out from their room. Nilu announced, 'Here at last, the lord has turned up!'

'Hope he is well; did you see how he is?' asked Tilu.

'*Looks* quite well! Let me ask you, O gallant! To which secret grove of Bindaban have you bin a-trysting'? Doesn't Bor-di appeal to you any more? Forget about the two of us—'

'The way all of you are going on—as though a Sunderban tiger has swallowed me up! Is there no way I can go out at night? I was at Ramkanai Kobiraj's.'

'An opium den opened up there recently?' remarked Nilu.

'What else could be happening to keep you there so late?' added Bilu.

Tilu tried to protect her husband from her sisters' teasing. She fetched water so that he might wash his hands and feet. 'Shall I wash your feet? They're caked in mud.'

'That patch around the jackfruit tree is terribly muddy.'

'What will you have to eat?'

'Nothing. Had some pressed rice at the Kobiraj-moshai's.'

'That won't do. You wanted some of that dish made with pumpkin. Nilu kept aside a whole bowlful for you—she loves you dearly.'

'All right, I shall have some. What did you feed Khokon?'

'Some milk.'

'Not coughing any more, is he?'

'Dosed him with ground dried ginger soaked in warm water.'

In the course of his meal, Bhabani shared his experience of the evening with Tilu.

'He is a very different sort,' agreed Tilu. 'Remember, he had asked the same thing the other day. You had said the other day, *purushanna parang kinchit*—there is nothing that is bigger than the One; isn't that the meaning?'

'Right.'

'I too wonder…but caught up with household work, I can't find enough time. You must teach me more. And yes, you must give us two annas each.'

'Why?'

'It's *terer paluni* tomorrow—the rite of the thirteenth. We must go for a meal in the woods, a picnic.'

'I shall come along too.'

'How is that possible? There'll be so many wives and daughters from other families. Do you know, it's bound to rain on the rite of the thirteenth?'

'Nonsense!'

'It is not nonsense, my dear. I'm telling you, it *is* going to rain.'

'Why do you get trapped into these superstitions? What connection could there be between the rain and eating out in the woods?'

'Alright, let's see how far your erudition will stand up.'

≈

It was the thirteenth of the month of Bhadra in the pleasant Sharat season. Along the bank of the Ichhamati the young women of Panchpota village had gathered to observe *terer paluni*. These rites were observed and celebrated beneath an ancient jiuli tree and a kadam tree. The two trees stood near each other and always had been there, or so it seemed. None of those still living recalled a time when they had not seen these two trees. Amongst the really ancient ones, Nilmoni Samaddar's mother used to say that some seventy-five years ago, when *she* had entered the village as a new bride—she, her mother-in-law and her grandmother-in-law used to celebrate the 'rites of thirteen' and have a picnic in the woods under the same tree. It was only last year that the eighty-five-year-old woman, Nilmoni's mother, passed away.

The women had fanned out according to the various localities they belonged to, although everyone was being deferential to Nalu Pal's wife, Tulsi, because her husband was wealthy. Nowadays they didn't do any cooking outdoors: each one brought whatever she could bring from her home; then, rolling out their banana leaf-platters they enjoyed the food in the merry company. They played rhyming games, sang all kinds of songs, ululated the auspicious sound, sounded the conch and indulged in all manner of banter and teasing. There was an ancient unwritten code that if you were from a prosperous family and brought along a lot of good food, you would share it with those from poorer homes. No one had to be reminded: it was simply understood and accepted as part of village life.

Such was the case today as Tulsi, in her broad red-bordered sari, walked up to Jatin's wife and his sister Nandarani. Although there was not much following of ritual pollution rules on this day, the women from the brahman homes tended to find themselves a place along the riverbank, while those of other castes would sit next to the field. Jatin's wife had brought some roasted rice, a couple of ripe bananas and a pot of buttermilk. That was all she and her sister-in-law would eat.

'O Swarna, how are you?' asked Tulsi, coming up to Jatin's wife.

'I'm well. And hasn't your little boy come?'

'No, I've kept him at home. He'll be really naughty if I bring him here. What will you be eating, O Swarna dear?'

'Here—got this buttermilk from home. Made it this morning from cream that I'd saved for three days. Why don't you take some to try it out, didi?'

Tulsi went to fetch a stone bowl to carry away some of the buttermilk; when she came back she was carrying four ripe martaman-bananas and several big feni-batashas.

'What's that you've got, didi?'

'Have some! Bananas from our garden: a big stalk came up in the month of Ashad, part of it got spoilt in the rains, though.'

Tilu and Bilu had also come to the woods, while Nilu was looking after Khoka at home.

Everyone was coming up to the sisters to offer them various things—milk, mothh sweets, murki coated in cane sugar, khoi, bananas and what not. They all spoke sweetly to the two and generally treated them with special attention. The more the sisters said they didn't need anything the more the others pressed them to accept their gifts. Whatever the sisters had brought they had already shared with the daughter-in-law of Nilmoni Samaddar, since he was the poorest.

'What will you have, O didi?'

'Brought some roasted rice, and there's a cucumber.'

'No milk?'

'Where would I get any? The cow hasn't calved yet.'

'Not yet? Then when?'

'In Aswin month, towards the end.'

At a slight hint from Tilu, Bilu brought them pressed rice, murki, batasha and sugar mothh. Shashti Chaudhuri's wife brought them about half a dozen ripe bananas.

'I have quite a large chunk of date palm jaggery, I'm going to get some of that,' said Foni Chakkarty's daughter-in-law.

'I won't take any more; give some to Aunty here,' said Tilu. 'I've got a whole pile of mothh-sweets and batashas. Well, Bidhu-didi, how come you haven't yet recited any of your rhymes this time? Let's hear you make up a verse or two!'

Bidhu, the widowed daughter of Foni Chakkarty and once the village beauty, was almost fifty years old. She promptly began reciting with vivid gestures of her hands:

> 'Asked me to come for
> some paan-supari:
> Anise grounds inside the paan,
> lively-lively pictures done.
> Shampoo from Calcutta,
> The comb from Medinipur,
> Such a coiffure I'll get up for you,
> Woven with champa flowers!
> My name is Swarabala:
> I'll garland you with a flower-mala!'

'So Bidhu-didi, you're composing verses at my expense. I'll show you!' said Bilu rolling her eyes at her in mock anger, for her formal name was Swarabala, which could mean the "melodic lass"! Bilu answered back with a riddle:

'Hornets nesting on a *chalta*-tree:
One without corners, cornered will be.
Bidhu-didi, why don't you sing us a song? I swear, how "bout one of Nidhu-babu's?'

Bidhu responded with a *tappa* composition which she sang turning around in circles:

> 'Is love merely a world of words, if the heart be
>   entwined with one?
> Would the creeper live, if the tree withers
>   In which it is entwined?'

The group now turned to a shy young woman and urged her to sing a composition dedicated to the dark goddess Kali. The singer was Nistarini, Bhajagobindo Barujje's daughter-in-law. She was the third daughter of Ratneswar Ganguli of Kamdevpur. Old man Ratneshwar was much in demand in evening soirées for he was among the well-known *dugi-tabla* players of the region. Dark-complexioned Nistarini was slim, with beautiful eyes and a melodious voice. In perfect pitch she sang

> 'Young and dark blue is she, the bride of the one
>   With the radiant topknot encoiled by snakes,
>   Blue-eyed, she wins over the three-eyed god—
>   O glorious consort of the Lord of the night.'

When Nistarini had finished singing, Tilu went up to her and slid an entire sugar mothh into her mouth. The shy young woman looked down in embarrassment; perhaps she was discomfited by the presence of so many pleasure-loving older women.

But she quipped, 'Didi, why don't you give one to *Thakur-jamai!*' She used the formal term to refer to Tilu's husband.

'Have you seen your Thakur-jamai then?' asked Tilu.

Bilu immediately came up and exclaimed, 'Why did you suddenly take his name—Thakur-jamai? Have you become greedy? Better be careful! You're not to look that way. The three of us are going to sit guard at the threshold with a broom, got it!'

Those who were standing close by began to titter.

Just then, an astonishing sight met their eyes: who should appear but Bhabani Barujje himself, a thin red towel slung on his shoulder and Khoka in his arms!

'Goodness! As soon as his name was mentioned, Thakur-jamai's turned up—' remarked Nalu Pal's wife, Tulsi.

'Did a fine thing—foisting him on us!' Bhabani was complaining. 'As though he'll stay with us! Started crying out for his mother as soon as he woke up. Tried to coax and cajole him—but would he listen!'

Khoka stared confusedly at the crowd and kept on saying 'Ma, Ma…'

Bilu rushed to pick up the boy and asked, 'But where is Nilu? Why do you say he's been thrust on you? I had put him in Nilu's lap—'

'She was sent for from your brother's home. He is unwell—so off she went, thrusting the little fellow on me.'

The gaggle of young wives and sisters had meanwhile joined forces, and were whispering away, since they couldn't speak to him directly. As the senior-most, Bidhu came forth as their representative, 'O Jamai-babu—of whatever exact denomination you might be, elder, younger or the middle one! All the womenfolk are a-sayin', now that we've got our Thakur-jamai in our midst we're not letting go off him, we—'

Before she could complete her words, Bhabani Barujje cut in, 'You must forgive me Bidhu-didi, I won't be able to manage all by myself. I'm quite old.'

His remark was met with torrents of laughter. Some laughed in a restrained manner, some giggled outright, one turned away her face and another muffled her outburst in her sari-end. The branches of the kadam tree shone rosy red in the afternoon sun and the feathery kash flowers on the other bank rippled in the flowing waves of laughter. Comforted by Nistarini, who had taken him in her arms, Khoka's happy babble merged with the distant comforting cooing of the dove. All in all, the rites of the thirteenth took on a different meaning for Nistarini. What a fun-loving person Thakur-jamai was! Still so handsome looking, even if he was getting on in years.

The new District Magistrate came over to inspect the Neelkuthi. No magistrate had set foot in the Neelkuthi since Mr Duncinson had been transferred. The welcome was therefore all the more ostentatiously organized with a grand bout of khana-pina and dancing—the works.

As he was leaving, the new magistrate, Coleman Saheb, took the Burra Saheb aside and said to him confidentially, 'Do you read native newspapers? You do? Hard times are ahead, Mr Shipton. Stuff some wisdom into the brains of your men. You understand? I hope you will not mind my saying so?'

'Explain that to me.'

'I will, presently.'

The truth of the matter, he said, was that things were getting worse. The native press had started kicking up a fuss. Harish Mookherjee was dishing out fiery pieces in the *Hindoo Patriot*, Ramgopal Ghose was making provocative speeches in public meetings against the indigo planters, the natives seemed to be coming into their own; the times were changing; one would have to do things more circumspectly. Secret circulars had been issued by the Government to act as far as possible in the interests of the raiyats—that was the gist of Coleman Saheb's advice.

The next day, the Burra Saheb shared this information with his junior.

David Saheb seemed to be rather upset: 'You see, I can work and I can do with very little sleep and I have never wasted time on liking people. Perhaps I am not clever enough—'

'No David, we have a stake down here, in this godforsaken land, you see? What I want to drive at is this—'

Sriram Muchi entered with urgent news: 'Saheb, the raiyats are a-sittin' and waitin' for you in the office. There's big trouble. The bagdis from Hingnora and Rasoolpur are mighty worked up. Believe they've let loose cattle to graze in the indigo lands and the cows are all eating up the saplings…'

'Where be they from—Hingnora?' demanded David Saheb as he sprung up in his agitation. 'I've got my eyes on those two scoundrels—headman Sadek and Chhihari Sardar for some time now. I know how to keep them disciplined.'

'The devil that is!' said Shipton, equally enraged. 'I will come in with you this time. Will you like to come on a mouse-hunt tomorrow morning?'

'Sure I will.'

'I wonder whether I ever told you these thieving people drove off some of our horses from the village?'

'My stomach! You never did.'

'Well, be ready tomorrow morning. Maybe we could kill off the mice right away.'

'Sure!'

≈

The next morning an unusual sight was to be witnessed.

Riding single file came two sahebs on their horses; behind them on a big white horse was Dewan Rajaram Ray, and after him, in a roan-coloured horse followed Prasanna Chakkarty Amin. Well behind them came Rasik Mallik, the master lathiyal of the Neelkuthi. The villagers sensed that something sinister was brewing; there was bound to be a terrible clash on this day.

Prasanna Amin suddenly dismounted at a particular spot. He called out to Rajaram, 'Dewanji, you go on ahead, my saddle seems to have slipped; I'll tighten it up a bit.'

He waited till the file of horsemen had moved out of sight. Tethering his horse to a *sondali* tree by the road he quickly moved to a hut a little further away.

'Gaya, O Gaya—' he began calling.

'Who be that outside?' came the voice of Gaya's mother, Barada Bagdini.

Prasanna Chakkarty waited in great trepidiation. The old woman was usually never at home at this time of the day. She would be at the Neelkuthi looking after the saheb children, running after them, bathing them and all the rest. Lord, did that creature have to be home—today of all days!

He cleared his throat and spoke up loudly, 'It's me, O didi—'

'Who be that? Amin-babu? What is it—at this time?' Barada Bagdini was saying as she came out of the hut. She had probably been boiling paddy: there were black streaks on her hands from the earthen pot in which the paddy was boiled. Her stiff stick-like hair was tied up in a high topknot over her head. She looked annoyed and suspicious.

'Oh, is that you, didi? Good you are here. There's something wrong with the horse's hoof; it can barely walk. Do you have a little coconut oil?'

'No, there's none. Coconut oil's dear.'

'Oh! I'll be on my way then.'

Barada Bagdini looked searchingly at Prasanna Amin. Who knows whether she actually believed his excuse? As though *she* wasn't aware of the many men who were after her daughter. She really had to sweep them away, with all the many pleas and prayers that they came to burden them both. Barada Bagdini was not born yesterday. Just because he was the 'Amin-moshai' didn't mean people like him were above suspicion; nor because he was getting on in years. There were the old ones, the young ones, the relatives—she'd seen them all. Couldn't trust any one of them!

Prasanna Chakkarty sped off on his horse.

Vast tracts of indigo fields surrounded Hingnora village. This was the season for the saplings to grow.

'See what they are up to!' said the Burra Saheb to the Chhota, pointing in the direction of the fields.

A crowd of people armed with sticks had come out of the bagdi-para and was moving towards them, running along the ridges separating the fields.

'Saheb, they are planning to surround us,' warned Dewan Rajaram. 'Come, let's go forward.'

'You get back,' said David. 'We've got to set fire to their homes; go and fetch some more people.'

'You won't be needing anything more,' said Rasik Mallik, the master lathiyal. 'Me, I'll go ahead—you must wait here.'

At this, the Burra Saheb said, 'You stay; the Chhota Saheb and I shall have be going. Did you bring along the *shorki*-spear?'

'No, saheb, won't be needin' the shorki-spear. A hundred men can't stand up to my lathi. You move away.'

Dewan Rajaram had in the meantime raced his horse towards the northern end of Hingnora village. The Burra Saheb shouted out, 'Rasik will go with you, Dewan.'

In a short while a hue and cry was heard. Inside the bagdi-para, women with their little children were screaming and running helter skelter at the charging horse. Seventy-year-old Ramdhon Bagdi was sitting by the roadside on a fallen trunk, smoking his tobacco. One blow of the stick and he fell howling and shrieking on the ground, his wife cried out in terror, people ran out of their dwellings. Within a few minutes there was pandemonium.

Soon, the bagdi-para was in flames. As the panic spread, the men who had armed themselves with sticks ran back to their homes trying to stave off the fiery devastation. This had precisely been Dewan Rajaram's intention. In any case, much of the crowd had already dispersed when they had sighted the Burra Saheb coming at them on horseback for they feared him like the devil. Wicked as the Chhota Saheb was and however oppressive, it was Shipton Saheb, they felt, who was the real scheming devil. He was capable of doing anything to get his work done. He stopped at nothing—seizing property, forgery, arson, murder...He was not hot-headed, though; not as impulsive as the Chhota Saheb. But, if he once realized that there was no option but a particular path, he would stick to it; would stoop to the lowest level to get his work done.

The fire was put out quickly by the villagers, but meanwhile, the objective of dispersing the crowd had been served. They all feared Rasik Mallik. A *namasudra* by caste, he was a professional lathyial—a terrific wielder of the stick and equally skilful with the spear. Some ten years ago he had accidentally killed one of his sons with his spear, mistaking him for a fox. It was the season for ripe jackfruits. They had a ripe one at home that was kept leaning against the wall made of matting. That evening, his nine-year-old had made a hole in the wall and was sitting outside the house eating stolen chunks of jackfruit. Rasik heard the muffled scratching sound and thought it was a fox trying to get at his fruit. He shoved in the spiked end of his spear with unerring aim through the hole in the wall. The mortal cry of the boy sent everyone running outdoors, lamp in hand. The little boy lay there with shreds of the ripe jackfruit all over his hands and mouth, and a gaping hole in his chest from which the blood spurted out, flooding the earth on which he lay. The eyes were already still, the hand unclenched; only the little legs moved spasmodically a couple of times as if trying to ward off something. Then, it was all over.

Rasik had not forgotten that night. But he was a fiend at heart, ready to do anything for money. It was he who had finished off Ramu Sardar with one thrust of his spear at the bundh. With a single blow of his stick he had finished off Satu Mondal, brother of Nevaji Mondal of Chalki village at Kharer Field.

The Burra Saheb and Rasik Mallik coming at them together proved too much for the people of bagdi-para. They slowed down.

'Call out your Chhihari Sardar!' Rasik roared out his challenge. 'Send him afore me. The Burra Saheb's ordered that I stick his head on the point of me spear and take it back to the Neelkuthi. Come on, you sons of vixens—if ever you've drunk a drop of your mother's milk, come out and fight with me! Come out—you sons of wild pigs. Come on—you son of a mongrel bitch! Bring your father and fetch him afore me, you *haramzada*, you bastard!'

Chhihari was indeed coming out to face him were it not been for his wife who clung on to his clothes—he wasn't a coward; but if had, he would most likely have lost his life. He couldn't have stood up to Rasik Mallik. How long could an ordinary householder with his stick stand up to a professional looter and killer?

'Rasik, can you fetch that rascal Chhihari and Sadek?' Chhota Saheb asked.

'I am afraid that would not be quite within the bounds of law. Let us return,' said the Burra Saheb whose temper had cooled somewhat by now.

A little later, he laughed and added, 'Sufficient unto the day—the evil thereof...'

The Chhota Saheb felt angry; he felt like adding an 'Amen' to the Burra Saheb's words; but finally, didn't have the courage to say anything.

Meanwhile Dewan Rajaram had turned his horse in the direction of the Neelkuthi. Prasanna Chakkarty was riding back with him, but when he glimpsed a firm-bodied sixteen-year-old bagdi wife hiding in the bamboo forest, her clothes in disarray, he halted. There was no one else in sight. The young wife was desperately trying to evade his attention and somehow disappear into the thicket.

'And who be you?' asked Prasanna Chakkarty, trying as far as possible to make his voice low and melodious.

No answer.

'I say, what's there to be afraid of? Am I a snake or a tiger? Who be you?'

No answer. Only terrified sobs.

Prasanna Chakkarty quickly looked around once more before he pushed his horse towards her, grazing her as he rode past. But she was a match for him; after all, she was from the bagdi community. Realizing her vulnerability the young bagdi-wife let out a terrified shriek and dashed right into the part where the jungle was the thickest. It was not possible to ride a horse through that thorny stretch of the jungle. Prasanna Chakkarty had no option but to turn back.

Why on earth were the females of the bagdi-para so beautifully built? Oh! The one or two he had sighted from time to time! No, really! Never amongst the bhadralok had he come across such build, such health—it was like comparing a tin whistle to a flute!

≈

'What is your game plan?' Burra Saheb asked Chhihari Sardar, quite directly.

'We're not goin' to be growin' any more indigo, saheb. You may kill us or punish us in any way you like.'

'And what be the reason for this?'

'What reason shall I say—there's no rice in our homes, no clothes to wear, all on 'ccount of this indigo! We've sworn by Ma Kali, our goddess Kali, that no more are we goin' to grow any indigo.'

'What if you will get, will then you be desirous of growing indigo?'

'No more sowin' of indigo—only rice. All our rice-growin' lands your amin comes and marks up, and we can't grow rice any more. No one's sayin' a thing if you buy your cows and your plough, and do your indigo growin' in your own land! But to seize the subject's land by force and make him grow indigo—why should that be, saheb?'

'I'll give you a reward of five hundred rupees. You don't put forth any obstacles in indigo cultivation. Tell the raiyats to back off.'

'Forgive me, saheb. Me alone tellin' them won't make any difference. I'm a-tellin' you, listen then—it's people from *thirteen* villages that have come together 'gainst this. Raiyats from the neelkuthis of Bhabanipur, Natabede and Hudo-Manikkoli—*all* come together. There's a furious wind a-blowin' from the west and the south.'

The Burra Saheb was already apprised of this information. That is why after the excursion of the other day into Hingora village he had sent for Chhihari Sardar and was now trying to sound him out in the premises of the Neelkuthi. The Burra Saheb had not imagined that Chhihari was going to be so stubborn.

Nevertheless, he ordered him, 'You shall come over to me. Go aheat and try it out. Much money will you get. Do you want a job in the cutchery?'

'No, saheb! Seven gen'rashuns of us have never worked for a salary. And let me tell you one more thing, saheb; me alone, can't deal with the storm that's a-comin'. It's a storm that's a-brewin' all over the district—what can one Chhihari do 'bout it? You have to understand, saheb—don't blame *me* alone. I've eaten the salt of the Kuthi; that's why I've open'd up 'bout these things.'

The Burra Saheb sent for his junior and instructed him, 'I say, David, this man swims in shallow waters. Let him go safely out and see that no harm is done to him. Not worth the trouble.'

Late that evening a secret meeting was called at the Neelkuthi.

The spies employed by the planters had brought in a good deal of information. The raiyats in the entire district were up in arms; they were not going to be forced to take the advance for indigo any more. All seventeen plantations were in great danger. There were sabhas and meetings taking place in every village, panchayats were being set up. It had gone so far that in some village clusters, the raiyats had uprooted indigo plants and had broken up the plots into smaller holdings where they were now growing edible greens like *danta-shak* and *tilu*.

At the meeting were some of the saheb managers of the neighbouring plantations, and of course, Shipton and David Saheb. They never invited a Bengali to any of their important or secret meetings. 'No native need be called,' Malisson Saheb had instructed, 'we shall make our decision known to them if necessary.'

'Ask the magistrate for more guns,' proposed Cauldwell Saheb. 'It's crucial that every plantation has a good stock of firearms.'

Cauldwell was the awe-inspiring manager of Bhabanipur. There was no one as cunning as he in appropriating land from the raiyats. He was unparalleled too in committing murder and indulging in reckless acts. However, a few days ago his wife had left with one of his friends and there had been no news since; the incident had left him rather crestfallen.

'Those blooming native leaders should be shot like pigs,' declared Shipton.

'I say, you can go on with your pig sticking afterwards. Now decide what we should do with our Impression Registers. That is why we have met today,' Cauldwell reminded the group.

Sriram Muchi entered with a tray full of decanters and a bottle of sherry.

'No sherry for me! I will have a peg of neat brandy,' said Cauldwell. 'Now Shipton, old boy, let us see how you keep your Impression Registers. This man of yours—is he reliable? Walls have ears, you know.'

'Oh, he's all right,' said Shipton casting a look at Sriram.

The dadon khatas recording the advances were the most important documents of the Neelkuthi. They held the thumb impressions of all the raiyats. The magistrate would personally inspect these registers. In most plantations two sets of books would be prepared; the District Magistrate would not be shown the real one. Shipton had already got the registers brought to the living room. He showed them to the others.

'Is this your original register?' Malisson asked.

'Yes, the other one is in office; this, I keep always under lock and key.'

'Sure. Do you have this week's *Englishman*?'

'I have.'

'It is funny, a deputation waited on the Lieutenant Governor the other day. The blooming old fellow has given them a benediction,' said Cauldwell.

'As he always does, the old padré!' was Shipton's reply.

Then they got down to some intense discussion. Clearly, the raiyats had started a rebellion; now the question was, to what extent were the plantations in danger of attack? And if they were, would the women and children be moved to the big Neelkuthi at Chuadanga or, should they all be transported to Calcutta?

'I don't think the beggars would dare as much,' said Shipton, 'I will keep them here all right.'

'Please yourself, old boy. You are the same bull-headed Johny Shipton,' said Cauldwell. 'Pass me a glass of sherry, Mallison, will you?'

'Funny, isn't it?' said Mallison with a frown and a laugh. 'You said you would have nothing to do with sherry, did you not?'

'Sure I did. I was feeling out of sorts with the worries and troubles, and also with the long ride through drenching rain.' Then switching to Bangla he said, 'Bearer, come hither here. Can a lime you get me?'

Shipton turned to Sriram and ordered, 'From the garden you will ged the lemons for saheb. One dozen—ten and two lemons you will bring, understart?'

The discussion went on for a while after Sriram had left. It was decided that the very next morning someone would be sent to the manager at the big plantation in Chuadanga, find out what quantities of firearms were stored there, inform the saheb that the womenfolk and the children from the different plantations were going to be sent there; he should be prepared to receive them.

To Shipton, Mallison said, 'You oughtn't to be alone at present.'

'What do you mean? Alone? Why, haven't I my own men?' said Shipton sipping his drink. 'I must fight this out by myself. Leave everything to me.'

'Well, all right then.'

The sahebs spent that night at the Mollahati Kuthi. At other times they would have set off on horseback for their own kuthis, but given the situation they didn't dare to travel singly in the dark.

Early next morning news came that the rebellious raiyats had come to loot Ramnagar Neelkuthi but had eventually left on account of firing from the Neelkuthi. The Ramnagar plantation was only thirty miles away. The manager, Andrews Saheb, was notorious for picking up any girl he fancied in his estate. He was looked down upon by some of his own race for the same reason.

'Oh, the old beggar!' said Mallison when he heard the news, frowning and wrinkling up his nose. To Shipton he asked, 'You don't see anything significant in that?'

'I don't see what you mean,' replied Shipton. 'I cannot carry on this indigo business here without my men, without that wily old dewan to help us, you see? They will not fail me at least, I know.'

'Very kind of them if they don't.'

The sahebs sat down to their distinctive breakfast that went by the name of *chhota-huzree*. It comprised huge bowls of fermented rice liberally garnished with lemon juice, cold ham left over from the night before, an entire cucumber and about four or five khoira fish fried in mustard oil, per man. Years of living in rural Bengal had turned the sahebs into rustics in matters of diet. They often ate their rice mixed with juice of mangoes or jackfruit. Many preferred the hookah to smoking tobacco in pipes. They cohabited with and even lived with women from the lower castes. Many a fresh arrival from England turned up their noses at these men, saying that they had 'gone native'. Not that these 'natives' cared.

The sahebs broke up soon after their repast and left for their respective kuthis. In another four days it became known that the women and children of the neighbouring plantations had been sent off either to the Chuadanga Neelkuthi or directly to Calcutta. Dewan Rajaram was forever on his horse riding around and through the neighbouring villages gathering all the information he could. It was he who came to know that people from seven villages were planning to band together and surround the Mollahati Neelkuthi late that night. And it was Nobu Gaji who gave him the news. Nobu had once been given a fair deal by the saheb, and for this he was grateful. 'Dewan-babu,' he said, 'I don't care what happens to the other saheb; this was not a bad man. Nothing should happen to *him*.'

The dewan informed the sahebs of the imminent attack so that they might be prepared with all their men. The two sahebs stood in front with their guns. The Burra Saheb had to inform the police.

After ten that night shouts were heard from the paths by the Ichhamati. The sahebs fired blanks. Dewan Rajaram was standing with his gun in the darkness between the two-storeyed *balakhana* and the cemetery, where there was a row of casuarina trees. Beside him in the darkness, spear in hand, was Rasik Mallik and his men.

'I beg of you, Dewan-moshai,' entreated Rasik Mallik, 'let me show off a bit this time and settle them. If I don't...this time, my father's name is not Tirbhongo Mallik.'

'Shut up you rascal. Hold your horses! Is it enough to simply kill a couple of people? It might have worked elsewhere. This is bang inside the Kuthi, the police will rush in to make an enquiry.'

'As if I won't make the bodies disappear overnight! *That* you can safely entrust me with, Dewanji.'

'All right, now you wait! Don't begin to wield your spear till I say so.'

It was a wonderful moonlit night. A strange sensation took over Rajaram. It was an entirely new feeling. On the dust road before them the moonlight came in shafts through the gaps between the serried casuarina trees. He had married off Tilu, Bilu and Nilu, had seen the birth of a nephew. All the major responsibilities of his life were over. If his body were to roll onto the dusty road, pierced by a spear in a face-off, would he have any unappeased longings, unfulfilled desires? None, he thought. As for Jagadamba, he had done enough for her. She would inherit large estates, various assets, as well as fertile rice-growing land—enough and more to run a large household. The annual income from his zamindari would be about four hundred rupees—luxurious. He could die without any worries. He wouldn't let any danger touch the sahebs. He had eaten of their salt for many years.

'Be ready Rasik, you rascal. But murder—you understand, only when they fall on you.'

In that path woven in moonlight and amidst the darkness beneath the casuarina trees there was a group of people coming closer, carrying torches, the glint of spears and lathis in their hands.

Rasik let out something like a war cry, 'Come on you rascals—come forward—and I'll pierce your guts—'

'Who be that?' said some people coming forward. 'Rasik-dada?'

'Not your brother, your father!' said Rasik with a curse.

'You shouldn't say such things, for shame. Come forward, dada.'

Dewan Rajaram suddenly could not see Rasik any more; he seemed to have melted in the play of darkness and moonlight. A little later he saw that the group was in disarray, people were fleeing, something shiny was whirling in their midst, something was flashing. What was happening? Was that Rasik Malik there? Oh no! What was he up to?

From outside the extended apron of the Neelkuthi there arose a huge cry. Then came sudden silence. Finally, all sounds died down. Now it seemed he could hear the sahebs' horses along the path to the north, where the balakhana stood. Rajaram went forward. Were people hiding here and there along the long avenue of trees?

No. But what was that?

Bodies lying on the ground. One, two, three, four, five. What had that rascal Rasik been up to? All had been felled by the spear. All dead. Five of them.

'O Rasik! Rasik?'

Rajaram felt dizzy. Rasik Mallik had made a mess. All these bodies had to be disposed off right away. The sahebs had to be informed.

Half an hour later the dewan and the Chhota Saheb were deep in discussion.

'Five of them!' asked David. 'Where will you hide them? First figure that out. The baur waters won't do. The bodies will only come up against the bundh—get stuck there.'

'Not that, saheb; we won't float them anywhere. Send orders to Hira Dom and his brother-in-law Kalu. I've found out a way.'

'What is it?'

'Let me carry through my plan first. And then I shall inform you. You order them right away. We must finish it all during the night; wrap it up before dawn. If there's blood on the path, it's got to be washed away. And slap a fine on that rascal Rasik tomorrow.'

Rajaram made sure that everything was done that very night; he was home and in bed before dawn.

'Goodness, is there no end to the work?' complained Jagadamba. 'Almost getting on to be daybreak...'

'It's all that accounting work that's going on. Books and registers to balance. Not easy!'

≈

Bhabani Barujje was out with his son looking to buy some fish. Khoka, a bright little fellow, was prattling away to his heart's content.

'O Khoka,' his father asked, 'will you have some fish?'

'Fish!' said Khoka shaking his head.

'Fish?'

'Fish.'

A little further Bhabani met up with Jadu fisherman, carrying fish for sale. Jadu made him a pranam and asked, 'Will you be takin' some fish?'

'What kind?'

'Got a bhetki, about a seer and a half'

'How much shall I pay?'

'Could give me three annas.'

'That's too much.'

Jadu fisherman put down the yoke from his shoulder and said, 'Babu, just think of how the rates are goin' up in the bazar. Could get a *pali*-measure of aush-rice for two paisa when I was a child. Went up to an anna. Now, it's six paise! Six mouths to feed at home: need at least one katha of rice for each meal. If I am goin' to give three annas for the rice alone every day—where am I to get money for salt, oil, vegetables, cloth, medicine, looking after guests and all the rest? Poor people like us, jamai-babu, how are we goin' to pull along?'

Bhabani Barujje did not argue any further and carried the fish home. Bilu and Nilu came running to meet him.

Bilu swooped on the fish in her husband's hands and exclaimed, 'Nice! What fish is it? Bhetki or chital?'

'An excellent fish!' said Nilu. 'O Khoka, will you have fish? Come to me now.'

Khoka clung to his father and cried out, 'Baba, Baba—' Probably because he rarely had a chance to be in his father's arms, Bhabani held a mysterious attraction for his son.

'So, you won't come?' said Bilu glaring at him.

'No.'

'Alright! As though your Baba looks after you and feeds you!'

'Baba.'

'So you don't want fish?'

'Eat.'

'If you *want* to eat, then come.'

Khoka looked up at his father and said in a weepy voice, 'Just see—' He was trying to say, 'Look, they're forcibly taking me away from your arms.' Bhabani knew that Khoka had learnt the phrase 'just see' only a few days ago, and he loved using it at every opportunity.

'Let him be with me, I'll make a quick round of Mahadev Mukhujje's chandimandap.'

'Tell us what we are to do with the fish,' said Nilu.

'Whatever you like. Where's Tilu?'

'She's gone to make boris and dry them in the sun on Bor-da's terrace. *Your* house doesn't have a terrace on the roof, you know. When are you going to build a proper house?'

'You should go to your brother and tell him that I have saved several kulin maids; he should now bring out some money from that iron chest of his. And I shall immediately get a double-storeyed mansion built. Had I not married you, you would have remained old maids; who would have married you?'

'Far better that Dada had tied water-pots around our necks and drowned us in the Ichhamati! What a marriage he has pushed us into! An old groom, over three-fourths of his life gone—'

'Well, he *could* have married you off to a young groom long ago. Why were you all rotting away at home all this time? Did I fall at your feet and beg you to marry me?'

'I'll box your ears!' declared Nilu and she quickly brought her hand dangerously close to Bhabani's ear, when Bilu reprimanded her, 'What's this!'

Nilu darted off with the fish, giggling.

Bhabani came out on the road with Khoka and began talking to him, 'Tell me, where are we going?'

'I going.'

'Where?'

'Fish.'

On the way to Mahadev Mukhujje's chandimandap they passed the babul tree which had a crowd of creepers smothering its top; in that dark shadowy place, a bird had made a nest in the upper branches. Bhabani put down Khoka in the shadow of the tree.

'Khoka, look! A bird!'

'Bird.'

'Want a bird?'

'Bird...'

'Very nice! I'll give you one.'

How beautifully Khoka smiled looking at his father. Bhabani loved the company of this pure, innocent child. He saw something deeper and greater in his smile.

'Will you, Khoka?'

'Yes...' Khoka said with a turn of his head. This was the first time that Khoka had said the word 'yes', and Bhabani enjoyed the way he said it. To him it sounded like the primeval first mantra of the *Rigveda*—bountiful and beautiful.

'How many?'

'One many.'

'All right, I'll give you one. Take it?'

'Yes,' said Khoka with another incline of his head. The next moment, he said 'Baba.'

'What?'
'Ma.'
'Meaning?'
'Ome.'
'But you've just come from home. Besides, Ma's not at home.'

Of the few words that Khoka had learnt, one was 'therey'. He liked using it for anything and everything. Right now he pointed with his finger and said 'Therey.'

'She's not there. Not anywhere.'

'Therey...'

'No, let's go for a walk; will you walk?'

'Wok,' he agreed, and once Bhabani put him down, trotted on quite happily for a while; then, came to a halt. He pointed to something ahead and said, 'Fox.'

'Where?'

It wasn't a fox, but a big snail lying on the path.

'Come on, that's nothing,' said Bhabani, holding Khoka by his hand. Khoka refused to budge and put up his arms wanting to be carried.

'No, come now, nothing to fear. Come on ahead,' urged Bhabani.

Khoka crossed the snail, albeit with some trepidation, but with complete trust in his father whose hand he clutched. His attitude was that of a devotee who has uncomplainingly surrendered himself to the divine. If only we could be so, thought Bhabani. How much his little boy was teaching him. It pained him to have to sit down at the chandimandap whiling away his time with the regulars.

A child was a marvellous creation of a great artist. How often he had been moved in contemplating the constellations in the sky. Gazing upwards at them was to be absorbed in meditation. How often, during the time he spent at his guru's ashram, Chaitanyabharati Maharaj would point to the heavens and say,

'Look upon the immortal Akshara Purusha:
The One whose head is Fire, the sun and the moon his eyes,
all directions his ears, all Vedas his speech,

the wind his life, his heart the universe, at his feet the earth—
that One is the inner spirit of all living creatures.'

It was Chaitanyabharati who had taught him to see the skies, had opened his inner eye. It was he who had taught him that just as millions and millions of sparks emerge from the fire, so too, from the Akshara, the indestructible Purusha, innumerable living creatures emerge, and into that they are absorbed—so went the immortal message of the Upanishads.

This child was a spark of that Fire; so was he not also the Fire? Was he *himself* not so too? And these wild bushes and jungle, these birds—were *they* not too a part of it? The laughter of this pure child and his meaningless babble brought to him signs of another world. Just as he became happy when the child loved him, he too, was a child of divinity, and if he loved the divine, would not bhagwan be pleased in the same manner?

It was many years now that he had left behind the life of a sannyasi, where all day and night they were immersed in discourse... there was no other talk but that of immortal being. Traversing the phases of infinite star-filled nights, the devout seekers of knowledge, sleeping not a moment, restrained their minds where they laid their souls at the feet of the Creator of the universe. Every leaf of every tree on the Himalayan forests was inscribed with a tradition of meditative search spanning across aeons; inscribed too, on the snow-fed silver rushing waterfalls; the quest fuelled with intense inward-looking fervour, of silent peace within hidden forests where the seekers would make their offering of love towards the supremely beautiful deity.

He had not seen with his own eyes those devoted seekers who had moved on to a higher level. But their signs had come down to him flowing down icy currents from the highest peaks. In the depths of those sombre meditative spaces, like the centre of the chariot wheel all those tranquil and self-controlled spirits had ripped away all ignorance, through the power of knowledge, the power of love.

Bhabani Barujje believed that such spirits existed. He had heard of them from the sadhus.

It is because they existed that there was still discrimination between good and evil; in this fraudulent world where deception reigned supreme, bhagwan was still remembered, the moon and the sun still rose, and the darkness made fragrant by the scent of wild flowers.

Having come to these rural places he had marked that everyone was engrossed in land, taxes and money, in oppressing peasants and gossiping. No one mentioned or ever brought up a topic that had to do with goodness. They appeared to be completely oblivious about bhagwan. They worshipped some weird object that they called bhagwan, seating him on the throne, or they shook in terror at his name, only stretching out their hands to ask for this and that. They never ever tried to know something of the Truth of that Supreme Being, his unwavering compassion. All they discussed was whether some young girl had spoken with someone in secret, or that someone's wife had walked with her head uncovered. There was not a single person with whom he could sit down and speak his mind. Only Ramkanai Kobiraj and the crazy sannyasini who had made her home by the banyan tree; there was some delight in conversing with them about bhagwan. They enjoyed his discourse. There was no one else in the entire village, for they had never stepped out of their village and seen any other land. How beautifully they embodied all that was narrow and insular in their philosophy, in their behaviour, their thoughts and their work.

How much better was the company of this child who did not know how to lie; who would not rake up questions of property or wealth, didn't know how to slander others; a transparent spirit just come from some unknown eternal bourne to take up its habitation in this tiny little body. No worldly taint had yet touched him; how would the ordinary person know how precious was the company of these infants?

Thick forests of scrubs lined both sides of the path. The child toddled along merrily. He stopped for a moment to look up at the sky and said something to himself.

'Khoka, what are you saying?' Bhabani asked him.

'No come,' said Khoka.

'What hasn't come, my dear? What is to come?'

'Moooon.'

'Would the moon come now, my son? Only at night. Come, let's go.'

'Foxy,' said Khoka, fear edging his voice.

'No, there's nothing to be afraid of. There are no foxes.'

'O, Baba!'

'What is it?'

'Ma!'

'Come, let's go. Ma's not at home now, let her come back. What will you have to eat where we are going?'

'Muki.'

'Good, come now. What will you eat?'

'Muki.'

There was quite a crowd at Mahadev Mukhujje's chandimandap. Foni Chakkarty who first spotted Bhabani, welcomed him profusely, 'Come babaji, how come you're here in the morning? Aah! You've come out for a walk with Khokon. Come, let's have a round of *pasha*—'

'I'm not going to be here for long, Uncle,' said Bhabani laughing. 'All right, I shall play a round. But Khoka is bound to make mischief; will he let me play?'

'Let me send him indoors,' offered Mahadev Mukhujje and called out, 'O Mungli, Mungli...'

'No, let him be, Uncle. He'll not want to go anywhere. He will start crying.'

The chandimandap was a quintessential institution of rural Bengal. It was the meeting ground for a group of ignorant, useless brahmans who sat there from morning to night, smoking up huge quantities of tobacoo, playing board games. They did not play cards, which were considered a 'furrin or ingriz' affectation in the villages. They lived off the revenue from the brahmottar land they had inherited. Only the well-to-do householder could afford the daily quota of half a seer of tobacco that made his chandimandap more popular than those of others. Chandra Chatujje, Foni Chakkarty and Mahadev Mukhujje were considered to be amongst the top rung of the brahmans in their village. Dewan Rajaram Ray was prosperous but he was usually caught up in the affairs of the Neelkuthi; there never was any such session at his chandimandap. These brahman men who simply gathered to chat and gossip, to play unending rounds of pasha and daba, knew nothing of struggle, cared nothing about earning a livelihood. They got the revenue that their raiyats gave them, got rice that grew in their trust land, they had orchards of mango and jackfruit, climbing vines of pumpkins and gourds; they bought fish on credit from the fishermen, paying them only a month or two later. So what did they have to worry about? Even the oil-presser brought them oil on credit, merely marking out the dues on the fence; to be sorted out only at month-end. Where life was so comfortable, these people had found it easy to fall into slothful ways...giving rise to frustration and evil doings.

All of this Bhabani had long observed from the time he had married and settled down in the village. He had not quite known what rural life in Bengal was. He had always been a traveller, wandering over hills and plains to the sound of the fast flowing waters of the mountain springs in faraway places. Marriage had now bound him to this place, and in particular, pulled him perforce into this lot of narrow-minded people. They were people who had no aim in life, who lived their entire lives shrouded in darkness. Nor did they make any effort or hold a desire to find out what lay on the other side of their familiar world.

'O Khokon, what is your name?' asked Mahadev Mukhujje.

Khokon kept looking at Mahadev Mukhujje, his big eyes filled with fear and surprise. He didn't say a word.

'What's your name, Khokon?'

'Khokon.'

'Khokon? Nice name! Hey, it's my hand—and what was the fall of dice...?'

After the game had gone on for a while, puffed rice and grated coconut was sent from the house for everyone. They fell back to their game with renewed vigour immediately after the snack. They played as though it was the sole reason for their existence.

Satyambar Chatujje's son-in-law, Srinath, now joined them. He worked in Calcutta, so enjoyed a certain status amongst the villagers. Not one of the brahmans of this village had ever been to Calcutta. And that included Dewan Rajaram. They had no real need to go to Calcutta; why would they want to venture to an unknown city, putting themselves into a sea of imaginary dangers? Their boys weren't interested in learning or education, for they knew that their livelihood was assured.

'Come in, babaji,' said Foni Chakkarty to Srinath. 'What's the news from Kolketey?'

Srinath often brought them strange and sensational news. He was their only link to the outside world. Today, he carried what seemed to them another such strange bit of news.

'The big news is that someone has murdered our Burra Laat!' he announced.

'Murdered? Who murdered him?' cried out everyone in a chorus.

'A Pathan, a Wahabi type.'

'And who was our Burra Laat?' enquired Madhav Mukhujje.

'Laad Meo.'

'Laad Meo?'

The game of pasha fell apart. Frankly, they didn't care whether Lord Mayo was alive or dead; in fact, many of them heard the name for the first time. But the great thing was that something novel had happened to stir up the everyday sameness of their lives. Srinath told the story with great detail and relish, how offices, the court—everything in Calcutta, was shut down on account of Lord Mayo's assassination.

By the time Bhabani got back home with Khoka it was quite late in the afternoon.

'Don't you have any sense?' Tilu scolded him. 'Where were you with Khoka all this time? Wouldn't he be dying of hunger? Where *were* you?'

'Ma, Ma,' cried out Khoka, extending his arms to her.

'Oh, forget all that for a moment! Do you know that Laad Meo's been killed?

'And who is that, my dear?'

'He is our Burra Laat.'

'And who killed him?'

'A Pathan.'

'Poor thing, why did they kill him? It makes me so sad.'

≈

Shortly after the assassination of Lord Mayo the situation worsened for the indigo planters. The plantation sahebs held meetings thick and fast. The magistrate saheb began sending his orderly with summons every now and then.

Rajaram was riding towards the Neelkuthi one day when he came upon Ramkanai Kobiraj standing beneath a tree.

'Dewan-babu, will you stop a moment?' requested Ramkanai.

'What is it?' demanded Rajaram, frowning.

'Just stop awhile. Listen to me, don't go ahead: the bagdis from Kansona have all gathered and are waiting for you by the Shashtitala field. They want to kill you—they're ready with their sticks. I'm telling you because I've come to know of it. I've been waiting here for you for a long while.'

'Who are the people in their gang?'

'That I don't know, babu. I'm a poor man. It came to my ears, so I felt I must tell you—I cannot follow the path of *adharma*. I'll have to answer to bhagwan one day, won't I? You are a brahman; it is He who has given me the task of warning you.'

When he saw that Rajaram was bent on riding ahead despite his words, Ramkanai Kobiraj began pleading with folded hands, 'Dewanbabu, please listen to me—it's dangerous for you to go that way! Don't go ahead at all. No, babu! O babu, do listen—'

But Rajaram had already galloped far away.

Rajaram was thinking, Ramkanai Kobiraj must be mad! How bitterly he had been humiliated by the people of Neelkuthi, and he, Rajaram, was the cause of it; and look at him now—trying to warn and 'save' that very person! A pack of lies!

As soon as his horse set foot on Shashtitala field he was ringed by a huge group of people armed with sticks and staves. Among those in the group Rajaram recognized the elder son, Haru, and Naran Sardar, brother-in-law of Ramu Bagdi who had been killed during the attack on his bundh.

The end was swift.

One in the group shouted out, 'Come on, you rascal, get off your horse right now. Won't let you get back today.'

'This rascal's a dog of the sahebs. Watch—we're going to play quoits with your head on this very Shasthtitala field.'

'Don't waste words!' called out someone. 'Just grab him by the neck and bring him down, make him sit down with his knees against his chest and send his head flying with a blow of the billhook—that's all!'

'You move away,' said Haru to his friends, 'Let me handle this. This bastard sent his men to beat my father to death!'

'Where's that Rasik-baba of yours?' a voice taunted the dewan. 'Call him—let him come and save you! You're about to enter Hell, my precious.'

With a swish a hand-spear came at him and grazed his left ribs. If his horse hadn't shied away in fright, Rajaram would have been finished right then. His head was spinning, he simply couldn't think, stars flashed before his eyes, a storm swirling around the coconut tree, strange things happening all around him. Where had Ramkanai Kobiraj gone? Ramkanai?

A stick came down on his head. He felt dizzy and weak.

Again, he felt a cold sharp touch inside his left ribs. What was happening to him? All this water…? 'Bastard—d'you remember Ramu!' he heard someone say.

Rajaram raised his hand to ward off the stick coming at him from someone facing him. How could he ward off all those sticks? Where was all this water coming from? Momentarily his gaze went to his own clothes; immediately, he felt nauseous. As though he had a high fever and his head was whirling, he was feeling weak and wanting to throw up. The very earth was reeling.

That beautiful little boy of Tilu's seemed to be sitting somewhere at one end of the field, smiling and chuckling to himself. How he was smiling! Then Rajaram did not know anything more. His eyes shut on their own.

The entire world was shrouded in the darkness of a moonless night.

It was all over by the time the villagers roused by Ramkanai's scared and terrorized pleas gathered around with their sticks and staves and came running to the Shashtitala field. Rajaram's bloodied body was found lying in the dust. It was lifeless.

≈

A year went by.

The turmoil in this region that followed Rajaram's death had recently died down. Jagadamba had stubbornly wanted to be cremated with her husband, but Tilu, Bilu and Nilu had with great difficulty dissuaded her. Jagadamba did not live long after her husband's death. She had turned slightly mad. The three sisters-in-law nursed her lovingly through this time. At the time of the Durga Puja, she lay feverish for three days and then passed away. She was cremated at the Kadamtala grounds, finally, beside her husband. Now Tilu's little boy became heir to the vast property left behind by Rajaram. The villagers had entreated the family to move into the ancestral home in which Rajaram had lived. Why Bhabani had forbidden this move, God alone knew. Therefore, it was still on that little plot of land given by Rajaram, in that little thatched hut, that the family went on living. Tilu finally brought it up before her husband one day.

'Tilu, why do you—even you, make this request of me?' asked Bhabani in turn.

'Why not? Explain it to me. Why will you not live in the house built by your father-in-law?'

'No, my son will never accept this house.'

'Not the property either?'

'No, Tilu, you must not be angry. This is wealth accumulated by oppressing countless people. I do not wish my son to be nourished on food that comes from such a source. Listen to me Tilu: I have kept the company of many good people; this much I've learnt—there is bound to be waste and evil, wherever there is luxury and excess. The spirit, the soul, is stained. Why else do think Chaitanyadeva instructed Raghunath Das, "Do not wear well and do not eat well"?'

'Whatever you think is best...'

'I've often told that mine is another path. Your Dada's work—don't mind my saying so—I never cared for. It was he who had Ramu Bagdi killed. Ramkanai's torture and humiliation—it was all ordered by him. It was the same Ramkanai who tried to warn him of danger. It is fated: he wouldn't even listen to the man! But let that be! If my Khoka lives, he will live a different life. He will not be greedy. He will be simple, following the path of dharma, of truth. If he wishes to know bhagwan, he has to live in simplicity, with humility. You cannot experience the divine if your mind is entangled in worldy affairs. That is how I shall raise him.'

'Will he become a sannyasi as you had?'

'You know that I had not actually taken the orders. My gurudev maharaj (here Bhabani bowed in reverence to his guru) had told me, "Son, you are yet to enjoy life." He had not granted me sannyas. He could see my future clearly. He had blessed me though, that even while living in the midst of *sansar*, I would not forget my love of God. I would not step on the path of untruth, greed or evil. What has been called in the *Srimad Bhagavad*: '*bittashathya no*', that is, forgery and malpractice for profit—I would never indulge in. Should I now push my son onto that very path? That is the inevitable outcome if he inherits and enjoys your Dada's wealth.'

'In that case, what will happen to Dada's wealth?'

'Why, there's you?'

'My son is not to accept it, and shall I? What do you think I am?'

'Your sisters, then?'

'Why would you push them onto the path of worldliness?'

'What if they wish to?'

'Even if they do, you are their husband, their supreme guru. They are ignorant women; why would you not explain it to them?'

'That is not how it is, Tilu: they are adults, if they desire to they should enjoy it. One cannot persuade by force.'

'Why should you force; you will explain. Let me first find out how they feel, and I will speak with you.'

'Well, do so. And if no one accepts it, you can offer the property and wealth in your Dada's name and in your Bou-didi's name in the service of the poor and the needy. That will help their souls, satisfy their spirit.'

≈

That very afternoon Hala Pekey made a sudden appearance.

'O Bor-di!' he called out from afar. 'Where's Khoka?'

Tilu called for Khoka and asked her son, 'Tell me, who is this?'

'Dada,' said Khoka looking at him.

'Not Dada, an uncle—your mama, your mother's brother.'

'Mama!' said Khoka.

Hala Peke took out a pair of gold bangles and tried to slip them on to Khoka's arms, but Tilu stopped him, 'No dada, I can't let him wear those.'

'Why, didi?'

'Unless he first consents, I cannot accept it.' She meant her husband.

'That time too, you didn't let him take it. If you don't this time too, won't I feel hurt, didimoni?'

'What can I do, dada? Why do you bring these things?'

'Because I feel like giving them, that's why. Khokon, do you love your uncle?'

Khokon, staring in amazement at Hala Pekey's face, said, 'Yes.'

'How much do you love me?'

'One much!'

'One much! That's good.'

Khokon stretched out his hands and took hold of the gold bangles that Hala was carrying. Clapping his hands in delight, Hala said, 'There didimoni, he's taken them! Khoka darlin' will wear them, and you won't be giving them to him; see how it is?'

In the meantime, Bhabani Barujje came home. 'And where have you come from?' he asked looking directly at Hala Pekey.

Hala Pekey arose and made a complete prostration before Bhabani.

'Ah, such devotion!' said Bhabani smiling. 'So how was the booty this time? Oh! What's that in Khokon's hands—bangles?'

'Hala-dada has brought them for Khokon,' replied Tilu.

Hala Pekey's face showed his anxiety.

'But listen to what your Khoka did,' said Tilu with a laugh. 'My darling, how much do you love your uncle?'

'One much,' said Khokon.

'An' will you be taking the bangles?'

'Yes.'

'No, no,' Bhabani cut in, 'take the bangles away. Why should we take them?'

Hala Pekey did not dare to say anything before Bhabani, but his face fell.

Tilu tried to intervene: 'You know, dada *wishes* to give them. You didn't take anything the last time he brought something—on the day of Khokon's rice-eating ceremony...'

Hala Pekey was silent. The dumb have no enemies.

'All right, you may leave them behind this time. But never again must you—'

Hala Pekey's face lit up in delight. He took the dust of Bhabani's feet and said, 'I won't be bringing anything anymore. I have now become wise. But this is not *that* sort of thing. This is my own.'

'Wisdom you will not have—that will come only with death. You are getting on in years. Why continue with the evil business? Aren't you afraid of the life to come?'

'You're not to scold him now. Can't you see there's hunger written all over his face?' said Tilu. 'Come now dada, come over to the kitchen!'

Encouraged by her words, Hala Pekey followed her and sat on the raised platform to the kitchen.

It was a mystery how Tilu and her son had managed to exercise such power over a terrifying dacoit like Hala Pekey. He followed Tilu around like he was her pet, pleasure and shyness bursting from his face.

The verandah made of clay and packed earth was polished and shiny with dungwash. Flowers of the bittergourd creeper peeked out from the thatched roof. Behind the hut lay the deep shadows cast by the bamboo grove of their neighbour, Shyam Chakkatty. Hordes of mynahs and babblers chattered and shrieked. Alighting on the slim end of a bamboo, a blue-throated barbet was having a nice swing. The dry bamboo leaves let off a particular fragrance. A creeper of wild nettle had wound its way along the kitchen window. Tilu put down before Hala Pekey one khunchi of roasted rice, some green chillies and half a ripe coconut. In a stone bowl she served him a big lump of date-palm jaggery.

The one khunchi of roasted rice disappeared in a few moments. Hala Pekey must have been ravenous. 'Didi-thakuron, if you have some more, you can give me some more!'

'Sit awhile, dada, and I'll get it for you. Tell us a story of your dacoity, will you, dada?'

Hala Pekey sat down to another bowl of roasted rice and began recounting his tale of how he and Aghore Muchi had gone to loot Nilmoni Mukhujje of Bhandarkhola village. He found only four or five men in the family, while there were about ten women. There were two hired helps, one of who lived along with his family in the room next to the cattleshed. They debated on whether they would lay siege to the house. Finally though, it was decided to go in for looting. They broke open the outer door with a pestle, and found that the men were ready with sticks and spears. The women were screaming away something dreadful.

'The poor things!' said Tilu.

'Hardly poor things! Listen on now, didimoni. My very life it was that was a-going to leave me that night. Little did we know that there was a widow called Dakkhayani inside the cattleshed who was handling the spear something powerful—she would've put old Nibaron Buno to shame! She it was who showed us her amazing hand! The men were all huddled indoors, not one showed himself.'

'Goodness! And then?'

'The men threw down the chanpa-shiri from the top and then they started to rain bricks and things at us. And the spear goin' at us at full tilt all the while. One of us got injured.'

'Died?'

'Not right away. Died by our hands. When we saw how Dakkhayini was going strong and we were in the open, we knew that we would cop it and be finished off one by one, so we sounded our *jhompo.*'

'What might that be?'

'Produced such a terrifying sound that a woman would drop the baby inside her—want to hear it? No better not…it would scare Khoka. We made sure that the men couldn't come down from the roof. Sent that spear slithering like a snake's tongue back and forth up and down, wrenching out their guts with each swoop—three or four of them went down. Meanwhile the villagers had surrounded us: no way to get out, and that Dakkhayini from the cowshed still at us with her spear. Aghore signed to us to get away—but how could we? Then, we tried our last trick—came out with a double-pronged stick that we call *dui hattha*—keeping the head held right, spinnin' and whirlin' like a potter's wheel, cut a path for my group through that crowd of people. The one who had been wounded, we cut off his head, and got away. He was Banshidhar Sardar, poor man—used to be great with the spear—'

'But that's strange! Why did you kill him?'

'If we *hadn't*, they would identify his body and get us all. And if he survived, he would spill the beans about the gang.'

'A disaster!'

'Would've been a disaster. Somehow we managed to get away. Looted a lot of gold ornaments that time—weighing thirty *bhori*.'

'How did you do *that*? You said the women were upstairs after they let down the chanpa-shiri.'

'Did what we had to long afore that. Can't stop fer a moment, can you, if you are going to do a dacoity? Look aroun', and snatch the stuff right away. Scream away all you like after it's done—you got the whole long night to wail.'

'You mustn't do this, dada. It's really wicked. How can you bear to eat food from what you've looted in this way? Stained with the tears of so many, it must be. For shame! Is it enough simply to fill your belly?'

Hala Pekey was silent for a while. Then he said, 'Don't say anything about grace and sin to me. It's all over now for us—not that rule any more, not that land. You know, when we were little we used to sing this verse:

> Hail Raja Sitaram, Bengal's Bahadur!
> At whose command all looting stopped.
> Lamb and tiger drink side by side,
> Safe the commoner on his pilgrim-path.'

'Oh, that one *we* know too!' said Tilu laughing. 'Heard old Dinu say it often when we were children.'

'Why wouldn't you know it! Sitaram was king of Nadia Pargana. The fort was in Masudpur, at my maternal uncle's: his home is in Hariharnagar, near Masudpur. I've seen them—Sitaram's fort, the stones and the broken bricks, that huge lake of his called Sukhsagar, the Sea of Happiness. Now of course, it's all forest and jungle, enormous snakes, tigers and what not. Used to be a huge madar tree in that jungle; I loved the fruits when I was a boy—real sweet they were—'

'Weet! I eat,' declared Khoka.

'Yes, you must eat them, Khoka. Won't I bring you some, won't I bring you mangoes when they ripe...'

'Eat mango.'

'Do eat. Why won't you?'

Bhabani sat down to his prayers after a bath. Tilu brought him a bowl of cucumber slices, half a coconut, grated, and some date-palm jaggery. Hala Pekey had rice amounting to a katha, after Bhabani had eaten. Dal, he had almost a tub full. Then he lay down to rest.

Some time later they heard the sound of wailing from the Mukhujje's house. 'Pekey-dada, will you go and have a look—find out who's crying?' Tilu requested Hala.

Bhabani went along with Hala. When they returned Bhabani said, 'There's been a shipwreck and Uncle Foni's elder uncle has perished. Ganesh just came back with the news.'

'Oh no!' said Tilu, 'A shipwreck?'

'Yes, a ship called *Sir John Lawrence*...'

'Do *ships* also have names?'

'Of course they do. This one sank on the way to Puri. Many people have died.'

'At least seven or eight from our village went on that pilgrimage. Togor Kumar's mother, Pencho milkman's mother-in-law, the eldest daughter Khenti who is a widow, Raju Sardar's mother, and Uncle Nilmoni's elder sister. What a pity, Khenti's little boy was with her! Only seven years old, he was.'

The village resounded with weeping and mourning. On the ghats along the river, in the chandimandap of the well-to-do, the granaries and threshing floor of the peasants, the crowd in the markets, in Nalu Pal's big warehouse and the grocery shop—everywhere, there was no other talk but of the unfortunate *Sir John Lawrence*.

A large number of ordinary folks from various districts of Bengal perished with the ship.

≈

Gaya-mem had barely come out of the Burra Saheb's kuthi and walked a little distance when she heard Prasanna Amin call out, 'O Gaya, listen, O Gaya—'

Gaya looked back and said, 'I've no time for any sweet talk now.'

'Listen, there's something I have to say…'

'What is it?'

'Will you be home later today?'

'What is it to you whether I'm there or not?'

'Nothing, just that—'

'Not one more word here! If you have anything to say, come to our house after evenin'. Whatever you have to say you can say before my mother.'

'No. No, what do you think I'm going to say now!' said Prasanna Chakkarty with a broad smile. 'But how are you these days? Looking a bit thin…that's why I'm asking.'

'Enough! No need for all this drama out here on the road.'

No! It was impossible to figure out this Gaya. Just when he'd start believing that she was beginning to look upon him favourably, she'd turn away her face.

After she had gone Prasanna stood there foolishly, somewhat in a daze. He heard the sound of hooves behind him and turned around: it was Shipton Saheb setting off from his bungalow. He got very scared and wondered if the Burra Saheb had seen him talking to Gaya-mem. No…

It took forever before evening fell. The rosy red of the setting sun shone on the big chatka tree along the Baur. *Jhinge* flowers bloomed on the field of the sandbank, the *shyamcoot* birds flew away from the Ichhamati towards Akai Lake…and it was still not evening.

'O Barada-didi,' Prasanna Chakkarty called out apprehensively, as he stood outside their door. He didn't want to call out Gaya's name right away. But he was fortunate: it was Gaya-mem herself who came and stood before him, thrilling Prasanna Chakkarty to the core.

'Well, Khuro-moshai!' said she by way of a greeting.

'Barada-didi—isn't she home?'

'Why?'

'No, just asking.'

Gaya-mem smiled mischievously and said, 'Ooh, was it *Ma* that you needed to meet? I better go and call her. She's gone to the *jugi*-para—'

'No, no! Why don't you sit Gaya, there's a couple of things I need to tell you.'

'Such as?'

'Tell me, how do you find me?'

'An old man—what else?'

'Am I really that old? Now don't say such unfair things, Gaya! Isn't the Burra Saheb getting on in years?'

'Oh! No point talking about *them*. Tell me whatever you want to say—'

'Can you tell me why is it that I can't stay a moment without looking at you?'

'Death's face! Aren't you ashamed to say such things to me?'

'It's because I'm shy that I've not been able to say them so far.'

'Now you've done it. Has it come to this that you will stop at nothing?'

'No, truly Gaya, I've seen so many women, but seen none with such hair, and such womanliness like yours…'

'Forget all that. Let me give you a piece of advice. Listen—'

'What?'

'Tell me that you are not going to tell a soul.'

Prasanna Chakkarty's face lit up. Gaya had never spoken so intimately with him ever before. What oblique messages lay in that dark pair of arched eyebrows! And the light in her smile! Had heaven come down to the earth on this autumn afternoon?

What was Gaya going to tell him? What would she...
Prasanna Amin's heart fluttered.

'What is it Gaya, tell me, what is this thing you have to say?' There was intense eagerness in his voice. 'And why should I go and tell others about what's happening *between the two of us*?'

The strong emphasis on this last part of the sentence was apparently lost on Gaya. She replied in an utterly casual tone, 'Then listen; I'm saying this for your own good. Cracks are showin' up among the sahebs. They're all leaving. The Burra Saheb's mem will soon leave. She's a good woman. When she's leaving, go and ask her for something. She'll give it. She's a good sort. Listen to my words.'

Prasanna Chakkarty was intelligent. It wasn't as though he had no inkling of the situation. The sahebs would be leaving. He had known something of it. But why did Gaya choose to tell *him* this, after so long, today of all days? Why should Gaya-mem care *at all* about his joy or sorrow, his progress or his decline? A thrill of pleasure ran down Prasanna Chakkarty's back. In the mellow light of the early evening, and in the evening of his own life, Prasanna felt as though something new and unexpected was awaiting him.

'Why are the sahebs leaving?'

'Their time has come, Khuro-moshai. Don't you know?'

'I've been hearing things.'

'The entire district is mad at them. Every day there's a letter coming from the magister saheb...warning the sahebs. After all, they're all whites. They're removing the mems beforehand. I'd like to warn you—move around carefully. Don't treat the raiyats as you used to before. It won't do if you carry on the same way—'

'Why, what is to you if I die, Gaya?' Prasanna Chakkarty's voice had suddenly taken on a deep note.

'Nyaah! What is one to do with the likes of you!' said Gaya bursting into peals of laughter. 'Here I am trying to telling you something for your own good, and you start spouting nonsense!'

'What did I say that was so wrong, Gaya?' His voice was as deep as before, perhaps deeper.

'Back to all that nonsense again! I'm a telling you—all that I've just told you; did you take it in? Now wait, wait!'

Then Gaya stunned Prasanna Chakkarty by coming up very close to him and giving him a tremendous slap on his back. 'A mosquito! Just see!'

Prasanna Amin's body trembled. Was that the earth spinning so madly?

'Remember now, what I've told you. And *fo-llow* it up. Have you heard it all?' Gaya went on.

'Yes, I have. Gaya, if I don't follow what you say, what would it mean to you? How would it affect you; would it be a loss?'

'A hoot I'd care!' said Gaya angrily. 'What would it be to me? If you don't listen, you'll die like Dewanji.'

'You're not angry, Gaya, are you? Better that I was dead. And would there be anyone to shed a tear if I die?' Prasanna Chakkarty let out a deep sigh at this juncture.

'Ooh! Look at him! Such a show! Makes me wild with anger. Speaking theatrically like those *jatra* heroes. Said something sensible and straight—and what do I get instead? Who will shed a tear at my death, who will do this, that, and the other! Why can't you talk straight, may I ask?'

'Well, let it be.'

'Good.'

'You go wild with rage whenever you see me, isn't that so?'

'What do I know? How can I keep answering such silly questions? As if I don't have any work to do! You better leave now—Ma will be back any minute now.'

'Well, I shall leave now, Gaya.'

'Yes, you'd better.'

A disgruntled Prasanna Chakkarty had turned back when Gaya called out, 'O Khuro-moshai!'

'What is it?' said he, looking back.

'Listen.'

'Why don't you tell me what it is?'

'Now, don't you be angry.'
'No, I won't. I'll leave now.'
'But listen, won't you?'
'What?'
'You are a mad one!'
'Whatever you say Gaya. Listen, come closer.'
'No, you had better tell me from where you are.'
'Will you listen to a tappa of Nidhu-babu's?'
'No. You leave now, Ma's on her way.'

When Prasanna Chakkarty had gone on a little ahead, Gaya called out, 'Come again another day—did you hear that? Come again.'

'Why wouldn't I? Of course I shall. Certainly I will.'

Prasanna Chakkarty went walking along the distant field. He had come away a long distance from Gaya's home. He hoped he hadn't been seen by Barada. How sweetly Gaya could speak if she wanted to; she had even made sure that he would be gone before her mother got back.

But even more astonishing, even stranger, the most amazing thing that had occurred—Ooh! It made him tremble in delight simply to think of it—was the way Gaya had slapped that mosquito dead. Coming up so close to him! And done with such a beautiful gesture!

But was there really a mosquito sitting on his back? Did she use it as a pretext to come up close to him?

True, she had shown him something at that time; but did he have the vision in that blissful moment to actually see a dead mosquito?

It was evening. The blue sky of autumnal Sharat was like an upturned bowl over the field. Like a series of golden spears in the bamboo grove of the jugi-para, the new shoots of the bamboo glowed in the rosy red sun. That was where Gaya's Ma was visiting. Thank God, she wasn't home; he wouldn't have had that talk with Gaya today otherwise. He wouldn't even have seen her. Such a beautiful day of Sharat would have gone in vain, in vain such a glorious evening.

Truly, it was a memorable day. All that he had been longing

for—had he got a taste of it today? Had he not been thirsty for a woman's love all these years?

≈

It was very late when Prasanna Chakkarty got home. It was a small hut he had in the Neelkuthi premises, with a tiny thatched room for a kitchen. Thank goodness, Amin Nakul Dhara was not there; he would've jabbered away in the most tiresome way. Prasanna was making himself some rice: he had put in whole plantains and bitter gourds to cook in the rice. Why cook at all? He didn't really feel like eating. Only wanted to dream about that...strange gesture of Gaya-mem's, her smile...Gaya had actually come up close to him and had slapped him on the back, to kill a mosquito!

Had a mosquito really sat on him?

What if...he was cooking, and Gaya with her smiling face peeked in to say, 'O Khuro-moshai, what are you up to?'

'I'm cooking, Gaya.'

'And what are you cooking?'

'Vegetables in rice.'

'Truly, yours is a hard lot...'

'What can I do, Gaya? There's no one I can call my own. Who cares about what I eat or do?'

'I've got fish for you. Good quality khoira fish.'

'Why do you worry so much about me, Gaya?'

'I keep fretting 'bout you...You live alone, suffer so much...'

The rice was cooked—it was getting scorched! He got a whiff of it. Prasanna Chakkarty sat down to eat his slightly burnt meal garnishing it with mustard oil. The flame from the double-layered lamp lit by castor oil flickered in the moist wind. When he was almost done, Prasanna realized that he had not sprinkled any salt on the vegetables and rice he had been eating.

But, the mosquito...had it really sat on his back?

≈

On his way back from his morning dip in the Ichhamati, Ramkanai Kobiraj discovered some lovely *nak-joaley* flowers that had bloomed atop the bushes bordering the river. They would be good for offering in his puja. He was greatly tempted to pick them. He was delayed coming back to his hut, as he had to make his way through thorny bushes to get the flowers.

It was his daily practice to have a bath before he sat down to worship his little Radha-Krishna, a doll-like image crafted by a village potter. He had bought it at the Charak fair at Bhashanpota. He loved arranging nak-joaley flowers around the icon, making sandalpaste and anointing the feet, lighting a couple of incense sticks before it. On some days he would offer slices of guava, pieces of papaya, or even a lump of cane sugar. If left undisturbed, he would be lost in worship for a long time. At times he would quietly weep. With a shy gesture he would wipe away his tears.

'Are you home, Kobiraj-moshai?' someone called out.

'Who is it? Coming...'

'I've been sent by Ambika Mondol from Sabaipur—his son has fever. You have to come.'

'All right, I'm coming. Just sit for a while.'

When he had finished his puja Ramkanai took some of the prasad and gave it to the man waiting outside.

'What is the illness?'

'Three days of fever.'

'You be on your way, I shall come there after looking in on two more patients.'

Ramkanai ate two pieces of cucumber and set off on his rounds. It was almost two in the afternoon by the time he got to Ambika Mondol's home at Sabaipur. He stood outdoors and called out. Ambika Mondol was a very poor man who lived by farming brinjals. His boy had been ill for three days and had gone without any medicine or food.

Ramkanai Kobiraj examined the boy with great care and then said, 'The pulse isn't very good. It will get disrupted.' The family members begged him to stay on. No one knew that he hadn't yet eaten. On an empty stomach, Ramkanai Kobiraj sat patiently by the boy's side until evening. He came home and performed his puja, cooked some food for himself and then went back to Sabaipur again to check on the boy.

Ramkanai's reading of the pulse was remarkably astute. The patient took a turn for the worse around midnight. Ramkanai had to use some medicinal poison and deal with the crisis. It was a small room; they spread out a mat on a low seat, and on this he rested until dawn. When he next checked the boy's pulse, he said, his face grave, 'The patient will not survive. The fever is marked by disturbance of blood, bile and phlegm, there are signs of delirium—it is enteric fever. I will be off. You needn't give me anything.'

He was not perturbed that he had not earned a cowrie from all the efforts he had put in; he only grieved that he hadn't been able to save the patient.

Lately, Ramkanai had acquired a pupil. He was twenty-two-year-old Nimai, the son of Akrur Chakrabarty of Bhajanghat. He found Nimai sitting on the patch of fine durba-grass outside his house, busy reading an old handwritten text of *Madhav Nidhan*. He got up and touched his teacher's feet as soon as Ramkanai came home.

'Come in my son Nimai, sit down. What is the nature of the pulse beat?'

'Sir, I didn't quite understand.'

'When is it a dangerous pulse?'

'When there is a pause after three, and a pause after four.'

'Why so? Won't it be equally so if it's after seven or eight?'

'Yes sir, it will be so.'

'That's right. I saw a patient today where there was a pause after seven. I've just come from his bedside.'

'Recovered?'

'Even the master of medicine, Dhanvantari himself, couldn't have cured him. As it is said in Sushruta: *kriti sadhya bhaveta sadhya*. I must tell you something, my son. You've come to study the art of medicine. You must not harbour any negative humour within. Never speak a false word. Never be greedy. Be contented with little. Treat the poor without charging them. Keep your faith in God. Do not indulge in any addiction. Only then will you become a good kobiraj. Our gurudev, Gangadhar Sen Kobiraj of Mangalganj, would always tell us so.' Pausing to make a gesture of respect towards his guru, Ramkanai went on, 'You see, I was his much loved pupil. I have not been worthy of him. He only had to read the pulse and speak out the diagnosis—and it would turn out exactly so. He would say, you need to have a pure mind; else, you cannot read the pulse. Now, will you have a bite to eat?'

'No, gurudev,' his pupil answered shyly.

'From the look on your face, seems like you've not eaten anything. What shall I give you—there's nothing at home. Ah yes, there's a coconut; why don't you husk it?'

'Is there a cleaver?'

'Get one from Batakrishna Samanta's, the house that's by the river in the bamboo grove. Will you recognize it or shall I come with you?'

'No, I'll find it.'

Teacher and pupil had some coconut slices along with a handful of roasted kalhai-dal before sitting down to their studies. They went on until it was two *prahar* into the afternoon. Even if the pupil was remotely aware of the passing hours, the guru was completely lost in another world. While teaching the text of *Madhav Nidaan*, Charak was introduced, from Charak he moved to *Kalpa-Vyakarana*, and finally to the *Srimad Bhagavad*. Ramkanai Kobiraj was a fine Sanskrit scholar: he had even studied the *upadhis* in grammar.

Ramkanai recited to his pupil several slokas which he explicated:

> 'Empty your mind of worldly thoughts and desires
> and with devotion meditate on God.'

'You understand, my son, the One is supremely compassionate. In the *Chaitanyacharitamrit*, Kaviraj Goswami has said,

> 'The One grants grace, it is only enough to seek
> refuge at His feet.
> Looking upon the ignorance of humans,
> who else but the One will grant them grace?'

His disciple came back with the kindling he had gathered in the bamboo forest.

The guru said, 'Why didn't you pick a tuber from the bamboo grove? Aren't there any?'

'Yes, there are lots.'

'Get one. You can borrow a spade from Batakrishna; have you returned their cleaver? Do so. Dig up a big-sized tuber, there's nothing to eat at home. We'll cook it in some rice and have it with mustard sauce. And listen, ask for a couple of green chillies when you are at Batakrishna's.'

'Gurudev, won't the tuber make our mouth itch?'

'Course not. With the mustard sauce, it won't.'

'One shouldn't eat a fresh ole; you have to dry it in the sun for a couple of days...'

'I know all that. But we'll have to eat *something* with the rice. Go and fetch one now. You'll be having your meal here with me...'

After a meal of boiled rice and tuber, garnished with the mustard paste, guru amd shishya went back to their studies. From the bamboo grove, the *piring piring* of a drongo heralded evening. Indoors, it grew too dark to continue with the reading; at his guru's bidding, disciple Nimai Chakrabarty tied up the manuscripts.

'Then I shall be on my way, gurudev,' he said, prostrating himself before the teacher.

'But how will you go? Clouds a-plenty over the bamboo forest; it's going to pour. You haven't brought your umbrella today.'

'The stick's broken. I'm making a new one. Brought some tender leaves of the palm and planted them in the clay; they'll ferment nicely in about a week's time. That will make a really strong umbrella—'

'Why, you can make just as good a one with keya leaves!'

'Doesn't last, gurudev. Nothing as good as those made with palm leaves—'

'Who says they don't? Not everyone knows how to tie one with keya leaves.'

Soon after, Gaya-mem entered with some ripe bananas. She bowed in respect from a distance and kept standing there.

'Come in my little mother, come in and sit down. What's that in your hand?'

'Bananas—from our tree,' said Gaya, somewhat reassured. 'I've come to offer some to you. I hope you will have them.'

'I can't; never take any gifts from anyone.'

'Take it with one cowrie, then.'

'I accept food from the patient's family. There's no harm in that. Batakrishna Samanta is a patient of mine. He's suffering from asthma: I do take a few things from his home. But my dear, you are not a patient of mine. And I pray that you never have to become one.'

'It's because of illness that I've come to you.'

'What illness?'

'A cold of sorts; can't sleep at night,' said Gaya hesitatingly.

'Is that right?'

'That's so. You are Shiva manifest. If one were to lie before you, wouldn't I have to rot in hell?'

'No, don't say such things,' said Ramkanai sounding distressed. 'I'm nobody. Let me give you some medicine...pound it in ginger and honey and have it.'

'Baba...'

'Yes?'

'Why aren't other people like you? Why are people so evil?'

'I too am of that group. How would I be any different? There's one good man in the village, that's the Dewanji's brother-in-law, Bhabani Barujje. Doesn't lie, looks out for the poor; his household is presided by Lakshmi herself, and his mind is absorbed in thoughts of the divine.'

'I've seen him from afar. Scared to go close—telling you the truth now. We've done nothing with our lives. You know everything. I needn't tell you...'

'Call upon the One. His mercy is all. Far greater sinners—you are after all nothing—have crossed over.'

'There are times, baba, when I'm filled with regret. Feel like leaving everything behind and going off somewhere. Can't do it because of Ma. It was Ma who spoilt me. If she had died, I would have gone away—honestly—that's how I feel from time to time...'

Ramkanai was silent. He didn't think it was right to respond to any of this.

'Will you take the bananas then?' asked Gaya.

'Leave them behind. Wait, let me give you the medicine. You do have honey? Else, I'll give you some.'

Gaya left him after making another pranam to Ramkanai. On her way home she suddenly came upon Prasanna Chakkarty.

'Here, Gaya, where had you gone to? What's that in your hand?'

'It's medicine, Khuro-moshai. Why are you standing here?'

'I thought you would come this way.'

'You must not do this again. Move away from my path.'

'What's up? Why have you turned against me?'

'It's got nothing to do with turning for or against you. Do let me pass.'

Gaya stormed on ahead taking care to keep a distance between them. Prasanna Chakkarty, unable to muster up enough courage, could only call her by her name. She didn't spare him a backward glance.

No! There was simply no saying what a woman...

≈

All across the districts of Jessore and Nadia the Indigo Revolt began to make its presence felt. The new dewan, Harakali Sur, brought the news to the cutchery.

Shipton Saheb was in the eastern part of the Neelkuthi cleaning the barrel of his gun, when Harakali Sur came and greeted him with a salaam: 'Saheb, thirteen villages are up in arms. The Chhota Laat is coming over himself to visit the places. The subjects will tell him everything...'

'Hear me, Dewan,' said Shipton Saheb with a shake of his head. 'I knows very well how to keep the raiyats unter control. Those who had killed the former dewan—I had deir homes burnt and razed to the ground. These people want a revolt—do they? All the sahebs of all the neelkuthis had come together for a meeting—you knows?

'Yes, saheb, I do. I was then working at the plantation of Ranabijaypur—'

'Oh, *that* Ranabijaypur—where Jeffries Saheb was murtered?'

'He wasn't murdered, huzoor. He had too much to drink and fell off his horse, and became unconscious—'

'Aah, that's the handiwork of the native *amlas*! It was a plot against his life—I knows it all. Who was the manager? Robinson?'

'Yes, huzoor.'

'Now listen, carefully and cautiously. I want a very intrepid dewan. Like Rajaram was. But—'

He pointed to his head and said, 'He was not a brainy chap—something wrong with his think-box—no indelligens. Didn't know how to be careful—that's why he dies. You see the gun?'

'Yes, huzoor.'

'Seven new guns have come. Shipton have been my name. How to keep them unter control—I knows. I will shoot them like pigs.'

'Huzoor.'

'It has been decided in our meeting. We are not going to back oud. We shall not lisden to the Government. Shall kill if need be. The memsahebs will not be kept here—I shall be senting the memsaheb away—'

'When, huzoor?'

'Monday next, by boat from here to Mangalganj. She will be leaving by boat, keep the boat ready.'

'As you command, huzoor. Everything will be ready. Who will accompany her, huzoor?'

'What need? I don't think that is necessary.'

Dewan Harakali Sur kept his ears to the ground and had information from various sources. But he hadn't yet figured out how much to let out and how much to keep to himself. He scratched his head and said, 'Huzoor, it would be good if you accompanied—'

Shipton frowned and said, 'She can take care of herself—she knows how to protet herself. I neetn't go; you organize everyting.'

'Huzoor, I would like Karim Lathiyal in the boat…'

'What! Is it as bad as that? No neet. You may leave. You won't be able to run the Neelkuthi if you are being so scared. All right.'

'As you wish, huzoor.'

'Listen to something. Are you sure there's as much as that? What have you fount oud?'

'Huzoor, if you will allow me to speak frankly. Karim Lathiyal and the paiks should accompany our memsaheb. The plotting has gone far.'

'Oh, this I never imagined possible!' said the saheb, whistling a tune. 'It will make me feel different—it is hart to believe such a thing. All right, you may go. Leave everything to me—whatever we have to do—will do all that. Got it?'

Harakali Sur had been mingling with many a saheb for a long time. He was an expert in decoding their strange mish-mash of Bangla.

'Let me say something, saheb,' he responded, 'you make your own arrangements and let me make mine. Salaam, huzoor.'

Three days later Shipton's memsaheb took leave of the Neelkuthi and got aboard the *bajra* that was kept ready at Kooltala ghat. Ten pikemen and Karim Lathiyal went along with her, and Harakali Sur himself boarded a separate boat, following the bajra.

Amongst the old employees, Amin Prasanna Chakkarty went up to her with folded hands and said, 'Ma, my own mother goddess Jagadhatri who sustains the world—you are leaving us! Now, it will be all darkness in the Neelkuthi…' At this point, Prasanna Chakkarty broke down and began sobbing loudly.

'Don't you cry my good man—' the memsaheb said. 'Amin-babu do not weep! Why weeping?'

'Ma, you are leaving me in such a state! Ma, is there anything left for me now? Before whom can I speak of my sorrow, my Mother Jagadhatri...'

The clever Harakali Sur turned his face away to hide his amusement.

Without a moment's hesitation, Memsaheb took off the thin gold chain she was wearing around her neck and threw it in the direction of Prasanna Amin.

Hurriedly and with great dexterity Prasanna neatly caught the necklace.

Everyone was amazed—Harakali Sur was stunned and Karim Lathiyal was left open-mouthed.

The bajra took off from the ghat.

Prasanna Amin stood for a long time at the ghat watching the bajra slowly disappear. Then wiping his tears with the end of his cotton scarf, he too slowly climbed up the flank of the ghat.

With the departure of the Burra Saheb's memsaheb, the goddess of wealth and prosperity, Lakshmi herself, abandoned the Neelkuthi.

≈

'Well, Khuro-moshai!' said Gaya-mem, laughing away, 'You'll have to go halves with me!'

Doves cooing above the tall treetops only made sharper the stillness of the afternoon. From the nearby bushes came the fragrant blossoms of the *shyamlata* flowers. The two happened to meet by the banayan tree. It wasn't entirely by chance; Prasanna Chakkarty had been waiting there for a long time.

'Do take it,' he said with a smile. 'It was because of you—'
'There, didn't I tell you?'
'You take it. I'll be giving it to you alone...'
'You must be mad! You think I'm such a fool? What would everyone say if I were to use things belonging to them sahebs and

memsahebs? You think I'd so much as touch it!'

'I really like you, Gaya...'

'That's fine.'

'There's such delight when I see you...'

'Was it to say such things that you were standing here?'

'Well...umm...'

'Well, I'm off now. Please listen, there's something I must tell you. Start looking for a job somewhere else.'

'I know all about that. You think I don't realize that their might isn't the same anymore? I'm not such a fool. It's just that I don't have the heart to leave you behind and move some place else.'

'There you go again!'

'Why don't you come along with me?'

'Where to?'

'Wherever our eyes take us...'

'Would be utterly fulfilled, wouldn't I!' said Gaya sarcastically, giggling all the while. 'I'll come with you wherever our eyes take us!'

Prasanna Chakkarty wasn't sure what to make of her reply.

'O Khuro-moshai! Not saying a word?' said Gaya smiling away.

'What can I say? Don't feel brave enough to speak to you.'

'You've shown enough of bravery, needn't show any more! Let me tell you something. Tell me, where shall I go leaving my Ma behind? And those who have given me food and looked after me, not a little, for all these years—it wouldn't be right, would go against *dhamma*, if I left *them* and went away. *You* should leave though; where do you eat these days? Who cooks for you?'

Prasanna Chakkarty is unable to reply. He stares at Gaya. What was she telling him? No one had ever spoken to him in this way. Once again he sensed a shiver of happiness run through him. It was a unique sensation, as though he was going to lose consciousness; almost made him weep.

'Who cooks for you...' he repeated in an absent-minded way.

'Well...you could say, well, I cook my food myself.'

'I'd like to see how you cook it.'

'Why, would it be some kind of a holy persad?'

'That it would be, by your grace. What will you be cooking now?'

'Brinjals boiled alon' with the rice; mugi'r dal. I'll fry some khoira fish if I can get some at the Khola river.'

'You really haven't eaten, so late in the day?'

'No. I've been waiting for you for a while now. Been waiting for you to come away from the Neelkuthi.'

'Goodness, never heard such a thing in my life!' said Gaya angrily. 'What nonsense! Am I to knock my head at your feet out of gratitude? You must go home right way. No excuses. Go, now—'

'I'm jest about to, but...'

'Not one word more. Leave right now.'

As Gaya looked ready to leave, Prasanna Chakkarty sidled up to her (as close enough as he dared to) and said, 'You're not angry with me, I hope? Tell me Gaya.'

'No, I'm not angry; quite comforted and dee-ligh-ted by all that's happened! Why are you so foolish! Now go.'

'Don't be angry with me Gaya. I shan't live if you do.'

His words were an entreaty.

≈

Bhabani Barujje was about to set off on his evening walk when Khoka began to cry, 'Baba, I want to come...'

'No, you'd better stay with me,' said Tilu scolding him.

'Baba, I'll come...' said Khoka stretching out his hand.

Bhabani pointed to the umbrella and said, 'Who umbrella? 'My umbrella,' went on Bhabani.

'Will rain,' said Khokon.

'Of course it will.'

At such times when Bhabani carries his smiling little boy and goes for a walk he thinks this indeed must be the company of the good, the pure. Khoka too does not want to leave him for a second. Bhabani begins to understand the nature of the emotional bond between father and child.

'Hap-ning! Hap-ning!' cries out Khoka in his father's arms.

Only *he* knows the special significance that the word holds for him. Perhaps he wants to say that something funny has happened. Perhaps everything that is happening is amusing to him. Bhabani only knows that every now and then Khoka raises both his hands and joyously shouts, 'Hap-ning!'

'What's happening, Khoka?'

'Hap-ning! Hap-ning!'

'Where are you going Khoka?'

'Get mukki.'

'Will you eat murki, my love?'

'Umm.'

'Come, I'll buy you some.'

The rains have filled the river to the brim. Bhabani took his little boy to the Ichhamati and settled him down in a boat. Dense green on both banks, stray creepers swaying above the water, golden flowers radiant in the overhanging branches of the babul tree. On the other side, piles of blue clouds slowly floating towards them, the blue-throated barbet flitting from one green branch to another...a master artist's creation.

On this melodious afternoon Sribhagwan was present in the tranquil waters of the river, on land, above, in all four directions. His presence was in the child's laughter, in the golden flashes of the blue-throated barbet...in the banakalmi flowers blossoming on bushes along the bank. In all such things one might find signs of divinity.

'What water! Water!' exults Khoka, stretching out his hand. He is trying out words he has just learnt and loves to use.

'Khoka, is the river nice?'

'Nice,' he agrees with a turn of his neck.

'Shall we go home?'

'Yes.'

'But you said it was nice.'

'Home, Ma.'

Khoka is very afraid to come through the dark bamboo grove. The two-year-old child does not understand everything; he is simply terrified. He clutches hold of his father suddenly and says, 'Baba, 'fraid. That?'

'Why that's nothing!'

Khoka continues to cling on to his father's neck.

To free him of his fear Bhabani reassures him, 'What's that swaying in the forest?'

Now the boy opens his eyes and says, 'Fiefies.'

'Will you go home and tell your Ma?'

'Umm.'

'Which mother will you talk to?'

'Tilu.'

'Why? Not Nilu?'

'Umm.'

'And another mother, what is her name?'

'Tilu.'

'You've said Tilu. Another...?'

'Nilu.'

'Another?'

'Ma.'

'Tell me the name of another mother.'

'Tilu Ma.'

'Oh oh! You've said Tilu Ma, you've said Nilu Ma; who is the other Ma?'

'Bilu.'

'Right.'

They were still moving through the thick bamboo forest, like an ocean it seemed. Darkness had settled in. Fireflies blossomed and faded. A bird was crying out in harsh notes from the jiuli tree. A thud: Was that a ripe palm-fruit falling off? From the thorny nata-thickets came the cry of crickets.

Khoka had fallen silent again, out of fear.

From far away came the sound of the conch, marking the evening prayers. Khoka, with his eyes still half-shut promptly said, 'Dugga Dugga nama nama...' He had learnt the auspicious salutation from his mothers. He looked around at the thickening darkness and said fearfully, 'O Bhabani—'

'What is it, my love?'

'Want to go to Ma, am afaid.'

'We're on our way.'

'Bhabani?'

'Yes.'

'Afaid.'

'Afraid of what? There's nothing to fear.'

Once again came the sound of the conch. Khoka quickly joined both his hands raising them to his forehead and chanted, 'Dugga Dugga nama nama...'

Bhabani laughed as he said, 'Let's see if reciting Durga's name will get rid of your fear this time.'

And it actually was so. They came out of the forest and began walking through the different neighbourhoods of their village. The cowsheds were thick with smoke that came from the evening fumigation, now winding its way through the foliage of the pumpkin creepers. Jhinge flowers crowned the hedges.

'There—our house is right there!' said Bhabani and, at that very moment, the first drop fell from the heavy mass of clouds as a cold wind began blowing. Nilu rushed out to gather Khoka in her arms.

'O my darling, my precious, where had you gone? All wet in the rain. Oh, don't you have any sense, bringing the boy home through woods and forests when it's so dark and rainy! What a thing to do! And that too on a Saturday!'

Khoka leapt into his mother's arms with a broad smile. He spread out both his hands and said in a tone of wonder, 'Hap-ning!'

≈

It was Bilu's turn tonight. Tilu, wearing her red-bordered sari, handed her husband the paan she had just made. 'Should I shut the window at the head?' she asked him before she turned to leave, 'Quite a wind tonight.'

'Won't you be coming?'

'No, Bilu will stay tonight.'

'Khoka?'

'He'll stay with me.'

Bhabani felt sad. Khoka stayed with them in the same room when it was Tilu's turn. He wouldn't see the child tonight. In his sleep the child would push his small legs and feet up over his body and sleep with his mouth slightly open. It was a marvellous sight.

Her lips reddened by paan, Bilu came in and sat down on one side of the bed. The paan-box was in her hand.

'Come, Bilumoni, come in,' said Bhabani.

Bilu appeared to be in low spirits. 'You don't want me, do you?' she said.

'Don't want you?'

'You don't—that I know. You were thinking of Didi just now.'

'Wrong. I was thinking of Khokon.'

'Shall I bring Khokon here?'

'No. Can he spend the night with you?'

'Wait, I'll get him. Of course he can.'

Bilu returned a little later with the sleeping boy in her arms. 'Didi had fallen asleep.' She laughed and said, 'I've stolen Khoka from her side.'

'Really?'

'Come take a look. Didi's fast asleep.'

'Didn't she shut the door?'

'She had kept it ajar for Nilu. Nilu's still winding up work in the kitchen. She'll sleep with Didi in the same room tonight. Didi spent the entire day grinding the dal to make boris with, quite wiped out. She does back-breaking work.'

'Why do you let her? She's Khoka's mother. Both of you should be working hard instead of her.'

'As if she would *let* us! You know that. All your concern, sympathy is for Didi. Who are we? Nobody. Just washed up in the flood. Here, would you like some paan?'

'Spread the quilt over Khokon, will you? It's cold tonight. Who made the paan?'

'Nilu. Do you know, Nilu wanted very much to be with you tonight.'

'Why didn't you let her then?'

'Exactly what I told you a moment ago: you only find fault with me over *everything*. Everything about Didi is wonderful, and so too with Nilu. Wish I were dead.'

Bhabani was aware that lately Bilu often expressed her hurt in this manner.

Why did she nurse such resentment? Perhaps she was very unhappy deep down. She was a quiet soul who rarely expressed herself; yet, every now and then came a sorrowful outburst. But why was it so? He had never consciously disrespected her. But with a woman's subtle sensitivity she had perceived through some gesture of his, some ordinary, simple word of his, that in his heart he always desired Tilu. Perhaps she understood this without him ever having said so.

Bhabani was saddened. He had made a mistake marrying three sisters together. He had not realized it then; what experience would a wandering sannyasi have had of the world? He had taken the decision with an overwhelming desire to save three fairly old kulin women. But it had never struck him that, having saved them, would he be able to make them happy?

He felt deep down that he had indeed not cared enough for Bilu. Not consciously perhaps, but however he had done it, Bilu had sensed it. He felt very sad for her.

He saw that Bilu had turned away from him and was weeping soundlessly.

He turned her face towards him and rebuked her gently, 'Bilu, what are you doing? Why are you crying so? Why are you behaving like a mad person?'

'I'm telling you truly—it's better if I were to die. I know that you are the guru, but there are times when I feel like I'm a thorn in your path, and I should be out of the way. You could be happy with Didi and Nilu.'

'You musn't speak like that. When have I disregarded you, tell me?'

'Let that be, I'm not telling you anything about that. It's my fate. No one is to blame. Now move a bit, let me make Khoka comfortable.'

'Perhaps I have made a mistake Bilu,' said Bhabani taking her by the hand. 'I didn't realize then...'

Bhabani's affectionate concern seemed to wipe away some of Bilu's sorrow. 'No, don't say so,' she replied.

'No, I mean it—'

'Here, have a paan, do. Don't take my words seriously, I'm a mad one.'

It needed so little to make Bilu contented. Bhabani felt deeply distressed. How joyous she had been at the time of her marriage, starry-eyed with hope. Why had he ruined her life?

He hadn't done it on purpose. Why had it happened so?

That night Bhabani spoke most tenderly and lovingly to Bilu. He painted a rosy picture of the future. Whatever *he* hadn't been able to do, Khoka would do for his mothers. Khoka would look upon each of his mothers in the same way. Bilu must not nurse any hurt or resentment.

Shafts of moonlight splintering through the clouds fell on the bed. It was very late. A night bird cried out from the fig tree.

Suddenly Bilu addressed him, using the intimate *tumi*, 'Listen, if I were to die, will you weep—my man-about-town?'

'What a thing to say!'

Bilu laughed and moving close to Khoka said, 'Just see, how beautifully he is smiling and moving in his dreams.'

≈

It was after Durga Puja. Feathery kash flowers had bloomed on both sides of the Ichhamati at the end of the rains, the waters of the river had spilled over into the fields and the morning sun fell on the bushes of nata-kanta.

Children had gathered to pick up the mandatory fourteen kinds of edible greens that would be needed for the ritual on the day before Kali Puja.

A little girl came up to Bhabani's son, who everyone called Tulu, and remarked, 'Oh! You've not been able to pick a thing! Better give me—'

'What shall I give you?' Tulu protested, 'I want to pick them too. Here, let's see...'

'See—there's a whole lot of greens that *I've* got here—gandamoni, bou-tuntuni, white-notey, rosy-notey, goyal-notey, tiny-noni, shanti-greens, matar-greens, kanchordaam, kalmi, punarnaba...and I'm going to pick rosy alu'r-greens, chola'r-greens and palang-greens—that makes fourteen! You're just a little boy, what would you know of greens!'

'You teach me. Ooh! Shoye-didi's come!

A relatively older girl came and drew Tulu close to her and said, 'Why are you bothering him, Bina? He's too little to recognize all the greens! Come Tulu dear, you come along with me.'

Foni Chakkarty's grandson Annada suddenly cried out, 'Look at the crowd on the other bank! So early in the morning too! Wonder what's up.'

It was true: large numbers of people had gathered on the other side of the river; some were carrying cloth banners. Soon enough, people started gathering along their bank as well.

Annada, who was a little older than the rest, went up to one of the adults, 'O Uncle Kapali, what's going to happen today?'

Those who had gathered there were mostly peasants who had come from the various outlying villages further inland. Some they knew, most others were strangers. One of them said, 'The Chhota Laat's machine-boat is going to pass us by the river today. He's heard that there's tyranny going on in the Neelkuthis and he's come to see it all for himself. The subjects are up in arms, not an indigo sapling are they going to sow anywhere in districts of Jessore and Nadia. That's why we've come to tell the Chhota Laat that we're not going to sow any indigo any more.'

Tulu, who was listening, stared at the river in amazement. Trying to absorb it all, he finally turned to Annada and asked, 'Dada, will you tell me what is indigo?'

'It's a kind of plant. Haven't you seen the Neelkuthi Saheb dash around in his tom-tom?'

'I want to see the machine-boat,' said Tulu, with a stubborn tilt of his neck.

'Not going to pick the fourteen greens, eh? Naughty fellow!' chided Annada, tenderly lifting the little boy into his arms in one sweep.

It wasn't only Tulu; all the village children stopped picking the fourteen greens as the crowd kept swelling on both sides of the river. Word spread that the Chhota Laat was going to appear before noon. Every now and then the peasants lined up on the banks let out successive chants of *jigir*. Many of the upper caste villagers such as Nilmoni Samaddar, Foni Chakkarty and Shyam Ganguly also arrived on the scene and waited by the kadam tree along the river.

'O Khoka,' called out Bhabani Barujje to his son.

'Here I am, Baba,' said Tulu running towards him with a smile.

'Have you picked the fourteen greens? Your mother was saying—'

'No—oh, Baba! Who's coming, Baba?'

'The Chhota Laat, Sir William Grey.'

'What's his name? Sir William Grey?'

'Good! You've picked it up quite well!'

'I won't go home now. Want to see Chhota Laat.'

'You will, but let me take you home and give you something to eat first.'

'No, Baba, I'll watch.'

The hours went by. The sun became fierce. Tulu was hungry

but in the midst of the waiting crowd he forgot everything.

'O Baba,' he began, 'What's the machine-boat like?'

'It's called an *ishtee-maar*. You'll see it soon. There'll be puffs of smoke.'

'*Lots* of smoke puffing out?'

'Umm.'

'Why, Baba?'

'There's fire inside, that's why.'

They heard a sudden cry from the populace gathered on the bank quite far away from them.

'Baba, take me up in your arms,' urged Tulu.

Bhabani put him up on his shoulder. 'Can you see now?'

'Ye...s...ss,' said Khoka, his eyes fixed somewhere far away.

'What can you see?'

'Smoke flying, Baba.'

'Did you see the machine-boat?'

'No, Baba, only smoke! Oooh, so much smoke!'

A little later, a huge steamer spewing out enormous quantities of smoke came into view. The sight quite overwhelmed the little boy. The populace sang out loudly as though they were calling upon Allah in a *jigr*, 'Indigo, we shan't sow, anymore, Laat-Sah'b, we beg our mother the Maharani.'

On board the machine-boat, several sahebs were seen seated on chairs. They all looked like the saheb who had been shooting birds by the river the other day.

'Baba?'

'Quiet now!'

'What is *that* saheb doing?'

'He is making a namaskar to everyone.'

'Who is he, Baba?'

'He's that Chhota Laat I spoke of. What's the name—do you remember?

'I don't, Baba.'

'You must remember Khoka, that's not right. Sir...'

'Uliam Grey,' filled in Khoka after a bit of thinking.

'William Grey—now let's go home.'

'Just a little bit more, Baba...'

'There's nothing more to see. They've gone now.'

'Where to, Baba?'

'They'll go down the Ichhamati to Churni, and from there to the Ganga. And finally they will go back to Calcutta.'

Tulu clambered down from his father's shoulder and trotted homewards. All around them were villagers, jostling and chattering. Tulu had never witnessed such a sight in all his four years. What a huge boat it was! How the water splashed right up to the bank as it went by, and what a lot of smoke! All those white sahebs sitting on their chairs!

'What did you see, my son?' Tilu asked him on return.

Khoka was thrilled to narrate all the marvellous sights he had seen, waving his little hands.

'That's enough!' said Nilu, 'Come and have your meal now.'

≈

Bilu was no more. On a rain-drenched night of Ashad month, after three days of delirious fever, she had passed away laying her head on her husband's lap and holding on to his hands.

Before her death, in the middle of the night, she had regained consciousness. Looking up at her husband's face, she cried out, 'Who are you, dear?'

'It's me,' said Bhabani, fanning her around her head. 'Now you mustn't speak. Just keep lying down quietly, that's a good girl.'

'Can I say something?'

'What is it?'

'You are not angry with me?' She was using the familiar tumi again. 'Listen, I've said so many things to you, my man-about-town...'

'Don't cry...you mustn't.'

'Fetch Khokon and let him sleep beside me. Will you please?'

'I'll bring him right away. Tilu was right by your side all this time; she's just gone to have a mouthful of food. Don't talk now.'

After they were both quiet for a while, Bhabani felt Bilu's forehead—it was damp with sweat. Did that mean the fever was coming down? As soon as Tilu returned, he would go off to fetch Ramkanai Kobiraj. A little later, Bilu suddenly turned towards him and said, 'Dearest, come closer, I'm calling you tumi: is that a sin? Even if it is, let me say it, won't be able to say it again. Will you be mine again in the birth to come? You must be, must be...Didi's forgotten to give Khoka his milk, call her...'

'What nonsense are you speaking! Haven't I asked you to rest quietly?'

'Where's Khokon? Khokon?'

Those were her last words. She turned her face to the wall and stayed that way even when Tilu and Nilu finally brought Khokon to her bedside. Bhabani Barujje left for Ramkanai Kobiraj's home. When they returned, Ramkanai examined the pulse and said—'It's been a long time; Tilu-ma, pick up Khoka from the bed.'

≈

The Indigo Revolt raged in three districts with equal ferocity. The report that the Chhota Laat, Sir William Grey, submitted after his tour has since become a famous document in the history of indigo plantation. Within a couple of years many of the indigo plantations located in the districts of Nadia and Jessore had been wound up. Most of the saheb owners either sold off their plantations or gave them on lease to some wealthy Indian before they set sail for England. Even if business did go on in a few plantations, there was not a mite left of their former power and glory. Shipton Saheb was amongst those who still held on to the Neelkuthi. David Saheb left with his wife and children, but Shipton was not the sort to let go easily. Mr Shipton tried to run the plantation as in former days, with the help of his new dewan, Harakali Sur. The old employees continued to work with him.

It was as if the poison had gone out of the fangs of the indigo planters. In the few remaining plantations in the neighbourhood, indigo cultivation was continued on a much smaller scale alongside regular farming—more like a zamindari.

However, in the interior of this stretch of the district, Shipton was still a man to be feared. He ran his business with the same tight reins, and once the revolt was over, much of the awe and fear that he used to inspire amongst the populace was back in force. Harakali Sur too could be found lording it over the subjects. The saheb in his tom-tom was still an impressive sight.

Shipton called over Harakali Sur one day and asked him, 'Dewan, when will Durga Puja be celebrated this year?'

'Around Ashwin month, after the rains, huzoor.'

'Arrange for a Durga Puja at the Neelkuthi this time.'

'That's very good, huzoor. If you permit me, I shall organize everything.'

'Whatever money it will be cost, shall I pay. Have to be a programme of the *kobi'r gaan*, the doggerel competition among poets.'

'Sir, if you would permit me, let me book Gobindo Adhikari's wonderful jatra troupe.'

'What be that?'

'Huzoor, it's a jatra performance. They come all dressed; for example, like Rama, Sita, Ravana—'

'Oh! I understand, like a theatre. Good, you go ahead, money shall I pay.'

'Where will it be held?' asked the dewan.

'In the hall, could be.'

'No, huzoor, we'll have to make the seating arrangements in the big field, with cloth tents and all. If it's Gobindo Adhikari's troupe, there's bound to be huge crowds.'

The village witnessed a most wonderful Puja that year. A massive and magnificent image of the goddess Durga (with her children) was fashioned right there in the premises of the Neelkuthi. Bishambar Dhuli, the drummer from Mansapota village, was hired to play for three days. Crowds poured in from about seventeen villages to listen to Gobindo Adhikari's troupe.

'Listen,' said Tilu to her husband, 'Nilu wishes to see the jatra at the Neelkuthi.'

'Would that look good?' asked Bhabani. 'Don't know if they've made seating arrangements for the women…Is there anyone else from our village who will go?'

'Nistarini was saying she might. And Nalu Pal's wife Tulsi will be going with her children.'

'They are rich people, no point discussing whether they will be going. Nalu Pal is the wealthiest man in the village these days. How are they going?'

'In a palanquin probably. It's a big one, and Nilu could go with them.'

'I'll arrange for a bullock cart. You go too,' Bhabani urged Tilu.

'I won't.'

'Why not? If everyone's going, you will too.'

Khoka was in seventh heaven to see such a big beautiful deity of Ma Durga, and he was thrilled by the jatra.

However, the women of the village could not go to the jatra after all. Kailash Chatujje, son of Chandra Chatujje, had recently set himself up as a patriarch—as an arbiter of social codes. Kailash did not give the women permission to attend the jatra.

≈

One afternoon in early *Hemanta*, shortly after the Puja, Shipton Saheb sent for Dewan Harakali Sur.

'Dewan, there hast been trouble.'

'What is it, saheb?'

'*Now* the Neelkuthi is finished.'

'Why huzoor? Has there been any fresh—?'

'Nothing. It is not been *that* trouble. No. This is another trouble. You knows there is a coundry called Germany? From that coundry indigo colour hast come to India, being sold in all coundries.'

'Are they growing indigo in *that* country too, huzoor?'

'Why that? You've not understoot. It is chemical indigo that is happening—not the real thing, fake indigo. Not from trees—some other means—by a synthetic process—you have not understoot.'

'Is it good indigo?'

'Excellend! That's why I've sent for you—look here, now!'

Shipton placed a blue coloured pill in front of Harakali Sur. That experienced man examined it carefully and checked out its dyeing quality. He was so astonished at the result that he couldn't speak for a few minutes.

'Dit you see?'

'Yes, saheb.'

'If *this* dye is in the market, why would people buy our indigo?'

'How much does it cost?'

'*That* why dit you not ask before?' laughed Shipton. 'I'm thinking that the Dewan has lost his mind. How much cout it be?'

'Four rupees a pound.'

'A *rupee* a pound; at the mosd—one and a half rupee for a pound! Wholesale hundredweight at ninety rupees. Our business has completely gone waste—ruined. Finisht and dead.'

Harakali Sur had been in this line for years. He was an old hand at the indigo business. He foresaw the implications and fell silent. What could he say? He saw the future clearly before his eyes. The indigo made from plants would not sell. And if the profits did not keep up with the cost of production, indigo plantations would have to wind up. 'The sahebs' boat is about to run aground,' he thought to himself.

On that Hemanta afternoon Burra Saheb Jenkins Shipton prophesied quite correctly that what Ramgopal Ghose's lectures, Harish Mookerjee's newspaper the *Hindoo Patriot*, Padré Long's agitation, the rebellion of the peasants in the districts of Nadia and Jessore and Sir William Grey's secret report—had failed to do, the little pills of synthetic dye from Germany would accomplish easily and soon enough.

Within a few years, indigo farming came to a complete halt in Bengal.

Shipton Saheb's memsaheb left for England, where she later died. Their only child, a daughter, was being raised by her grandfather. Shipton Saheb alone did not wish to leave this land of Bengal.

Some time later in the small room adjoining the big verandah of the Neelkuthi, Shipton lay on a bed looking out at the white clusters of fragrant flowers of the Indian cork tree just outside his room. He was thinking of the old days, of another time and place.

A tiny village of Westmoorland…no one he used to know lived there anymore. His old mother had died some years ago. His brother had moved to Australia where he lived with his children.

The many inns, some of them former pubs in his village, came to his mind. In the one owned by landlord William Ritson—what a crowd there'd be of an evening! Langdale Pikes and Great Gable before them—about fifteen hundred feet high, all those who climbed those hills eventually ended up at the pub.

On the water's edge grew willow and mountain sage; from the village of Borrowdale the path wound its way through hill and dale. How often as a boy he had walked down the winding path with his huge dog as a companion. So many fishing trips to Elterwater…the name sounded so old and so odd to his ears now. Elterwater—of huge pikes and salmons, what fun he had fishing; by then, Rhino's Pass would be shrouded in darkness. He's coming back home from Elterwater, fishes dangling from his hand, his pet Great Dane trotting behind him…

'—the eagle is screamin' around us, the river's a moanin' below—'

Rhymes that they used to sing as children. Andy would sing that one. He too, humming it as he sat waiting for the fish to bite near Elterwater.

Dreams of his boyhood…

'Gaya, Gaya?'

'What is it, saheb?' asked Gaya coming up to him.

'Sit beside me, dearie. What have you been up to all day? Where have you been? What were you toing?'

'I've been a-sitting. What's there to do?'

'If I die here—what will you do if I dite?'

'What a thing to say! You're not to say such things, for shame—'

'I want to give you some money, but where will you keep it? Will be stolen and looted.'

Shipton Saheb burst into sudden laughter, 'Gaya, listen to the song, listen carefully to the words—listen to the word. Modern, you know.'

'Go on! Why don't you sing it? Don't like all this ittr mittr that you're saying.'

'Well, listen...

> Yes, Yes, the arm-y
> How we love the arm-y
> When the swallows come again
> See them fly—the arm-y!'

Gaya stopped her ears with her fingers and exlaimed, 'Oh, my ears are deafen'd! Don't roar so much. Is that a tune?'

'Aah, you did not care for it,' said the saheb. 'All right, *you* sing one, that one—*tomar bodon chande jodi dhora nahi pabo*. If I cannot aspire to you, one beautiful as the moon.'

'No, sahib, better not sing now.'

'Gaya?'

'Yes?'

'What will you do when I am deat?'

'Don't speak of such things, for shame!'

'No, I am no milksop, I tell you, I understant business. The Neelkuthi's days are over. Shall I leave or shall I stay on here?'

'Where will you go, saheb? Better stay on here.'

'You will stay wit me?'

'I will, saheb.'

'Nowhere will you go?'

'I won't, saheb.'

'Right, you will not go away? May I take it as a pledge? You have said your heart's thoughts?'

'I'm saying so, saheb. You have done a lot—fed me and looked after me; now, when the times are bad for you, where shall I go leaving you alone? Can I live with my dhamma, if I were to do that, saheb?'

Drawing Gaya-mem to him in a close embrace, Shipton said, 'Oh, my dear, my dearie—you are not afraid of the Big Bad Wolf! I call it a brave girl!'

≈

Nistarini had gone bathing in the Ichhamati. It was the rainy season and the river was full, lap-lapping on both banks. Big yellow flowers of the titpalla creeper brightened the tops of bushes, on the sandbank across, white kash clusters were swaying in the golden wind; the jungle of *saibabla* and *keya-jhanka* was overrun by the blue flowers of the *bonkalmi*; by the water's edge you saw the wild kochu buds and the little wild purple flowers of *chanda*-grass on the edges of the banks; matar creepers dangling and swaying over the river, as the restless waters came in waves and resounded splash-splash against the half submerged branches of the bonnyeburo tree.

When she saw that the ghat was deserted Nistarini felt a great desire to put her water-pot against her chest and swim in the river. In the fast running brimming waters of the Ichhamati in the month of Bhadra, even a straw was torn in two in a few moments; people were afraid of bathing during this time for fear of sharks and crocodiles. Nistarini never bothered about any of this; those who have never swum with a water-pot against their chest—what would she tell them of the pleasure! You are swimming, almost borne along by the ebb tide, surrendering yourself to the current and along with you come clusters of floating vegetation—*toka-pana*, the bright ripe fruits peeping out from the *telekucho* creeper, the river-mynah chirping and shrieking from the mossy floating islands that went by you—such bliss! The joy of liberation! What if the crocs take you? Let them!

That too, would be a kind of liberation, unique and varied—sheer joy.

After she had been swimming for a long time, Nistarini realized that she had left behind all the ghats in their village. She had almost crossed Panchpota village and before her was the Goylapara ghat in Bhashanpota village. Dense jungle lay on the right, on the left, fields of vegetables, pointed gourd and serrated gourd, farmed by the peasants of Aramdanga. She had made a mistake—shouldn't have come so far all by herself. What would people say! It was not possible for her to swim against the fast flowing waters and go back all that way. She shouldn't go ahead either. Would it be right for her to head for the southern bank that was all but smothered in jungle? She'd have to walk home along the bank, though she didn't know the way.

She struck out for the shore. A line of bonnyeburo trees had drooped down almost touching the water, trees and creepers, leaves and tendrils densely entwined; chattering wild birds hopped about, greedy to eat the telakucha fruits that had ripened all over the place. What was that scratching noise, the rustling of dry leaves? Was it some small beast running away in alarm, perhaps a vixen?

Before she got on to the bank she pushed up the bauti-bracelet on each of her arms towards the elbows, wound her wet sari firmly around her body, pushed away her mass of black hair from her forehead; when her right foot fell on the sand, she happened to step on an oyster. She picked up the oyster from beneath her foot and held on tightly to it. Then, she fearfully pushed and wound her way through the narrow overgrown jungle path along the bank, stung by the coarse nettles, her sari end torn to shreds by the thorns of the *sheya*-berries, until she came to the kaora locality. The kaora womenfolk stared curiously at her, with a degree of astonishment as well. She—a wife from the brahman-para; how had she come so far, *alone*? In wet clothes, her hair all wet too?

Then, as she drew near her home, she could hear sounds of wailing, a confusion of voices. Her mother-in-law and aunt-in-law were loudly sobbing. They had decided that she had either drowned or had been pulled under by a crocodile. When she hadn't returned from the bathing ghat those who had gone running to look for her came back to say that there was no trace of her. They were all delighted to see her. Her mother-in-law came forward and embraced her, stroking her head most tenderly. Her neighbours came and affectionately began upbraiding her.

After she had eaten, she called her sister-in-law Sudhamukhi and the two of them went to the tree behind their kitchen. There, Nistarini prised open the oyster. The two of them took turns to probe the inside with their fingers, as all the villagers did if they chanced upon an oyster. She found something like the seed of a berry.

'Thakurjhi, take a look at this...'

'O my! This is a pearl sure enough!'

'Nonsense!'

'I'm a-telling you Bou-didi, I swear to you. It's a pearl.'

'How do you know it's a pearl?'

'Come let's show it to Ma.'

'No, Thakurjhi, don't show it to anyone.'

'Come on now. Why should you be ashamed?'

Soon the entire neighbourhood got to know that the daughter-in-law of such and such a house had found a precious pearl in the waters of the Ichhamati. At the old men's hangout in the chandimandap nothing but her find was discussed for days on end. Bidhu the jeweller turned up one day, and after examining the pearl offered a price of sixty rupees. Nistarini's husband had never set eyes on so much money at one go. Just before Bidhu jeweller was about to set off with the pearl, Nistarini had second thoughts, and she declared, 'I shan't sell this pearl.'

That very day a Musalman trader came to their home wanting to see the pearl. He too examined it carefully and offered a price of a hundred rupees. But Nistarini still refused to sell the pearl.

Meanwhile there was tremendous excitement in the village. Such and such's wife has found a pearl worth a hundred rupees in the waters of the Ichhamati. How many in the village of Panchpota had ever seen a hundred rupees in their lifetime? Fortunate they were indeed. A crowd of wives rushed to Nistarini and put on the auspicious vermilion on her forehead. Her mother-in-law went to Naraharipur, where she offered puja at the Shyamrai temple. Someone sent a ripe banana, another a papaya, and so on.

Nistarini came to visit Tilu one day. She had brought the pearl with her.

Khoka put in in his hand and looking at his mother with questioning eyes, wanted to know what it was.

'A pearl.'

'What is a pearl, Ma?'

'It's found inside an oyster.'

Nistarini took Khoka on her lap and said, 'I could give this away to him, Didi.'

'No, what would he do with it, my dear?'

'Really, I shall; I seem to forget everything when I look upon his face.'

Tilu had to work very hard to dissuade Nistarini from gifting away the pearl. Nistarini was not a great beauty but she was very attractive. She had none of the shyness and diffidence of the village wife—there was a kind of masculine aura about her; as a girl she had been adept at climbing trees and swimming. She didn't care much for others, certainly not her mother-in-law, and not even her husband.

Tilu loved her. This young woman had not been trapped in the web of narrow-mindedness, superstition, cowardice and ignorance of the other village folk. Nistarini was like a woman from a different era, mistakenly born at least half a century before her time.

'Will you have a bite?' asked Tilu

'No.'

'Khoi and cucumbers?'

'All right then, they're nice to eat.'

≈

It was the same Nistarini that Tilu discovered one afternoon behind a bush, engrossed in intimate conversation with Gobindo, son of Krishnakishore Ray of Ray-para.

Tilu had gone to the river with Khoka for a bath. It was early Hemanta, the last of autumn. The river had just began to dry up, the air was filled with the smell of the dry black grass, flying kash flowers along with the seeds were getting stuck in the mud on the river bank. The chhatim tree by the riverside had brought forth innumerable clusters of white flowers; the slightly cool afternoon breeze was fragrant with the smell of the flowers of the chhatim.

Bhabani often chose this time to go to the river with his wife and son. In the peaceful atmosphere by the river it was natural to think of bhagwan. He believed it to be the appropriate time to speak to Khoka, awaken him to divinity beneath the generous blue skies. He felt that it was in the bosom of that broad flowing river under the expanse of the blue skies with the forest line as a horizon that he could initiate his son into the presence of divinity.

When Bhabani joined them a little later, Tilu asked him to explain the meaning of a particular sloka.

'From the *Prashanupanishad*? Is this the sloka: *sa evam yajam nam ahar ahar brahma gamayati*?' he recited.

'Yes.'

'It leads the sacrifice, *yajmana*, to Brahman every day.'

'Who is the One?'

'Bhagwan.'

'Who is the yajmana?'

'The one who worships the One with devotion.'

'Isn't it being said here that the mind is the yajmana?' asked Tilu.

'Yes, it is so, wait—whose voices do I hear? Behind those bushes... Let me go.'

'Don't go any further. First find out what...Here, let me go...'

They found Nistarini and Gobindo with their backs to them engrossed in conversation; and it did not seem like it was either the Upanishad or the Vedanta that they were discussing, sitting so intimately. For Gobindo held strands of Nistarini's thick black hair in his right fist, while he was gesturing with his left to make a point. Nistarini with her neck slightly bent was looking up at his face with a smiling face.

Hearing footsteps behind them, Nistarini turned around and grew rigid with fear when she saw Bhabani and his wife. Gobindo promptly melted into the forest. Bhabani Barujje slowly walked backwards. Nistarini stood before Tilu, her head bowed like a guilty person. Tilu pointed to the forest and said, 'Who was that who went away? What are you doing here?'

Nistarini's throat had dried up. Beads of sweat had come up on her forehead. She did not reply.

'Who was it? Tell me, won't you?' persisted Tilu.

'Gobindo.'

'What is it with him and you?'

Nistarini was silent.

'And to come away so far from your home into the middle of this jungle—bravo young woman!'

'I like to,' replied Nistarini, in a mild and low tone.

'I'll break every bone in your body,' said Tilu angrily. 'You naughty girl! I'll show you all about "liking". She's come to this jungle by the river, half a kos away from her home—why? Because she *likes* to! No knowing whether a tiger or a snake will get you. Grown-up creature that you are—aren't you ashamed to say so? Go on now, get home…'

'Why don't you come away, dear?' said Bhabani Barujje from a distance, getting a hint of her anger.

'Now you be quiet,' was Tilu's response.

'Don't you have any sense,' she said turning to Nistarini, 'it will be all over the village in a second. How will you show your face, you wretch?'

Nistarini wept soundlessly.

'Come, come along with me, you wretch. A treasury of talents! Do you still have the pearl or have you already bestowed it on Gobindo?'

'No, I haven't. It's with my mother-in-law.'

'Come with me now. Imagine the two of them sitting here in the middle of stinging creepers and nettles. Have I ever seen such an unthinking creature like you—if Kunti-thakuron ever got to know would she let you stop for a second in this village!'

'What if she doesn't? There's still the waters of the Ichhamati.'

'There she goes with her nonsense! I'll break all your bones; you dare to speak back? Take a dip in the river, quick. Come, I'll give you fresh clothes.'

Tilu brought her back home and gave her a dry set of clothes and something to eat. When Nistarini was somewhat restored, Tilu asked, 'For how long have you been meeting him?'

'About five or six months.'

'And no one has got to know?'

'He comes secretly to that part of the forest, and so do I.'

'A fine thing to do! How can you say it just like that! Grown-up creature that you are! Tell me, that you are not going to see him again.'

'He won't be able to bear it if I don't meet him again.'

'Again! You are not to go there, do you understand?'

'H'mm.'

'What does that "h'mm" mean! Will you or will you not go?'

Nistarini turned her face away and muttered, 'Gobindo has given me something...'

'What is it?'

'Shall I bring it to show you? It's a pair of makri earrings.'

'Where is it?'

'With me,' she replied fearfully, 'Tied up in the end of the wet sari. It was today he gave me those...new ornaments. No one in this village has a pair like that. Just come out in Kolkata city. He got them made for me; his cousin works somewhere in Kolkata.'

Nistarini untied the end of her wet sari and showed Tilu her new pair of makri. Tilu held the earrings and turned them around, 'They *are* new, *and* well-made too. But you can't accept them. You have to return them. You return them to him and tell him you won't ever see him again. I shall keep it all to myself, this time. No one else saw you, only us. We're not going to tell a soul. But I won't let you commit such a sin. Don't you like your husband? Deceiving your husband and—'

'He does not love me,' broke in Nistarini, her head bowed low.

'I'll beat you up good and proper! How is he going to love you? If you are going to be gadding about in this manner?'

'It's not that. He never did like me. He doesn't know anything of this.'

'Doesn't it hurt you to cheat on your husband and do all this?'

'Didi, you have a husband who is like Shiva himself. We would have said the same thing if we had got a husband like Shiva. I asked him for a sari, and such a scolding he gave me, both my mother-in-law, and that precious creature. My parents had given me a *gurjaripancham* anklet, even that was given away to Nalu Pal to borrow money against; they've no thought of redeeming it even now. So often I've begged them, but they don't listen. And how would they? You see how poor we are. There's been no paddy; whatever little there was, we managed somehow to stretch for three months. I've been working such long hours on the pestle that my sides are about to crack open. Even after I do so much work, there's no way I can make any one of them happy. Tell me didi, why should I stay with such in-laws?'

Nistarini the beautiful rebel's face reddened in anger and outrage. Her face glowed with the pride and energy of youth, her mass of hair spread all over her back. Tilu was filled with tenderness for this courageous young wife. She seemed to have no inkling of what a turmoil it would cause in the village if anyone got to know of her affair.

Tilu spent a long time explaining and talking to her, comforting her. She escorted her home well before evening, told her family that Nistarini had gone bathing with her and had been chatting with her all this time at their home.

'How strange!' said Nistarini's mother-in-law suspiciously. 'We went *twice* to scour the ghat and couldn't find her, and then went to all the neighbouring houses—what a wife and a half! Left when it was broad daylight and she comes back home now, when it's evening an' dark. What can I tell you dear, I'm shot to pieces with this daughter-in-law of mine...And you should hear her retort to everything that we say!

'Indeed! Every one of you is a precious treasure, aren't you? And you, of course, don't have any faults, there can't be any...' said Nistarini in a low but audible tone,

'*Did* you hear that, my dear? Just listen to her! You barely get a word in edgeways, she gets at you right away.'

'Good!' said Nistarini.

'Now my dear, is that the way to speak to your mother-in-law?' scolded Tilu.

It would soon be evening. Tilu went back home. Darkness had gathered in the bamboo forest, fireflies flitted in the gaps between the *kaalkasunde* trees.

'You understand, times are a-changing,' she said to Bhabani on her return. 'What happened this afternoon makes me think so. Never heard a wife from a respectable family going to meet another man in the jungle and sitting and chattering away with him. When we got married, we were told not to talk to you during the day. Even now, young brides in our village go to their husbands only very late at night, when everyone is fast asleep.'

'Didn't I tell you the other day,' responded Bhabani Barujje, 'that Khoka will be able to walk with his wife beside him in daylight, in this very village?'

'Goodness! The things you say!'

'It will be so. The time is not far off. You saw for yourself with this young wife. The times are changing very fast.'

≈

Prasanna Chakkarty hardly got to see Gaya-mem these days. Since

Memsaheb's departure Gaya was more or less living in the Neelkuthi on a permanent basis. Even if she did come outdoors at times, and they happened to meet on the road, it didn't seem like before. Sometimes though, it *was* like former times. With the whimsical Gaya-mem you couldn't quite predict. If she felt like it, she would happily chat away with Prasanna Chakkarty standing there on the path. If she didn't feel like it, not a good word would she have for him!

Business was bad at the Neelkuthi. The cultivation of indigo went on as before. The subjects looked up to the Burra Saheb and the Dewanji in much the same manner as before, but business had touched an all-time low. Even the available stocks didn't sell in the market. Prices had plummeted so low that it wasn't worth growing the crop. A large stock from last year was still stored in the godown for lack of demand. The Neelkuthi job had lost its aura; but where would the present employees go? None of them had been thrown out of the Burra Saheb's Neelkuthi; he even continued to pay the same salary, but there was nothing of the frills of former times. They couldn't count on commanding the same respect. The Neelkuthi was in its last gasp.

'O Amin-babu,' said Sriram Muchi to Prasanna Chakkarty one day, 'do ask saheb to give me my piece o' land.'

'I'll do that. Is he giving *all* the servants a plot of land?'

'The Burra Saheb's asked for land to be given to Bhoja and Nafar and me. You are to measure out a bigha each from the khas-land belonging to the Neelkuthi and give it to us.'

'I'll do it as soon as saheb orders me. And we are not to get any?'

'You could speak to saheb. Said he'd give land only to us servants. Won't give you people; Gaya-mem is to get fifteen bighas.'

'Eh! What's that you're saying!'

'Wouldn't it be she who'll get it? Certainly not you! She's the favoured one.'

Exactly two days later, Dewan Harakali Sur got the written order from the Burra Saheb: he was to get Gaya-mem's land surveyed and measured by the amin. The saheb also sent for the amin and told him that Gaya-mem was to accompany him, see the land for herself and choose the plot.

'From which land is the plot to be given?' the amin asked the dewan.

'Look at the survey for the Beledanga Lot Number Eighteen,' ordered the dewan. 'First find out how much of the land is good for growing paddy.'

'Only five bighas of that land is good for paddy, Dewanji. I would suggest the strip that starts at from the bend around Chhutorghata to the wooden bridge at Natidanga—the land we had confiscated from Shashi Muchi; that's excellent for young paddy. If she's given *that* land—'

'Aah, shut up will you!' said Harkali Sur with a wink.

'Why, babu?'

'That's prime land—the head of a meaty goat! What's the saheb going to live on? The Neelkuthi's done for. Sixteen to eighteen maunds of special udi-rice good for murki you will get from that piece of land. Saheb has to get into farming in the *khas-khamar* plots. Why should *we* want to give it to Gaya? In time, the two of *us* might well share the land between ourselves.'

Aah, ignorant worldly-wise Harakali Sur, what would you know of the pangs of love?

The very next day Prasanna Chakkarty waited for a long time under the neem tree before he caught sight of Gaya-mem. Gaya never ate her meals at the saheb's; she walked home to her mother's every day at mealtimes.

'So, Khuro-moshai? What is the news?'

'Hardly see you! You've become so elusive.'

Gaya-mem came up very close to Prasanna Chakkarty and said with a smile, 'What are you standing here for, in the scorching afternoon sun?'

'For you.'

'Go on with you. The same nonsense again, Khuro-moshai!'

'Haven't seen you for five whole days.'

'How would it matter if you didn't see this wretched face?'
'Meaning...?'
'Tell me, of what use will I be to the likes of you now?'
'Listen, Gaya...'
'Yes?' she said and immediately burst into giggles. Hiding her face with her sari end, she turned to leave.
'Listen! Listen; why are you off! There's something I have to say,' said Prasanna Chakkarty hurriedly.

Gaya half turned as she kept walking away and said, 'Your "something" is always this and that, Khuro-moshai. Only things like I like lookin' at you, I'm a-waitin' for you and thinking about you—that sort of stuff and nonsense. How often have I told you that I call you "Khuro-moshai"; should you be saying such things to *me*? Don't say them. But you seem to get friskier by the day. Your tongue seems to run away with you.'

'Why would you say my tongue's "frisky"? What have I said to you?' asked Prasanna Chakkarty all smiles.

'Only, how nice it is to look upon you, how long I have not seen you, I can't live if I don't see you—'

'Not one of them is a lie.'

'You better go home. Don't keep standing here in this hot afternoon sun. Will make me sad.'

'Is that true, Gaya? Will you really feel sad? You really mean it, Gaya?'

'Yes. Yes. Yes. Now go home. Don't go on with your crazy stuff, standing here...'

'One word...'

'Again! "One word more, one thing more, O Gaya, listen to me do; O Gaya, let's sit down for a chat",' she mimicked him.

'No. It's not that.'

'What then? Some cock and bull story?'

'It's nothing to do with any of that. I swear to you Gaya. You *must* listen, it is very important for you. But you have to keep it absolutely secret, no one should hear a word.'

Within a few days of this meeting, Prasanna Chakkarty had measured out fifteen bighas of the prime land confiscated from Shashi Muchi—land which yielded excellent paddy; he got Sriram Muchi to dig in stakes at the right places, planted babla trees to mark the boundaries, and finalized the entire transaction to his satisfaction.

Gaya was present when the measuring was going on. She noticed a little fig tree and requested him, 'Khuro-moshai, will you include this fig tree in my land? I shall eat figs...'

'And if I do put in, will you remember me, Gaya?'

'Tee-hee-hee...there you go again!'

'Must you speak like that if I speak straight out? What's the harm in replying to what I asked? O Gaya...'

Another outburst of giggles followed.

'Oh, let it be! Forget it! I'm not going to say a thing more. Here, I've given a turn to the chain, and the fig tree is now yours!'

'Shall I take the dust off you feet, or not? A berhaman god, and on top of that a Khuro-moshai! Oh, it will be sin upon sin for me.'

Gaya went down on her knees and made a pranam from a distance. There was such a smile of contentment on her face! Such a smile! That tender young fig tree would live long. That tree was a witness to Prasanna Chakkarty Amin's happiness on this day. Prasanna Amin would die, but on this afternoon, missives of an exquisite happiness were inscribed forever beneath the shade of tender young leaves of the fig tree. Whose eyes glisten in the moonlight, whose deep sighs float around in the hot stillness of a *Falgun* afternoon—would anyone care to remember some fifty years hence, the sorrow and joys of their inner lives?

≈

A few months later.

Bhabani was sitting with his son at Bonsimtala ghat where there was a bend in the Ichhamati. Not yet three in the afternoon, only the occasional squawks and cries of the little cormorants and the ducks broke the dense shadows and silence of the forest. The fishermen who had dived into the river and brought up shells last winter had left them behind in scattered heaps. From the babla and wild juggidumur trees creepers swung out to dangle over the waters. Behind the dense green foliage the baggy rosy-red fruits of the *kakjongha* peeped out.

'Khoka, if I were to die, would you look after your mothers?' asked Bhabani of his son.

'No, Baba. I'll cry...'

'Why should you cry? I am old. How long shall I live?'

'For v-e-rr-y long.'

'Only because *you've* said so? You're mad!'

Khoka burst into peals of laughter and hugged his father, exclaiming, 'My Baba!'

'Listen to me. Will you look after your mothers after I'm dead?'

'No. I'll cry.'

'Tell me, who is bhagwan?'

'I don't know.'

'Where does he live?'

'There, up there,' said Khokon, pointing to the sky.

'Where, my son? Above the treetops?'

'Yes.'

'Do you love him?'

'No.'

'Really! Why not?'

'I love you.'

'And who else?'

'I love Ma?'

'Why don't you love bhagwan?'

'Don't know him.'

'What you've said Khoka, isn't wrong. You cannot love without knowing them, understanding them. Only if your love is based on knowing and understanding, does your love become strong. That is why most people cannot love bhagwan. They fear bhagwan, but they do not love. Well, I shall try to make you understand, shall I?'

Khoka didn't understand any of this, but responded

enthusiastically to the last question of his father.

'Khokon, how do you like that bird?'

'Nice!'

'Do you know who has made this bird? It is bhagwan, you understand?'

'Yes,' said Khoka with a nod.

'You didn't understand anything, did you? All that you see—it is bhagwan who has made it all.'

'Yes, Baba. Ma said bhagwan made the stars.'

'What else?'

'And the moon,' said Khoka.

'And?'

'And the sunny.'

'Yes, the sun. Where have you learnt so much? From your Ma? Good. Do you love the moon?'

'Yes,' said Khoka.

'Then, wouldn't you also love someone who had made such a wonderful thing?'

'I will love,' said Khoka.

'Certainly. Love some.'

'And *you* will love?' Khoka wanted to know.

'Yes.'

'Will Ma love too?'

'Yes, she will,' assured his father.

'And I will?'

'Yes.'

'And will Chhota Ma?'

'Yes,' said Bhabani again

'Then I shall love,' declared Khoka.

'Certainly! Come, I shall show you the moon in the sky.'

'Who is sitting on the moon?' asked Khoka.

'There's no one on the moon, my dear. That's the stain on the moon.'

'What is 'tain?'

"It's like the stain on a metal plate, you know,' explained Bhabani.

The son looks at his father in amazement. His lovely innocent face is without a stain. The moon has stains, but not his son's face.

Bhabani also looks in wonder at his son. Where had this child been all this time?

What was that bond touching his heart, moving him, something from the far away past? The world that was so familiar and visible everyday, where Foni Chakkarty sat reckoning his interest, Chandra Chatujje's son, Kailash Chatujje politicked and bargained trying to be a social leader, a world mired in endless pettiness, greed and sin—it was as though momentarily he was not part of this world. Seemingly so very familiar at one level, it was completely unknown, deeply mysterious, in tune with the unheard but tangible rhythm of the universe, the cosmos.

The air behind them was fragrant with akanda flowers, as though the still blue space was immersed in meditation of the eternal. The music of life, that pure unstruck sound he was hearing in so many voices today; five hundred or a thousand years later…where would those voices disappear? In the flow of time new histories would unfold on the riverbanks by the restless waters of the Ichhamati. Father and little son sitting here by the river on an afternoon today and the immense love and affection between the two—no one would know of it. Only the One would be ever unchanging, in the midst of all flux. It was human beings who wanted to imagine bhagwan as Brahman, like Light itself. Revealing itself in such lovely afternoons, in every flower and fruit, every spring, in the millions of births and deaths, in hope, love and compassion revealed only in faint glimpses… no religious scripture in the world could say what the One's form was. Even if a sage had experienced it from within, he had not expressed it…Who could say what it was?

But it also seemed that however infinite, however great bhagwan is, he is like us. There is some link between my heart, the heart of a child and bhagwan. It was not only that bhagwan has created me;

I am related to the divine by close intimate ties. I have the right to look upon His face without fear and with love...in the countless stars of the night sky. For bhagwan is as a loving father to me. I am not just a doll created by bhagwan, but his child, flesh of his flesh. This little boy before me is also a manifestation of the divine. His meaningless laughter, his childish prattle are all a part of cosmic play, joy manifested in the realm of sound.

This little boy too, will grow up and have a family with a wife—and children will be born to them. Bhabani Barujje would not be present in that future. Just as one forgets an incident from one's life that happened some ten years ago, he too would be forgotten. This cane grove, the ancient flowering saptaparna tree, perhaps *they* would still be there, but not him.

Bhabani's heart filled with the mystery of the cosmos. The rays of the setting sun, Nistarini's intelligent enquiring eyes, Tilu's loving gaze, the blue-eyed wonder of the child before him were a part of the mystery that filled Bhabani and they were part of the most mysterious deep and secret power of creation itself.

He was startled by Tilu's voice from behind him. She had her towel slung over her shoulder and the water-pot in the crook of her arm. She had come to bathe in the Ichhamati.

'I *knew* it—that he would be sitting here with Khoka,' she said with a smile.

'Come to bathe?' asked Bhabani smiling back at her.

'To see you both, too.'

'Where is Nilu?'

'About to begin the cooking.'

'Come sit.'

'No one will come this way, I hope.'

'Who would—at this time of the day?'

Tilu sat down, her body resting against Bhabani's. She had put down her water-pot and now almost embraced her husband.

'Khoka is looking very astonished; don't behave so—he's growing up,'

Tilu turned to her son: 'Khoka, what have you learnt about bhagwan?'

Looking at his mother Khoka said, 'Ma, O Ma, I want to bathe.'

'Won't you answer my question?' she asked him.

'Want to bathe.'

Glancing around, Tilu said, 'I'll wash him and then we shall bathe. Come, let's go for a swim.'

'Sit down, Tilu,' said Bhabani. 'I've been talking to Khoka about bhagwan and you know, I felt something—that he was there in the sky, the wind, the river waters...in this boy. To give him pleasure, is to delight in him.'

Tilu was listening intently to her husband with a serious expression. She never took his words lightly. 'So you experienced Brahman?' she asked eagerly.

'You're making me laugh,' he protested.

'Then, what was this experience about?'

'His shadow crosses across my heart once in a while. He comes close to me, as it was today—we are his, not separate. However great he might be, vast as he is, he is not another, but our father. *Divyehamurta purushya*—do you remember?

'But that is precisely to experience Brahman. I am sure of it. Whatever brings you so close to bhagwan, is it not *Brahmanubhuti*?

'I shall come to the river with Khoka every day and speak to him about bhagwan. How else will he realize his own humanity?'

'You must do as you think right. Come now, let us bathe first, and then go for a swim. Khoka, sit here on the bank.'

Khoka, who was a most obedient fellow, signified his assent.

'Don't get into the water.'

'Won't.'

Husband and wife had a glorious swim, bathed and dried Khoka and came home by the grass path just as the evening sky was about to be lit up by the moon and the fireflies beginning to be visible.

It was the waning of Chaitra, moving into summer. The fields and the forests were radiant with flowers. On that empty stretch of grassy land, the flowers of the ghentu swayed in the sprightly south wind. In the still silent blueness suggesting the meditation of the eternal, Bhabani Barujje felt that on such a beautiful and lonely evening just behind the horizon, intimations of that unknown land, a life yet to be experienced, were approaching them. True that he had found refuge in his guru and had then come away, had finally not become a sannyasi but a householder, and true too, that he had married three women at one and the same time, getting further entangled; but did that matter? The field, the river, the wild foliage and greenery, the cycle of seasons, birds, evenings and moonlit nights all had brought to him such exquisite *ananda*, as though a new Upanishad was being composed within his own heart. This was the fulfilment of his life...he could sense him even in his little Khoka.

The village women had just left the river ghat, carrying back water for their homes, their wet footprints now invisible on the dusty path; flocks of river-mynahs and magpie-robins had stopped singing only a while ago. Some beautiful young village woman must have bent the *nagkesar* tree with its flowering branch a little before evening to pluck its flowers...beneath the tree, stamens tipped in golden pollen lay scattered, emerald green shining leaves lay like a carpet on the ground...

Suddenly, remembering Bilu, he felt very sad. He must have neglected her in some way, but had not done so consciously. Was it possible to understand always how a woman might feel? There is no happiness in this world without sorrow—real happiness can only be experienced after deep sorrow...the happiness that comes without sorrow is superficial and shallow. The joy that may come after sorrow has been experienced is of a cleansing nature, giving one a true taste of life. Those who have called life only sorrowful know nothing of life, but to believe that life is only full of sorrows is to deny the divine. The world was a joyous state of experience—ananda. However, one needed the right kind of vision to experience. These were some of the truths he had begun to apprehend.

Khoka lifted up his arms to Bhabani, 'Baba, I'm afraid,'

'Why my dear?'

'A fox! Take me in your arms.'

'No. Come on, keep walking.'

'I'll cry then.'

'We're both in wet clothes, my love,' said his mother. 'What do you want to get wet for so late in the day? Come now, you must walk along.'

Nilu was waiting for them; she had already performed the prayers and had kept ready a place for Bhabani.

The verandah had been freshly wiped and polished and now sparkled clean. As soon as the prayer was over Nilu came to ask if she should get some food. She brought some murki in a bell-metal vessel and two slices of coconut for Bhabani.

'You will have to spend some time with me too, talking to me...' she said to them.

'Do sit down Nilu. What are you cooking?'

'No, I don't mean *that* kind of conversation. You're too clever by half! The kind of conversation you have with Didi, that kind.'

'I see you are very jealous of your Didi. What kind of conversation is that, may I know?'

'Samaskrita and all that stuff about gods...Brahma or something like that...'

Bhabani laughed heartily and looked at her affectionately. 'It's because you've never *wanted* to listen that I never spoke to you of these things. Well, let it be so from now onwards. But you know how you acted just now? In ancient times there was a sage who had two wives, Gargi and Maitreyi—you behaved like Gargi: if my co-wife wants realization of Brahman, whether I understand or not, I too want the same, that was Gargi's real intention.'

'What are you eating, Baba? I want some...' said Khoka.

'Come, Khoka.'

Bhabani fed him a bit of murki. Khoka looked at the bowl and said, 'Coconut.'

'No. It will give you a stomach ache.'

'Stomach bite?'

'Yes, my son.'

'Baba, O Baba, stomach bite?' repeated Khoka.

'Yes, dear.'

'Baba?'

'Yes?'

'Stomach bite?'

'Stop it now!' scolded Nilu. 'What a fellow he is—to go on and on once he gets started on something.'

Khoka looked from the one to the other without quite comprehending her words.

'Who is she talking about, Baba?'

'Oh, about Nilu Bagdi who lives yonder. Now explain it to him, who we are talking about!' exclaimed Nilu and ran to pick him up.

Khoka expressed his displeasure by crying out, 'Let me go, I want to go to Baba...'

'No.'

'No, let me go, I'll go to Baba.'

'Put him down...here's a slice of coconut for you.'

Khoka was deeply attached to his father. He didn't like to let go of his father even for a minute. He took the coconut slice from Bhabani and put his head on his lap. 'O Baba, Baba!' he kept babbling.

'What is it Khoka?'

Khoka could only stroke his father and say, 'O Baba, Baba!'

'Here I am,' said Bhabani.

'Babaji, are you home?' came old Shyamchand Ganguly's voice.

Bhabani, getting very agitated, welcomed him, 'Yes, Uncle. Do come in.'

'Won't come in. I've got a light. Come along with me to Chandardada's chandimandap. That widowed daughter of milkwoman Bhani is going to be tried today—a verdict has to be given. It's going to be a tough one.'

'I don't think I'll come there, Uncle...'

'How can that be! You *must* come. Everyone's waiting for you.

It is society that is going to judge, and you are undoubtedly one of the leaders of our society. Don't *mind* my saying so, babaji, but you seem to be forgetting all your responsibilities.'

Nilu had already disappeared into the kitchen with Khoka.

It was not possible to refuse Shyamchand Ganguly—he was irascible and quick to take offence. Like Sage Durvasa of yore, he was free with his curses.

Bhabani went into the kitchen to inform Tilu and Nilu; it was a knotty business, that village trial, he wouldn't get back until late. Khoka ran up to grab his father's hand and said delightedly, 'Baba, come, we'll eat,'

'And what shall I eat?'

'Come Baba, sit. Lots of fun.'

'I'll have to go, dear; there's some work. You have your food.'

'I shall cry. You don't go. Don't go. Come sit. Lots of fun.'

An ecstatic smile shone on the child's face as he said these words. He tugged at his father's hand and made him sit on a stool—actually, the wooden base for rolling out *luchis*.

'Sit here. You eat.'

'H'mm.'

'I will eat.'

'Good.'

'Will you eat?'

From outside the kitchen, the-ready-to-curse Shyam Ganguly let out another shout, 'I say, is babaji going to take some more time or what?'

No, it wouldn't do. One couldn't keep Sage Durvasa waiting outside. Bhabani had to get up. Khoka clutched at his garment, 'Don't go, O Baba. Sit down, O Baba. I'll cry...'

Bhabani had to disentangle himself from those eager but feeble little hands and rush out. All the way Shyam Ganguly, who was considered to be a 'head' of society, kept on an unending patter about the trial. At Chandra Chatujje's chandimandap, someone's young widowed daughter was accused of having a secret affair.

Nothing of this remotely affected Bhabani; all he could think of was the loving intense look in Khoka's eyes, the pair of little fists that had tried to keep him back in vain, that he had disregarded and torn himself away from. He remembered an incident from Khoka's infancy...

He had been visiting somewhere and had not seen Khokon for long. He thought that when he came back in the evening Khoka would be fast asleep, wouldn't wake up the whole night. They would not be able to talk. But when he got home he found that Khoka was still up, waiting for his Baba. The moment he entered the room, the little fellow cried out joyously, 'O Baba! Come, come—picture—'

'Go to sleep. I shall come back from the other room.'

'O Baba, come, I'll cry.'

Bhabani loved the infant. He was not yet two at the time, and he spoke so beautifully, so tenderly. Bhabani felt as though the very spirit of his life was drenched with a tender emotion of nurturing. He lay down beside the child, who promptly embraced him by the neck and kept saying, 'My Bor-da, my Bor-da—'

'Indeed! How am I your Bor-da?'

'My Bor-da,' the child insisted.

'Am I your Bor-da? Well, all right.'

Since he had settled down in the village of his in-laws, all the younger people including the children addressed him as their elder brother, 'Bor-da' or 'Mej-da' the middle brother. If the child believed that the person he called Baba, also had another name, such as Bor-da, then so be it.

'Khokon, *my* darling Khokon,' said Bhabani caressing his child.

'My Bor-da.'

Bhabani felt it was a unique kind of love he sensed in that tiny little human heart. No one had accepted him so unreservedly and with such ease, in so little a time, without any attempt to judge him. That was the difference between thinking of the other as oneself. No discriminating between the self and the other.

'I'll tell you a story, Khokon. There lives an old wicked witch who lives in a t-a-ll palm tree, like that one—there. Her ears are big as baskets, her teeth like radishes—'

Before he could go any further, Khokon quickly hugged him and said, 'Af'aid. Af'aid...don't tell me more, I'll cry then.'

'Will you cry?'

'Yes.'

'All right, I won't then.'

A little later Khoka did something funny. Shaking his little head, spreading out both his arms and clenching his tiny fists he suddenly said, 'There's a wickitwitch...such big big ears—'

'Oh my goodness, Khokon!'

'Eee-eee-eee. There's a wickitwitch.'

'Oh no Khokon, I'm so afraid! Don't tell me any more. I'm afraid...'

'Hee hee!'

'Oh! I'm so very scared.'

'There's a wickitwitch—'

'No. No. Don't tell me any more!'

Peals of innocent delighted laughter came from Khoka. Bhabani was most amused; he pretended to hide his head under the pillow in fear.

Khoka again embraced his Baba who was so afraid and said to him in loving soothing tones, 'My Bor-da, my Bor-da.'

'Yes, you give me a hug, I'm so very afraid.'

'My Bor-da.'

'Come Khokon, come to sleep beside me.'

'Tell me the *jonti* tree...' demanded Khokon.

Bhabani started reciting the rhyme...

> 'The jonti-tree on the other bank has many jonti fruits,
> My heart goes a-hurtling eating the go-jonti's head,
> My life goes pit-a-pat, my throat goes dry;
> When shall I ever get past Hara-Gauri Field?'

Khoka suddenly flung his arms apart and opening his eyes wide began, 'There's a wickitwitch—'

'My goodness!'

'Big big ears...there's a wickitwitch.'

'O Khokon, don't tell me any more.'

'Hee hee!'

'Oh, I'm so afraid. Khokon, don't scare me so.'

'My Bor-da, my Bor-da...'

This evening, trying to appease Shyam Ganguly, he had sadly neglected Khokon.

≈

An unexpected event took place in the village. Nalu Pal became much too wealthy. Of course, in recent times, he had moved up from being just a grocer to becoming an owner of a big warehouse, doing a brisk trade in paddy, mustard and mung-kalhai dal at the trading centres, both at the *mukam* and district level. But this was on a different scale altogether.

It was Dinu Bhatchaj who brought the news to Foni Chakkarty's chandimandap one day. That ancient chandimandap, constructed in the days of the late Shivasatya Chakravarty, had turned dark with the fumes from coarse tobacco. The brahmans of the villages were by and large an idle lot; they wouldn't step out of their respective regions in their entire lives, for the simple reason that they did not need to. From morning to evening either Foni Chakkarty's or Chandar Chattuje's or Shyam Ganguly's chandimandap became the venue for a whole lot of idle, useless brahmans who managed to spend their time spinning yarns, gossiping and politicking against others who were vulnerable to their 'trials' and 'judgements'. They pounced on a hapless 'offender' who was then forced to treat them all to a feast for having done something that the collective pronounced 'anti-social'.

When Dinu Bhattchaj goggled at the ready audience and announced, 'Have you heard what our Nalu Pal's been up to?' everyone eagerly crowded around him.

'What is it? Do tell us, what's up?'

'Satish Kolu and Nalu Pal have made a fat profit from buying up tobacco. Not a trifling amount. Ten or twenty grand!'

'Amazing! You don't say!' cried out everyone in astonishment.

'The two have been quietly doing a lot of trading at the mukam for quite a while now. And *this* time, they bought up one lot of goods on credit at the Bhajanhaat-mukam and sent it to Calcutta. Satish Kolu's brother-in-law is a wholesaler at the Bhajanhaat, you see. And *he's* the one that's tipped them off. Otherwise, what would those two know of business! And that was enough to make them rich and red!'

'*I've* heard something as well,' insinuated Foni Chakkarty. 'That's not the real story: nothing to do with Satish Kolu's brother-in-law or father-in-law! It's to do with *Nalu Pal's* father-in-law—it's *he* who has lent them the money. Nalu puts on a certain face, but his situation is *quite* different in reality.'

Hari, the village barber, had come to shave the group. He would come to the chandimandap knowing that he would find his clients all in one place. He came on an appointed day and would first have a smoke before he got down to the business of shaving.

Now, he put down the earthen pipe he had been puffing on and said, 'No, Khuro-moshai, Ambik Pramanik is not rich—*that* I know. He's a small-time trader; where would he get so much money from?'

'Oh, he's got the money all right; just keeps quiet about it, that's all. Loves his son-in-law, and that's the *one* daughter he has. He's somehow managed to put that money together for his son-in-law. Can you run a business without any capital?'

Whatever they might or might not be able to put together from these conflicting versions, what *was* certain was that Nalu Pal had turned a wealthy man. Within less than a year this fact became well established when it was known that he had bought up a huge consignment of rice grains at the Patpatitala ghat. He leased out the ghat from the zamindar, and daily had ten to twelve big traders who transacted business alongside the loading and unloading of bulk purchases during the paddy and mustard season. The professional weighers he had employed for this purpose barely managed to keep pace with the rapid turnover of goods. He must have made a profit of at least twenty-five thousand from the Patpatitala warehouse in a single season. He employed a whole lot of people including a mohuree, a *gomasta*; and, in addition to the grocery store which was now transformed into a retail warehouse, he set up another shop for selling cloth.

From being a prosperous householder he was now a wealthy merchant, a *mahajan*. But you wouldn't know it to look at Nalu Pal. He wore a nine-yard dhoti worn above his knees in the manner of working people, and went about bare-bodied and barefoot. If he saw a brahman he would quickly join his palms together and bow down and take the dust of his feet. Tulsi beads strung around his neck, a sling-bag marked with the auspicious name of Hari in his hand—all in the manner of a humble Vaishnav. You would have to admit that what Nalu had achieved in one lifetime was a dream for most.

You might ask him, 'Pal-moshai, all well?'

And he would reply in the humblest manner, 'My salutations to you this morning! Do come in and be seated. No, Thakur-moshai, my business is in a bad way. All this show—I'll have to wind up. It's practically come to a halt. Can't run it any more.'

Going by the expression on his face, the naïve might start feeling sorry for Nalu. But this was merely Nalu's profession of Vaishnav humility; it had nothing to do with the real situation. About fifteen thousand rupees worth of business was transacted annually at the ghat. The capital for his cloth business alone came to thirty thousand rupees.

Nalu Pal had a partner, and that was Satish Kolu. There was a time when the two of them had hawked their goods, Nalu selling paan-supari and Satish, dealing in mustard oil, ferrying the load on his head to various weekly markets. Then came Nalu's little grocery shop that he had set up with his savings. However, it was Satish who had advised Nalu to buy up mustard, potatoes and tobacco in bulk from Teghora Sheikhati and Bandmura-mukam and sell them in the countryside. Satish was a partner, though without any capital; his job was to identify the business centres. Satish was a master at buying up goods at the opportune moment. A big-time merchant had only to look at Satish to know that here was a genuine buyer. This quality of Satish's lay at the root of their success. On his part, Nalu had earned a good name for fair dealing. Together, they had built up an impressive network running into tens of thousands of rupees.

When Nalu came home one evening, Tulsi began, 'We are nearing Kali Puja, dear, and look at you sitting so tight, all frozen up like!'

'Too much pressure at work! There's five hundred maunds worth of goods lying at the mukam; simply can't find a way of transporting them here.'

'I'm not going to listen to any of that. It is my desire to feed all the berahmans of the village, offer them a fruit feast, with luchi and sugar. You had better organize it. Also, I want an ornate gold bracelet—a *jasham*.'

'Whew! That's a lot of money!'

''So what! You have to do it for the sake of your children, bring down blessings on them. And for the little boy, you'll have to get a lot of ornaments—*pata, nimphal* and—'

'Now hold on a bit, wife; don't go rattling off the list so fast. Just wait.'

'No. There's no need to wait! You've got to bring Moyna-thakurjhi from her in-laws: let me send Shaw's mother this very day to get her.'

'We shall have her over for Kali Puja anyway, so get her across any day you wish. But wait, where will the brahman-thakurs have their feast? Now that Chandar Chattujje is dead...'

'I'll tell you...you can have the feast at Bhabani Barujje's home... Of my two desires, this is one.'

'What's the other, may I know?'

'Course you can. You'll have to make Ramkanai Kobiraj the *tantradhar*, the chief officiating priest—he shall recite the mantras.

Not one like him hereabouts.'

'Got it. But wife, what you want is very difficult to get. He's *not* the type that you can bring home with money. Bhabani-thakur is inclined the same way. Our only hope is Tilu-didimoni: have to get *her* on our side. You go and make her agree first thing. If it's held in *their* home, all the berahmans are sure to come.'

As an outcome of this discussion between husband and wife all the brahmans of the village were invited to Bhabani Barujje's house on the night of Kali Puja.

Tilu's Khokon kept greeting all the guests with a 'How are you?' To some, he said, 'Do come, come. How are you?' happily blurring the different forms of address, the honorific with the familiar. When he saw Tilu and Nilu serving salt on everyone's platter, he too demanded that he be allowed to help. He would stand before a guest and looking at him with his eager expressive eyes would ask him, 'Will you have some salt? Some salt?'

With his beautiful face he was quite a favourite. 'An' wouldn't it be so? The mother's a beauty and the father so handsome!' they said to each other. Only to see him one more time and hear him speak they would cry out, 'Here, Khokon, we need some salt here... this way, baba!'

'C-o-m-i-n-g!' Khoka would respond most busily.

Ramkanai Kobiraj recited the mantras for the Kali Puja. He was also partaking of the feast, seated slightly apart from the others. Tilu plied him with hot fluffy luchis, even as he protested, 'No, my Didi! Why are you giving me so many! Can't eat so much, you know.'

Ramkanai Kobiraj was getting old. Even if he was a good doctor, he wasn't worldly at all, so he hadn't been able to save anything. He remained as poor as in former times. Burra Saheb Shipton had sent for him once, wanting to give him some money as a gesture of penitence for the earlier treatment meted out by the Neelkuthi, but Ramkanai did not want to take any gift from a mlechha. He had refused the money.

Nalu Pal, now known by the more formal name of Lalmohan

Pal, was standing at a distance gazing at the brahmans feasting. It was a fortunate day for him indeed that he had managed to feed so many kulin brahmans with luchi and sugar. Half a maund of flour, ten seers of ghee made from cow's milk, and ten seers of sugar. A gargantuan affair of gifting and feasting!

'O Tulsi, come stand here and have a look, a worthy sight!' he called out to his wife who was standing shyly beneath the jackfruit tree. Her sari-end pulled over her head, her face almost invisible, Tulsi came and stood not too far away from her husband.

Husband and wife gazed in a mesmerized manner at the invited brahmans. The joy in Nalu Pal's heart was indescribable. Hadn't he suffered in his uncle's home as an adolescent and in the early years of his youth? His aunt would grudge him even a few drops of oil. He had kept his hair long for a while—a teenage fancy; his hair would always be rough and wild-looking for lack of oil. If he ate a bit more rice than usual he would be told, 'For how long are we going to provide fodder for an elephant!' But had he *ever* sat idle? Huge quantities of rice from the Bhathchhala market, some two kos away, he had carried back on his head. His aunt had given him the responsibility of drying all the rice that was boiled in their home. Half a maund and twenty-two seers of rice was boiled every day! One day, on his way back from the weekly market, he had lost a silver two-anna coin; it must have fallen off from the knotted end of his garment. For three days running, each time his aunt served him food, she would say, 'There's no more grain...all 'bout to finish. For how long are you going to devour the stack your uncle has saved up, huh? Better find your own way!' He had wept bitterly that day.

The same Nalu Pal was now able to organize a grand fruit-based feast along with luchi and sugar for such a large number of brahmans...He wanted to shout out loud and clear, 'Tilu-didi! Give lots to everyone, give to each one whatever he desires—there was a day when I suffered so much for a mouthful of food!'

When the brahmans were leaving after their meal, Tulsi came and stood beneath the jackfruit tree, the sari-end covering her head in deference to their age and caste. Lalmohan addressed each and every one of his guests with folded hands: 'Thakur-moshai, did you have your fill?'

People in the village loved Nalu Pal. The guests left saying nice things, blessing him. Sambhu Ray, the distant relative of Rajaram Ray who was a copyist in the Amuti Company in Calcutta, even said, 'Come on Nalu, come with me to Calcutta on Monday. There's going to be a festival this coming week, you'll enjoy all the celebrations; no one in this village is interested in anything new—frogs in the well that they are! They've started a rail line from Howrah to Bardhaman, you'll see that too—'

'I know about the railways. My goods came on the railway from somewhere that side. That's what our mohuree was telling me.'

'But have you *seen* it?'

'When did I ever go to Calcutta that I'd see it?'

'Come and you'll see it this time.'

'I get scared. Heard that Calcutta's a real den of thieves and gamblers, that city.'

'You'll be coming with me. You're rich people, what do you have to worry! I'll fix you rooms in some good Bengali inn. You'll never see anything like it, ever. The Sarkar is celebrating their victory in the Kabul war.'

≈

So that was how Nalu Pal and his wife Tulsi set off for the celebrations in Calcutta. There was a lot of opposition to Nalu taking his wife along with him. People said that the sahebs would make them eat beef and turn them into *Krishtaans*—scary things like that. Sambhu Ray was the one and only person of this village who was experienced about life in Calcutta. He somehow managed to convince everyone and successfully took Nalu and wife away on their tour of Calcutta.

In Calcutta they rented a little thatched hut in the Kalighat area. The rent was a bit steep, at one anna per day. Tulsi bathed in the Adi Ganga, offered bel-leaves plated in gold, and a sacrifice of a pair of goats at the Kali temple. They went to bathe in the Ganga every day for all the seven days they were in Calcutta, offering puja afterwards.

As to the houses, the horse and carriages of Calcutta—how could Nalu and Tulsi even begin to describe them! The high and mighty came for their promenade to the Maidan in their carriages of four horses, they had huge bungalows in the suburbs of Calcutta, along the rivers, where on Saturdays and Sundays *baijis* came to perform *nautches*—all this and more they were told. As to the innumerable sweet shops and all the eateries in the city! They'd never set eyes on such a range of food in their lives! On the day of the celebrations, there was a show of fireworks at the Maidan. Such a crowd there was of people jostling and shoving. The sahebs were making merry with their canes, hitting out at the people to clear a path for themselves. People fled to the side at the blows of the cane; Tulsi also got a whack of the cane; she turned around and saw two sahebs and one memsaheb behind her. The two men were swinging their canes from left to right, the people scattering away in fear. 'Mother dear!' exclaimed she, and skittered to the side. Sambhu Ray held them by their hands and steered them through. Another day, Nalu Pal went shopping. Vegetables were far more expensive than at home. For the first time he saw vegetables being sold in small quantities. Two paise for a seer of brinjals! How on earth did people live in the city? Milk cost one anna and six paise per seer; that too, not pure milk, but mixed with water. Sambhu Ray explained that the steep prices were partly because of the celebrations. Round potatoes were being sold quite cheap and in abundance. That was something he didn't have in the villages, and the potatoes were quite tasty. The rare occasion when the local grocers would bring it to the villages, they charged very high prices.

'Must buy up some of these round potatoes on our way back,' said Nalu to his wife, 'If it's profitable enough, I'll get them wholesale in future.'

'That's food that the sahebs eat, not fit for cooking through the year and at all times.'

'Who has told you that it's the sahebs' food? They're being grown in our land too. I keep in touch with what's happening at the mukams. Kalna and Katowa in Bardhaman district—that's where potatoes are cheap, a lot are grown in the region. Just that they don't sell in *our* village; else, couldn't I've got them from Kalna now? They do sell in the cities; but in the village, who'd be buying them?'

'You're impossible!' replied Tulsi, 'Like the pestle that goes on grindin' even when it rises to heaven it's only business, buyin' and sellin'! The same when you've come here too.'

≈

Nalu Pal had to recount stories of his wondrous visit to Kolketey for days on end to the villagers. But soon an even more wondrous event took place.

Around mid-winter, Dewan Harakali Sur and Narahari Peshkar turned up one day at Nalu's warehouse. Nalu Pal and Satish Kolu welcomed them, stiff with anxiety, eager to please. The guests were promptly served paan and tobacco. They were the higher ups from the Neelkuthi, not the sort to visit commoners. Satish Kolu dashed off to Nobu confectioner's to organize the food. A little later, Dewanji informed Nalu about the reason for his visit: the Burra Saheb wanted some money on loan. The 'Bengal Indigo Concern' was selling off its interests in the Mollahati plantation. They didn't want to continue, given the current low prices for indigo in the market. Shipton Saheb wanted to retain the plantation for himself; he would have to pay fifteen thousand rupees to the Bengal Indigo Concern. The Burra Saheb was offering to mortgage the Neelkuthi in return for a loan of the money from Nalu Pal.

'That's the only way out to keep the Kuthi going,' explained Narahari Peshkar. 'Otherwise, the plantation business will be over this summer, by Chaitra month. We'd lose our jobs of course, and Saheb too, would have to leave.'

'The Burra Saheb is very keen on trying to run the Kuthi himself,' Dewan Harakali confided to Nalu. 'He's spent so long in these parts;

he doesn't want to go anywhere else now. Besides, he doesn't have anyone in his own country. Memsaheb died, and the one daughter he has—she's never set foot here.'

'Dewan-babu, can't say anything right away,' Nalu Pal replied with folded hands. 'Got to ponder over it. Besides, I'm not the only one in the business, have to get my partner to agree. I'll let you know in three or four days.'

'Why three, take up to fifteen days if you need to, Pal-moshai!' said the dewan graciously, as he took his leave. 'We'll need the money around March; there's still a lot of time.'

'My goodness!' said Tulsi, when she heard about the visit.

'Set me wondering too. How things have changed!'

'Will you give the money?'

'I'm not too unwilling. Such a huge Kuthi house, a hundred and fifty bighas of khas-land, mango orchards with such delicious grafts, horses, carriages, tables and chairs, and the chandeliers—all that will be part of the mortgage. Even in its last days, that Kuthi has a lot to offer. But Shotey Kolu is not keen on it. Says, we're people who trade; why get into all of this? Who knows whether we'll have to get into legal issues, maybe have to go to court?'

Nalu Pal was unable to sleep the entire night. Fragments of memories drifted in and out...Burra Saheb Shipton on his tom-tom... the paiks and lathiyals—the Kuthi's private army; fear and terror... Lay down strokes of the Shyamchand...Burn down the villages... and him making his way back and forth to the Mollahati weekly bazar with his load of paan and supari...

Such a strong desire he had to lend the money to the Burra Saheb.

≈

That very year, besides the celebrations for victory in the Afghan war, something noteworthy took place.

After only a few days of fever, Burra Saheb Shipton breathed his last at the end of March.

No one had ever dreamt that the saheb would die so suddenly.

Gaya-mem's devotion in nursing him was unparalleled. She was by the patient's bedside from the first moments of his illness. In his delirium Shipton was sometimes babbling, sometimes singing snatches of this and that. Gaya-mem could not understand all that he was saying.

'Gaya, listen…' he would say.

'Yes, my dear?'

'Givv me brandy. You will have to givv me.'

Gaya had been up for several nights in a row. Her eyes were red, her clothes and hair dishevelled. The entire entourage of the Kuthi's employees—dewan, orderly, amin and the small fry, were on their feet attending to their master's wishes. Even in the waning days of the indigo business, they considered themselves salaried employees of the Bengal Indigo Concern. But Gaya was the only woman in the household. It was she who attended to every little thing, staying up nights.

Gaya would not let him drink. 'Doctor's told you not to. You won't get any,' she said, in a scolding voice,

Shipton turned to look at her. 'Dearie, I adore you—you undertand? I adore you.'

'Now, don't speak nonsense.'

'Brandy, just a little, won't you? One little bit.'

'No. I'll give you some candy water.'

'Oh! To hell with your candy water! When am I getting my peg? Givv brandy…'

'Shh, be quiet. Your cough will get worse. Your head will ache.'

Shipton Saheb lay down quietly for a while. Two days later, the fever took a turn for the worse. Dewan Harakali Sur tried very hard to get his master over to Calcutta. But the saheb was adamant about not leaving his home. Senior doctor Askhay was called over from the sub-divisional town; he too advised that the patient should not be moved at this stage.

Gaya-mem sent for Ramkanai Kobiraj.

Ramkanai Kobiraj, carrying his little bundle of roots and herbs, was sitting in a chair near Shipton's bed.

'Ah! The old medicine man!' Shipton said to him, 'When did I meet you last, my old medicine man? You will be obliget to reply, a reply I will want...'

Then, after falling into silence for a while, he said, 'You will not be looking at the moon, will you? Your name and profession?'

'That's how he has been, Baba, for the last couple of days. Only nonsense he's been saying since yesterday,' said Gaya to the kobiraj.

Ramkanai was examining the patient's pulse with great concentration.

'*Kshine balabati nari, sa nari pranaghatika*: that pulse which is faint...is mortal indeed,' he pronounced. 'Give him some anise seed water from time to time, my child. You will have to get the accompanying dose for the medicine I shall give. This dose will be more critical than the anupan, which must be given prior to the medicine. I too shall try and get you some of it; I know where they are to be found, I will need another person to help me.'

Shipton Saheb was trying to get up from his bed, 'You see, old medicine man, I have too many things to do this summer to have any time for your rigmarole—you just—'

Sriram Muchi and Gaya-mem gently laid him down on the bed again.

'No, you're not to say such things, for shame...' Gaya-mem said to him in a loving tone.

The saheb was still looking at Ramkanai. He said after a while, 'Shall I get you a glass of vermouth, my good man—will you have a glass of liquor? It's good stuff. Oh, that reminds me, when am I going to have my dinner? When will my khana be servt? Bring my khana—'

The next two nights he tossed around restlessly, upsetting Gaya with his continuous babble and crying out from time to time. From the afternoon of the third day he fell into a kind of doze. Only once, very late at night, he stared ahead and cried out to Gaya, 'Where am I?'

'Saheb, what are you saying?' Gaya asked, bending low over him. 'Don't you recognize me?'

The Burra Saheb kept gazing at her and finally said, 'What wages do you get here?'

Those were his last words. His breathing became harsh and difficult and it went on like that for a long time. Gaya began weeping. Around his bed stood the old employees—Sriram Muchi, Dewan Harakali Sur, Narahari Peshkar, Prasanna Amin, and Nafar Muchi.

'Oh, it's unbearable to see such suffering!' said Dewan Harakali. 'Isn't there anything one can do?'

But Shipton Saheb was not suffering.

No one beside him knew that he was then far away in his native land—in Alderry village of Westmoreland, walking along the narrow winding mountaneous path of Rhino's Pass in the shady glens of oak and elm with his ten-year-old younger brother, out hunting rabbits; sometimes, on a boat rowing on Elterwater—that huge lake in the hills; with them, their faithful Great Dane; or, quite absorbed in drawing up on his fishing line a huge carp or a pike, trying to land it; and always, always…he could hear the pealing echoes of their village church bells that came wafting through the cold mountain wind blowing and rustling through the branches of the beech trees.

≈

Tilu served her husband the entire lot of the dish she had cooked with dumur-figs, 'It's for you, eat it up.'

Bhabani, a wet towel still draped over his body, tried to protest. 'Stop, stop.'

'You enjoy it, why won't you have it?'

'Has Khoka eaten?'

'He's out playing. O Nilu, will you bring the fish? Will you have the prawns first, or the fried khoira fish?'

'Who gave the khoira?'

'Who would *give* it? Nimai and Bhim fishermen brought some over. Paid them two paise. They're not accepting cowries in the market any more. They say give us copper coins.'

'Everything is changing over time, and so much to come! And have you heard—?'

Just then Nilu came with the fried khoira fish; Bhabani invited her to listen to his tale. The rail was coming to their land—tracks had been laid upto Chuadanga. That machine-gari would be there either this year, or latest by the next year. Tilu was listening spellbound, her face resting on her bauti-ornamented arms, when there came a clattering sound from the kitchen. Nilu, who had just put down the plateful of khoira fish and was listening wide-eyed to these marvels, her clenched fist against her chin, ran towards the kitchen with the plate.

'Get out! Out you go, you wretch!' they heard her cry from the kitchen.

'Taken it all?' asked Tilu craning her neck.

'Taken that big beley-fish I'd fried for Khokon—he was to have it for dinner!'

'Was it that tomcat?

'The tom it was!'

'Don't let him come in, beat him and shoo him away with the broom.'

'Well, he too, is a living being. Who will feed him if he doesn't get anything from you or me? He's taken it, well done,' said Bhabani. 'O Nilu, come now and listen to my tale. If I live a little longer, we shall not only see the rail lines, but we can go to the Raas fair at Santipur, riding on the rail machine!'

Once Nilu came back Bhabani told them about the large numbers of coolies who were clearing the jungle and laying the 'lines'. He had seen those long strips made of iron that they joined up and made into tracks.

'Let's go to see them,' said Tilu.

'Why would you only want to watch them lay out the lines? Best to go next year: we must actually ride the rail. Where shall we go to?'

Nilu promptly chanted, '*Jyoshti jugal*! Will Didi go too?

If in the month of Jyestha you see a pair,
In heaven will you be with your husband dear.'

'Ooh! Utterly devoted to her husband, I see,' joked Bhabani.

'What's there to laugh! You should rather say, "May the auspicious symbols of marriage stay with you." Mej-di was blessed indeed: she passed away with sindur in her parting, wearing her broad red-bordered sari. How long it has been already.'

'Couldn't you find anything better to say, while he is eating! The older she's getting in years, the worse she gets!' Tilu reprimanded her sister.

It was almost five years since Bilu's death, but Tilu knew that any reference to her made her husband absent-minded; why bring it up while the poor man was having a meal?

'O Didi, has Thakur-jamai finished his meal?' came Nistarini's anxious voice from the courtyard. She had draped her sari over her head out of respect for Bhabani.

'Why, my dear? What do you have in those bowls?'

'I've made a sour chutney of hog-plums, and this is cooked with kochu-greens. He'd said he liked them, so thought I'll cook him some and bring them along. Is he done?'

'No, come in and give them to him.'

'Why don't *you* give them, Didi? I feel shy…'

'Issh! His daughter's age you must be, and all this shyness! Come, bring them.'

'No, Didi.'

'Yes. You must.'

Nistarini came in awkwardly and put down the bowls near Bhabani's Barujje's plate. She didn't say a word. But her face was radiant with excitement and intense apprehension.

Bhabani tasted some of the vegetable and said, 'Excellent kochu-greens! Who has cooked this, bou-ma?'

Nistarini was considered an oddity in the village. She walked alone along the main paths, from one house to another, she spoke freely with many, and often behaved in a way that might be seen as dangerous—such as now, coming to their home in the afternoon, carrying home-cooked food from one locality to another. There was no other such wife in the village, no such daughter-in-law who had come from elsewhere. People loved to gossip about her, pointing her out with their finger, but Nistarini, who was not a child-bride, was made of strong stuff; she didn't much listen to her mother-in-law. She had been a beauty; now she was just a little past her youth, the sun moving westwards as it were.

Bhabani felt very compassionately towards her. What a strong and powerful woman, embodying the energy that moves the world; and yet, there was so much gossip and scandal about her. These parts of rural Bengal seemed to be made up of men who were not men—a group of ignoramuses! How would *they* begin to appreciate a beautiful strong intelligent woman as a marvellous creation! This lot of the supremely stupid spent all their time creating new rules and regulations in the name of saving their social world, what they called 'samaj'.

He had seen two such women, Nistarini and Gaya-mem, in this part of the world. Gaya-mem was another strong woman who had experienced much, embodying the struggle and aspirations of life.

Bhabani had heard of Gaya-mem from Ramkanai Kobiraj. After the death of the Neelkuthi's Burra Saheb she would come every day to listen to him recite the *Chaitanyacharitamrita*. Whatever she had by way of money, clothes, food—even a tiny measure of rice—she would not hesitate to give to anyone who seemed needy or sad. Many had tried to tempt her, but she had been resolute and had turned them away. Now she had fallen into very difficult times. Her own people had cast her out, wanting to have nothing to do with her once her patron, the Burra Saheb, had passed away. The same people had once flattered her greatly when a word from her would help change the fresh marking of land for indigo on this one or that one's plot, or would secure them odd jobs at the Kuthi. A lot of cowards they were!

≈

That evening Bhabani went over to spend some time at the sannyasini's ashram. Khepi was delighted to see him and attended to him with great deference.

'So how is it going?' asked Bhabani after a while.

She was another of those women—this Khepi. About forty years old, she had never been a beauty, but she was strong and determined—a sannyasini living alone in the dense forest. There were tigers, evil men, but she didn't care; would probably send them flying with one touch of the trident she held so firmly in her hand—that much confidence she had in herself.

'I'd like to listen to some good and true words,' she said, coming to sit beside Bhabani.

'Have I said anything untrue then?' said Bhabani Barujje with a laugh.

'How are the mothers?' she asked after his wives.

'Hmm.'

'Is Khoka well?'

'He's well. Goes to the village school. He wishes to come here.'

'Bring him over the next time.'

'Certainly, I shall.'

'Will you tell me, which do you like better—the divine manifested as Form or the Formless?'

'Let's not get into those big-sounding terms, Khepi. I'm a simple householder. If at all you wish to, you must listen to my guru-brother Chaitanyabharati.'

'Then you must tell us something about your travels in the western regions. I enjoyed it so much, that time when you were telling us on that rainy day.'

Bhabani Barujje often visited Khepi's ashram. Dwarik Karmakar was a devotee; he had recently donated money to get a little hut built for the convenience of all those devotees who were also devoted to their fix of ganja. Dwarik Karmakar had paid for the straw, the bamboos and the rope. Another devotee, Hafez Mondol, had put up the hut working very hard on it. They gathered every evening; soon, the pipal tree would be shrouded in smoke from cannabis. No one smoked in front of Bhabani Barujje though, for he was regarded with respect.

He began his narrative: 'A river flowing through a forest of sal forest, the hills above us full of gooseberries and wood-apple trees. Not a few, but many. My gurudev lived on gooseberries, wood-apples and custard apples. It's been a long while, time has moved swiftly. After all, it has been almost fourteen years since I've settled down in your land. Now I'm almost sixty-two years old. So much has happened in this time. But I feel that that my gurudev is still alive and deep in meditation beneath that gooseberry tree.'

Khepi sannyasini who had been listening intently asked, 'Is he not alive then?'

'One of my guru-bhais called Chaitanyabharati had come here a couple of years ago. Our guru was still alive then. I haven't had any news since.'

'A guru who initiated you with mantras?' Khepi wanted to know.

'Sort of. He didn't give anyone mantras; he was a guru to give good counsel.'

'I'd greatly desired to go and see him. But I've become too old; how would I walk to such a far-off land?'

'Have you heard—we're going to have the rail in our part of the country?' Bhabani asked.

'So I've heard. If the rail comes, will they let us get on, or is it only for the sahebs and such like?'

'I believe that all of us can get on. But you have to pay for it,' said Bhabani.

'Thakur-moshai,' declared Khepi, 'my god appears to me beneath this very *ashwath* tree. We're poor folks, if we don't have money enough to spend to go to Gaya, Kashi and Bindabon—would he not grant us grace simply because we are poor? Most certainly he will. He is there in Form, and as the Formless too, he is everywhere. Under the shade of this very tree he comes to a poor person's hut like mine and has ganja with all of us—'

'Ehh?!'

'Forgive me, Thakur-moshai for saying so. It was wrong of me. These are hidden and mysterious things. But it's only to *you* I've said this, not to anyone else.'

Bhabani smiled and kept quiet. It was wrong to try and break someone else's belief. Who was he to disabuse them of the belief, if they actually believed that bhagwan mingled with them and smoked ganja with them? These people of little wisdom did not try and begin with the vast; they had already limited the eternal in their own way and come to terms with it. Even if one could not meditate on the Boundless, surely there was an aesthetic pleasure, a certain *rasa*, in that *attempt* to imagine. They did not know how to experience that rasa; rather, they were eager to bring the Boundless within the bounds of the known and trivialize it.

'Are you angry?' asked Khepi. 'I know the kind of person you are, so I get scared of what you might think.'

'What's to be scared? Let people believe in whatever they wish to. What's the harm in that? Should I quarrel if it does not tally with my beliefs? I must leave now.'

'Have some fruits?'

'No. Not now. I must leave.'

Dwarik Karmakar came up with a gourd: 'Will have to cook a *shukto* dish with this gourd.'

'What's up, Dwarik? Are you going to have some?'

'Sir, would I do that ever?' said Dwarik modestly. 'Wouldn't even eat food cooked by my daughter! Had gone to her in-laws in Bhajanghat that time, so her mother-in-law said to me, "I've cooked some green gourd in mung-dal: will you have some?" "Forgive me, I can't," said I. Cooked everything myself in the verandah outside their kitchen.'

Dwarik Karmakar was considered a master at fishing with a line. Bhabani Barujje said to him, 'You are so good at fishing; why don't you tell us a story about your experience?'

'Why not, jamai-thakur?' Dwarik responded in the same modest manner. 'For two score years or so, I've been fishing alon' the river, by the lakes, ponds and waterbodies in these parts. Why *wouldn't* I be a good fisherman? If a man keeps at something with all his heart and soul, wouldn't he become ripe at the job?'

'If you had been after bhagwan for all these years, you would have realized *him* by now. Why did you waste the precious gift of human life on fishing?' Khepi retorted.

Dwarik looked embarrassed and ashamed at her words. He had never reflected on such things. It was only now, when he was sixty-five years old, that he was hearing of such new things. He walked away listlessly to the edge of the akanda bushes and put down the gourd.

Bhabani felt for him. He turned to the sannyasini: 'Now Khepi, what are you saying to Dwarik? *I* had a wonderful guru and yet, I've come here to your village and become a householder. Why? Can anyone figure out why? Let each one do what he is capable of doing. But he must do that well, with all the truth in his heart, not deceiving anyone, not hurting anyone. If everyone is going to be special, what would happen to our everyday life? Not every stone is sacred and worthy of worship; don't we also need stones to grind spices with?'

'I can't bear ignorins at all! Dwarik, don't you be angry. Where is that gourd now? Won't I be giving you some shuktani that I'll cook? Once it becomes Ma Kali's persad, where's the question of losing caste!' said Khepi.

Bhabani's presence created a certain uneasiness, for the regulars felt obliged to stop smoking ganja in deference to his status. Hafez Mondol came and stole a look at Bhabani, as though saying god knows from where this nuisance of a jamai-thakur has turned up! No way can we enjoy even a bit of ganja.

'Look at all these creatures!' said Khepi, 'All they'll do now is to puff away.'

'It is you who has encouraged them; would they dare otherwise?'

'It's true that I smoke some, helps me take my mind in a direction,' admitted Khepi.

It began to rain a little. Bhabani tried to leave but the others wouldn't let him. So they all took shelter in the thatched hut. They were thrilled to hear from his lips the story of Sankhya-Likhit from the Mahabharata. Sankhya and Likhit were two brothers, both practicing austerities, each one in his own ashram. The younger, Likhit, went one day on a visit to his elder brother's ashram and found no one there. As he waited for his brother's return, his eyes fell on a ripe fruit amidst the foliage of the fruit trees in the hermitage. Marharshi Likhit promptly picked the fruit and devoured it. A little later when his brother returned Likhit told him about eating the fruit. Sankhya's face fell when he heard this. What! To be an ascetic—and steal someone else's belongings! Even if it was from a tree belonging to his brother, it was still not his own. To take someone else's possession without telling them was as good as stealing, however trifling the object might be. And for an ascetic, it was a major sin.

'Dada, what shall I do?' asked Likhit most humbly.

His elder brother counselled him to go to the king and seek judgement on the charge of theft. Likhit followed his words unconditionally. Astonishing the entire array of people assembled at the court, he begged the king to be punished. The king too was stunned. How could he punish a sage—Maharshi Likhit—on charges of theft? When Likhit told him the story, the king tried to laugh it off. But Likhit was adamant. 'My brother is wise and a seer,' he told the king. 'Since it is *he* who has instructed me to seek punishment, I beg of you to do so.' After many pleas and much persuasion, the king pronounced the same punishment that was meted out to thieves—to have both his hands cut off. Likhit returned to his brother's hermitage in that condition; Sankhya wept when he saw him. He embraced his brother and said, 'An ill wind blew you here today! How did you succumb to greed and eat a mere guava to commit such a sin?'

It was the hour of twilight. The Sun God was on his way down. 'Come my brother,' Sankhya said, 'let us perform the evening ritual.'

'But I don't have hands to make the offering with,' said Likhit helplessly.

'You have always been a follower of truth. You made a mistake and have even accepted the punishment for your act. If the Sun God does not receive the offering from your hands today, will there be any truth or dharma left in the world? Come with me.'

Just as he was about to make an offering in the waters of the Narmada, Likhit's chopped arms became whole again. The two brothers embraced each other and came home. The way back was enveloped in darkness. Laughing, Sankhya said to his brother Likhit, 'Let's see how many guavas you manage to eat tomorrow morning!'

Dwarik Karmakar exclaimed with delight at the story.

Hafez Mondol expressed his appreciation with 'Ahaaa...such a tale!'

While Khepi, who was sitting behind them, broke out in emotional sobs.

It was as though the ashram way of life from ancient India came alive for a while in that obscure little village—a Bharatvarsha with the spirit of meditation and aspiration, ready to renounce all for the rigour of truth. It was clear to everyone present...Likhit with his outstretched bloodied arms walking all the way from the court to his brother's ashram through the forest, crying out 'Dada'.

Just the other day he had cheated a customer of an anna when he was doing up his sickle, thought Dwarik Karmakar.

Hafez Mondol remembered that last Wednesday evening he had quietly slashed off two long bamboos from Kuranram Nikiri's bamboo copse to make some fishing rods with. He often did so. He wouldn't, any more. Aah! Those were worthy people indeed who had lived in former times! How enjoyable it was to listen to jamai-thakur tell these stories.

Khepi brought out two bananas and some slices of cucumber for Bhabani Barujje. Placing them before him she said, 'Please have some.'

'Bhagwan is like a mother to us,' Bhabani was saying as he ate, 'his disciplining is the same way. The mother might forgive others making mistakes, but she does not indulge her own too much. She cannot bear if others should criticize the one she considers to be her own. This too, is the path of love. The devotee has to be moulded to perfection. He or she realizes that the fiery visage of the divine is but another manifestation of his loving contented face—one that is always there for the devotee.'

Coming back from Khepi's, Bhabani saw Nistarini on her way home, alone and in the dark. When she saw him, she stepped away from the path, and stood by a tree. Where was Nistarini coming back from so late at night? Perhaps she had been visiting Tilu. She rarely visited other women of the village.

They were the women of the future, sounding the notes of the life yet to come. Only a few could hear the tidings that barely sounded in the footfall of their bare feet—the soles ornamented with red lac. Some did hear the imminent sound. In the overwhelming darkness that enveloped rural society such brave young women were treated badly, barely accepted. In every chandimandap ancient brahman males were cooking up machinations and conspiring against them, but it was *these* women who were ushering in a new kind of life.

He remembered too, those distant western regions where he had seen many such brave women in Brajadham, in Bithoor, in the Valmiki hermitage...There, in the evergreen leaves of keli-kadamba as though intermingled with yellowish neem leaves, the deep blue covered by the red flowers of the *atimuktalata* bush, peacocks danced in a flock while beneath shady trees ghaghra-clad, the slender and strong young women of Braja sport in the dark waters of the Yamuna also known as Kalindi...

When would the women of Bengal arise? When would daughters

and wives full of radiant energy like Nistarini be born in the homes of Bengal?

≈

'Nistarini has got into a fix again,' confided Tilu to her husband that night.

'What is it?'

'She's got involved with someone again...'

'Gobindo?'

'No. Not him. Someone from her natal home, comes to see her every now and then.'

'Don't worry. Nothing will happen. Who told you?'

'She did, herself. She was here quite late this evening sharing her thoughts with Nilu and me. She was quite open about everything, nothing secretive. That's what I like about her. But she was younger then, she's getting older now. I scolded her today.'

'No, you shouldn't scold her too much. Let each one do what he or she thinks fit.'

'And you know what, she loves you greatly—'

'Me?'

'Are you surprised? No trusting the male of the species. Who knows in which direction you turn and when! But listen, she really has a lot of respec' for you. She tells me, "Didi, it's a matter of great fortune to have a husband like yours." If I say you are old, she gets very angry. "He's hardly old. Show me how many among the *youth* there are who match up to Thakur-jamai!" she challenges me. Things like that, you know...hee hee! Wonder if she's taken a fancy to you. It's to look at you she comes to this house.'

'For shame! You musn't say such things. She's my daughter's age.'

'Well, *we* are young enough to be your daughters. What's that got to do with it! I'm telling you—she absolutely has a—'

'Now let that be. Where is Khoka?'

'He just got back from playing. Must have fallen asleep. He was reading something. He kept telling me, "Ma, I want to have my meal with Baba." I told him that you would be very late coming home. Shall I set your place?'

'Do. But first let me finish my prayers. Will you call Nilu?'

≈

Nilmoni Samaddar was in great difficulties. His household was in dire straits. The price for one katha of rice had gone up to three annas. Dewan Rajaram had been one of his major patrons; after he was murdered, Nilmoni was left in an awkward situation.

Rajaram-dada had not been a good man—he was full of wicked plans; a frontman of the sahebs. That's what brought about his death. It was common knowledge these days that he had gone secretly one night to hand over Kusum to the Burra Saheb; he'd told her all kinds of stories, deceived her and taken her along. To think that Shyam Bagdi had left his daughter at Rajaram's home so that she might turn out to be a good woman! But it must be said that the Burra Saheb had turned her away—didn't so much as let her step in. The times had changed, he told Rajaram, the raiyats were unhappy and ready to rise, they would do so at the slightest pretext, the Government would be angry too; the new magistrate was quite hostile to the planters. Take her back, he said. Who'd asked you to bring her anyway?

Rajaram had gone back home with Kusum.

It was Kusum who had narrated this tale to her kinsfolk. This was why the bagdis and duleys in particular were incensed with Dewan Rajaram. This was why he lost his life at the hands of a group of bagdis.

Nothing remained secret for very long in the village. Nilmoni Samaddar had learnt of this from the Kansona bagdis, who were the dominant group in the region. It was they who had come together and murdered the dewan. That Burra Saheb had refused to accept Kusum was also common knowledge; it raised the saheb's esteem in the eyes of the common man. But all that was history now. The real question was, what was Nilmoni Samaddar to do? His wife

Annakali was at him morning and night—'There's no rice at home. Do something, I can't do any more beyond telling you that there won't be any rice cooking from tomorrow.'

It was for Kansona village that Nilmoni Samaddar now set off, a little after noon, to the same house where Ramu Bagdi—murdered by the Kuthi's men—used to live. Ramu Bagdi's son Haru was seated beneath the jackfruit tree twisting and twining jute strands to make a rope. Haru had become prosperous in recent times: two stacks of grain and a stack of hay for his cattle lay heaped up in the yard.

As he came up to greet Nilmoni and welcome him, Nilmoni felt as though he was a drowning man who had just been thrown a rope.

'Baba Haru,' he said, addressing Haru in the familiar *tui*, 'get me some tobacco, will you?'

Haru went off to prepare the tobacco and brought back the kalke-pipe on a banana leaf, in accordance with the rules of caste pollution.

'And what brings you this way?' he enquired.

In the meantime Nilmoni had thought out a plan.

'It's to meet *you* that I've come,' he replied.

'What do you need?'

'Last night I had a bad dream...about your boy it was. Is Shashthi Narayan home? Call him over.'

A little later Narayan arrived, puffing away at his *thelo* hookah. Naran Sardar, as he was called—was the hand behind Rajaram's murder. He was magnificently built, tall and strapping—the headman of this village.

'Come, Narayan,' said Nilmoni, 'I've come to you because of a bad dream I had. I've always thought of you as my own, never considered you as another. That dream was about Haru's boy, Badal... it was as if I saw—' Nilmoni stopped abruptly.

'What did you see?' Haru and Naran cried out simultaneously.

'No point in your listening to what I saw. On top of everything, today is a Friday that is moonless. Oh no! It is said, *tadardhang krishi karmani*...half of it goes to husbandry. Disastrous! No! *That* won't work!'

Naran was the chief of his village, the sardar, and an intelligent man. He immediately came up to Nilmoni and said, 'In that case, Khuro-moshai, what is the prescribed way out?'

'Isn't that *pre-cisely* why I've come! You are not strangers. I've always been coming here, thinking of you as my own. Would today be an exception? No, my son—that wasn't the kind of father who had given birth to me...' Silence again, on Nilmoni Samaddar's part.

Naran Sardar might quite justifiably have asked why had the question of his birth come into the conversation in such an irrelevant way, but without quite comprehending all that Nilmoni had said, he responded with great agitation, 'Then you *must* perform the antidote. Forget about us, we neither see nor hear...what do *we* know! You do whatever has to be done.'

'But it is a grave matter,' replied Nilmoni. 'You see, we shall have to perform the *sharanga matrisadhan*. What day is it today? Now hold on...Friday, Saturday...Aah, Sunday is the second day of the moon in its bright phase, *shuklapaksha*! It's all worked out! But let me think it through.' Nilmoni fell silent again, apparently absorbed in a weighty problem.

Uncle and nephew stood stockstill in order to give Nilmoni the benefit of uninterrupted thinking.

'Got it! Think they can get away with it, huh!' Nilmoni announced with a beaming face, a little later.

'What is it, Khuro-moshai?'

'Not a word now! Just give me two grains of kalhai-dal, but be sure to first touch Khoka's forehead with them.'

Haru ran off and came back with the two grains of kalhai-dal that he handed over to Nilmoni. Closing his fist over them, Nilmoni made as if to leave.

'What! Are you off?' Haru and Naran called out in alarm.

'Must leave now. According to the almanac, Wednesday is in the phase of *ashtottori*. I'll have to perform the *sharanga* sacrifice with these very grains. Not a moment to waste.'

'Khuro-moshai, stop a moment—won't you please take two kathas of sonamung-dal for your home?'

'No time, my son! Not now. Let me at least get you the amulet tomorrow morning and we shall take it from there.'

Nilmoni walked back home with renewed energy. The fish had bitten. For years this was how he had been keeping his household afloat—travelling to this village and that to wheedle out something from one family or the other. Of course, you had to try different ways of getting the job done; it turned out differently each time.

On the edge of his village he came across Khetro Ghosh who was coming back from his field, a basket of brinjals on his head. Khetro stopped on seeing him, put down his basket, and twirling his thin towel to fan himself, complained, 'Too many rabbits, creating havoc they are! An' the moment I set a net to trap them, they're gone. Only ten gondas of brinjals I get from my two bighas of land! Do somethin' to help me. I was a thinkin' of comin' to you anyways.'

'Your work will be done. Tonight, at two *dwanda*, come to my home with one *haritaki*-berry. It's a moonless night; makes it even better,' said Nilmoni reassuringly.

'I'll certainly come,' said Khetro. 'I say, why don't you take home a couple of brinals?'

'Bring them along when you come; can't be carrying a load of brinjals home,' replied Nilmoni.

Approaching his home, Nilmoni heard unfamiliar voices. Who could they be?

Before he could enter, his daughter-in-law came running to the door, 'Baba—'

'What is it daughter-in-law? Who is that talking?'

'Shhh! Aunt Sarojini's arrived from Bhararkola along with her daughter and son-in-law. Two little grandchildren, too! Ma's told me that there's no rice at home; you must do *something* right away.'

'All right, go and tell her it will all be managed. Have the guests been given some snacks?'

'What *could* one give them? What's there at home!'

'That's true. Let me see what I can do.'

Nilmoni Samaddar walked up to the mango tree outside their house and began pacing up and down in a frenzied manner. What *was* to be done? As for his cousin Sarojini—couldn't she have chosen a better time to come? In any case, what was the need to come at all? Nothing but a nuisance! Never sent anyone to make enquiries about them, and all-a-sudden brimming over with love and affection!

While he was racking his brains Khetro Ghosh turned up. He had about five gondas of brinjals slung from a rope bag, an entire stalk of ripe bananas and a little pot of date-palm jaggery.

'The jaggery is made from my *own* date-palm trees,' said Khetro, handing over all the gifts to Nilmoni. 'My eldest has made it himself. Please accept it. And here are those two har'taki-berries you wanted. Brought those too.'

'Well, that's fine. But just now Khettar, I badly need a couple of kathas of rice. Guests have come, you see, and my son's not at home. He's supposed to bring two maunds of rice when he returns tomorrow. But what am I to do until then?'

'Not to worry! I'll get the rice right away.'

Khetro Ghosh was a full-fledged farmer; he did not lack anything by way of food at home. He came right back with the rice and then gave him the two berries. Nilmoni went in with the rice and the berries. He was back within half an hour.

Handing back the berries to Khetro Ghosh, Nilmoni instructed him, 'Now go and string up these two on a black thread and tie them to your fencing on the *eastern* side of your brinjal plot. That'll do it! I've just purified them with mantars. Not a son of a rabbit will dare enter your field!'

Nilmoni was back at Kansona the next morning. His daughter-in-law had hunted out an old amulet that he had filled with some resin from the jiuli tree and packed with mud. He took some sindur along with him, and picking up some bel-leaves on the way smeared them nicely with the sindur.

Haru and Naran were looking out for him anxiously. Haru hadn't slept a wink at night, he said.

'Then too, I told him not to breathe a word of this at home,' Naran Sardar added. 'Else, the womenfolk would have made a racket howlin' and weepin'.'

Nilmoni Samaddar handed over the pounded bel-leaves smeared in sindur and the amulet to Naran Sardar.

'You are like the little fellow's grandfather,' he said. '*You* go and tie this around his neck and feed him the juice of the bel-leaves. Didn't I stay up all night long to perform the appropriate sacrifice—*sharanga homa*! Plenty time to sleep later, I told myself. Haru is no different from *my* son. Let me first do *him* some good. It was hard work, my son. You take it to him now; Yama himself wouldn't dare to touch the boy. I'm feeling mighty relieved too…Phew!'

It would not be difficult to guess as to what transpired subsequently.

Haru's hired help, Goopley Bagdi, carried a load of one dhama of autumn rice and two kathas of sonamung-dal on his head to Nilmoni Samaddar's house.

And Nilmoni's household carried on in its usual fashion.

≈

Gaya-mem was making dung-cakes and putting them out to dry on the yard one morning when she sighted Prasanna Chakkarty Amin heading in her direction, Quickly, she pushed aside her basket full of dung and stood up to arrange her sari.

'What's up?' said Prasanna Amin as he approached her. 'Haven't I told you, Gaya, you are *not* to do this kind of work! Oh, it makes me sad just to see it. Once a queen and now a maker of dung-cakes!'

'If it's something one has to do for all time to come, best get started on it.'

'If at least your mother was alive…' sighed Prasanna Chakkarty. 'Died suddenly, didn't she? Wasn't yet her time…'

'It's one's fate, Khuro-moshai,' said Gaya. 'Otherwise…' She looked down at the ground, a melancholy expression on her face.

Prasanna Chakkarty glanced at where she lived. The house comprised two thatched rooms. One was an old-fashioned kitchen; in their days of prosperity, the ever-vigilant Barada Bagdini had rebuilt it with strong wooden beams, windows and a door made of the solid wood of a jackfruit tree. Gaya appeared to be using this as her bedroom: through the window Prasanna Amin could see a wooden bed. But the other room was in a wretched condition: the thatch was almost blown away; rat holes had erupted all over the place; the floor had not been smoothened and washed with dung for a long time, even the walls were beginning to crack.

'How did the room get into such a state?' asked Prasanna Chakkarty.

'What state?'

'It's about to collapse.'

'If it does, so be it! I'm a lone soul; how many rooms will I need to live in?'

Prasanna Chakkarty continued to speak, as if to himself, 'Those sahebs and all, you know—whatever it is, they are from a different land—what would they know about *our* joys and sorrows? *You* are to blame as well. Why didn't you ask for something at the time? You were at his side all the time. That's when one grabs and puts aside something for a rainy day.'

Gaya-mem was silent. It looked like there were tears glistening in her eyes.

'No! Never seen such an unthinking creature like you in this day and age! A currrsse on it!' said Prasanna Chakkarty emphatically.

The right to say such things and in such a manner came from Prasanna Chakkarty's genuine fervour for Gaya-mem, and she knew this better anyone else. Did she have any option but to listen silently?

Just then Bhagirath Bagdi's mother made an appearance.

'Ah, isn't that Amin-babu?' she cried out, stepping into the yard. 'Heard all that you said. Right you are! I tell her mornin' and evenin' the Burra Saheb's gone after makin' a mem out of you. Folks called you "Gaya-*mem*"; but I say—did he give you property to make you a *real* mem? Your Ma's dead; not another left in the family, not a cowrie to your name—only that bit of land in the Kuthi. Some rice you got out of it the past year, so you're still alive; else wouldn't you be starvin'? Not *one* among the bagdis will have any truck with you—as good as dead you are to them. No one will eat along'er you. Where will you go now? Raised you in my arms I did when you were a child. Who's goin' to tell you anythin' now that your Ma's dead? That woman's heart broke in two—that's how *she* died. Used to weep and tell me, "Didi, if that daughter of mine had a bit o' sense, we would be livin' right royal. But she came back empty-handed from the Neelkuthi."'

Provoked from both sides, Gaya replied in desperation, 'How does it matter to you both whether I eat or starve? I've done the right thing. Whatever I thought was right I did!'

Bhagirath's mother grimaced and made as though to leave.

Turning away she said, 'Hurts me bad, so I tell you. Don't I know you—you were *always* a stubirn nuisance. When you ruined your caste at the saheb's home, shouldn't you have at least sorted out your affairs? There was reason enough for her mother to weep her heart out this past year. No one's going to drink a sip of water touched by you; you can lie ill and dyin', an' who's a-goin' to give you a drink of water? You think on it Amin-moshai—the Neelkuthi's changed hands and gone to another; the saheb, he's kicked the bucket, and what's to become of you!'

'Whatever I could do by way of the paddy-land—that's the saving grace,' replied Prasanna Chakkarty. 'Otherwise, she wouldn't even have a place to stand on. At least she'll get *something* from those five bighas of land, even after paying off the sharecroppers.'

'An' is it *so* easy to get her fair share, babu?' retorted Bhagirath's mother. 'Is *she* capable of it? She's a *mem-saheb* you see! If they cheat you, what are you going to do, may I ask?'

After Bhagirath's mother left, Gaya-mem asked Prasanna Chakkarty, 'Khuro-moshai, did you come to quarrel with me? Are you going to be leaving or will you sit down?'

'No, why should I quarrel? Just that I keep longing for you, so I keep coming...'

At this, Gaya-mem began to laugh as in former times, covering her mouth with the end of her garment. Prasanna Chakkarty saw that she was already changed: sorrow, and a hard life had left their mark on that burnished beauty of hers. It was a good thing that he had been able to give her the land, measuring it out with his own hands. Otherwise, she would have surely starved to death.

Prasanna Chakkarty sat down on the palm-leaf mat that Gaya gave him.

'What will you have?' she asked.

'What do you mean?'

'Why Khuro-moshai, just because I'm from a low caste, can't I offer you any food? Got bananas, got a papaya. Won't cut the papaya; *you* can cut it yourself. Can't let you go without eating a morsel if you've come to my home.'

Gaya brought out two bananas, a whole papaya and half a coconut and placed them before Prasanna Amin.

'The water, I can't give you, Khuro-moshai,' she said with a smile. 'Wait, let me show you something,' she added, turning to go into her home.

'What?'

'I'm bringing it out. Just wait.'

A little later she was back with a small printed book and placed it in front of the amin.

'Take a look. And here—let me get you a cleaver, nicely washed. You can have the fruits then.'

'Wait, listen to me. Where did you get this book? A *book* in your home?' Prasanna Chakkarty couldn't hide his surprise.

'*You* take a look. Do I know how to read and write?'

'Did that old kobiraj give it to you? Can't read; what would he give *you* a book for?'

'He gave it, and I took it. *The Hundred Names of Krishna.*'

Prasanna Amin was astonished beyond measure. A printed book in Gaya-mem's home, and that too a sacred book with the hundred names of Krishna. Impossible!

He cut up the fruit with the cleaver and sat down to relish them. He left half of the papaya for Gaya.

'I enjoy coming here. When I come to visit you, I forget all my sorrows, Gaya,' he said with a smile.

'There you go again, spouting your nonsense. Come, if you want to. Have I ever told you not to come?'

'Say that. Let me be at peace.'

'That's good if that's so.'

'What will you do with that *Hundred Names of Krishna*?'

'I keep it by my head when I go to sleep. There's no one at home. Would've been different if Ma were alive. Gets rid of my fears of demons, spirits and all of that. I live alone.'

'That's so.'

'The entire neighbourhood—they've turned into enemies,' Gaya went on. 'When Saheb was alive, they'd flatter me. Now if I were to call them at night, not one will come to help me. That's why he's given me the book. Said all my fears would go away if I kept it by my side. Such a good man he is. Do you know, if I don't go to thresh the paddy today, there won't be a grain of rice for me to cook? Not a pestle will they lend me hereabouts; I'll have to go to Kenaram Sardar in the other locality. They're good people: bunos by caste they may be, but *they* have humanity in them, Khuro-moshai.'

Prasanna Chakkarty lingered till quite late in the day. Gaya's plight had sorely grieved him. On his way back he stopped beneath a madar tree in the Ganeshpur field. Ganeshpur was the name of Gaya-mem's village. Only bagdis and a few families of fisherfolk lived here. The tree was shady though the sun had climbed high.

He thought about Gaya's difficult situation: 'If I had some money on me, would I have let her suffer like this? We'd have set off, the two of us, wherever we wished to. But I don't dare to. I'm getting on in years, and there's no money, no food at home either...'

Were the fruits on the madar tree ripe?

Prasanna looked up to check. No, the fruits hadn't yet ripened.

≈

Late in the afternoon, Bhabani completed his reading of the *Bhagavat*, a difficult text. What a magnificent composition it was—in its poetry as well as in its philosophical import. After his long reading session, while he was tying up his manuscript, he noticed that Nistarini from the neighbouring locality had stepped into their yard.

Lately, Nistarini had begun conversing directly with Bhabani, although of course, she would do so only inside their home, not outdoors.

'Thakur-jamai?' said Nistarini, as she came up and took a seat.

'Come, daughter-in-law. All well?'

'As you have blessed me, I've come to tell you something.'

'Yes, what is it?'

'There are religious discourses that take place at the old kobiraj's home, songs too; may I come to listen? I'd like to, very much.'

'No, daughter-in-law; his home is outside the village, on the edge of a field. No one goes there.'

'What if *Didi* did so?'

'But your Didi doesn't go there.'

'What if I arranged that?'

'What will you do there?'

'I shall enjoy listening to him. There's no one in the village that speaks of anything good. At least I would listen to a good book being read, songs—it would make me happy.'

'Have you consulted your mother-in-law or your husband?' asked Bhabani.

'*He* will allow me. As to whether my mother-in-law does or not...The old woman's a hard one. What do I care if she doesn't! I'll go all the same.'

'For shame! This is where you are wrong, daughter-in-law. Shouldn't behave in this way.'

'I've a great desire to hear you speak of the scip-tures.' She added, with a touch of hurt pride in her voice, 'But that you don't want—I know it.'

'What do you know?'

'That you don't desire I go there.'

'And how would you have learnt of such a thing?'

'I know.'

'All right, if your Didi ever goes, you come too.'

'Is it bad to do what one's heart wishes to?'

Bhabani found the question rather strange. 'Daughter-in-law, you are mature enough now; you ought to understand if one does *whatever* one desires to, one might even do things which are bad.'

'Is that sinful?' she asked.

'Yes.'

'Then I shan't do them anymore. If you say so, it *must* be right.'

'You are intelligent; what can *I* tell you?'

'Whatever you tell me is very important to me, Thakur-jamai. I was about to step onto another path, but only came away because of the counsel I had from you and from Didi. Whatever you tell me, I will have to follow even if it makes me sad, even if it makes me happy—you are my guru.'

'I'm no one's guru, daughter-in-law. That's all rubbish.'

'Will you have some twice-fried pressed rice with grated coconut? I've just made the pressed rice; I'll get you some tomorrow.'

'Bring some, daughter-in-law,' said Bhabani.

Khoka, who had just come back from playing, immediately asked his mother, 'Aren't we going to the river?'

'Where were *you* all this while?'

'Playing a game of *kapati* with Habu. Let's go now. That's why I came running home. I'll come back and study English. I know how to read it now!'

Very often, before evening fell, Bhabani along with his two wives and his son went down to the river. All of them loved swimming, washing and cleaning themselves. Then they sat down to *upasana*.

Khoka loved doing both at the river—bathing and meditating. It was he who hurried his parents to the river every day. Today, Nistarini demanded that they take her along as well.

Bhabani was reluctant to take along any third person, an outsider; it made him uneasy. Upasana was to be practised either by oneself, or in the company of like-minded people. But Tilu entreated him on behalf of Nistarini. And so she came as well.

All of them had finished swimming and bathing. The last rays of the sun shone on the tips of the forest of kash and over saibabla bushes; water birds were winging their way westwards carrying the glint of the blood red light on their wings. They were headed towards a waterbody, possibly Samta Lake, in Nakashipara.

'Daughter-in-law,' Bhabani enjoined her, 'join your hands as they have and then say, either in your mind, or after them, or simply listen:

> The One who is in fire, in water,
> Who is in the beautiful;
> Who is in the grass, in fruits and flowers—
> To that One I salute.
> The One who is within and without,
> The One who is wherever I look,
> To that One I salute.'

Khoka joined his parents in chanting the Sanskrit verse in his melodious voice.

'Khoka, who has created this world?' Bhabani asked his son.

'Bhagwan,' replied Khoka in the tone in which one recites a memorized table.

'Where does he live?'

'Everywhere, Baba.'

'In the sky too?'

'Everywhere.'

'Does he speak?'

'Yes, Baba.'

'Will the One speak with you too?'

'Yes, Baba. If I wish to, so does the One. Without me the One is not.'

It was Bhabani who had taught all this to his son.

He would not be able to leave behind any possessions for his son. He was getting old. He would have to depart on the final journey while his son would still be in his teens. What could he leave behind for this son, so that one day, the boy would realize that it was an invaluable gift that he was slowly coming to understand, learn, recognize and internalize?

It was belief in divinity; and an abiding love for the divine, Iswar.

He knew of no more valuable gift.

One did not need great intelligence to arrive at this understanding; it was possible to do so by being simple and natural. This was the truth he had arrived at, sitting and meditating by the banks of the Ichhamati day after day. In the evenings the rosy red of the saibabla bushes ringed by kash-reeds would slowly fade, above him, the first star would show itself, in the distant kash forests he would hear the dove calling out as the fragrance of the wild silk-cotton flowers came to him in the breeze...

It was in those moments while sitting on the riverbank, that he had travelled along a joyous path of experience, receiving in the depths of his heart this truth—an ancient truth, but always to be realized anew: bhagwan was not limited by any one form. In him the play of Lila and of Form entwined. One could not be without the other. The child, the river, the river bank were part of this cosmic oneness.

Nistarini was very moved. She had riches within her. But she was the daughter-in-law of a humble householder: she was forced to spend her days cooking, eating, labouring—a life bound by chores. There was no occasion for her to listen to anything that was different, that would take her elsewhere. She had never experienced such moments.

'Didi, can I come again?' she asked Tilu.

'Why not?'

'Will Thakur-jamai let me?'

'No. He will beat you!'

'I was so happy today. Who will ever speak of such things, Didi? It's only blows and kicks for me. Only my mother-in-law cursing me day and night! After all that I do, don't even get to eat my fill. Yes, it's true that I did wrong. I sinned. But did I have any wisdom then! For whatever I've done, I tell bhagwan, you give me whatever punishment you wish to.'

'Now, let all that be. Whenever you wish, you come along with us.'

'Thakur-jamai is like a god. Not one like him in our parts. I am really fortunate that I have the company of people like you. I greatly desire to invite Thakur-jamai and serve him food that I've cooked.'

'So go ahead, what's there to it?'

'You know everything—our home is not that sort. I have to bring the vegetable dishes I've cooked secretly. No one knows, they'll start gossiping if they do.'

'You invite me or Nilu along with him, and no one will gossip.'

They had just climbed up the ghat when they saw Ramkanai Kobiraj come their way. He was on his way back from another village where he had gone to see a patient. Barefoot and dusty, his dhoti tucked high up to his knees, he was carrying his precious little bag of herbs and roots in his hand. Tilu went up to him and touched his feet in salutation; Nistarini did the same, imitating Tilu.

Ramkanai shrank back in embrarrasment. 'What are you doing, Didi! No need for all that. Makes me ashamed. Come, all of you, come to my little hut. Now that I've met up with Barujje-moshai, our evening is bound to pass well.'

Ramkanai Chakrabarty lived in Chorpara; you had to go beyond the big field on the northern part of the village to get to Chorpara Field.

'You must get back home,' said Tilu to Nistarini, 'We're going to Chorpara Field.'

'I'll come too.'

'Won't they scold you at home?'

'What do I care if they do? I'm coming for sure.'

'Come then. But it will be very late before we get back, I warn you.'

'No one will say a thing if I am with all of you. And if they do, fat lot I care! I don't listen to all that.'

So they had to take Nistarini along. Once at Ramkanai's home, he spread out a cane mat for them and lit a double-storeyed lamp of castor oil. He then had a wash and completed his prayers.

'You must eat something, though there's nothing much. Just some roasted rice. Will the Ma Lakshmis mix it or shall I?'

After their frugal snack, he read out a chapter from the *Chaitanyacharitamrit*. Bhabani recited from the *Gita*.

Seeing a handwritten manuscript kept carefully on the low table, Bhabani asked, 'What is this—the *Bhagavat*?'

'No. It's *Madhav Nidaan*, copied out by my gurudev himself. Whoever wants to learn the Ayurveda scripture must begin with the *Madhav Nidaan*. This one is glossed and edited by Bijoy Rakshit. His commentaries are hard to find. I use this book to teach my student Nimai. He's been ill for the past few days, hasn't been coming.'

Ramkanai opened up the manuscript for Bhabani. The handwriting was clear and radiant like pearls on the handmade paper that was already half a century old. At the end were some old-fashioned *shyamasangeet*, composed to honour the dark goddess Kali or Shyama. Perhaps it was Gurudev Mahananda Kobiraj who had also composed the songs. At Bhabani's request, Ramkanai sang one of those songs, in his rather poor voice:

> 'So deep this love of the naked one:
> Why do I call out her name with such passion?'

Then Bhabani sang one of Dasarathi's Ray's songs:

> 'Surrender yourself at his blessed feet'

Ramkanai enjoyed the song very much, he shut his eyes in joy as he exclaimed on the alliteration: '*Uthe bar bhubon jibon, e pap jiboner jibonanto*...at the end of this sinful life, Aaha-ha!'

Enthused by their appreciation Bhabani made Tilu sing another song by the same poet: *dhoni ami kebol nidaane*...Rich am I only in my knowledge of the root cause...'

Tilu was not a bad singer.

After the song Ramkanai said, 'Oh he's written marvellously, this Dasarathi Ray; where does he live? I've never heard such alliteration, such language...wonderful!'

> 'What mischievous play, O daughter of Braja
> Krishna is of my creation:
> I am the doctor Hari who cures all sorrows
> In the skies I reside.'

'Will you write down the words for me?' asked Ramkanai Kobiraj. 'One has to be blessed by the gods, else you cannot write so!'

'Lives somewhere near Bardhaman, the poet,' replied Bhabani. 'He had come last year to a gentleman's house in Ulo to sing his panchali-verses. That's where I heard him, and learnt the song. I've taught it to Khoka's mother too.'

After a couple more songs they took their leave of Ramkanai and headed back in the moonlit night towards Panchpota village. The vast expanse of Chorpara Field glistened in the moonlight and the waters of the canal were luminous beneath the moon.

Pointing to the canal, Bhabani said, 'Look Tilu, when your brother was the Neelkuthi Dewan there was a terrible fight at this bundh; the Neelkuthi's lathiyals murdered people here.'

Suddenly, they saw a man striking across the field with immense energy.

'O Didi, look! Someone is coming this way!' said Nistarini.

'It's a very lonely spot,' said Bhabani. 'Everyone, wait...'

The man had a big stick with him. It was clear he was advancing directly towards them. They became fearful at the way he moved. When he had come closer Nistarini said, 'O Didi! Hold on to Khoka's hand, Thakur-jamai. Don't go on ahead—'

The man was right before them. In a moment, when he had carefully seen them all, he cried out in a voice of surprise and joy, 'What's this! Isn't it didimoni? Thakur-moshai? An' here's Khoka...'

Tilu had recognized the man by then.

'Hala-dada? Where have you come from?' she cried out.

Hala Pekey seemed to immediately conceal an expression on his face. 'Was just goin'...you know, to Chorpara...' he stammered out. 'Someone...that's all. Wait, all of you. Let me pay my respecs.'

Hala Pekey's appearance was not as formidable as before. His hair had whitened somewhat; overall, he looked quite old.

'Where have you been all these years, Hala-dada?' Tilu asked him. 'Haven't seen you in ages.'

'In the Sarkar's jail.'

'And why in the jail again?'

'There was a dacoity at the Biswases of Habibpur; the daroga came and picked up Aghore Muchi and me, sed you've done it.'

'And *hadn't* you done that dacoity? Hadn't you?'

Hala Peke did not reply.

Tilu was not one to let go so easily, 'So you are innocent?' she said.

'No. Done it,' came the reply.

'Where is Aghore-dada?'

'Died in jail.'

'Shall I say something?'

'What is it?'

'What were you thinking of just now—when you were heading towards us with that stick, from the other end of the field? Tell me the truth. Supposing it wasn't *us*?'

Hala Pekey was silent.

'Hala-dada, come home. Come along with us,' said Tilu in a gentler tone.

Hala Pekey appeared to get all worked up, 'No didi, won't come now. I'm not worthy of the dust of your feet. When I die, will you remember me as your elder brother?'

He came up to Khoka and said, 'My darlin', come close to me, my Khoka-thakur. My precious moon, my bit of gold, how big you have grown! Can't even recognize you. Live long, may you live long—learn how to read and rite, like your father!'

Hala embraced Khoka with deep emotion and affection. Then, without saying another word or throwing a backward glance at anyone he strode across the field, vanishing into the moonlight.

'Who is that, Baba?' said Khoka deeply wondering. 'I've never seen him. Why did he embrace me?'

Nistarini's heart was still beating fast. She had realized what had happened. Everyone had.

'Oh! What if it hadn't been us...not a soul anywhere...in the middle of this field!' said Nistarini.

They began walking again, homewards. Deep in the groves of mangoes and jamun trees a woodpecker could be heard. Fireflies flickered over the thick bushes of bonmorche. Bats flapping their wings hung around the big silk-cotton tree. You could spot some of the constellations that had risen in the moonlit sky. Something else came to Bhabani Barujje's mind: This very Hala Pekey who killed people, waylaid them and looted them—was there not the divine even within him? Which Hala Pekey was this? Was he bad? Was Nistarini bad? Who would judge them? Who had the *right* to judge them? There was a supremely mysterious force unseen by anyone, who works silently, guiding us all; letting each one come to fruition in his or her way, each one following the way as it came naturally to him or her. It was along this path that a supreme power—with the loving regard of a mother and a father, watched over us with infinite compassion. No one—whether he might be a Hala Pekey or a Nistarini—would be left uncared for. Each life was precious and needed.

Along this path eternal, through the flow of lives and deaths, even the lowest of the low would be guided with infinite love to their realization. The tender love that he felt for his little son was reserved for all living beings by that cosmic power. What amazing comfort Bhabani Barujje found in trusting that cosmic power. There was nothing to fear. Do not fear—*ma bhoi*—said the Sanskrit sloka. Was the One not everywhere? Where was it not?

≈

Dewan Harakali Sur was seated in Lalmohan Pal's establishment showing him the accounts of the farmland in the Neelkuthi's estate. It was quite late in the afternoon.

'Dewan-moshai,' said Lalmohan Pal, 'the accounts of the khas-khamar, why don't we do those later? It's really very late. Where will you be eating?'

'At the Kuthi.'

'Who will do the cooking?'

'Our Narahari Peshkar will. He cooks well.'

'Oh! By the way, my wife and sister have been wanting to see the Kuthi; they've never seen the inside.'

'You *must* visit. Why not come tomorrow? I shall make all the arrangements. How will you be coming?

'By bullock cart.'

'Why, the Kuthi has its own palanquin. I can send that over.'

It was now two years since the Bengal Indigo Concern, through the mediation of Innes Saheb, had sold their Mollahati Kuthi for eleven and a half thousand rupees to Lalmohan Pal and Satish Sadhukhan (known more familiarly as Shotey Kolu). After Shipton's death, Innes Saheb had tried to run the plantation for two years; finally, he had to report that it was no more profitable to continue. Of the one hundred and fifty bighas of khas-land the Kuthi owned, the primary business was now agriculture, and the remaining thirteen bighas within the precincts of the Kuthi had now been planted with saplings of mangoes, jackfruit, guavas and other fruits. It was only the farming that continued from former times; the two sole employees from earlier days were Dewan Harakali Sur and Narahari Peshkar. Amin Prasanna Chakravarty and many other employees had already been served notice. The huge bungalows of the Neelkuthi along with their furniture still stood. There was no option but to keep them, for they had come with the land sold by the Bengal Indigo Concern. The entire sale took place at a throwaway price—no doubt about that! But in these provincial backwaters where would they find buyers for fancy furniture? It would be too expensive to cart it elsewhere. The Bengal Indigo Concern was going through difficult times; they were happy to get what they could. Innes Saheb had transported two big almirahs to Calcutta; that was all.

Dewan Harakali Sur had come to Nalu's home and explained: 'The khas-land of one hundred and fifty bighas—precisely, one hundred forty-two bigha, nine kathas, seven chatak—consider it one hundred and fifty...of that, there was provision for seventy bighas for *otbandi jama bybastha*. In addition, the waterbody in Nowadar had been taken on rent from the Raja of Natore at the time of McNeil Saheb. It would yield a hefty water tax. Pal-moshai, you can buy the Neelkuthi without a second thought—not as an indigo plantation, but as a landlord's estate.' Harakali Sur had offered: 'I shall look after your zamindari, and a couple of old employees you will have to keep; we shall run it amongst us, the accounts will be at your disposal, down to the last cowrie.'

'Along with the furniture in the Kuthibari?' Lalmohan had clarified.

'Absolutely.'

'All right, done.'

That was how the Kuthi changed hands. At some point, Innes Saheb had created a problem, said he wouldn't let go of the two carriages and the two pairs of horses. Lalmohan Pal had raised an objection. Eventually, a trifle more was added to the price. Once the Kuthi was bought, the horses and the carriages were sold to the Gosain-babus of Rayganj for almost a thousand rupees. Dewan Harakali had correctly estimated that they could make a big profit if the khas-land and the water taxes were well supervised. In some small plots of the estate indigo was still being cultivated.

'Why don't you ask the Dewan-moshai to send us the sahebs'

tom-tom with the horses and all—we shall go for a ride,' Tulsi had asked her husband, after the sale was complete.

Lalmohan's reply was, 'No, Boro-bou. The Burra Saheb used to ride all over the countryside on this very tom-tom, and we'd run away to the fields with loads on our heads if we heard him coming—that scared we'd be; and if you were to ride that *same* tom-tom, you know what people would say? They'll say, they're all puffed up because they've made some money. The dewan *had* offered to send the tom-tom for me to visit the Kuthi; I begged him with folded hands, "Forgive me," I said, "all that high-class stuff, that's for the babus. We are simple merchants. If *we* begin to put on airs, our business will go to the dogs."'

≈

Eventually, one fine day Lalmohan's elder daughter Saraswati, her mother Tulsi, Nalu's sister Moyna along with their flock of children set off for a tour of the Kuthi. Dewan Harakali, Prasanna Amin and Narahari Peshkar walked them around the premises and inside the bungalows.

The visitors plied their escorts with questions at every turn.

'O Dewan-uncle, what is *this* room for?'

'This is where the sahebs would sit and have their meals, my child.'

'What are these h-u-g-e chandeliers for?'

'When they danced, all of these would be lit up.'

'And *this*?'

'This is a glass *mogg*: the sahebs would drink from this. Look at this: it's called a de-canter, they would drink liquor from it.'

'Don't *touch* those things, don't go that way—you'll have to bathe again at this time of the day, come away!' Tulsi warned her children.

Most of the servants had been served notice; a few paiks and *peadas* still remained. The entire retinue of lathiyals had long been disbanded and sent away. Overrun by creepers and all kinds of foliage, the gardens were now almost impenetrable. People were scared to go that way even during the day for fear of snakes. The other day a dead cobra had been found in the jungle to the west of the Kuthi.

Amongst the older servants there remained the old brahman cook, Banshibadan Mukujje. He still did the cooking for the dewan and some other employees.

Moyna's daughter Shibi, begged the dewan, 'O Grandpa, O Dewan-gran'pa, the sahebs used to have a room to bathe in, didn't they? I want to see it—'

Thereupon Dewan Harakali Sur gathered his flock and took them to one of the big *gosulkhana*s. They were all astounded to see the huge bathtub inside the room. Moyna's daughter was dying to get inside the tub to figure out how exactly the sahebs bathed; but she didn't dare say so. For a long time they moved around examining all the furniture, touching and pressing this or that object, exclaiming over it all.

What on earth had the sahebs done with so many things?

As the day waned, they headed home in their bullock cart; the employees of the Kuthi had all come out and waited on them respectfully until they left.

≈

That night, exhausted after a day of work, Lalmohan Pal was lying on their bed made of the strong wood of the jackfruit tree,.

'Went and saw the Kuthi today,' announced Tulsi, coming in with a boxful of paan that she placed near the pillow by his head.

Lalmohan Pal was rather preoccupied. They had bid for two hundred and fifty measures of *gachhtamak* at the Bhajanghat trading centre; the goods had still not arrived, so he was in a bit of worry.

'What are you thinking of?' asked Tulsi, when she got no response from him

'Nothing really.'

'*Bound* to be business!'

'Well, something like that,' admitted Nalu.

'Went to see the Kuthi today...saw it.'

'What did you see?'

'Goodness! No end to what we saw! Have you seen it, dear?'

'Me? Don't have a moment to die, and *I'm* going to go and see those things at the Kuthi? You're mad, wife! We're people in business—all that elegance and style, that's not for *us*! Right now for instance, that lot from Bhajanghat, it's still not come. Worrying about it.'

'Will you fulfil a desire of mine, dear?' Tulsi made her request in the demanding tones of a nine-year-old girl, and came up smiling to her husband's side.

'What is it?' said Lalmohan Pal, irritably.

'Angry with me, are you? Won't tell you then,' said Tulsi in an aggrieved tone.

'Oh! Say it anyway.'

'No.'

'My dear didi, say it, say—'

'Oh! Oh! What's going to happen to me! So much water down the bridge, and he calls me his *didi*! Is that how you should speak? Just been bringin' in money with your business, that *you've* learnt to do, but to behave and speak like a bhaddarlok—you know nothing of that! Whoever calls his *wife* his elder sister?'

Lalmohan grew rather embarrassed. It was true he had been thinking of other things.

'Tell me, wife, what do I have to do?' he said placatingly.

'You'll have to pay a penalty.'

'How much?'

'I have a desire; you have to fulfil it. Tell me you will?'

'What?'

'Winter is coming' on, all the poor and the destitute in the village—you have to give them a quilt each; and as to the *bamunthakurs*—I'd like to give each of them a warm shawl. On the day of equinox in the month of Kartik.'

'The poor will be given the quilts, but the bamuns won't accept your gift. Don't you know the brahman-thakurs of our village! All right, let me first do an ishtimit of how much it will come to. I'll have to send someone to Calcutta after that's done. '

'And, *one* more thing?'

'What is that?'

'Dewan-moshai has sacked an old bamun from the Kuthi. His name is Prasanna Chakkarty. The dewan's told him we don't need you any more.'

'So the fellow's come and pleaded with you, has he? This is wrong of you, wife. What do I understand of the work at the Kuthi? There's no work for him, so he's been asked to leave. Is one to keep paying out a salary even when there's no work?'

'Yes, you have to. Where is he to go at *this* age, may I ask? Who will give him a job?'

'You're so childish; whyever do you get into this? What do you understand about business?' said Nalu Pal, annoyed. 'You think money grows on trees, don't you? Just because *he* asked! Why does he come to you, may I ask? A scheming bamun!'

'Listen to me, let me tell you something,' said Tulsi in a calm voice. 'Don't just say whatever comes to your tongue. Don't go overboard just because you've made a bit of money.'

'Now, how have I gone overboard? All I said to you was what do I understand of this Neelkuthi business. Whatever the dewan does, you and I should not go over his head. You are a woman, what do you understand of all this? That's how work is done!'

'Well, whether you give or don't give him back his job, one shouldn't say *whatever* one likes about others. That makes people feel that you are swollen with pride, and have become arrigint and hoity-toity. For shame!'

Tulsi went off in a huff, looking very displeased.

This conversation had taken place some two years ago. Since then, no one knew where Prasanna Chakkarty Amin had gone to, leaving the Neelkuthi where he had worked for decades. He had no option. Harakali Sur had trimmed away all those employees who were no longer needed, to save the zamindar's money. They had scattered off in various directions. Once their jobs at the Neelkuthi were gone,

Syce Bhoja Muchi and Bearer Sriram Muchi began farming on the land they had been given by the Burra Saheb. This rainy season Sriram Muchi had died of snakebite on his way back one dark night from the Mollahati market.

Sri Lalmohan Pal's granary now stood right in front of the big bungalow of the Burra Saheb. The paddy from one hundred and fifty bighas of prime farmland was threshed and winnowed there; heaps of cattle fodder was bound and piled up there too; and, in the big verandah where the sahebs once had their chhota hazree, the labourers and farmhands who worked in the fields sat chatting with one another as they smoked their coarse tobacco.

'You know,' one of the farmhands remarked, 'those dang sahebs sat *right here* and devoured hunks of roast chicken and spoke their Injiri. No one had the right to step this way—an' look now, right *there* is Rajabali sitting on the same bless'd place and a-scratchin' away at his itches and scabs!'

≈

One late afternoon Bhabani set off with his son to visit Ramkanai Kobiraj. Khokon didn't want to let go him of him, wanting to go wherever his father went.

They passed a row of big babul and silk-cotton trees, bushes of shyamlata; you could hear the bats, and weasels were scampering about as darkness fell over the forest. Fireflies flickered around the termite mounds, some of which looked exactly like men seated in the bamboo forest.

'What's that, Baba?' cried out Khoka at one point.

Inside Ramkanai Kobiraj's mud hut on the southern fringe of the Chorpara Field, his double-storeyed lamp was shining away. He was very happy to see them. Khoka loved to come to this old man's mud hut. In the peaceful light of the lamp the room looked magical and wonderful, the floor shining and smooth. A poor bagdi girl from the neighbouring bagdi-para came to wipe clean his home with dung-water every day. She did it out of grateful love, for the kobiraj had cured her of a serious illness.

In a little niche in the wall there was a picture of a deity decorated with flowers. There was no bed, only a woven mat on the floor, a couple of books and some papers, three or four cane baskets. The baskets were not for his clothes or any other possessions, but to store his medicinial plants, powdered herbs and the like.

Bhabani cherished these evenings with this poor brahman who was in many ways a renunciate. There was none to compare with him in the village. Ramkanai enjoyed reading out the *Chaitanyacharitamrit* and Bhabani listend to him attentively. As he listened, he remembered something of his days as a wandering mendicant. On the banks of the river Narmada atop a little hillock was a humble ashram established by a sannyasi he knew. He was called Swami Kaivalyananda, a direct disciple of the 108th Srisri Madhavananda of Puri. He lived by himself while a couple of his disciples lived below the hill in another hut, tending to their guru. A milch cow gave them enough milk; the dung was used for fuel and so on. The little hut was thatched with grass from the hills, and strips of fencing encircled it.. An unknown fragrant flowering creeper had climbed over the fencing. You could hear wild parrots squawking in the heights of the tunth trees, the gurgling of a mountain spring came from the forest on a plateau on the Mahadeo hills across the Narmada. Kaivalyanandaji's disciple, Anup Brahmacharya, would sing beautiful bhajans. Waking up at night Bhabani could hear the strains of the sorrowful ragini *Tilak-kamode* wafting from the hut below...*ek ghari pala chhina kala na parata morey*...not for a moment do my eyelids shut awaiting you...

On awakening, his eyes would fall on the huge kusum tree and the tamarind tree beside it that grew on the slope further below. From the cracks between huge rocks, innumerable wild flowers pushed their way out; some looked like the *dash-baichandi* found in Bengal. These had no fragrance, but the air was drunk with the scent from the yellow flowers of wild creepers. How amazingly peaceful it was on that riverside. No one came to destroy the stillness enlivened only with bird song; how wonderful it was to meditate in such surroundings. He would go down to the Narmada to bathe and afterwards climb up the rock face, step by step.

It was only when he came to Kobiraj-moshai's home that memories of those peaceful days came back to him. At Foni Chakkarty's chandimandap—it was always gossip and talk of worldy affairs. In fact, wherever he went, the conversation was circumscribed within the boundaries of the village. It made him unhappy.

He also felt that if one ever built a temple it should be a little rough hut as this, amidst the silent forest. Monumental grand temples, marbled floors, courtyards made of huge stone slabs were replete only with grandeur: could bhagwan be found there? In many such places he had found greedy worldly sadhus; white marbled floors bereft of the spirit of divinity.

'Barujje-moshai,' Ramkanai wanted to know, 'have you been to Brindaban?'

'No, I haven't.'

'You've been to so many places, why not *there*?'

'I do not care for Brindavan-lila,' said Bhabani shortly.

'What shall I say with my limited knowledge?' replied Ramkanai. 'But it seems to me, that caught up in the worries and responsibilities of sansar, the devotee cannot really enjoy the love of the divine, that is why a pure transcendental space—a *chinmaya dham,* has been spoken of, where there is only the eternal love play of the devotee and the divine. *That,* for me, is Brindavan-lila.'

'How well you've spoken! The Brindavan *you* have spoken of—it is present before our eyes at all times, everywhere. One may see the presence of the divine in the flower, hear it in the cry of the bird, in the laughter of the child...'

'Is such vision granted to everyone?' asked Ramkanai.

'That is why they grope around in the dark. The ancient Vedas are inscribed on every aspect of nature. I feel that flowers, rivers, the skies, stars, the child...are all sacred texts. One experiences the wonders of eternal play through and in them. Wherever the One may reside is naturally a temple, not stone monuments alone! As I was on my way here, I saw *kumud* flowers blossoming in Chorpara Lake; that too, is a temple. One has to love the nature that surrounds us. In rhythm with nature, loving every aspect of it, nature herself will inspire us with a greater energy, and take us to a realm of inner spirituality.'

'This same thought finds expression in the Vaishnav scriptures as: *jahan jahan netra parhe, tahan tahan Krishna sphure*: wherever the eye falls, Krishna springs forth from thence,' endorsed Ramkanai.

'That is so. Can the One be present only in the temple or the pilgrimage place? It would be madness to believe so! The One is everywhere: *vanaspatau bhuvriti nirjhare va kuley samudrasya sarittatey va*...in the trees and plants, in waterfalls, in the seas... If the One is before me and I do not open my eyes to see; yet again, in the guise of the child it is the One who comes to embrace me, and I run away terrified thinking that I am getting entangled in the coils of *maya*—would I ever be able to experience the divine? There is liberation in those very objects that *appear* to be to be bonds. Is liberation to be attained by running away and screaming "*Mukti*"?'

'Barujje-moshai, do you think that bhagwan desires our love?'

'I've begun to experience a little of this...bhagwan desires our love. Earlier, I used to place too much emphasis on the path of knowledge,' admitted Bhabani. 'I now feel that he is my father. I've taken birth in his family. The same blood runs through my veins. Never will he push us into the path that will not bring good to us. Like a wise father he will hold me by my hand, for he is our very wise, very ancient, very experienced, very knowledgeable, very powerful father. We are his very ignorant, superstitious, cowardly helpless sons. How would he knowingly push us into a path that is not beneficient, holy?'

'Quite so! Quite so!' exclaimed Ramkanai enthusiastically.

For a few minutes Bhabani Barujje remained silent, as though hesitating to speak further. Finally, he said, 'Kobiraj-moshai, this is from my own experience; I've told you I didn't understand any of this earlier. The truth is that even an atom that emerges from one's own experience is richer than a thousand sayings told by others. It is only now that I have become a father myself, after Khoka's birth, that I have begun to understand the love of the father in the divine. How would I have known all these years how a father might feel!'

'So it comes to this, that our Khoka here is a sort of guru to you?' said Ramkanai smiling.

'Right. Tell me, who is not a guru? If I can learn something from someone, that person is indeed my guru; the One is in everyone. Listen to the song that goes:

> In the form of the father born as a child,
> As the mother gifting the breast,
> As the child having my fill of the breast,
> In all of this I am made manifest.'

'Whose song is that? Nice!'

'A new poet; can't recall his name. This is how it begins... the I in myself all are that me and I that is all, all belong to me.'

Ramkanai Kobiraj was an excellent listener. So was Khokon who sat quietly with a look of astonishment and reverence on his face as he listened to his father.

'A lovely song!' said Ramkanai Kobiraj, 'But a bit too advanced—Advaita-Vedanta. Not for the ordinary person.'

'As you say. But there *is* no high or low in Truth. These are serious matters. My guru used to say that it's not so easy to become a believer of *advaitavad*. The real seeker of advaitavad will consider the joy of all living creatures as his. He will immerse himself in the service of *all* living creatures. He will consider each one's body is his, each one's spirit his own. At that stage, there is no separation of the self and the other. He can give of Himself completely, even to remove a little thorn from someone's foot. In a waking state, *ato mama jagata sarvang*—all those in the world are mine, all of them me; when in the highest state of consciousness: *athava na ch kinchan*—nothing is mine; there is nothing, only this self. At that stage, there is no world. You understand, Kobiraj-moshai?'

'It's very advanced discourse for the likes of me. But also very good! Difficult to digest though; I cure people by grinding up little pills; what would I do with the Vedanta and all that? Do I have the brains for it? But I do *enjoy* it. You come to this poor man's hut—can't tell you how happy you make me. But wait—let me get a mite for Khoka...How wonderful it has been today!'

'Why are you bothering about food when we are having a nice discussion? Don't get up...'

'Let me give him *something* to eat. A patient had brought me some cottage cheese; can I give him some? Here, Khoka, have some. '

'I won't eat till Baba eats too. First Baba.'

'Oh, the little fellow is worthy of his father!' said Ramkanai clapping his hands. 'Who be that outside?' he called out.

It was Gaya-mem who came in with some bananas. She prostrated herself to make her pranam and said to Ramkanai, 'Baba, do have these.'

Bhabani was astonished at seeing her. 'Do you come here?' he asked.

'I do come to Baba now and then,' said Gaya humbly. 'But I had not thought that I would be seeing you here.'

'How do you come from so far away?'

'Whenever I come here, I spend the night at the home of a distant cousin sister of mine—she lives in Chorpara.'

Suddenly her eyes fell on the silent attentive form of Khoka sitting in his father's lap.

'Whose Khoka be this?' she said going up to him. 'Oh, is he yours? A precious thing he is for sure. How nicely he is growin'. May he live long! May he be the pride of the Dewanji's family!'

'What do you do these days?' Bhabani asked her.

'What am I to do? Do what I can to get by, in sorrow. It's been very difficult since Ma died. So I come running to Baba, to listen to him read me *Chaitanyacharitamrit*.'

'You don't say! I've not heard most brahman women say what I've heard you say today.'

'That is your kindness, baba. Once my mother died, the world seemed empty...'

Then, very embarrassed, as if she was guilty, she slowly said, 'Baba, whatever I have done when I was young and raw—there's nothing to be done for it. Now I am older, I understand a bit. If people like you were to give me a little compassion—'

'Who are *we*? And as for compassion—the One will not abandon any one, let alone you. Are you not a part of him, you're not a stranger!'

Turning to Ramkanai, Bhabani said, 'Kabiraj-moshai I see you have now become a healer of those stricken by the illness of *bhobo*. It makes me happy.'

'And what is this illness of "bhobo"?' asked Ramkanai.

'Well, there's a song about it...

> I'm the healer who treats worldly ills;
> I don't come home until I'm invited by love.'

'I see. Tell me more.'

'I think *bhoborog* is a state of ignorance. It afflicts those who run after wealth rather than believing—as you do—that a handful of rice and greens is enough to fulfil their needs. It's like if one brother is very poor and the other very rich.'

'Forget about me,' replied Ramkanai. 'I simply don't have the means and the skills to become rich. Would have done it if I could!'

'You wouldn't have. You are *made* differently. You haven't seen evil-minded people, steeped in worldliness, that's why you speak so—you know, the sort who fill themselves only with concepts. They mistake theory for a true knowledge of the self, which is far deeper.'

'Now, son-in-law, let that be. Each to his own, I say. I like living in this little mud hut, and so I live here. As for the one who does not—well, he does something else.'

'Are they living in a *greater* state of happiness? Are they more contented than you? Not at all! The *atman* delights in *ananda*; the closer one moves to the atman the greater the joy; the closer towards wordly affairs, the greater the sorrow. There is no such thing as joy in the external world; joy and peace lie within. Not knowing this, man chases chimeras. The musk deer maddened by his own scent rushes blindly in search of it. Happiness is never theirs.'

'That is for them to know. What can I say? This is what gives me delight and joy, only that I may say. Only this much I've understood that ananda lies *within*,' said Ramkanai.

Khoka was listening to this difficult conversation with the same attention as before. His big eyes were wide open with intelligent curiosity.

Gaya-mem quite fell in love with him. She came up close to him and whispered, 'What is your name, my little boy?'

'Tulu.'

'Will you be a comin' with me?'

'Where?'

'To my home. I'll give you papayas to eat.'

'I'll go, if Baba says so.'

'And wouldn't he say yes, if I asked him?'

'Yes, you may take him. Is it far, your home?' said Bhabani

'I shall take him with me. Will you come, little fellow? Sure?'

'Papayas?' said Khoka after some thought.

'Aren't there many! A papaya as big as this!' And Gaya spread her arms wide to a size that seemed a trifle exaggerated for a papaya.

'Baba, o Baba,' asked Khoka of Bhabani, 'Shall I go to this aunty's home? She'll give me a papaya.'

He kept looking at his father with enquiring eyes, waiting for his permission.

≈

Gaya-mem spent the night at her distant cousin's in Chorpara. She would leave for Mollahati the next morning; not exactly Mollahati, but her village, Gayeshpur. Her cousin's name was Nirada; she was known in the village as Niri Bagdini. She wasn't well off, and when Gaya turned up saying she would spend the night at her place, Niri got alarmed. What would she offer her cousin for a meal? At one time Gaya-mem was renowned in the area. She had lived well and had shared her good fortune with others. How could she be served such humble fare? Finally, Niri had to offer her some red autumn rice and vegetables cooked with a sprinkling of tiny shrimps. Then she laid out a mat and gave her cousin a thin quilt to cover herself with.

Gaya could not fall asleep that night.

She kept seeing that little Khoka. If only she had a little boy like him…She wouldn't have felt so lonely, empty and finished, if she had something or someone to live for. Who could be her anchor? Several years had passed since the Burra Saheb had passed away. The Neelkuthi was finished; it now functioned as the estate cutchery of the new landlord, Nalu Pal. In the space of these few years Gaya-mem had become a pauper. The Burra Saheb had given her a lot of jewellery, much of which she had to sell off when her mother had fallen ill. The rest she had sold or pawned bit by bit to eke out a living. There was little left.

The old days seemed like a dream. But they were not so old either. It was only a few years ago that the business of the Kuthi ended, that Saheb died.

She learned the hard way that the world was cruel, that there were few, if any, to look after her. Her near ones were all dead.

Niri came to sit beside her. She had been chewing on paan that carried a strong smell of tobacco. It made Gaya nauseous; she couldn't bear the smell.

'O Gaya-didi,' said Niri.

'Yes, sister?'

'Fall'n asleep?'

'Can't sleep 'cause of the heat.'

Niru unrolled her woven mat of palm leaves and lay down beside her.

'Couldn't give you anythin' decent to eat. You never did come before…' she began.

Perhaps Niri was being sarcastic. Why would people spare you if they felt that the time was right? Even a frog could kick out at her in her present condition, and Niri, after all, was her cousin sister.

'There's something, Niri...I don't have anything left. How shall I manage, sister?'

'That is so, Didi, what can I tell you?' said Niri in a tone of sympathy. 'Would you ever be able to husk paddy? 'Twould at least fetch you a bellyful of rice.'

'I thresh mine. But I've never done it for others. What would one get?'

'*Panchadorey*.'

'What's that? Didn't get it.'

'My, look how the memsaheb's a talking!'

It was true that Gaya-mem didn't know any of these terms; she had been brought up in the shelter of a big tree from the age of fourteen. She had kept no track of any kind of distress labour.

'Tell me Niri, do, what *does* it mean? Won't you?'

She was hurt by the sarcasm that she thought she heard in the high-pitched laughter that came from Niri. She determined to leave this place first thing in the morning.

'Why do you laugh so much?' she said sadly. 'Truly, I don't know. Would I lie 'bout it, Niri?'

Niri began explaining what it meant—it was back-breaking work—you had to be at the pestle from morning to late afternoon. Then you boiled the paddy. You had to gather the kindling for the fuel. In the month of Chaitra you went back and forth to the bamboo copse for dry bamboo leaves, enough to last the whole year to keep the fire going. Just winnowing the pressed rice for hours together made your arms ache so...'You won't be able to do it, not *you*,' said Niri, at the end of her account. 'Aunty raised you differently, spoilt your chances. You didn't become a memsaheb and you didn't become a labouring bagdi girl. How will you live? You've lost out both ways.'

Gaya did not say another word.

It was her destiny. No one was to blame. They were bound to

tell her off now that she was going through bad times. Never again was she going to bare her sorrows to anyone else. They were not her near ones. They would only enjoy being sarcastic, take pleasure in her sorrow.

'Have some tobacco to chew on?' offered Niri.

'No, sister.'

'Are you sleepy?'

'I'll try and sleep now.'

'You're too delicate like. If you'd had body like *ours*—used to staying up nights, you'd have known what's what! Whenever there's a puja, a festival, I've been up all night making pressed rice, making *chhatu* with gram flour, husking paddy. How else can you keep your customers? Can't even stay *awake* one bit, and you think *you* will thresh paddy!'

Gaya wasn't very good at quarrelling. Unlike the typical village girl, Gaya couldn't fight back. Otherwise, Niri and she would have gone for it hammer and tongs by now. For a moment she thought that she *would* respond to Niri's jibes. But the next moment her sense of propriety made her feel that it would be useless to do so. Go to sleep, let her say whatever she wants. Her words won't wound you really. What would Niri know of her heart?

Her thoughts turned elsewhere. How long had she not met Prasanna Khuro-moshai! Where had he gone after he was dismissed from the Neelkuthi? At least he was someone who used to look in on her. He was one person who had regarded her with affection in this cruel world. Gaya had ignored him, toyed with his feelings. The strong *dokta*-tobacco in Niri's mouth that assailed her now only reminded her of those days. He too was absent from her life now.

Visiting the Kobiraj-moshai had brought her a kind of peace, after a long time. There were people who spoke of good things here. She felt a sense of solidarity.

≈

Tulsi had given her children coconut sweets and puffed rice for breakfast that morning.

One of their servants came to ask if she should clean out the big cowshed.

'Not now,' said Tulsi. 'The cows need to be milked and taken out for grazin'. No sense cleanin' up now, it will only get messed up again.'

For the past two months Moyna had been visiting at her brother's home. Her youngest son was very ill. It was to get him treated by Ramkanai Kobiraj that Moyna was here with her children. Lalmohan Pal had not been able to get Moyna married into a wealthy family because at that time he was still Nalu Pal, struggling to break even. Now that he had enough, he tried to have her over very often, so that she and her children might enjoy something of a good life during their visits. Tulsi's innate goodness had made this possible. If Moyna didn't come soon enough, she would be at her husband: 'Have you *frozen* up or something (this was a favourite phrase of hers)? What if her parents are dead—you, her brother, are still alive, why don't you go and fetch your sister?'

At the time their mother died, Nalu had already a shop, his store of paddy stacks and his warehouse, but he had not yet become such a big merchant. Nalu Pal nursed a sorrow that his mother hadn't been able to see him make it to his present status. Tulsi took extra care of her sister-in-law, almost as if she was trying to make up for a mother's love. Moyna was the quarrelsome one; she had always been a bit spoilt since her childhood. If she felt she had been slighted in any way, she would immediately let Tulsi have an earful. Tulsi, however, with her remarkable store of patience, would never be put out. What happened this morning was yet another instance of her forbearance.

While the children were having their morning snack, Tulsi's daughter Habi slapped Moyna's little boy for some reason or the other. Moyna needn't have meddled in what went on between the children, but she went up and demanded to know from the children as to who had slapped her Keshta. She was told that it was Habi; something to do with sharing the puffed rice. Moyna began smacking and hitting Habi, then scolded her loudly: 'Become too big for your boots, have you! You *dare* hit that thin child of mine—all skin and bones as he is. You'll be at peace only if he dies. Your Ma must have encouraged you, else how could such things happen!'

Tulsi overheard her tirade and came out to protest, 'Thakurjhi, what makes you believe that *I* have encouraged this? You think I'm going to tell her to beat up your son; is he not my own?'

Moyna embarked on a bitter round of abuse. She ended up by slapping her sick boy and screaming at him, 'Why can't you die, you wretch! It's because my brother has to spend money on *you* that they're all so angry. Just go and die—'

Shocked by Moyna's behaviour, Tulsi ran to pick up the boy in her arms. 'Have you gone mad or what? Why are you beating the thin creature so cruelly?' she upbraided her sister-in-law. 'Oh! The poor thing, his back's covered with red welts!'

'Good if it is!' retorted Moyna, in a shriller voice. '*You* don't have to show such love for him. They say it's a witch who loves a child more than his mother! Put him down, now!'

'No, I shan't,' said Tulsi. 'You're never going to touch that sick boy while I'm around!' Tulsi entered her room with the boy and locked herself in.

When Lalmohan Pal came in home from work quite late in the afternoon he found that Tulsi was still cooking, though the children had been fed. Moyna burst into tears as soon as she saw her Dada. She had better be sent back to her in-laws, she sobbed; she had had enough of her parental home. The day her mother had died, the door had been shut on her face. She went on in the same vein.

'Now what have the two of you cooked up again? I come back dog tired and weary; and not to have a moment's peace once I'm home!' said Nalu.

Tulsi did not say a word, did not reply to anything anyone said. She arranged the oil and the towel for her husband's bath, instructed the maid to prepare the water and the bathing stool. 'Why don't you have a bath and eat something first?'

'No, you tell me first what happened, I'll eat only then.'

'Are *you* going to be difficult too? Who shall I turn to? Please eat first I'm a-tellin' you.'

When he heard everything Lalmohan Pal said, 'Can't bear so much trouble. I'm going to separate the two of you, right away. Since you can't get along with each other...'

Tulsi's patience was immense. She didn't say a word to her husband. With much coaxing and cajoling Moyna was persuaded to have her lunch. Only after everything was sorted out did Tulsi sit down to have her meal, in the third hour.

A little before evening Jatin's sister Nandarani, who lived in a neighbouring locality, came to visit.

'O Bou-didi, I've come to say something...if you are willing to listen...' she began.

Tulsi put out a stool and made her sit. Made a special paan and offered it to her visitor.

'You will have to give me a rupee as a loan. I've nothing on me,' said Nandarani. 'Don't know what I'm going to feed my son tomorrow—you know everything about our affairs, Boudi. My father didn't have any means; just married me off to a good-for-nothing. He passed away, and now it's sink or swim—'

Tulsi never sent back empty-handed anyone who came with a request. She too, was from a poor family. Her father Ambik Pramanik used to run a very modest little shop and their childhood had been full of hardship. Tulsi had not forgotten those years.

'Whenever you need anything, you must come and tell me,' she reassured Nandarani. 'You're not to feel shy. I'm happy that you've come, thinking of me as one of your own. Do have another paan—and would you like some dokta-tobacco too? No? And how is Swarna-didi?'

Nandarani went home happily with the one rupee. Tulsi asked her maid to escort the visitor up to a certain point in the path through the village.

≈

Tilu and Nilu were busy shelling heaps of tamarind. It was a hot afternoon in the month of Chaitra. Seated on palm mats, Nilu was doing the shelling and Tilu was sorting them out into separate piles.

'Which tree are they from?' asked Tilu

'Don't know, Didi. Gopal Muchi's boy, Bengta—he's picked them for us.'

'By the river where it broadens out?'

'They're very sweet. Here try one, Didi.'

'Yes, very,' said Tilu after putting some in her mouth. 'Must be that big tree by the river.'

'Better hurry! Khoka's about to get back from school; you know he'll want to eat it all up.'

'Listen, do you remember Bilu? The three of us would sit around shelling tamarind so often, remember?'

'Very much.'

The two sisters sat silently thinking of many things. It was only a few years ago that Bilu had died, but it seemed like an age. On such Chaitra afternoons, the rustling of the bamboo grove, the melancholy cries of the hawk-cuckoo brought back a rush of memories. They remembered too, their Dada who had brought them up with love and care after their parents' death, their sister-in-law…

'What are you upto, bou-didi? Shelling tamarind?' It was Hemlata, their neighbour Sarat Barujje's wife, who sauntered in, mouth filled with a paan.

'There's still two baskets full. Come, draw up the mat and sit down with us,' Tilu invited her.

'Won't sit now, just came to find out is today the thirteenth day of the moon? Is one allowed to have brinjals?'

'Of course! It's the twelfth now, will carry on till two prahars at night—your Dada was saying.'

'Is Dada home?'

'He's out somewhere. How is Dada?' (Both of them referred to the other's husband as 'Dada'.)

'He's well. You know—as well as old people can be. He's recovered from his cough and fever. Where's Tulu?'

'Not back yet from school.'

'That's a whole heap you have there! We picked some from the two trees we have—worthless they were, riddled with worms. Do give me a couple of shelled pods of tamarind; I'll cook with them in the rainy season. Your Dada loves having a sour dish made with khoira fish…'

It was late in the afternoon. In the bamboo thicket a cuckoo cooed away sitting atop a tall bamboo. From somewhere wafted the smell of pickled berries. Two ploughing bullocks that belonged to Noley the barber were grazing beneath the *kamranga* tree. Birajmohini, daughter-in-law of Uncle Shotey Chaudhury from the neigbouring locality, was seen on her way to the ghat, towel in hand.

'O Biraj, Biraj!' called out Nilu.

'What is it?' said Biraj, one finger on her nose ring, as she turned towards them.

'Wait!'

'Will you come, Didi?'

'Yes.'

Biraj came from Shantipur in Nadia, from a village called Baghachra. She liked emphasizing how her speech was quite distinct from that of the rustic women of Jessore Bangal.

The sisters joined Biraj after latching their door.

There were only two bathing ghats in this part of the Ichhamati—the Raypara ghat and the Saheb's ghat. Bonsimtala ghat lay further ahead, at the bend in the river. Women rarely went there because it was very far away although it was the best of the lot, with thick green foliage; even the flow of the river was more beautiful, the bird calls melodious, and a myriad wild flowers blooming, changing from season to season. You would find at least a couple of fifty-year-old *chhanra* trees with solid trunks, and delightful resting spaces beneath the trees.

'Let's go bathe at the Bonsimtala ghat,' urged Tilu.

'This late?' said Biraj.

'It's not *that* far away.'

'Would've come, but my ma-in-law's not at home, and she's laid out these two branches in the sun, forget to stow them away—if a cow or something were to get at them, she'll skin me alive!'

'I'm not listening to any of that! You must come to Bonsimtala with us. Come.'

'Why, is there a fancy man hidden away and waiting?' shot back Biraj with a smile and a coquettish look in her eyes.

'Are we going to have a fancy man in our dotage! That's for you—the tender young ones! Why one, you'll have one at every ghat!'

'*Ishh*! You can still turn heads around with your beauty at *this* age—I can tell you that, didi. Come, come, where are you going to take me? That fancy man is going to be goggle-eyed!'

Eventually however, they had to go to the Raypara ghat, almost dragged along by all the other women who were on their way to bathe. At the end of a hot afternoon, the cool waters of the river seemed to have freed the women of their daily burden; there was much laughter and teasing. No one seemed anxious to get out of the water in a hurry.

'Ah, here you are Bor-di, haven't seen you in ages!' cried out Sitanath Ray's daughter-in-law, Himi.

'I don't come to this ghat anymore,' said Tilu.

'Which one do you go to, then?'

'Would you give away your secret man? Why should she tell you? I wouldn't, if you asked me,' chipped in Biraj.

'Bor-di is my mother's age,' retorted Himi, 'don't speak to her like that. You are beautiful and young—it's *your* turn now. What do you have there?'

'I've got some husk...thought I'd scrub myself with it. Would you like some?'

'No, thanks! You are a beauty, *you* go ahead.'

The response drew a round of giggles. The ghat resounded with the sound of happy young voices. A little later the seven-day moon would rise above the *shirish* and *puon* trees. Flowers from the *potpoti* tree had cascaded down into the water. Biraj felt a mysterious happiness, as though there was no sorrow, no struggle in the world... people would always praise her beauty, everyone would forever respect her status as the eldest married wife. Forever, they would hold out only for her the plateful of feni-batasha; for her little son's life's ceremonies—from childhood to his adulthood—they would crowd around her with auspicious sounds of the conch on a mist-laden early dawn soft with the chirping of birds; wearing a finely woven Shantipuri sari, a plateful of flowers in one hand and a bowl of turmeric paste in another, her heavy anklets ringing out their musical rhythm, her golden poinché on her arms, and gurjaripancham on her ankles—she would lead the line of married women... All this and so much more she keeps dreaming and seeing before her eyes, as she dives in again and yet again; once, after she surfaces after her dip, she seems to see her mother's smiling face on the other bank beneath the open skies, and once, it is her wedding night...she and he—playing the ritual wedding games with shells, and he stealing a look at her—a bashful smiling face...

Only happiness. A life of bliss! Only sporting in the water, eating, pleasures, only endless leisurely rounds of playing *binti*-cards...hee hee hee, what fun!

'O Biraj-didi what *are* you up to? Diving and dipping so late in the afternoon?' asked Himi looking most astonished.

'Oh no! You've wet all your hair too!' added Nilu. 'How on earth will you dry that mass of hair! Honestly, don't you have any sense?'

Their words escaped her completely. Absorbed in her own reflections, she said, 'Listen, shall I sing you a song? My heart's desires shall I tell you every one of them?'

'Hush!' said Himi, 'There's someone coming to the bank. Someone with a heavy tread.'

It was Nistarini who walked up cleaning her teeth with gul-powder. The others gave her a quick look but no one said a word of greeting. Many of the women from this village chose not to speak with her for there was a lot of scandal about her. No one had actually seen anything to incriminate her, but her fearless walking around by herself, her stopping to talk to whomsoever she wished to, everything had provoked gossip. By not speaking with her, the others wished to protect themselves from gossip.

Tilu and Nilu were exempt from all the customary restrictions. They also knew that if Tilu wanted to, she would do whatever she wished. No one had ever gossiped about the three sisters.

'Come, my dear,' said Tilu welcoming Nistarini with a loving glance. 'Come very late?'

Nistarini gave a disdainful look at the ghat full of young bathing beauties and said, almost as if to herself, 'Got busy shelling the tamarind, didn't realize it was so late.'

'Oh, we were busy doing the same thing today—Nilu and I. Have you been upset with us?'

'Why would I be?'

'You haven't visited us for a while.'

'When would I have the time, Didi? Boiled the starch, then washed the clothes. There's only me to make the pressed rice, thresh the paddy... Ma-in-law doesn't put in *that* much now-a-days.'

Although she was older than the others, Nistarini was still beautiful, and her manner of gesticulation, the smile on her lips as she spoke made the others smile. Himi and Biraj started giggling and slowly the others joined in till everyone was laughing.

'Oh, that Nistarini-didi can really make us laugh! She's too much. Come Nistarini-di, come down to the water, do!'

'Will you sing us that song, one of Nidhu-babu's? How wonderfully you sing it—the one that Bidhu-didi used to sing,' said Biraj.

It was well known that Nistarini was a fine singer. And how she could liven up a gathering with her funny stories. That too, was one of the reasons for the gossip. Some said it wasn't right for a woman to be so boisterous and free.

Nistarini began singing with appropriate gestures:

> 'My friend, is love only a matter of words,
> When one heart is in the other entwined?
> Will the creeper thrive if the tree dries?
> When one life is threaded with the other?'

There was a stunned silence of admiration. Such a melodious voice, such beautiful gestures to go with the lyrics! And how lovely she looked as she was singing.

'How wonderfully you sing, Nistarini!' said someone finally.

Nistarini too felt very happy. At that moment she forgot how she had been practically sold off by her father when she was only seven to a *shrotriyo* brahman family. It was a lot of money—seventy-five rupees—that he had got. She had never been able to come to terms either with her lame husband, or with her mother-in-law. Her husband was an honest man though, and her father-in-law, Bhajagobindo Barujje, a really good person. He had never gone against her. They had become poor in recent times; never had enough for themselves or to give the children, but Nistarini kept up her spirits. She knew that they said unpleasant things about her in the village—what did she care! The whole lot of pure blessed chaste *satis* that they were! A curse on them!

She went into the water. Biraj embraced her strong and firm wet body and said, 'Nistarini-didi, my golden lovable didi! What a lovely song, and sung with such lovely gestures. Had I been a man, then, didi—I swear to you—I would've a-fallen for you! Come, shall we go for a picnic to the forest?'

Before Nistarini's eyes came up a vision of long ago, who knows why it was so. The mind was a strange thing; who could ever predict its flow? She saw herself with her lover, sitting by the riverside. And then she did something daring that no one ever did in the village, no woman ever did. She asked Tilu, 'Bor-di, how is Thakur-jamai?'

It was against the social codes to speak of a man in this direct manner. But then everyone knew Nistarini. They had become used to her strange and outlandish manner.

≈

It was getting closer to the Pujas. The good people of the village who gathered daily at Foni Chakkarty's to while away the time were busy in their usual manner. Vast quantities of smoke from the freshly-cut tobacco threatened to darken the chandimandap. There was a better quality mat laid out on one side for brahmans, and palm-mats for other castes, with a narrow passage in between for walking through.

'Such changes the times have brought along!' sighed Nilmoni Samaddar.

'It's what the newly rich do! What are you and I going to do about it? If you don't like it, just don't go. That's all there's to it.'

'*You* won't go, but the brahmans of Abaipur will be coming. And what will *that* do to your prestige?'

'Why, what have you heard now?'

'He's going to be inviting all the brahmans of the village to his home during the Durga Puja.'

'The rascal's forgotten himself, dares too much. Turned newly-rich, that's why!'

Without paying any heed to any criticism from anyone in the village, Lalmohan Pal, formerly known as Nalu Pal, celebrated Durga Puja in his home with great fanfare. This year there were many pujas in their village and in the neighbouring ones. As always, this was a time when the poor and the dispossessed could eat their fill of coconut sweets, fine pressed rice and murki. How many homes could they be visiting for the food? Shuktani, kochu-greens, fig curry, sonamung-dal, fish and meat, yogurt and sweets offered a-plenty in every home.

None of the brahmans of his own village had accepted Nalu Pal's invitation. So far, Nalu Pal had been sponsoring feasts for brahmans by paying for the expenses, but the feast itself was always hosted in another brahman's home. But to want to do the same in *his* home! The patriarchs could not agree to this audacious move. Nalu Pal went with folded hands from door to door: the 'full bench' court in Foni Chakkarty's chandimandap spent a whole day in deciding the finer points of the case. At the end though, Nalu's 'appeal' was dismissed.

On the sixth day of Durga Puja, Tulsi came to visit Tilu and Nilu. She had on a broad red-bordered sari, a golden murki-maduli necklace, and the promised gold jasham ornament on her arm.

She made a full pranam to Tilu and complained, 'Didi, just listen to the kind of injustice that the village brahmans have visited on me!'

'I've heard about it.'

'Rice, they said they won't eat; so, I've got the best kind of ghee there is to make luchis and fry them.' She requested Tilu to speak to her husband. 'Can't I have a simple desire—to invite berahmans to my home and feed them? Don't I wish to have the dust of your feet in *my* home? What's wrong in having fruits, and luchi with sweets?'

Bhabani Barujje had seen something of the world. When he heard about the problem from Tilu he said, 'It's beyond me. It won't happen in *this* village of kulins. But the brahmans of Angrali Gadadharpur and Nasrapur will accept the invitation. They are shrotriyo brahmans.'

He visited Nalu Pal, explained the matter to him and advised him accordingly.

'Jamai-thakur, will *you* be there or not?' Nalu wanted to know with folded hands. 'You promise, you will?'

'If I wouldn't, would I have come to your home?'

'That's enough. I don't need any of *them* godly brahmans any more, if you and my didi come to my home. My life will be fulfilled.'

'That won't do, Nalu. You send someone to the brahmans in the villages I've mentioned; better still, go yourself. Take their counsel.'

From Angrali came Ramhari Chakrabarti and from Nasrapur came Satkori Ghoshal. They were brahmans who negotiated and mediated social codes. They came to broker a deal with Nalu Pal, laying down their terms and conditions.

Ramhari Chakrabarti was in his mid-fifties—short and dark, with a bushy beard and moustache. A little amulet was tied to his topknot, and another tied around his arm. His erudition was limited to basic mathematical tables and so on, much like the typical village schoolmaster. He was the head amongst those brahmans who would teach the loud recitation of tables.

Ramhari heard it all out and said, 'Here's brother Satkori who has also joined us. Pal-moshai, everyone knows that you are a wealthy man. But *never* in this land has it happened that brahmans have come and actually dined in a home such as of your caste. But between us both, we shall get it done. What do you say, eh, Satkori?'

Satkori was relatively younger, fair and tall. You might take him for an innocent good-natured chap, but he was clearly a needy person in worldy terms.

'That's so,' he agreed.

'What do you say?' asked Ramhari of Nalu.

'Whatever you say, dada,'

'In that case, shall I speak out the terms?'

'Please do.'

Ramhari spread out the fingers of both hands before Nalu Pal and said, 'Five rupees it will cost you for each of us.'

'Done.'

'You'll have to give one rupee to each brahman as the ritual gift, *dakshina*.'

'*That* you will have to bring down to eight annas.'

'Also, one bundle of foodstuff to take away—luchi, sugar and coconut sweets. That's to be organized *before* the meal.'

'Done. But bring down the dakshina-fee to half a rupee, please.'

'And, you have to give us our five rupees, *before* the meal. Not less than that.'

'I'll do that. But *you'll* have to get a hundred brahmans to come, at the very least. If it's less than that, won't be able to keep my promise about your fee.'

'Course I shall,' said Ramhari Chakrabarti with a vigorous shake of his topknot with the dangling amulet. 'Got enough in my home to begin with—a nephew, nephew-in-law, three cousins from my uncle's side, my own four sons, two little girls—they'll all come. By the grace of god, brother Satkori too has five, and *they'll* all come. Well, that makes almost half of a hundred, doesn't it now?'

≈

Ramhari Chakrabarti was powerful all right. He turned out to be as good as his word. On the day of the feast the brahmans started pouring in, little children in tow. The tented enclosure that had been set up in the big courtyard did not suffice to hold all of them. It was a feast of gargantuan proportions! The sheer quantity of ghee-rich luchi and sugar that each one of those brahmans polished off was quite a sight! No one had ever held such a large feast with food of such a high quality in these parts. The invitees were served as much as they wished to eat of luchi and sugar, and delicacies like *malpua* and coconut-*raskara*. A special treat was *sukho doi*—a kind of condensed yoghurt made by renowned Sona Goalini of Baikanthapur. Even as they were eating, the brahmans began praising and applauding the splendour of the feast. One ancient even went so far as to quote from that well-known play—*Kulinkulasarvasya Natak* to express his sentiments:

> 'Piping hot luchis puffed in ghee,
>   A few strands of ginger
>   'long with kochuree...

I'd only *read* of such things, Baba Nalu; never had the good fortune to taste any. After all, who would treat us in such poverty-stricken parts! But my son, having come to the feast at your home today...'

A chorus of endorsement arose from the others, 'You are so right, grandfather! So right!'

Eventually, their bellies filled to bursting, the eight-anna obligatory gift *and* a bag of goodies in hand, groups of brahmans left Nalu's home, deeply satisfied.

'So, Pal-moshai,' said Ramhari Chakrabarti, coming up to Nalu Pal, 'didn't I tell you? Lay out the rice and the crows will come flocking!'

'No, no, don't say such things! It puts me in the wrong,' replied Nalu Pal, somewhat embarrassed. 'I am so blessed that my home has received the dust of your feet today. Go ahead with your brokering. You've got some might, I'll say!'

'Got nothing to do with my might, Pal-moshai. Ramhari Chakrabarti does not speak anything but the truth and the right thing. Or I'm not my father's son! You tell me now—how many in these parts have ever offered a feast of luchi with sugar? They heard what was going to be served, and they came running. I believe no one's come from *this* village? That they won't; they think no end of themselves.'

'There's one who has—Bhabani Barujje-moshai.'

'Is that so?' said Ramhari in astonishment. 'Dewanji's son-in-law?'

'That's the one.'

'Pal-moshai, won't you introduce me to him?' requested Ramhari.

Bhabani Barujje had sat down to eat in a quiet corner with his son after all the brahmans had been fed. For the first time in his life, Khoka tasted that delectable thing called luchi.

'Baba, is this called *nuchi*?'

'Eat well, my son. Would you like some more?'

'Umm,' said the boy, inclining his head in assent.

At a sign from Bhabani, Tilu who was serving them, put a couple of freshly fried puffy hot luchis on Khoka's leaf plate. Just then Nalu Pal came in with Ramhari Chakrabarti and stood about ten hands away from where Bhabani was seated.

'Yes?'

'This gentleman has come to make your acquaintance.'

Ramhari made a pranam and said, 'One look at you and I know I must have got up this morning to an auspicious sign.'

'You mean a bad omen!'

'Don't even say such a thing! Had I known that you and my

mother (he meant Tilu) were to come and eat here this afternoon, I would have told Pal-moshai that it wouldn't have mattered at all whether any other brahman came or not. Spending so much money to feed so many bamuns when such a direction has been given! Where is my mother? Do allow your son to have a glimpse of you, my mother; he will not go home otherwise.'

At this entreaty from Ramhari, Tilu came out with her sari-end partially covering her face. Ramhari made her a namaskar and exclaimed, 'Like the divine consorts Shiva-Shivani—the two of you! What a wonderful day it has been, Pal-moshai! Ma, do remember this son of yours.'

Tilu whispered loudly to her husband, 'Will you grace my home this coming full moon? It is to celebrate Khoka's birthday. Come and have a meal.' It was customary not to address a stranger; you had to keep someone as a 'middleman' when speaking to another male.

Before Bhabani could say anything, Ramhari said, 'I shall do so, Ma. I shall indeed come to have the festive meal, *parabanna*. It's my good fortune. I shall have to share the news with your daughter-in-law once I go home.' He was referring to his wife.

'Why don't you bring her as well?' Tilu extended the invitation.

'She is old-fashioned. She is not the same like you, who are with the times. She never comes out before any man. But I shall come and share the special meal with Khokon here, and I shall sing your praises.'

≈

'Bouma, have you heard anything in the village? About that...?' Nilmoni Samaddar's wife Annakali discretly asked her daughter-in-law Subasi.

Subasi understood that her mother-in-law was obliquely referring to the invitation given out by the wealthy people in the other part of the village who had commissioned the extravagant Durga Puja festivities this year. The question was whether *they* would be able to take advantage of the invitation or not. They were very poor and rarely had an opportunity to eat well, so they had to keep a sharper lookout than others as regards the feasts and festivities to which they might be invited as brahmans.

Subasi was a docile daughter-in-law. She had once been a shy thing, but their family circumstances having forced her to borrow all the time from the neighbours had blunted the edge of her diffidence. She shared with her mother-in-law all the news she had managed to gather: not *one* of the brahmans of their village was going to have a meal at Nalu Pal's.

'Find out what's happening at Swarna's home,' instructed her mother-in-law.

'Will you come, Ma?'

'I'd better grind the dal. I'd soaked the dal in water, if I don't grind it now, it'll go waste. We've not been able to get enough for the year, as it is. Listen, daughter-in-law, let me tell you…'

'Yes, Ma?'

'Tell Swarna,' whispered Annakali looking around furtively to make sure she wasn't being heard, 'that even if no one else goes, we two families will go secretly late at night. What do you say?'

'Will you be able to live it through if Uncle Foni or his wife happen to see us?'

'We'll only go late at night. How would anyone know?'

'Even trees have ears in this village,' said Subasi.

'But why don't you find out anyway?'

Subasi went to visit Jatin's wife, Swarna. They too, were amongst the poorest in the village. She found Swarna busy cutting a huge pile of the inner pulp of a plantain trunk. By her side, were two branches full of ripe drumsticks, ready for cooking.

'What are you cooking, Swarna-didi?' Subasi asked.

'He's not at home, so I thought what's the point cooking anything special for us women—let me make something with the drumsticks and kalhai-dal.'

'True enough.'

'Sit down, won't you, Subasi?'

'Can't now. Mother-in-law sent me to ask if you were going to take up that invitation from Tulsi-didi?'

'Well, my sister in-law was asking me if I would. But if none of the village bamuns go to their place, how do we? Will all of you be going?'

'*We* will, if all of you do.'

'Will you call Nandarani here for a bit?'

It was quite some time since Jatin's sister, Nandarani, had been abandoned by her husband. They barely managed. Jatin's father, the late Rupchand Mukhujje, had got his daughter married off to a kulin with a great difficulty. But the groom had contracted several other marriages; he would come once in a while to collect a lot of money and things from his in-laws and then set off on his marital rounds. For the last four or five years he had simply disappeared. Nandarani had to bear the burden of raising three kulin daughters—a common enough tale in kulin households.

Nandarani was seated on a low stool, drying her spread-out hair in the sun. She came away when Subasi went to call her; the three women sat down to figure out how they might accept the invitation.

'If we go *very* late at night, who's to see?'

'Then, let's go,' said Subasi. 'No point annoying Tulsi: after all whenever we are in trouble, it's Tulsi who looks after us, who else? But when it comes to pushing us around and ostracizing us, everybody's ready to gang up.'

Very late at night the two families secretly left for Tulsi's home. Tulsi served them with great care and gave each one of them a bundle of food to carry home as well.

When Swarna returned she discovered that while they were away her husband had come home. He had unlatched the door and lit a lamp, and was now waiting for her.

'Where had you gone to?' he asked his wife. 'What's that you have in your hand? I've brought two measures of sonamung-dal from a family that I officiate for at Gaighata, asked them for it. At least the children can have a good meal. And what do you have in your hand?'

'Don't you worry about that. You will have something to eat, won't you?'

'I'm very hungry. There's some rice.'

'Do sit down. Eat whatever I'm going to give you now.'

Swarna was delighted that after a long while she was able to serve her husband some delicious food. Married into a poor family, even when her father-in-law was alive, she had seen that the most even he could expect for a snack was coarse grains of roasted rice. Lately, she had been pounding the roasted rice for the toothless old man.

'My! Where did you get all this food from?' asked Jatin.

'Don't tell a soul—from Tulsi's. Tulsi herself came the other day and invited us with folded hands. A lovely girl she is. Not a speck of pride in her.'

'Who else went?'

'Nandarani and Subasi went...and all the kids. How happy Tulsi-didi was! She stood there and supervised the serving and everything. Insisted on giving us an entire pot full of luchi and sugar to bring back home.'

'You did the right thing. There's never enough to eat. Whoever gives us any food?'

'If they get to know in the village...?'

'Will they hang you or put you on the stake! Good you did it. They *invited* you and you accepted it. It's not as if you went there uninvited!'

'Thakur-jamai was there too. So were Tilu-didi and Nilu-didi.'

'No one will dare say anything to *them*. We're poor—all the wrongdoing will be dumped on us. Doesn't matter. Did you eat your fill of luchi? Were the children fed properly? Put aside the rest of the food for them; they can have it once they get up in the morning. Only don't go around talking about it in the village; and that's the end of it. But tell me, did you enjoy yourself and eat well?'

'Would Tulsi-didi let us go if we didn't eat our fill! She's a-standin'' there with folded hands. Keeps sayin', "O, you're not eating properly, please have some more, do..."'

≈

On Khoka's date of birth, celebrated as per the almanac, Ramhari Chakrabarti came with his two sons to Bhabani's home. For Khokon, he had brought khoi made from special grain and a thickened milk dessert cooked by his wife. Mats had been laid out for the guests on the raised section of western portion of Bhabani's home. The guests were few—Ramkanai Kobiraj, Foni Chakkarty, Shyam Mukhujje, Nilmoni Samaddar and Jatin. Amongst the women there was Nistarini, Jatin's wife Swarna, and, Nilmoni Samaddar's daughter-in-law, Subasi.

'Ah, it's Ramhari! How are you?' said Foni Chakkarty.

'My pranam to you, dada! How are *you*?'

'What's there to say? Getting on in years; time to go. Amongst the old ones, it's me and Nilmoni-dada who are still around, doing well; the rest have all gone one by one.'

'And how old might dada be?'

'About sixty-nine.'

'Goodness! No one would believe it to see you. Your teeth all there too!'

'I eat half a seer of rice, even now. Half a katha of fruit with pressed rice. Half of a ripe jackfruit I can manage at one go. Drink two and half seers of milk twice a day, drink and digest it all.'

'There's something about all that food, that's why you are in such good shape. Otherwise—'

'Ramhari, there's something I want to say. What *did* you do the other day! Do the bamuns of Angrali and Gadadharpur lack *all* propriety? Just because you've been invited, do you *have* to go and eat at a shuddur's home? *Chhi chhi!* For shame, you're brahmans, after all! Don't you wear the sacred thread? No matter that you're not kulins. Not everyone is a kulin; but as to a sense of pride and dignity—*that's* for everyone to maintain.'

Nilmoni Samaddar had begun to feel very uneasy at Foni Chakkarty's diatribe. He was worried that people would get to know that *his* wife and daughter-in-law had secretly gone late at night and eaten their fill at the same place. He would be in great trouble if it were ever made public. But by God's will, Bhabani Barujje came in exactly at that moment to usher them to the meal.

Foni Chakkarty and the others wouldn't sit in the same row as Ramhari Chakrabarti, for the latter was a shrotriya brahman, considered inferior to kulins. He was seated elsewhere, but the honour of feeding Khoka the birthday dessert, payesh made with rice and thickened milk, was given to him. Khoka's seat was just next to Ramhari's. Tilu, part of her sari draped over her head, began fanning the two of them.

'What is your name, my little fellow?' Ramhari asked him.

'Sri Rajeswar Bandyopadhyay,' said Khoka very shyly.

'And what do you study?'

At this question, Khoka spoke up enthusiastically, 'I study at Haru gurumoshai's village school. Sambhu-dada, who lives in Calcutta, has promised to teach me English.'

'That's wonderful. Such a little boy and he's going to study Ingleesh! Then you will turn out to be a hakim at the court. That's good. You have the looks to be a hakim.'

'Ma's asking, won't you have some more?'

'No, no, I've had enough. Taken three helpings of the birthday payesh, what more do I need? May you live long, little one,' Ramhari blessed him.

No one from a kulin brahman family had ever accorded such respect to Ramhari Chakrabarti, the broker of feasts for brahmans. As he was leaving, Ramhari touched Tilu's feet as a mark of respect and said, 'I shall take your leave now, mother. Shall remember this forever, the way you looked after me. I've come to know today that you are not like any old Ram or Shyam hereabouts. Two arms and two legs alone don't make a human being. And hanging a sacred thread round your neck doesn't make you a kulin.'

≈

So many changes had taken place in and around the village. The railway was running from Chakda to Chuadanga. One Jyestha month Tilu and Nilu went with their husband to Aranghata, to offer puja to the local deity. They went by bullock cart to Chakda, where, after bathing in the Ganga, they cooked and had a meal. Khoka who was with them was terribly keen to see the railway. Finally, the train arrived. They all boarded that wondrous machine at Aranghata. For over a year they talked to each other and to others about the astonishing rail journey.

Meanwhile, Khoka had finished his studies at the village school. Bhabani sat down one day to discuss with Tilu whether he should apprentice Khoka to become a *muktar* at the court, or whether the boy should study Sanskrit at the local school for brahmans. If he were to do the former, Bhabani would have to consult Satish Muktar.

'Call Nilu,' said Tilu.

Nilu was no more the Nilu of yore. She had become a real matron, organizing every detail of the household to perfection.

'Really, why don't you ask *Tulu* directly?' suggested Nilu when she joined them.

Tulu had grown to be a handsome looking boy, grave for his years. And devoted to his father.

'Baba, why don't you decide? How would I know?' said he. 'As for Chhoto-ma, she knows nothing. Remember what she did when we got on to that rail-gari? Sat down with her betel leaves to make paan. We were there in a jiffy from Ranaghat to Aranghata, and how that upset Chhoto-ma! "I've just begun makin' these paans and three kos distance the carriage has already come!" she kept complaining.' Tulu began to laugh heartily recounting the tale.

'What would I know, my son!' replied Nilu. 'We're old folks. I remember travelin' to bathe in the Ganga at Chakda, and it would take forever...you could make as many paans as you want. You needn't burst your sides laughin'!'

'What's wrong with what I said? What do you know of studying and learning? Ma's at least studied some Sanskrit, but you're quite ignorant.'

'*You* teach me, Khoka.'

'Me teach you? At this age she's going to go learn the alphabet!'

'I'll make you some lovely milk dessert later in the day,' Nilu said.

'Truly?'

'Truly.'

'In *that* case you are very nice. Not at all stupid,' declared the boy.

'Now, stop all that teasing, Tulu,' said Bhabani, 'and give me a reply to what I asked you.'

'Baba, why don't *you* say?'

'What do you wish?'

Nilu spoke up again. 'Don't let him get into that muktari business. Teach him Ingriji. We have to send him to Calcutta. Look at that Sambhu—how well he's doing after he got a job in Calcutta. Is our Tulu any less intelligent?'

'What do you say, Khoka?' Bhabani asked his son again.

'Chhoto-ma is quite right. Let's go ahead. What do you say Ma? Isn't Chhoto-ma right?'

'Supposed to be stupid, aren't I? What would *I* know!' exclaimed Nilu.

'No, Chhoto-ma,' Tulu reassured her, 'I didn't laugh at you. What you said means a lot to me. I too want to study English; Baba, you go ahead with that idea. But who will teach me English?'

'How would I know anything about that?' said Nilu. 'You'll have to find out.'

'True enough. Khoka is right: who is going to teach him English? No one in the village knows any English, only the Ingriji-copyist, Sambhu Ray. He's been working with the Amuti Company House for years; speaks English with the sahebs and all. Spouts English in front of the villagers to show off.'

'Khoka, how does your Sambhu-dada speak English? Give us a sample,' said Tilu laughing.

'Ittseistmuttfoot-it suntu-fut—fit—'

'Wonderful!' said Bhabani, 'When did you learn all this?'

'Learnt it from listening to him. He says all this and I listen to him. And then I say it *exactly* as he does.'

'It's amazing how well he has learnt English. Just listen to him speak!'

'Really, he's speaking it so wonderfully,' chimed in Nilu.

The three were delighted at Khoka's intelligence. Enthused by their admiration, Khoka said, 'I know some more; shall I say it, Baba? "Sit a hipp-sit-foot-a pot I my"—you know Baba, he says *these* two words a lot: *I* and *my*—really he does, Baba.'

Nilu marvelled at how brainy their boy was.

≈

Prasanna Chakravarty suffered a lot for two years after he lost his job at the Neelkuthi. It wasn't easy getting an amin's job. And how would he get by if he didn't have a job? After a lot of searching, he had got his present situation, but where would he get a job with all the comforts of the one he had enjoyed at the Neelkuthi? The Bengali landlords could hardly match the wealth and prosperity of the sahebs. Nevertheless, it was four years now that he'd been working for his present employers—the Pals of Bahadurpur cutchery.

That morning Ghanashyam Chakladar who was the estate *naib*, went off in a palanquin to look into and supervise the affairs of the khas-land at Chitalmaari. Prasanna Amin felt a little relieved. These were new masters; you had to deal cautiously with them—no Rajaram Dewan here, no Burra Saheb.

Ratilal, the naib's servant, came into his room and said, 'Amin-babu, what are you doing?'

'Sitting around. Why?'

'The Naib-babu's duck, did it come this way? Seen it?'

'No, haven't seen it.'

'Will you have a smoke?'

'Get some tobacco ready for me.'

Ratilal came back, having prepared the tobacco. Prasanna Chakkarty didn't have the courage to ask for any on his own unless the naib's servant offered to do so himself.

'Amin-babu, I don't think that Girey fisherman delivered the fish he was supposed to this morning.'

'Was he supposed to? I saw him selling fish at the weekly market yesterday. *Aar*-fish, it was.'

'Brings it over everyday; who knows why he didn't come today? Naib-moshai, he needs his fish, can't have his meal without it. Let's wait and see. If he doesn't bring any, I'll have to run over to the fishermen's locality.'

Prasanna Chakkarty did not care for this continuous chatter. He was in low spirits today. Besides, he didn't feel like talking for too long with the naib's servant. True, the vagaries of fortune had brought him to his present state, but it wasn't easy to forget the power and the glory of his life at the Mollahati Neelkuthi.

Wanting to get Ratilal out of the way, he quickly retorted, 'If it's fish you need, you'd better rush; they'll take it all to the Sonakhali market later in the day.'

'I'll set off then, what do you say?'

'Right away! Don't dawdle.'

In a little while, Ratilal was seen leaving the cutchery, carrying a container to bring back the fish. Prasanna Chakkarty immediately felt a sense of peace. Now to sit in the sun and massage some oil all over himself, and then for a leisurely bath... He sat down under the jackfruit tree and draping himself with a bright red thin towel began the oil massage. He would have to cook after he finished bathing.

It was that time of the year when the raiyats of the Neelkuthi would bring over heaps of brinjals. Radishes and serrated gourds too, they'd bring. Not just him, all the amins would get their share. Narahari Peshkar would bring over all the stuff that *he* had got from the rayiats and tell him, 'Prasanna-dada, you're a brahman: cooking is part of your hereditary skill. Cook something for me too.'

It was a convenient arrangement. Cooking for two was the same as cooking for oneself. The monthly expenses didn't add up to more than three or four rupees. Narahari would bring him all the rice and dal they needed. Such superb milk he would be gifted by someone or the other; never had to *buy* a thing. And yes, there was Gaya... he remembered her...

Gaya...Gaya-mem!

Why was it that thinking of her made him so sad?

Gaya-mem had looked upon him with favour. He had been dogged by sorrow all his life. Not a kind word, not a smile, not anything ever said to him in a sweet voice. It was Gaya alone who had fulfilled these longings. Such a shapely beauty, with her cascade of black hair! Could one ever find a reason why Gaya-mem, beloved ayah of the Burra Saheb, would look upon a creature such as him with such favour? But she had done so.

'Khuro-moshai, O Khuro-moshai!' How sweetly she would call out to him...

True, he was old enough to be an elderly uncle of hers, but Gaya had never been contemptuous of him. Why *hadn't* she? Why had she found out all sorts of pretexts to banter and joke with him? Why did she get so much pleasure teasing him, making him dance to her tune? How was Gaya doing now? How long it was since he had seen her. Who knows whether she had fallen into difficult times? How many nights he had lain awake missing her. Hadn't seen her for a long time.

'O Amin-moshai, couldn't get any fish!' Enter Ratilal, container in hand.

Prasanna Chakkarty felt a wave of anger. A curse on you! Am I your bosom buddy! Am I the *same* as you? A mere servant—scouring pots and pans, running errands; and you dare come to chat, grinning away like a fool, with Prasanna Amin!

How would Prasanna Chakkarty—now a water-snake without any venom—a person without power, respond to such a question! Gone was the Mollahati Neelkuthi, gone was Burra Saheb Shipton, and gone too, Dewan Rajaram Ray.

There had been law and order in the days of the Neelkuthi: people trembled in fear and awe on beholding a red face. It was the devil's own domain in *these* estates run by the local landlords. Did anyone care! A plague on them!

'H'mm,' said the amin irritably, in response to Ratilal, almost indifferently.

'Havin' an oil massage?' enquired Ratilal.

'Umm.'

'Goin' for a bath?'

'Umm.'

'What are you planning to cook?'

'Nothing special...dal and bitter gourd. There's buttermilk.'

'Sonka the milkwoman has dropped off some marvelous buttermilk. Like some?'

'No, I've got my own.'

Before Ratilal could come up with anything more, Prasanna Chakkarty had slung his thin towel over his shoulder and headed off to bathe in the Icchamati. Oof! What a trap he'd fallen into! Having to natter away with the fellow, as though he had nothing else to do. The rascal's effrontery was the limit.

How long it had been that he had been cooking for himself... twenty years? No, more than that. His first wife Saraswati had passed away even earlier. Ever since, he'd been dealing with pots and pans. So it had gone on. He cooked what he did daily—kalhai-dal with lots of green chillies and fried bitter gourd. That was it. There was the buttermilk, of course.

'Did you cook the dal?'

He almost choked on the water he was pouring himself from the tilted water-pot above his mouth. What a ghoul this fellow was; can't you see a man's sitting down to eat his meal! Did you have to start speaking just as a man is pouring some water down his throat? Wretched rascal!

'Umm, why?' he answered, palpably annoyed.

'What dal have you cooked?'

'*Maskalai.*'

'Will you give some to me? Shall I get a bowl?'

'There's nothing left. Finished it all—the one container I'd cooked.'

'But I've brought you some buttermilk.'

'I've *got* buttermilk. I'd bought some.'

'This is special. Sonka milkwoman is famous for her buttermilk. She's the widowed sister of Bishtu Ghosh. There's no one else but her who knows how to make *mathawala*-buttermilk. Have a taste,' urged Ratilal.

Nice sounding name…might as well give it a try. H'mm! Not bad, quite tasty. So Sonka milkwoman lived in the same village, did she? How old would she be?

He had a smoke and then lay down on his none too clean bedding. He'd barely shut his eyes when the paik messenger came in to announce, 'Naib-moshai's sent for you.'

Prasanna Chakkarty struggled to his feet and hurried to the cutchery. It was crowded with raiyats. About ten of them had copies of the official surveyor's document known as the *chitha*. Naib Ghanashyam Chakladar was a man of a serious disposition, not someone you could treat lightly. He had gathered the pleats of his coarse dhoti around him and sat half-reclined, on the thinly carpeted floor, leaning against a slightly dirty bolster. Ratilal handed him a silver-plated hubble-bubble with a long extended pipe to smoke.

'Have the chithas for the khas-mahal been prepared?' he asked, looking up at the amin.

'Almost done; just a few left.'

'Can you give it to them? There, you can go along with Amin-moshai,' he said to the waiting raiyats. To the amin he said, 'Do what you can for them, their chithas. They've come from far away and will have to return today.'

Prasanna Chakkatty had been at this job for decades, you didn't have to teach *him* the niceties of the business. As if it was only a question of getting the chithas for the khas-mahal ready! There would be problems galore—with the measurement of boundaries, this and that, and the chithas would have to be signed by the naib—all sorts of things. And at this late hour—how was it all going to get done? It was hard to say. Of course, he would *try*.

In the days of the Neelkuthi some money could be made out of these deals. But those were days of yore...like a dream.

One of the raiyats came up to him and requested, 'Please do it, Amin-babu. We'll give you something...as paan-money.'

'How much of something?'

'One anna per head, we'll give you.'

Prasanna Chakkarty put down the stitched account book he held in his hand and declared, 'In that case, it won't be done now. You can go tell your Naib-moshai. The chithas have been done, but they've not been tallied with the original records, and the signatures not done either. You can reckon on another fortnight or perhaps a month's delay. A lot of gruelling work involved.'

'So what would be the sum you are quoting?' the headman of the group said most humbly. He too was an experienced man, knew the very pulse of the law, the niceties of the zamindari cutchery, and all that was involved. No one had to tell *him* why the Amin-babu was acting difficult.

'No, no, that won't do,' replied Prasanna Chakkarty looking very displeased. 'You had better go to the naib. The work isn't done yet. Another fortnight or so it will take me to wind it up.'

'Don't be angry with us, Amin-moshai,' entreated their headman with folded hands, 'Aren't we giving six paise per head?'

'Not a cowrie less than two annas per head.'

'We're poor folks...it will kill us—'

'No. Impossible.'

The headman was forced to collect five quarters from the ten members of his group and hand it all over to Prasanna Chakkarty in the most docile manner.

You'll have to come around my precious creatures. Prasanna

Chakkarty doesn't have to be told how to do his job by a Ghanashyam Chakladar. Would *he*—former amin of the Neelkuthi—have to learn from a third-rate zamindari's estate official on how to make money on the side? Come to order me around, huh! Ever seen a Shipton Saheb!

It was three in the afternoon. Ghanashyam Chakladar sent for him again. The naib was an extremely hard-working man, no question of him having an afternoon siesta. A bolster against his chest, he was about to sign the collection registers; the *peshkar* was standing before him, turning the pages.

'Handed them the letters?' he asked Prasanna Chakkatty, looking directly at him.

'Yes, sir.'

'Can you ride a horse?'

'Sir.'

'You'll have to set off for Rahtoonpur right away. You are going to be the chief witness in the lawsuit between Bilatali Sardar and Osman Gani. Go and do a thorough investigation. Nakur Kapali is waiting there on behalf of the cutchery. He'll explain everything to you. There's a silk-cotton tree behind Osman Gani's dwelling: measure how far away that is from the main road. Measure it with the surveying chain, will you?'

'Shall I take the chain then?'

'Yes, do. Take my horse—the one with the cropped ears. Don't give it free rein; just a light tap on the belly with your left foot. He'll speed up.'

Now, at this time of the day, to set off for Rahatoonpur! So far away! Who knows how late it would be before he got back home. And was Nakur Kapali to teach him what had to be done? Laughable it was. What would that fellow know about surveying and measuring! His job had been to run after the amin with a peg—the fellow was simply what the sahebs would call the 'pinman'. That same Nakur Kapali was to teach *him* the finer points of surveying—he who had served under the stern gaze of the sahebs for an uninterrupted quarter of a century? Nakur Kapali indeed!

The horse galloped away on the Jessore-Chuadanga road, a proper road. Almost eleven kos it was. Everyone in these parts knew him. How often he and the karkoon would come this way to mark out plots for indigo cultivation during the days of the Neelkuthi. A riot had taken place here during Dewan Rajaram's tenure; it had turned into a big affair. The district magistrate had come to investigate after receiving complaints from the subjects.

The elder headman Abdul Latif was now dead; his son Shamsul came forward to escort Prasanna Chakkarty to their home. There was still some daylight left. He'd really raced his horse in the afternoon sun.

'Salam, Amin-moshai!' Shamsul greeted him. 'How are you these days?'

'How are things with all of you? Abdul dead? When did that happen? Aaah, he was a good man. I'm in Bahadurpuri these days. It's too far away; hardly a chance of meeting up.'

'Have a puff. I'll get the tobacco ready.'

'Do you know where I could find Nakur Kapali?'

'The thatched hut by the Baur that was built for the amin during the surveying—that's where he is.'

Prasanna Chakkarty had been brooding over something for a while now. He realized that he had a deep desire to see the old place—the Kuthibari.

The light was waning. Soon it would be evening. Mollahati Neelkuthi was a good three kos from here. If he galloped hard it would take an hour. He could still make it before evening. After some deliberation he set off for Mollahati. Hadn't been there in a while. Yellow flowers had blossomed in the *dhundul* thickets, the sap from the jiuli trees was racing down. The wind whistled through the open fields from the Morighata Baur, bringing with it the fragrance of kumud flowers. Beneath the thorny bushes of the sheya-berries, weasels and mongooses scurried around making peculiar hissing sounds.

Life was empty, quite meaningless. Like that vast Morighata Field it was. Nothing really appealed to him anymore. Merely earning a living, eating and drinking—every move like a clockwork toy. No pleasure in anything; doing something only because it had to be done.

The light waned. In the western sky a five-day old moon had risen like a slice of pumpkin. God! What strong tobacco those rascals smoked. And to offer it to their guests! He was still racked by spasms of coughing.

The cloudy line of the horizon had melted into the bluish haze of the forests. The horse was spent after galloping all that distance. He could feel the sweat all over its body. Now, finally, between the tall casuarina trees he caught glimpses of the white Neelkuthi in the distance. His heart swelled with mixed emotions. The playing fields of his youth, of pleasures and gossip, large sums of money changing hands...so much had happened in this place. It wore a haunted look now. Lalmohan Pal was a businessman turned zamindar; how would *he* uphold the honour and prestige of the Neelkuthi?

With a start Prasanna Chakkarty realized that he had somehow moved away from the Neelkuthi and come to the graveyard that lay some distance away from the house. Luxuriant gardens had once been planted on either side. Huge trees, English trees that Robson Saheb had planted—all of which now made the graveyard heavy with darkness. That one there was Robson Saheb's daughter's grave. And the one next to it was Daniel Saheb's. Prasanna Chakkarty hadn't seen either of these sahebs. He had heard stories of the huge white Kuthi being built during Robson Saheb's time.

The graveyard was running wild with overgrown bushes and uncut grass. In the heyday of the Neelkuthi you could pick up a drop of red sindur off the graves—so spotless and shining the place was. Who gave a hoot for it now!

All of a sudden his horse seemed to falter and shy away. Prasanna Chakkarty looked up and a shiver ran down his entire body. He'd forgotten that Shipton Saheb's grave was hereabouts. What was that white thing moving? Behind the white flowers of the tall clumps of *ulukhagra* that grew wild around Shipton Saheb's grave?

He was in the lonely abandoned graveyard, draped in hazy moonlight. However courageous Amin Prasanna Chakkarty might be, he couldn't help but think of ghouls and evil spirits.

'Who is that? Who? Who are you?' he cried out hoarsely, his voice distorted in fear.

From behind the waves of the ulukhagra flowers that surrounded Shipton Saheb''s grave, a woman's figure rose up with a start, hurriedly, and stood still in that hazy moonlight like a marble statue.

'Who is it? Who are you?'

'Who? Khuro-moshai! O Khuro-moshai!' said the person in a tone of extreme incredulity. A little later, and she had come forward: 'I am Gaya.'

For some time Prasanna was dumbstruck in amazement. Then, hurriedly placing his foot on the stirrup, he dismounted. 'Gaya!' he exclaimed in a tone of delight. 'It's you! And here? Come quick, get out of this jungle now—what had you come here for?'

In the faint moonlight Prasanna saw traces of tears on her face glistening. It looked as though she had been weeping there alone for quite some time now.

'Come Gaya,' said Prasanna, 'let us go out that way. Terrible jungle this side.'

It was as though Gaya-mem barely heard him. 'Come, Khuro-moshai, won't you see the Burra Saheb's grave?' she replied. 'Do come. Since you've come, might as well take a look at it,' she went on. And holding him by the hand, she almost pulled him towards the grave. Someone had strewn freshly plucked *sandhyamalati* and *bok*-flowers from the overrun garden all over Shipton's grave.

She picked up a bunch of sandhyamalati and handed it to him, said, 'Come now; offer some of this. Don't your remember, today is the day Saheb died? You've eaten his salt once upon a time. Pluck some of the ulukhar flowers and scatter those too. Offer those too, all together...'

Prasanna Chakkarty saw a fresh flow of tears run down both her cheeks.

Slowly they emerged from the wilderness of the graveyard and sat down beneath an English tree. Neither said a word for some time. But that both were deighted at the unexpected encounter was evident from the expression on their faces. As though emerging from within the stony walls of a palace of an ancient civilization, beneath that ancient juniper tree brought there by Robson Saheb, a man and a woman had come to life on this evening-turning-into-night by the abandoned Mollahati Neelkuthi.

Gaya had become thin; she had none of the beauty of former times. Her front teeth had fallen. She was visibly aging. Signs of sorrow were writ on her face, all over her body, in the glance of her eyes and in her wan smile.

Gaya silently gazed at the amin's face.

'How are you, Gaya?' he asked.

'Well. Where are you coming from? Where do you live these days?'

'I live very far away, in Bahadurpuri. I'm the amin at the cutchery. Let me hear you talk about yourself first. Why are you looking so poorly?'

'Don't talk to me about looks. Would've been starvin' if Saheb hadn't gifted me the land and if you hadn't measured it out for me. People respected me and cared for me when the times were good, when I could get some work done for them. Who is to ask after me now? Instead, they get after me, treat me like an outcaste in our neighbourhood—I'd told you about it, that time when we met.'

'Is it going on in the same way, even now?'

'For as long as I live, you think, Khuro-moshai, there's going to be a way out of this? I've lost my caste, you see. If I'm lain down with fever no one will give me a drop of water, no one will stop by to look in on me. What can I tell you 'bout my sorrows! With whom will I quarrel! So much has changed for me.'

Prasanna Chakkarty listened silently. He had tears in his eyes. The moon could be glimpsed through the gaps in the branches. Like her, his days too were steeped in sorrow.

He got up and firmly tethered the reins of the horse to the English tree, then came down to sit down beside her once more. Such joy there was in his heart. There were few who would want to listen to stories of sadness: could one speak of sorrows to anyone and everyone? It was as though she was his kin. There was comfort in relieving himself of the burden of his unspoken sorrows.

'I've become old, Gaya,' he said with something like a laugh. 'My hair has whitened. There's always something like fear inside of me. Wanted to do well in life; and now, I feel that there's another who's employed me, and if I were to lose this job, who will give me a fistful of rice? I've lost faith in myself. The way things are moving, Gaya, there won't be a soul to pour a drop of oil to soothe our matted hair.'

'Don't you worry, Khuro-moshai, you shall stay with me. That paddy field you had measured out for me will be enough to keep the two of us. What *more* can people say of me? Haven't I already drowned, or am I still going to drown? There's One above us all who won't abandon you or me. It's my Baba who had given me the sign. I used to believe there was no one. Till as long as I live, you will get the care and devotion of this poor woman. Even if I do come from a low caste.'

Old Prasanna Chakkarty's being was filled with an exquisite sensation. He had never experienced such feelings in his most glorious days. As though having lost everything he had been given everything, sitting here in the abandoned graveyard.

He got up abruptly and said, 'Gaya, I'll be off now.'

'Where will you go so late at night, Khuro-moshai?' asked Gaya, taken aback.

'It's another's horse that I'm riding, will have to get back to the cutchery while it's night. Since I fill my belly working for others, it is *their* work that I've got to attend to before everything. If I don't see you again, remember this old man. You go home; there could be snakes in the dark.'

Without a moment's delay, Prasanna Chakkarty untied the horse and setting his foot on the stirrup jumped on to the saddle. As he tugged at the reins, giving direction to the animal, he muttered, as though to himself, 'Gaya at least said what she did, that's enough. Whoever will say as much in this world? Only those who are close to one! Think of you as my own...'

Above the juniper tree the five-day moon was now moving towards the Morighata Baur. From within the dark undergrowth that had overtaken the old broken graves of the forgotten sahebs of the old Neelkuthi, the crickets were sending out their shrill cry.

Generations of leaves, bushes and creepers have come to life in every bend of the Ichhamati, in every fork of its forests. Above Balaram-Bhangon where the bank is prone to erosion, in a few years tiny saplings of sondali turn into a jungle; on many fallow fields there first springs up thickets of ghentu, then a jungle of kakjongha, *koonchkanta-nata* and *bonmorich*, innumerable wild flowers sprout anew on every bush...and above, the clamorous cries of flocks of migratory birds. We have seen the flight of geese winging their way in effortless grace over fields of tender green paddy beyond the line of clouds, foraging lotus stalks. We have seen the beautiful violet-purple of the *bonsim* flowers flood the river banks every year at the end of rains.

It is also at the end of rains that the kash-flowers drift in the wind and fall into the muddy banks where year after year their seeds take hold and burst into clusters of kash. In time, the thickets of kash too make way for thickets of sheora, then come the *sodali* trees—and then, innumerable creepers of pumpkin, *kantabash*, wild chalta. Creepers of gulancha, of matar, the small and the big goaley blossom and thrive in turn. On the deserted char-land of Ichhamati fragrant spring comes into life yet again in the clusters of ghentu-flowers...in the same months of Falgun and Chaitra, trading boats drop anchor and fishermen cook their meals in the shadows of the wild trees; they will soon move along the broadening river towards Sunderban to collect beeswax and honey—*benehar*-honey, *pulpati*-honey, honey from *geyon*, garan and sundari trees and honey from the first blossoms of *keora* trees, as fishermen spread out their nets in the Ichhamati to trap lobsters and *itey*-fish.

As soon as indigo cultivation stopped on both banks of Panchpota village, the profusion of bonnyeburo, pituli, *gamar* and *tittiraj* trees grew rapidly into a jungle. No more do the fishermen tie their dingies in the area; no more is there a path to come down to the water's edge: innumerable creepers, saibabla and bushes of sheya-berries have flourished, forming an impenetrable forest. Pearl seekers wait for the constellations of Swati and the northern Bhadrapad to shed water that they believe will give birth to pearls in the wombs of mussels and oysters; cherishing wild hopes, they heap up the shells beside the clumps of okrafruits where the yellow flowers of the radhalata softly shed their petals over the discarded piles of mussels and oysters.

And still, how many people have been cremated and turned to ashes that are washed away by the Ichhamati and taken to the sea, flowing backwards and forwards in the ebb and flow of tides, finally merging into the heart of the blue sea. The one who had planted with great hopes his banana orchard in the northern field, the one who split the bamboo to weave a fishtrap by the bend of the Gholduburi, the ashes and bones of his body might be lying bleached on the bank of Ichhamati. The footprints of beautiful young wives mark the path down to the river ghat on either bank, and the footprints of old women gradually disappear; in every village the auspicious sound of the conches joyously announce a wedding, the rice-eating ceremony of a child, an adolescent taking on the sacred thread, of Durga Puja and Lakshmi Puja... In time, the red lac bordering the bride's feet fades and is washed away, the smoke from the incense grows faint...Who can recognize death, proud Mother Death? Like the deer of illusion, as a *mayamriga* she guides us through the paths of life, her mysterious veil parts sometimes for a child, sometimes for an old man, the call of the eternal infinite comes in the gentle quivering of the telakochu flower, in the bitter sharp fragrance of medicinal plants in early Hemanta or at the end of Sharat. There are a few who on rainy days see in the swelling waters of the Ichhamati, in her mood of sensuous plenitude, dreams of that distant unknown boundless ocean...These fields, these abandoned stumps and mounds of former habitation layered in history, a mother's smile now vanished still traced in invisible lines.

Perhaps the first star of the sky knows something of it all.

Flowing past all of them, the restless waters of the Ichhamati move towards the big salty river, going past the mouth of the river, past the Raymangal, and Gangasagar towards the mighty ocean.

Translator's Note

Ichhamati was only partly serialized in the magazine *Abhhudoy* in mid-1947 before it was abruptly stopped. It finally came out as a book in January 1950.[1] Bibhutibhushan Bandyopadhyay passed away at the age of 56 on 2 November 1950.

When this translation was commissioned in 2012 it was believed that the novel was being translated into English for the first time. I completed a first draft in 2013, based on the paperback edition published by Mitra & Ghosh Publishers, BS Bhadra 1419. It was while revising this draft in early 2014, when I had moved to the Centre for Studies in the Social Sciences, Calcutta, that I found an existing English translation called *Ichamoti*. This translation by Arup Rudra was published posthumously in 2012. The reader will now have a choice of two English translations.

≈

Bibhutibhushan's diaries show that he was deeply attentive to speech patterns;[2] but in *Ichhamati*, which is set in Jessore district (in present-day Bangladesh), showcasing the local language is not his primary intention. Dialect is foregrounded in certain intimate moments, as when the specific ending of verb declensions becomes a matter of jesting between insider Tilu, a native speaker, and Bhabani who comes from neighbouring Nadia where the language is closer to standard Bangla. Bhabani's reflections, which are prioritized in the novel, are in standard Bangla, as is the narratorial commentary. I have used a mix of English dialects, idioms and accents to suggest deviations from standard speech, both in pronunciation and syntax.

Ichhamati is composed primarily in direct speech, indicated by the long dash, a convention followed in most Bengali novels: I use quote marks for direct speech by the characters, a convention familiar to the English reading audience. I have only indicated the range of Bangla spoken by each of the sahebs and the memsahebs, i.e. deviations from standard Bangla and, in the case of the sahebs, quaint grammatical errors. Speech patterns are constantly destabilized through juxtaposition: one jostles the other, or rests cheek by jowl. The Burra and the Chhota saheb speak two very different versions of Bangla—the former an archaic version, the latter grounded in the local Jessore patois. The memsaheb speaks yet another kind of Bangla. Often their sentences are a mix of English and Bangla, indicated in the orthography of the original as a mix of roman and Bangla script. For example, 'And what is it you neet? Any particular work? I am very busy now. Little time I have.' (There is a switch to English and then back to Bangla again.) I had intended to use slightly different fonts to indicate where the English occurs in the original, but it proved to be cumbersome.

I have taken into account the bilingual/multilingual reader who might not know Bangla but would be familiar with the nuances of kinship terms prevalent in much of the Indian subcontinent. Forms of address signifying kinship, social and affective ties or hierarchies have been retained as in their generic form, they suggest the shifting shades of deference in a village economy. They appear in lower case in the translation: for example, *huzoor, sir, didi, didimoni, babaji, baba, baba-thakur, dada-thakur, jamai-thaku* and so on. The suffix thakur indicates that a brahman is being addressed by a lower caste: Gaya addresses Ramkanai Kobiraj as 'Baba-thakur' as does Bhoja Muchi to Bhabani; Hala Pekey refers to the assembled brahmans as 'baba-thakuron'. Bhabani is called 'Jamai-thakur' by the village woman; jamai signifies his relationship as a 'brother-in-law'. When flirting with her admirer Prasanna Amin, Gaya enjoys emphasizing that he is an elder, a venerable uncle or 'Khuro-moshai'. Rajaram Ray is addressed variously as Dewanji, Dewan-moshai and Ray-moshai by underlings, and as 'my Dewan Roy' by the English planter. Dimunitives are common, used either affectionately (Tilu from Tillotoma), or to a person of lower strata (Rajaram calls Sriram Muchi, Remo).

An individual may have many names or various versions of his name. Abbreviations are used interchangeably, or as in the case of Nalu Pal, signal his rise in the village when he becomes Sri Lal Mohan Pal or Pal-moshai. Ramkanai pleads with the *daroga* (policeman) as 'Daroga-moshai'. I have therefore retained suffixes which signify gender, status, kinship terms, e.g. moshai, -bou or -babu.

Rustic or local turns of speech, sometimes cutting across caste and class lines, is indicated by a separation of consonantal conjuncts of the more Sanskritic pronunciation: *prasad* becomes *persad*, *berahman* instead of *brahman* and *suddur* instead of *sudra*. Variations of brahman include *berahmon* and *bamun*; similarly, vaishnavs (*baishnabs*) are often referred to as *bosthom* (e.g. Sayaram Boshtom the pin man) and Christians as *Kishtaans*. By the same linguistic rule, Srihari is pronounced *Chhihari* (Sardar).

I have retained the Indian months and six seasons (*Sheeth, Vasanta, Grishma, Varsha, Sharat, Hemanta*), the English orthography reflecting the Sanskrit pronunciation (e.g. *Sravan* or *Hemanta*, rather than the Bangla *Srabon* or *Hemanto*) and local variations of cooked dishes (*shukatani* rather than *shukto*).

≈

Ichhamati is packed with terminology from the revenue system, derived from Persian and Arabic. Specialized terms such as *khas-jami*, meaning land that is under direct control of the landlord, appears sometimes as *khas*-land; they have been explained in the Glossary. Also included in the Glossary are official titles (also signifying status) such as *Amin, Dewan, Mohuree, Peshkar* which are invariably appended to proper names, e.g. Prasanna *Amin*, but the latter is also referred to by his full name, Prasanna Chakatty or Chakravarty.

Anglo-Indian terms found in gazetteers, memoirs and fiction of/from colonial India, such as *baksheesh, khana-pina*, as well as titles, such as *khansama*, have been retained since they occur quite naturally in the period. (The *Hobson Jobson* is an invaluable guide in this regard.) As a general rule, non-English words—Arabic, Bangla, Hindustani, Persian and Sanskrit—are italicized only at the time of first appearance.

Sanskrit *slokas*—both popular couplets as well as passages from the Upanishads—are embedded in long conversations between Bhabani, Chaitanyabharati and Ramkanai Kobiraj. Bibhutibhushan first provides the Sanskrit verse in Bangla script and then gives us *his* Bangla rendition of the Sanskrit. I have privileged the author's Bangla renditions and translated them into English, while cross-checking wherever possible with the original Sanskrit.

The word used in Bangla by Bhabani is consistently '*bhagwan*' (holy, the exalted one), while in the Sanskrit verses he cites, the word is Brahman. The latter has been translated as the Absolute, the Supreme, the Supreme Being and the One Truth, the underlying reality of the world, that which has no form and shape and is beyond discourse and cognizance. One can 'apprehend' Brahma only by the ceaseless process of Negation, as in the *Brihadaryanyak Upanishad*, (II.3.6). As has been noted, 'early translations of the Upanishads have distorted their meaning by introducing the word 'God' or the word 'Lord' when no such dualism was meant.'[3] I have retained *bhagwan* (in lower case), with occasional references to the divine, when the ungendered pronoun in Bangla is an honorific.

I have attempted internal glossing wherever possible, without retarding the narrative flow. These include material objects of everyday use, some still in use in early twentieth century and others now obscure or rendered obsolete, such as pieces of jewellery, e.g. specially tuned musical anklets known as *gurjaripancham*.

There are several instances of repetition and numerous internal contradictions (the latter mostly to do with names and kinship), as well as a few historical inaccuracies (as in Bhabani's gloss on the Grand Trunk Road) in the original novel. I have made a few 'corrections' for internal consistency; but have not edited out inaccuracies, as these do not affect the overall theme.

Like all of Bibhutibhushan's writing, *Ichhamati* is a celebration of flora and fauna, particularly of the profusion of commonly found plant life that flourishes in most regions of Bengal. So as not to impede the syntactical flow and the aural rhythms, I have retained most of the Bangla names of plants, flowers and trees, except when they have a familiar equivalence in English (e.g. banyan, silk-cotton or mango tree or barbet, drongo and cuckoo in the case of birds). In a departure from my earlier translations of Bibhutibhushan's novels—*Aranyak* (2002) and *Making a Mango Whistle* (2005)—*Ichhamati* does not provide an exhaustive glossary of plant names in Bangla, English and Latin. In part, this is because this immense range of creepers, thorny bushes, trees and shrubs with their seeds, flowers, fruits, nuts and thorns thriving on land and water do not simply comprise a 'landscape' in *Ichhamati*; they imbue the narrative with a subjective undercurrent, linking the moment of the conscious thought with an awareness of the surrounding foliage, even if it is a small cluster of floating vegetation moving in the river's flow.

In the deliberate shift of diction in the poetic-prose of the epilogue, Bibhutibhushan privileges synaesthesia, seeking to move between land, water and space—finally, beyond the visible and tangible. As though leaving for the modern reader a leaf from the Upanishads that pervades the phenomenological realm of the novel, of his protagonist's consciousness, and as the author himself had internalized them.

≈

In living with this novel for several difficult years I have been helped in numerous ways by Sibaji Bandyopadhyaya, Jiji Bhattacharjee, Lalita Devi, Aditi Lahiri, Henning Reetz, Kumar Shahani, Sudeshna Shome Ghosh and Swathi Sukumar. Bratati Bhattacharya, Reeta Bhattacharya, Arunima Chakraborty, Nandita Das, Lily Ghosh, Ishita Gupta and Himanshi Sharma have helped with readings, proofing and meanings at different times, and my thanks go to all of them. I am grateful to Lavanya Mani for illuminating the text.

The translation is dedicated to Kumar Shahani with the strong hope of seeing him create his 'Icchha-mati' (as he persists in calling it) inspired by the vignettes I have read out to him in Bangla and English.

Notes

1. *Bibhuti Rachanabali*, vol. 6, p. 802. According to Rusati Sen in her biography of Bandyopadhyay, the date of publication is BS Paush 1956.
2. *Urmimukhor*, p. 382.
3. M. Ram Murthy, *Isa Upanishad*, p. 19. Accessed on www.mast.queensu.ca/-murty/ind3.pdf.

Glossary

Calendar

The Bengali Era (BS or *Bangla Son/Sal*) is 594 less than the AD or CE year in the Gregorian calendar if it is before the 1st of Baisakh, or 593 less, if after.

Months		**Seasons**
Baisakh	first month of the Bengali year, mid-April to mid-May	Grishma/Summer
Jyestha	mid-May to mid-June	
Asharh	mid-June, mid-July	Varsha/Rains
Sravan	mid-July to mid-August	
Bhadra	mid-August to mid-September	Sharat/Autumn
Aswin	mid-September to mid-October	
Kartik	mid-October to mid-November	Hemanta/Fall
Agrahayan	mid-November to mid December	
Paush	mid-December to mid-January	Sheeth/Winter
Magh	mid-January to mid-February	
Falgun	mid-February to mid-March	Vasanta/Spring
Chaitra	mid-March to mid-April	

Forms of address

baba	father
babaji, baba	used to address an older man; also a male child, affectionately
babu/babuji	common honorific suffix in northern India
boro-bou	eldest daughter-in-law in an extended family
bou-didi	often shortened to *boudi*, to brother's wife
bou-ma	daughter-in-law, even if not related
bou-thakuron	used to address a brahman wife
moshai	honorary suffix for a male, abbreviation of *mahashay*
thakurjhi	a wife's address to husband's sister

Measurements

anna	one-sixteenth of a rupee
bhori	unit of weight a little over 11 grams
bigha	land measure, 01.3 hectare
chhatak	a little over 58 grams; also a measure of area, 4.18 sq. metres
gonda	a unit in fours
dwanda	little less than half an hour
katha	measure of cereals
kathha	measure of land, about one third of an acre, 66.68 sq. metres
khunchi	vessel for measuring rice paddy and other grains weighing 2.5 seers
kos	measure of distance equal to about 2 miles
maund	measure of weight, about 37 kilograms
pali	a local measure
poa	measure of weight, one-fourth of a seer
paisa/pice (pl.)	small copper coin, quarter of an anna
prahar	3 hours
shiki	coin valuing a quarter of a rupee; a fourth part
seer	measure of weight, about 933 grams; one-fortieth of a maund

Select general glossary

amla	employee of a zamindari estate
amin	surveyor, evaluator, revenue collector or contractor
arat	warehouse where goods are stored to be sold on a commission basis
aratdar	agent who earns a commission selling goods, regularly advances money to cultivators for seeds; lends money to zamindars
bagdi	cultivating and fishing caste, bagdi men were also used by landlords for their private armies
baur	where the bend in the river creates a natural pool
burkandwaj	armed retainer, unmounted escort
boshtom	popular version of baishnab/vaishnav, one professing vaishnav faith
brahmottar	land endowment to a brahman, exempt from revenue
buno	literally meaning wild; here, jungle clearers
chandimandap	covered temple courtyard adjoining a rich landowner's home, originally dedicated to the goddess Chandi, but usually a place

	for brahman males to 'hang out', also open to villagers on special occasions
chitha	memorandum stating the measurement of a zamindar's estate based on actual measurement
char	new 'depositional land' emerging from a shifting riverine situation; settlement in the floodplains of Bengal
cutchery	an administration office, court-house
dadon	advance value for producing estimated goods; here, advances forcibly given out to peasants to cultivate indigo
dadon khata	registers showing loans given as earnest money
dewan	minister of a native state
dom	traditionally made to work as scavengers, untouchable caste
duley	primarily agricultural workers, often considered to be a sub-caste of *bagdi*
ganj	commonly used as suffix (also prefix) indicating neighbourhood or market
faujdar/i	district under faujdar; the office & jurisdiction of a faujdar; criminal as opposed to civil justice
goladar	one who stores paddy or cereals in his warehouse and advances the same to cultivators; money-lending may be a supplementary profession
gomasta	local agent or steward
hakim	district magistrate
Horu Thakur	(1738-1812) iconic *kobiyal* or versifier, who sung his compositions in 'kobi' contests in Calcutta
jama-bandi	land assessment, settlement
jama byabastha	annual tax from renting out a bathing-ghat or market place
otbandi jama byabastha	rents for tenants-at-will with a specific period of occupancy
jamanabish	accounts clerk in the receipts branch
jigr (from Arabic. zikr)	successive chants or cries in praise of Allah, recital of attributes
kaora	hog keeper; name of one of the lowest castes among Hindus
kapati	outdoor game involving teams, holding one's breath and running to 'touch' other members
karkoon	clerk or lower level manager
khamar	land which is still to be distributed or rented out
khas-jami/	agricultural land not let out to the tenants, but cultivated

khas-khamar/	directly by the owner, a demesne; *khas jami* could also mean
khas-mahal	to bring the land from the rayiat's occupancy to the zamindar's control
khansama	house steward, table servant
kulin	system of hypergamy, practiced among kulin brahmans in Bengal
lathi	a stick or pole usually of bamboo, sometimes bound with iron rings
lathiyal	one who fights with his lathi or stick, often a hired mercenary
mahakuma	part of a district, munsefi court; subdivision
mahajan	wealthy trader who advances loans against interest
mauja	a cluster of villages
mark khatian	ledger with account of the land 'marked out' for indigo cultivation
mohuree	accountant
mothh	sweets made of congealed sugar, shaped like a temple
muchi	a caste working in leather, either as shoemaker or saddler
mukam	business or trading centre
mukhtar	attorney
munsif	Indians appointed to try suits at the lower civil courts
naib	deputy
nakalnabish	copyist; clerk
namasudra	members of a caste mainly engaged in boating and cultivation
nikiri	Muslim community of fishermen
panchali	narrative genre comprising music and poetry, usually about the love of Radha-Krishna. Dasu/Dasarathi Ray (1806-1957) considered a master of the form
paik (also spelt *pyke*)	footman, an armed attendant
para	neighbourhood, locality, settlement based on caste identity
peshkar	bench clerk; agent; deputy; minister; assistant; manager
pinman	person employed to drive pegs or stakes into the ground for surveying
praja	peasant cultivating the land; also meaning subject, tenant
rayiat (also spelt *ryot*)	cultivator, landholder paying revenue to zamindar or directly to government
raiyati	belonging to a *raiyat*, land of which the revenue is paid in money; in this sense, opposed to *khamar*, and of which the

	revenue is paid in kind
sadgope	cultivating caste of Bengal
sandad	grant
Sarkar/ Sarkar Bahadur	popular Hindustani reference to the British Government
seresta	chief record-keeper
shamla	formal headgear, usually worn by lawyers in 19th century Bengal
shorki	short spear
shyamasangeet	devotional hymn to goddess Kali, also known as Shyama, the dark one
suchikabharan	medicine in Ayurvedic pharmacopoeia containing a minute quantity of snake-poison
sudder amin	chief judge; designation of the second class of Indian judges
Swati	fifteenth of the twenty-seven zodiacal stars according to Indian astronomical calendar, the star Arcturus
syce	groom, mounted attendant
thak-naksha	a cadastral survey
thelo hooka	coconut-shell water container used for a hooka
tom-tom	one-horse carriage or a buggy; popular corruption of the word 'tandem'
udi-dhan	special lightweight rice to make 'murki'
Uttarbhadrapad	one of the twenty-seven zodiacal stars according to Indian astronomical calendar
vakil	pleader

Compiled in part from *The Cambridge Economic History of India, Volume II, c.1757-c.1970* (1982), Dharma Kumar (ed.) (New Delhi, Orient Longman in association with Cambridge University Press, 1991).

Religious & philosophical references

Advaitavada	pure Monism / Absolute Non-dualism
Advaita-Vedanta	one of the three major systems of thought, formulated by Shankaracharya
atman	from the 'breath of life', the meaning extends to soul, self or Ultimate Reality within the individual
Brahman	word used in the Upanishads to indicate Supreme Reality; derived from the root *brh* 'to grow, to burst forth', suggesting

	ceaseless growth. Hence, Absolute Consciousness
bhuma	the omnipresent Supreme Being; Absolute Consciousness
Brahmavad	the doctrine of non-dualism, awareness of the Oneness of the universe
Charaka	believed to be the principal compiler of *Charaka-samhita*, the oldest text on Ayurveda, with a code of ethics for the physician
Chaitanyacharitamrita	the most important hagiography of Sri Chaitanyadeva by Kaviraj Goswami
Chitsukhi	an Advaita-Vedanta text attributed to Sri Harsha, also known as the *Tattvapradipika*
Dhanvantari	physician of the gods to whom is attributed the science of medicine, Ayurveda
Kalpa-Vyakarana	*Kalpasastras* (rituals) and *Vyakarana* (grammar), two of the four limbs of the Vedangas
Madhav Nidan	a diagnostic medical treatise, considered a pioneering compendium based on knowledge sourced from *Charaka-samhita*, *Sushruta-samhita*, etc. named after Madhavacharya, an Ayurvedic physician of the of the seventh century CE
Moha Mudgara slokas	verses attributed to Sri Shankaracharya, intended to break the illusions of the ignorant; popularly known as 'Bhaja Govindam'
Mimamsa	lit. 'investigation', school of Hindu philosophy primarily concerned with ritual
Narad Bhaktisutra	text attributed to the sage Narad, on the nature of selfless love and the means to achieve a state of pure devotion
Nyaya	investigation through logical proof, one of the philosophical systems of Hinduism
Patanjali	second century BCE, founder of the yoga philosophy based on Sankhya, composer of the *Yoga-Sutra*
Sankhya	one of six orthodox doctrines of philosophy, founded by Kapila
Srimad Bhagavad	also known as the *Bhagavata-Puran*, c. 10 CE, devoted to Krishna; the most important of the eighteen puranas
Sushruta	ancient physician (c. 600 BCE), author of *Sushruta-samhita*, one of the foundational texts of Indian medicine and surgery, with description of medicinal plants, minerals, etc.
Upanishads	one of the major components of the Vedas (along with the Brahmanas, Aranyakas, Mantras)
upadhi	concept referring to everything that is superimposed on, conceal *Brahman*